Praise for

SUPERNORMAL

"This extraordinary book taught me more about resilience than anything else I've read. With the ear of a therapist and the voice of a novelist, Meg Jay delves deep into the human condition to illuminate how we find strength after suffering. It's impossible to read SUPERNORMAL without seeing yourself in it—and without seeing yourself more clearly too."

—Adam Grant, *New York Times* bestselling author of *Give and Take*, *Originals*, and *Option B* with Sheryl Sandberg

"This powerful book sheds light on the secret shame that so many children and adults hide, and reveals why those who often feel abnormal are actually supernormal. Jay casts light on this important, rarely considered issue in this must-read for educators, physicians, survivors of childhood adversity, and all who wish to understand how our childhoods shape ourselves and our lives."

—*Booklist*

"Adversity is much more common than we think. But so is resilience, as Meg Jay reveals in this remarkable book. With a storyteller's grace and a clinician's insight, Jay explains how everyday superheroes triumph over traumas of every kind—and how you can use their inspiration and lessons to transform your own life."

—Daniel H. Pink, *New York Times* bestselling author of *Drive*

"Both disturbing and inspiring, [SUPERNORMAL] offers an unretouched picture of the profound challenges facing millions of American youth and a map of the path some may be able to follow out of their despair...SUPERNORMAL's inspiring message and Jay's portraits of how to act on it make this a valuable and important book."

—*Shelf Awareness* (Starred Review)

"On our long journey through life, sometimes we get knocked down by adversity. Meg Jay's brilliant analysis of how to rise up even stronger is essential reading for all of us on the path of every-day heroism."

—Philip Zimbardo, PhD, president of
The Heroic Imagination Project

"Compelling and hopeful. [Meg Jay] amply shows that though internal battles may not end, the joy that comes from living a balanced life is always possible. A well-researched, abundantly documented, readable work of social science." —*Kirkus*

"SUPERNORMAL is a compassionate, optimistic, yet realistic tale of resilience. We can bounce back from adversity. Even so, the bounce hurts. I recommend this book to anyone seeking guidance, or inspiration, for coping with everyday stress—or a once-in-a-life-time trauma."

—Robert E. Emery, PhD, University of Virginia;
Director of the Center for Children, Families, and
the Law and author of *Two Homes, One Childhood*

"With SUPERNORMAL, Meg Jay takes us into the secret world of friends, neighbors, and colleagues, where many are fighting their own private battles. You will understand resilience quite differently after you read this book, and the world would be a more compassionate place if everyone did."

—J. Stuart Ablon, PhD, director of Think:Kids

"SUPERNORMAL puts an end to the 'happily-ever-after' tales we tell ourselves about resilient children. But it does not stop there. Deeply researched and full of insight and wisdom, it is a book for anyone thinking about how we navigate the vicissitudes of life."

—Steven Lagerfeld, public policy fellow at
the Woodrow Wilson Center

"In a world where quick fixes masquerade as the secret to health and happiness, SUPERNORMAL saves the day with an inspirational account of resilience that never shortchanges the pain, risk, or complexity of the challenges involved. Masterfully researched, eloquently written, and deeply felt, SUPERNORMAL satisfies at every level."

—Daphne de Marneffe, PhD, author of
Maternal Desire and *The Rough Patch*

"Meg Jay offers the supernormals among us—those masses forged by adversity—both self-awareness and community. They will see themselves, and one another, in her pages, exhaling with the relief of recognition."

—Joshua Prager, author of *The Echoing Green* and *100 Years*

"Jay...challenges the idea that [people who have experienced trauma] are damaged and abnormal by redefining them as 'supernormal' heroes. [Jay] uses her [superhero conceit] to help make the people whose stories she shares more relatable, in the way that children, especially children in difficult situations, look to their fictional heroes for...affirmation."   —*Publishers Weekly*

"Gripping, evidence-based, and inspiring, SUPERNORMAL brings to life the surprising numbers of kids and adults who overcome adversity. Be prepared for a tour of everything from brain science to community empowerment, enriched by real-life stories. Five stars!"

—Stephen P. Hinshaw, PhD, author of
*Another Kind of Madness: A Journey Through the
Stigma and Hope of Mental Illness*

ALSO BY MEG JAY

The Defining Decade

SUPERNORMAL

THE SECRET WORLD OF THE FAMILY HERO

MEG JAY, PhD

TWELVE

NEW YORK   BOSTON

Cover design by Jarrod Taylor
Jacket photograph © Colin Anderson/Getty Images
Cover copyright © 2017 by Hachette Book Group, Inc.

Twelve
Hachette Book Group
1290 Avenue of the Americas, New York, NY 10104
twelvebooks.com
twitter.com/twelvebooks

Originally published in hardcover and ebook by Grand Central Publishing in November 2017
First Trade Paperback Edition: January 2019

Twelve is an imprint of Grand Central Publishing. The Twelve name and logo are trademarks of Hachette Book Group, Inc.

The publisher is not responsible for websites (or their content) that are not owned by the publisher.

The Hachette Speakers Bureau provides a wide range of authors for speaking events. To find out more, go to www.hachettespeakersbureau.com or call (866) 376-6591.

Library of Congress Cataloging-in-Publication Data

Names: Jay, Meg, author.
Title: Supernormal / Meg Jay, PhD.
Description: First hardcover edition. | New York : Twelve, [2017] | Includes
   bibliographical references.
Identifiers: LCCN 2017022618| ISBN 9781455559152 (hardcover) |
   ISBN 9781478993865 (audio book) | ISBN 9781478929741 (audio download) |
   ISBN 9781455559145 (ebook)
Subjects: LCSH: Resilience (Personality trait)—Case studies. | Resilience
   (Personality trait) in children—Case studies. | Adjustment (Psychology)—
   Case studies.
Classification: LCC BF698.35.R47 J39 2017 | DDC 155.2/4—dc23
LC record available at https://lccn.loc.gov/2017022618

ISBNs: 978-1-4555-5913-8 (trade paperback), 978-1-4555-5914-5 (ebook),
978-1-4789-2974-1 (audiobook, downloadable)

CW

10 9 8 7 6 5 4 3 2

For Jay and Hazel

supernormal (adj.) exceeding or beyond the normal or average; exceptional

CONTENTS

AUTHOR'S NOTE

"The most basic of all human needs is the need to understand and to be understood."

—Ralph Nichols

As a clinical psychologist and educator, I listen to people for a living, and recently I have begun to write books about what I hear. This is why: Much of the time, people come to a therapist or teacher with problems they feel they have no one to talk to about, or they fear no one else will understand. For two decades, then, my days have been spent behind closed doors hearing about events that, often, have taken place behind closed doors, too. One thing I have learned is that many, many people feel isolated with similar problems, unaware that they are not as alone or as different as they think.

Also, therapy and the classroom are not for everyone, and there can be financial, logistical, or cultural barriers to each. I have gained a lot not only from listening, but also from researching and reading about the problems that have been brought to me. I want this information to be accessible not just to those who can afford schools or therapists but also to anyone who can access the Internet or a bookstore or a public library. Education is an intervention, said feminist theorist Gloria Jean Watkins, better known by her pen name "bell hooks."

What follows, then, is a work of narrative nonfiction. Throughout this book, I draw on hundreds of studies from hundreds of researchers, only some of whom, for the sake of readability, are named in the body of the text. Please consult the notes at the end of the book for full citations, and for information about where you can read more. I also quote from dozens of memoirs and autobiographies, as well as from a few biographies and novels. In most cases, quotations are provided in full. On a few occasions, quotations are abbreviated, but—again for readability—rather than use brackets or ellipses, I made certain the meaning of the words was not altered. For more complete quotations or context, the notes can point you to the primary sources.

As I worked on *Supernormal*, the question I was asked most often was this one: "Where will you find people to write about?" As you will soon see, family heroes are all around us, and many have populated my private practice—and the community clinics and lecture halls where I have supervised and taught—for twenty years. In the chapters ahead, I tell the stories—in a disguised fashion—of family heroes with whom I have had the privilege to work. The narratives that follow have been chosen not because they are the most shocking, unusual stories of hardship one might find. Rather, they are stunning examples of just how powerful and poignant our most prevalent adversities are, the ones that millions of children and teens wake up to every day.

Each story in this book is based on real events and endeavors to be emotionally true. To protect the privacy of those who have shared their experiences with me, identifying details have been changed. The fundamental aspects of the stories I share—the hardships my clients and students faced and what they thought and how they felt as they made their way through them—have not been altered. The dialogue I include consists of others' words as I remember them. I hope every reader sees himself or herself in the pages that follow, but a resemblance to any particular person is coincidental.

CHAPTER 1

Supernormal

There is no greater agony than bearing an untold story inside you.
—Maya Angelou

Helen looked as put together in person as she had sounded on the phone. Precisely on time for her first appointment, she sat on the couch with her back straight and her hands resting on top of each other, the bottom hand clenched. We exchanged some pleasantries, which included my asking if she had found my office without incident. To this, Helen replied, almost offhandedly, that she had been late getting out of a meeting at work, rushed over in her car, gotten a flat tire on the way, rolled into the closest service station, dashed in to drop off her keys, dashed back out yelling over her shoulder that she would return in an hour, jumped on a bus heading in the right direction, hopped off a mile or so later, and ran the last couple of blocks.

"You sound like a superhero," I said.

Tears began to fall down Helen's cheeks, and she looked at me wryly, sadly. "You don't know the half of it," she replied.

Helen told me she had spent most of the last several years since college—"How many has it been?" She paused to count. "Ten?

Eleven?"—crisscrossing the globe with nongovernmental organizations fighting for a better world. Social justice in Africa. Climate justice in Southeast Asia and Latin America. Juvenile justice in Eastern Europe and the Caribbean. Helen went wherever she was needed and then, one day, her mother sent word she was needed back home.

Helen's father had killed himself in the house where she grew up. Theirs was a modest home in a suburban neighborhood about two hours outside San Francisco. It was a place where there had been a yard to run around in, and Helen and her two younger brothers each had a bedroom of their own. Maybe this was why, many years ago, no one heard the youngest boy sneak out of the house in the middle of the night and head for the backyard pool. Maybe this was why no one saw him drown.

Before she was even a teenager, Helen had begun to sneak out of the house at night, too. At first, she wanted to know what the world had looked like to her brother just before he died, but then she kept doing it because it felt like getting away, at least for a while. Her father was not arguing for a fresh start somewhere else. Her mother was not crying, refusing to leave her memories of her youngest child—and the marks she had made on the kitchen doorway as he had grown taller—behind. During the day, Helen walked down the halls at school where she earned good grades with a smile—her parents needed her to be "the strong one," and she was. In the dark of night, though, Helen could walk for blocks and blocks, and as she moved in and out of the cones of yellow light from the streetlamps, there was no one to be strong for, no one to save.

Back from her work around the world, Helen drove her rental car down those same streets, unsure of what she hated more about her neighborhood: the fact that the houses were all supposed to look alike or the feeling that hers never had seemed like the rest. Next, she went to her father's office, where she packed his personal items into a cardboard box, among them an empty water bottle stashed suspiciously in the bottom desk drawer. When she unscrewed the top and put her nose to it, it smelled of alcohol. Helen felt like drinking, too, as she sat back and swiveled side to side in her father's desk chair and eyed the hundreds of files stacked haphazardly in chairs around the room. On her way out, Helen politely thanked her father's colleagues as they fumbled with awkward condolences, and with congratulations, too, about her many good works: "Your father was so proud of you. He talked about you all the time, you know." Helen did know. She was, and had always been, living proof that her family was all right.

In a flash, Helen had a new job near her hometown, this time as a fund-raiser for a presidential campaign. There was work that needed to be done right here in the United States, she reasoned; besides, her mother needed her, too. At the office, friendly, impassioned calls with donors were interspersed with weepy calls from her mother: her house—the one she vowed never to leave—might go into foreclosure. It was on a day like this one that she made her way to my office and told me her story.

"I've never said all this to anyone before," Helen confided as tears rolled in steady tracks down her cheeks. "Some people know some of it, but no one knows all of it. People look at me and they see all these great things I have done—and they are sort of astonished when they find something out about my family but no one really knows me. I don't think anyone has ever really known me. It's lonely."

Helen sat silent for a long while, folding and unfolding a tissue.

"I'm so tired," she continued. "I feel embarrassed to say that, to be sitting here crying, when I think about all the people in the world who have had it so much harder than I have. It's like I don't have the right to be as worn out or as sad as I am. I don't know what's wrong with me. Sometimes I feel like I don't fit anywhere, like there isn't a word for...whatever I am. I just have this feeling that I'm not like other people," she concluded. "That I'm not normal."

Then, with impeccable timing, Helen glanced at her watch and interrupted herself to say, "Our time is up. I'll see you next week." She wiped the tears from her face and walked out the door, off to race back to her car.

* * *

Helen is what is called a "family hero." In families or communities where there are problems, the role of the hero is to be well and do well. "The strong one" in the bunch, his or her job is to be helpful in the home and successful in the world. Some become honor students or class presidents whose achievements bring much-needed distinction and positive attention to their loved ones. Others become star athletes or accomplished artists whose trophies and talents offset the troubles around. Still others become activists or doctors who set out to do good. Family heroes cannot just be normal, they must be supernormal. If they are good enough or smart enough or kind enough, or they work hard enough, then maybe all will be well—or at least they will be well. Family heroes always seem to be saving someone, if only themselves.

So it was for Helen, who overcame hardships, both big and small. The loss of her brother. Her parents' grief. Her father's death. International injustice. A flat tire. Helen leapt into action no matter what. Strong and determined, compassionate and brave, she was a hero to her family, and maybe to some others, too. Tirelessly, it seemed, she came to the rescue of those who needed her and she stood up for strangers around the globe.

To those who knew her, Helen was a marvel, and maybe few would have guessed that, behind closed doors, she felt different and alone. But, of course, Helen was not as different from other people as she imagined.

What follows are the most common adversities that children and teens wake up to every day. If you are wondering if you might have been one of those children or teens, ask yourself the following questions. Before the age of twenty:

- Did you lose a parent or sibling through death or divorce?
- Did a parent or sibling often swear at you, put you down, humiliate you, isolate you, or act in a way that made you feel afraid?
- Did you live with a parent or sibling who was a problem drinker, or who abused other drugs?
- Were you ever bullied by, or afraid of, kids at school or in your neighborhood?
- Did you live with an adult or sibling who struggled with a mental illness, or some other serious illness or special need?
- Did a parent or a sibling often push, grab, slap, or throw something at you, or ever hit you so hard that you had bruises, marks, or other injuries?
- Did you live in a home where you went without clean clothes or enough to eat, you could not afford a doctor, or you felt you had no one to protect you?
- Did someone in your household go to jail?
- Did a parent, sibling, or another person at least five years older touch your body in a sexual way or ask you to do something similar?
- Was a parent or sibling in your household sometimes hit, kicked, or slapped, or ever threatened with a weapon?

If you answered yes to one or more of these questions—or if you lived with an adversity not mentioned just above—you are not the only one. Considered individually, each of these experiences may affect only a minority of the population, but considered together under the umbrella of childhood adversity, multiple studies in the United States and around the world suggest that up to 75 percent of children and teens are exposed to one of these events—or more—as one problem may lead to another and another.

Yet, as we all know, many young people, like Helen—and maybe like yourself—grow up and do well in the world, not just in spite of the difficulties they have known, but maybe even because of them. They are family heroes, and here are a few well-known examples we will hear a bit about in the pages ahead, women and men who show us that those like Helen are, in fact, in good company:

Andre Agassi, tennis champion
Maya Angelou, author
Alison Bechdel, cartoonist
Johnny Carson, comedian
Johnny Cash, country singer
Stephen Colbert, comedian
Misty Copeland, ballet dancer
Alan Cumming, actor
Viola Davis, actor
Viktor Frankl, psychiatrist and Holocaust survivor
LeBron James, basketball champion
Barack Obama, 44th president of the United States
Paul Ryan, 54th Speaker of the House
Oliver Sacks, neurologist
Howard Schultz, chairman of Starbucks
Akhil Sharma, author
Elizabeth Smart, child safety advocate
Sonia Sotomayor, US Supreme Court Justice
Andy Warhol, artist
Elizabeth Warren, US senator
Oprah Winfrey, media mogul and philanthropist
Jay Z, rapper and businessman

Of course, most family heroes aren't celebrities. Most are everyday people hiding in plain sight as doctors, artists, entrepreneurs, lawyers, neighbors, parents, activists, teachers, students, readers, and more. As we are about to learn, theirs is a powerful, perilous, lifelong saga, one that, after decades of interest and research, still amazes and confounds.

* * *

In 1962, psychologist Victor Goertzel, along with his wife, Mildred, published a book titled *Cradles of Eminence: A Provocative Study of the Childhoods of Over 400 Famous Twentieth-Century Men and Women.* Their famous men and women were those who had at least two biographies written about them, and who made positive contributions to society: Louis Armstrong, Frida Kahlo, Pablo Picasso, Eleanor Roosevelt, to name a few. What was "provocative," or at least surprising, about the Goertzels' book was the revelation that, as children, three-quarters of these prominent individuals had been burdened by poverty, broken homes, abusive parents, alcoholism, handicaps, illness, or other misfortunes. Only fifty-eight, or less than 15 percent, seemed to have been raised in supportive, untroubled homes. "The 'normal man,'" concluded the Goertzels, "is not a likely candidate for the Hall of Fame."

Perhaps former First Lady Abigail Adams was right when she said, "The habits of a vigorous mind are formed in contending with great difficulties. When a mind is raised and animated by scenes that engage the heart, then those qualities which would otherwise lay dormant, wake into life and form the character of the hero and the statesman." Or maybe it is simply true that no matter where one looks, if one looks closely enough, adversity is more common than not. Rather than the freakish burden of the unlucky few, hard times can be found in the personal histories of both eminent and everyday family heroes.

Social scientists initially stumbled upon these everyday family heroes mostly by accident. For almost a hundred years, since the founding of the field of psychology, researchers had largely concerned themselves with mental illness, and especially with how problems in childhood led to problems in adulthood. Sigmund Freud is probably best known for popularizing this notion late in the nineteenth century, but it was, in fact, a point of view that was already well established. "Everywhere I go I find that a poet has been there before me," Freud purportedly said, and indeed it was eighteenth-century poet Alexander Pope whose words became this popular adage: "As the twig is bent, so is the tree inclined."

Yet in and around the 1970s, small, disparate groups of researchers began to observe that as the twig was bent, the tree did not always incline. At the University of Minnesota, psychologist Norman Garmezy set out to study children who, because their mothers were mentally ill, were at risk of being ill, too, only to become intrigued by those who showed few signs of trouble. At the Institute of Psychiatry in London, Michael Rutter studied boys and girls who seemed similarly unaffected by poverty or deprivation. Emmy Werner, a psychologist at University of California at Davis, launched the Kauai Longitudinal Study to follow at-risk infants across time, only to become captivated by those who seemed to rise above childhood disadvantage and family discord. At the Menninger Foundation, Lois Murphy and Alice Moriarty co-directed the Coping Project, a research program that identified children who handled hardship well. And Swiss psychiatrist Manfred Bleuler—the son of Eugen Bleuler, who coined the term *schizophrenia*, and who himself worked with adult schizophrenics—noted with surprise that most of his patients' children were quite accomplished. He proposed that their difficult early experiences had a "steeling effect" on who they were, making them remarkably strong.

As British psychoanalyst James Anthony wrote in 1987, "One would have thought that the picture of children triumphing over despairing, degrading, depressing, depriving and deficient circumstances would have caught the immediate attention of both clinicians and researchers, but [until recently] the survivors and thrivers appeared to pass almost unnoticed." Suddenly, though, enthusiasm for these survivors and thrivers ran high. Young people like Helen were called "keepers of the dream" because, from the outside at least, they represented the promise of the American Dream: triumph over hardship, scrappy self-sufficiency, hope for a better future, and a seeming equal opportunity for success.

Family heroes captured the imagination of professionals and laypeople alike, and many early descriptions in academia and the popular press suggested there was something truly incredible about them. Headlines, journal articles, and book titles rang out with superheroic superlatives: "Superkids." "Invulnerable." "Invincible." "Children of steel." "Supernormal." Family heroes displayed an almost otherworldly ability to adapt and succeed, but how?

* * *

Family heroes are often counted on to save the day at home or at school, and, for a time it seemed, researchers thought that they just might save social science, too. These "children who will not break," as trauma expert Julius Segal referred to them in a 1978 book, had to have some special strength, it seemed, and if only scientists could discover their secret, then they could reveal to the world the secret of success. "The invulnerable children!" exclaimed Segal in his writings about such boys and girls. "They may be our best research hope."

Segal was not the only one who thought so. All around, scientists delved into the lives of family heroes with zeal and, by the 1980s, "resilience" research was born. Laypeople wanted to know—and still want to know—the "secret" of resilience, or what exactly is that superpower that allows some to rise up when others fall down. Maybe not surprisingly, no simple answers have been found.

The quest for a short list of personal qualities that seemed to make a person resilient generated a pretty long list of purported assets, not all of which need be present in any one individual, or else that person would be super indeed: at least average intelligence, a pleasant or engaging temperament, problem-solving skills, self-control, independence, self-confidence, good communication skills, humor, determination, ability to form friendships, optimism, attractiveness, a sense of faith or meaning, conscientiousness, and some talent or hobby that attracted the attention of others.

Yet as tempting as it was to believe that these superkids used their superstrengths to fight back against what was bad about their surroundings, it soon became apparent that many had help from what was good about their environments, too. The most fortunate were sustained by having at least one parent or adult who loved them, and who provided consistent warmth and supervision. Some survived and thrived not because of their parents but because of siblings who cared, or who looked after them. Others were propped up by supportive relationships outside the home, such as with teachers or coaches or mentors or relatives or friends, or by resources in their communities: good schools that fed their minds or fed them lunch; safe neighborhoods or community centers where they could go and just be kids; libraries or churches or gymnasiums or music centers where they could escape and even be inspired.

As renowned resilience researcher Ann Masten so aptly described, those like Helen do not really have superpowers. Perhaps even more surprising, they use, she said, the "power of the ordinary"—or the everyday attributes that can be found in minds, families, and communities—to make something out of nothing, to make a lot out of a little, to pull a rabbit out of a hat. As is usually the case with magic, however, things are not quite what they seem.

The closer—and the longer—scientists followed the lives of family heroes, the more they found that resilience is something that goes in and out of view depending on how and when one looks at it. Most often, researchers look for an "observable track record" of good performance, the most easily observable of all being doing well at work or school. But what about those parts of life that researchers cannot see so easily? Soon it was discovered that many kids who woke up to hard times at home yet did well in the classroom felt stressed and lonely on the inside, making their difficulties tough to spot. Similarly, many adults who excelled at work seemingly unfazed by years of troubles were found to be struggling covertly with their relationships and their health. Perhaps decades of research had revealed the secret behind childhood resilience after all: that no one—not even a family hero—is invulnerable.

*   *   *

In the middle of the twentieth century, Heinz Hartmann suggested that normal development takes place in what he called an "average, expectable" environment. Something like what pediatrician and psychoanalyst Donald Winnicott referred to as a "good-enough" upbringing, the average, expectable environment is a home—or a school or a neighborhood—where there is enough safety, enough food, enough affection, enough peace, enough discipline, enough supervision, enough role modeling, enough attention, enough love, and at least one good-enough parent or adult who cares. In the good-enough childhood, life need not be without problems, as moderate, age-appropriate challenges are good for us. Still, according to Hartmann and Winnicott, those problems ought to be predictable and they ought to feel normal, whatever we as a culture think that might be.

Ironically, the average, expectable environment that Hartmann envisioned may be neither average nor expectable. Many more people than we might like to think grow up with what Hartmann called "above-average environmental burdens." A 2010 report from the Centers for Disease Control and Prevention estimates that, as children, about 25 percent of adults were the targets of verbal abuse, 15 percent suffered physical abuse, and 10 percent were the victims of sexual abuse. About 30 percent watched their parents divorce. Approximately 30 percent lived in a home where a family member abused drugs or alcohol, and 15 percent witnessed some form of violence. About 5 percent grew up with a parent in jail, and 20 percent shared a home with a family member who was mentally ill.

These might sound like problems that "other people" have, or ones that reside only below the poverty line, and financial hardship can surely lead to or result from problems in the home. Yet the landmark study that stunned the medical community with just how prevalent and harmful these early stressors are—the Adverse Childhood Experiences (ACE) Study, begun in the late 1990s and sponsored by the CDC and Kaiser Permanente and conducted by co-principal-investigators Vincent J. Felitti and Robert F. Anda—was an examination of nearly eighteen thousand mostly middle-class families. Of these, nearly two-thirds reported at least one of the aforementioned adversities, and almost half reported two or more.

What this means is that, for all kinds of children and teens, adversity has a way of piling up. Tough times may come bundled together in what has been called an "adversity package," such as in Helen's childhood, when one misfortune sets off other problems. In a 2004 study that examined the interrelatedness of hardships, 80 percent of children who lived with one adversity were also exposed to at least one more, and 50 percent were exposed to at least three more.

On top of this, the most prevalent early adversities aren't one-time events; they affect the life of the child over and over and over again. Rather than "shock traumas"—to use the words of psychoanalyst Ernst Kris—the most common troubles are "strain traumas" in that they burden the child, and then the adult child, in an ongoing way. They are what fellow psychoanalyst Masud Khan called "cumulative traumas," or problems that build up across childhood, the full weight of which may not be realized until adulthood: "only cumulatively and in retrospect," Khan said.

What makes most childhood adversities so dangerous, then, is not necessarily their gigantic proportions but their wear and tear on the daily lives of children, and on developing bodies and brains. Difficult experiences get under our skin in the form of what is now widely known as toxic stress, or chronic stress. Chronic stress takes its toll—metaphorically—much in the same way as do repetitive blows to the head. When, for example, an athlete is struck once seriously enough to lose consciousness— when he has incurred a concussion—we intervene, we take him out of the game. When a player receives a lesser blow, however, maybe he seems all right and we send him back to the game, back to his life. But, as neurologists have found, the hits, big and small, add up.

In 2011, Robert Block, the past president of the American Academy of Pediatrics, testified before a Senate subcommittee on children and families that childhood adversity "may be the leading cause of poor health among adults in the United States." This is because the chronic stress puts us at risk for all sorts of ailments down the line—from ulcers and depression to cancer and autoimmune diseases. And make no mistake, family heroes are not impervious to this kind of stress. They may be more successful than others at battling back against it—at putting together a life in spite of it—but here is the rub: Battling back is stressful, too.

A 2017 article in the *New York Times* titled "Why Succeeding Against the Odds Can Make You Sick" profiled the work of scientists who study resilient strivers, those who worked to overcome childhood disadvantage. The more likely strivers were to agree with statements like these—"When things don't go the way I want them to, that just makes me work even harder" or "I've always felt that I could make of my life pretty much what I wanted to make of it"—the more likely their health was to suffer, leading one researcher to suggest that, when it comes to our health, resilience may be only skin-deep.

* * *

So here we are in the twenty-first century, some fifty years after the accidental "discovery" of the everyday family hero. What began as a quest to follow some superkids and uncover their superstrengths became a journey that researchers surely did not anticipate, one that offered no simple answers but did reveal some important truths: More of us face early adversity than not. Many of us use the ordinary powers at our disposal to fight back against them—and some triumph. And such victories are almost never as easy or decisive as they may appear. These days, few people refer to family heroes as superkids or invulnerable or invincible or supernormal, but maybe those early researchers were onto something with their superhero comparisons. Because let's not forget, superheroes are complicated characters.

The world's first superhero—Superman—is an iconic American creation, an enduring symbol of the American Dream. Rocketed to Earth as an infant from his home planet of Krypton, Superman first landed on the cover of a comic book in 1938. He is "faster than a speeding bullet. More powerful than a locomotive. Able to leap tall buildings in a single bound." And of course he can fly, too: "It's a bird! It's a plane! It's Superman!" Only a chunk of kryptonite from his home planet—a piece from the past—can bring him down.

Yet as the world would also come to learn, it is not so easy to be the Man of Steel. An orphan and alien, Superman is taken in and cared for by some good people—the Kents—but still, he feels different from those around him, because of his history and the special powers even he does not understand. As he comes of age, he hopes to use his abilities to help others, and to this end he moves from Smallville to Metropolis, where he begins a long—and thus far unresolved—struggle to make the world a better place. As much as Superman may like to live an everyday life as Clark Kent—and maybe even find love with Lois Lane—the world just keeps calling him into action. Peace, it seems, can only be found in his Fortress of Solitude.

Superman was the prototype for almost all superheroes to follow, and the defining features that are common among most can be found in the lives of many family heroes, too. Like superheroes, they dodge bullets and leap over tall buildings in their way when so many other people around them—even those who have been presented with fewer obstacles—do not. They fight back against the dangers at hand with what looks like ease. Yet as Helen suggested on that first day we met, this is only half the story. Many go on to achieve what feels like high-flying success only to wonder how long they can keep going, or when it all might come crashing down.

* * *

As the culture that imagined both Superman and the American Dream, we romanticize upward mobility in all forms and sometimes forget about its difficulties. Naturally, we are amazed by family heroes, yet as we have focused on *How do they do it?*, we have forgotten also to ask, *How does it feel?*

How it *feels* to be a family hero is what *Supernormal* is all about. It is the untold story—the secret world—of those who soar to unexpected heights after hardship and heartbreak in childhood. It shows the world that fighting back against one's past is as courageous—and complex—as are family heroes themselves.

The family hero is an everyday superhero, and sometime antihero, who has strengths and secrets that even those closest to him may not know. Donning a cape in the service of others, he may use his powers to be good and do good even as he struggles with exhaustion. Wearing a mask in service of himself, he may live with incredible alienation even as only relationships can save him. Ultimately, *Supernormal* will take seriously the questions of whether life must be a never-ending battle, whether good can win out in the end, and where exactly love fits in all this. But first, we begin where such sagas always do—with an origin story. There is a moment or a circumstance that sets everything in motion.

CHAPTER 2

Origin Story

I don't really miss God, but I sure miss Santa Claus.
—Eric Erlandson and Courtney Love, "Gutless"

The sound of hangers scraping woke Sam up. It was a familiar sound, one he had heard through the thick haze of sleep on weekday mornings for as long as he could remember. Sam's father was a businessman—a manager of some kind—at a paper mill in the next town over, so he started his day sooner than the rest of the family, pushing and pulling his suits and shirts along the metal bar in his closet as he chose what to wear. By the time Sam got out of bed to get ready for school, the only evidence his father had been in the house at all was a nearly empty cup of coffee that sat at the head of the breakfast table. Cold when he got to it, the coffee was sweet with sugar and rich with cream and Sam loved to start his mornings by drinking it up.

This time when Sam heard the hangers, it was different. It was too dark to be morning, and the screeching and scraping went on for longer than usual. Plus there had been that fight—one that seemed worse than usual—between his parents the night before. When he heard his father walk out of his bedroom and start down the hall, Sam knew he was leaving—not for work, but for good. He padded to the doorway and peeked out, just in time to see his father moving through the last few feet of the shadowy corridor, his brown hard-sided suitcase in hand. As he watched his father go, Sam thought about calling out and saying something: maybe *Wait, don't go!*

Instead, he said to himself, *It's for the best.*

Betraying his more complicated feelings, Sam tiptoed to his sister's room, where he knew his mother would be sleeping, and he shook her shoulder until she grunted a groggy "Huh..."

"Dad's gone," Sam whispered to her, feeling someone should be informed of this significant turn of events.

"Go back to bed," was all she said.

Sam did.

He was nine years old and it was a school night.

* * *

Every family hero has an origin story. This is a story that does not begin with "I am born"; instead, like Superman's being sent away from his home planet Krypton or like Spider-Man's spider bite, there is an event or a circumstance that places the child on his desperate and courageous path. In the words of pediatrician and psychoanalyst Donald Winnicott, "a change occurs which alters the whole life of the child." Something happens that is so consequential that life simply cannot go back to the way it was, and the way it is now feels broken somehow. "My seven-year-old world humpty-dumptied, never to be put back together again," writes Maya Angelou about being raped as a child. Sometimes, though, there is a circumstance that is not like a spider bite at all in that it is there from the start, such as when a baby is born into extreme poverty or to a parent who is mentally ill. For the supernormal child, in one way or another, continuity and connection are splintered: There is a before and an after. Or a then and a now. Or a me and an everyone else.

Most often, changes that alter the life of the child take place over months or even years—such as when a sibling becomes ill, when a town deteriorates, or when a parent starts drinking—but the changes feel abrupt and cataclysmic nonetheless. "No one hired a skywriter and announced crack's arrival," rapper Jay Z remembers about growing up in Marcy Houses in Brooklyn. "But when it landed in your hood, it was a total takeover. Sudden and complete. Like losing your man to gunshots. Or your father walking out the door for good. It was an irreversible new reality. What had been was gone, and in its place was a new way of life that was suddenly everywhere and seemed like it had been there forever."

For Sam, his father's leaving was that total takeover, that origin story. When he thought about his life, the story always started there. That night was not Sam's earliest memory, but it was his first memory—the first moment—of his irreversible new reality. It was the change that rearranged Sam's family and the roles his family members would play for decades to come. And as he stood there in the doorway and watched his father walk away with his old life, Sam tried to be reasonable—and strong—by telling himself that it was for the best: Mostly his parents seemed miserable together. Yet as he tiptoed off to find his mother, Sam had the foreboding feeling that things were about to get worse.

* * *

One-third of marriages end within the first fifteen years, making divorce the most common adversity children face. An estimated one million children watch their parents split up each year, yet the fact that divorce is widespread does not mean it is without consequences for the child, any more than the fact that an estimated 350,000 babies are born each day makes childbirth any less painful or momentous for the individual. As commonplace as it may seem, divorce has the potential to, as Winnicott said, change the whole world of the child because, usually, parents are the child's whole world. Divorce shows a child that his world can be torn in two, not just by rare, extreme acts of abuse or terror, but by something as ordinary—and sometimes even as well intentioned—as two parents going their separate ways.

In 1969, California governor Ronald Reagan signed the first no-fault divorce law in the United States. Prior to no-fault divorce, to be freed from marriage, one spouse had to prove that the other was clearly to blame for the breakdown of the union, with adultery, abuse, desertion, insanity, and lack of intimacy among the most common grounds for dissolution. To many legal scholars and advocates for women's rights, these conditions made divorce unnecessarily complex and adversarial, and the burden of proof seemed too heavy, especially for wives who may have had less access to money and other resources to support their case. After California, no-fault statutes swept the nation in the 1970s and 1980s as men and women embraced the prospect of being able to liberate themselves from dysfunctional, loveless marriages. By 1985, no-fault divorce was available in forty-nine of our fifty states. Freedom and choice, it seemed, would help partners and parents make healthier decisions and lead more joyful lives, and this appeared to be in the best interest of children as well.

Without a doubt, sometimes divorce is necessary and in the best interest of all parties—parents and children included. Not every divorce is an adversity. But not every divorce is a "good divorce," either, and sometimes, even when "it's for the best"—as Sam said in the doorway that night—there is change and loss. Large national studies report that, after divorce, about 20 to 25 percent of children experience emotional or behavioral difficulties—such as depression, anxiety, aggression, disobedience, or academic problems—compared with about 10 percent of children in intact families. While this means that children of divorce are twice as likely as their peers to have noticeable and even diagnosable troubles, such data also suggest that 75 to 80 percent appear to do just fine. "The kids are all right," we may be relieved to conclude, but the absence of disorders is not the same thing as the absence of distress. "The key," says psychologist and divorce-expert Robert Emery, "is to separate pathology from pain."

Clinical and empirical research over the past four decades suggests that children of divorce are "resilient but not invulnerable." From the outside, many seem to adapt gamely, taking on more chores at home, keeping up with their own homework, looking after siblings and themselves, and being go-betweens for their parents; yet they may do so as they live with unspoken struggles that are not revealed for years and even decades after the breakup of their families. Psychologist Judith Wallerstein argues that "divorce is a cumulative experience. Its impact increases over time and rises to a crescendo in adulthood." This may not be the case for every young adult whose parents have divorced, but many live with painful feelings and memories.

According to research by Robert Emery and colleagues, compared with those from intact homes, adults from divorced families are three times more likely to feel they had "harder childhoods than most people." About half agree that their parents' split relieved tension in the family, while the other half do not, instead feeling that one set of problems was traded for another. Adult children of divorce tend to have more negative feelings, memories, and beliefs about their families, and they are three times more likely to wonder if both of their parents love them. Unable to don the rose-colored glasses they see some others wear, they view life and love through the "filter of divorce." This sort of filter was what brought Sam to therapy as an adult: "I feel like a piece of Scotch tape that has been stuck and unstuck and now I'm not sticky anymore. I have relationships that look like everyone else's but there is no naïveté. If your own parent can leave you, then anyone can leave you. Life happens. Things change. Things can start off good and wind up bad. I can't pretend I don't know that."

Many children seem to take divorce in stride, even though later they may say that their parents' split was *the* formative event of their childhoods—the origin story of their lives.

Three-quarters of children of divorce say they would be different people today had their families not broken up. They are twice as likely to feel that their childhoods were cut short, and some say they lost the ability to play. Their happiest days, it seems, were before their families fell apart. Their best days, they worry, are behind them.

* * *

Sylvia Plath's father passed away when she was nine years old, and she later remembered that time like this: "My father died, we moved inland. Whereupon those nine first years of my life sealed themselves off like a ship in a bottle—beautiful, inaccessible, obsolete, a fine, white flying myth." Sam's father was still living, but much as in Sylvia Plath's case, the nine years they had spent together now suddenly seemed like something in a bottle, maybe not something as fancy or as put-together as a ship, but perhaps something like a few old pennies that clinked around inside. Those old pennies were the happy memories Sam had of his father and maybe even of his life so far, and while he once thought he would keep dropping pennies in that bottle year after year, now it seemed like those few red cents were all he had.

Sam's father hailed from Brooklyn—which, in Virginia in the 1970s, was more foreign than it was hip. He was a Yankee, which Sam understood to be bad, but he always had the feeling his father had been exposed to some special things that maybe those around him did not know. This seemed deliciously possible on Saturdays, when they would spend lazy days clicking through his father's old slides of Coney Island or poring over the stamp collection that once had belonged to his father's father. Sam loved how important and official the smooth, plastic-covered pages felt under his fingertips, and the crackling sound they made when he turned them. Sam marveled over all the old-fashioned pictures and prices—1c! 3c!—on the stamps, and how the dates went way back.

Other Saturdays, "the boys" made the short drive to the tidewaters where Sam's father taught him to ride ocean waves on a red-and-blue canvas float. For the biggest ones, they kicked out and bodysurfed, Sam riding on his father's back with his arms around his neck. Sam's father taught him how to dive under the waves that scared him, and to hold his breath until the swell rolled over his back past his ankles. When the tide was low, they hunted for clams by looking for little air bubbles along the wet sand and then digging as deep and as fast as they could. When the tide was high, Sam and his father went crabbing, tying chicken necks on nets and lowering them over the side of a pier. Sam's job was to hold the string and wait for a nibble; when he felt a tug or two, he hopped foot-to-foot in excitement as his father swooped in and pulled the line up hand-over-hand, quickly closing the net around the unsuspecting crabs.

Once they had a dozen or more crabs scratching around inside their Styrofoam cooler, father and son triumphantly took them home to boil them alive. Sam's father dropped the scrambling crabs from the cooler into a tall pot of steaming, bubbling water, and they made a hissing sound when they hit the surface. Sometimes, when a crab managed to jump out of the pot and scamper across the kitchen floor, Sam fled and watched from the hall, shouting while the disoriented crab scurried sideways, this way and that, banging into the cabinets or the refrigerator, free for a few seconds until his father could step on its shell, pick it up by its back two legs, and pitch it again into the pot, this time for good. Sam was the kind of kid who made faces at the thought of hurting animals but he was his father's favorite and his father was his, so Sam figured, those crabs—with their sharp, jagged claws that once drew blood from his father's big toe—they got what they deserved.

*   *   *

Psychologist and renowned family therapist Virginia Satir suggested that "most people prefer the certainty of misery to the misery of uncertainty." As an adult, Sam did not think he would have preferred for his parents to have remained in a miserable marriage, but the uncertainty that followed had been difficult, too. When parents break up, foundational assumptions about love and family and order and permanence are shattered, and children begin to ask themselves devastating questions about bedrock: Is it my fault? What will happen next? Who will take care of me? If my parents can stop loving each other, can they stop loving me? Where will I live? Who is going to take care of the parent who lives with me? Who is going to take care of the parent who lives alone? Who is going to buy our food? Will my marriage break up one day? As comforting as one or both parents may try to be, reassurances that everything is going to be fine—or even better than before—are not always backed up by reality.

Children fare well when their newly single moms or dads fare well, too, but sometimes parents and parenting deteriorate after divorce. As difficult as it is for modern families to juggle careers and children, single parents tend to struggle even more. Parents who once shared homes, bills, cooking, bath times, bedtimes, weekends, and sick days feel overloaded as they try to go it alone. Nearly two-thirds of adults live in a community other than where they were raised, which means that reinforcements in the form of Grandma and Grandpa and aunts and uncles may be miles or even an ocean away. Almost half of adults report they have only one person—at most—with whom they discuss important matters, and because this one person is usually a partner or a spouse, divorce leaves parents alone not only with their logistical needs but with their emotional ones as well. As some children become the shoulders for their parents to cry on, they are confronted with grown-up problems they are helpless to solve, such as who will drive the car pool or pay the bills.

About half of custodial parents receive all the child support they are due, while about one-quarter receive some and one-quarter receive none; support is especially unlikely to be paid if there is not shared custody or regular visitation, or if one parent leaves the state. Yet even when parents both pay their fair share, finances are still likely to become strained. According to bankruptcy expert Senator Elizabeth Warren, in the twenty-first century, when two-income families who pool their money struggle to stay in the middle class, "today's newly divorced [parent] is already teetering over a financial abyss the day [he or she] signs the divorce papers." About one-third of single-parent families live in poverty, and because women are seven to eight times more likely to raise children after a divorce, they and their children are especially at risk. "Having a child is now the single best predictor that a woman will end up in financial collapse," Warren writes. And she should know. Though Warren's parents did not divorce, her own origin story begins when her father lost his job and she and her mother went to work to keep the family solvent: "I know the day I grew up. I know the minute I grew up. I know why I grew up," she recalls.

Sometimes even more wrenching than the day-to-day worries about where the childcare or the money is going to come from is wondering where the care will come from. Psychoanalyst Adam Phillips and historian Barbara Taylor suggest that "today it is only between parents and children that kindness is expected, sanctioned, and indeed obligatory," and whether or not this is a sweeping truth, it does tend to be how children feel. One of the most robust findings in research on resilience is that a leading factor that protects children against hard times is the number of high-quality relationships in the child's life, and divorce can cut this number in half. Sometimes the number is halved because where once there were two parents, now there is one. Other times the number *feels* halved because, even though both parents remain committed to the child, they are now preoccupied with new jobs, new lovers, new stressors, new responsibilities, and their own feelings about the divorce, and each parent may be only half as available as before. In an effort to cheer up their children and themselves, parents may tout the benefits of growing up with two bedrooms, two families, and two sets of everything. Life will be twice as good, some may say, but children are not fooled. "Even a good divorce restructures children's childhoods and leaves them traveling between two distinct worlds," says author Elizabeth Marquardt. "It becomes their jobs, not their parents', to make sense of those two worlds."

None of this is to say that unhealthy, unhappy families ought to stay together. There are no easy answers to troubled partnerships. This is simply a recognition of something that as adults we may be pained to acknowledge but that children already know: Like marriage, divorce is for better and for worse. In one study, 80 percent of young adults agreed that "Even though it was hard, divorce was the right thing for my family." Children do best when parents are willing to talk about breakups from the other side, too: that even though divorce may be the right thing, it is hard. Otherwise, adolescents are left alone with their grievances and young children are left alone with their grief.

* * *

On the October morning Sam's father left, no one in his family spoke of it. As odd as this may seem, it is not unusual. Twenty-three percent of children report that no one talked to them about divorce as it was happening, and 45 percent recall only abrupt explanations such as "Your dad is leaving"; just 5 percent of children report feeling fully informed about what was happening between their parents and being encouraged to ask questions. So off Sam went to school that day—and on all of the days that followed—as if nothing had changed. This was easy to do because, unlike home, where he simply pretended nothing had changed, school was a place where this was actually true. Mornings still began with the same Pledge of Allegiance. At snack time, Sam still ate cheese crackers and drank chocolate milk from little cartons. Playing soccer at recess was still the best hour of the day. School was still where new things came in the form of fun and faraway facts, like about weather or Egyptians, and these new things were presented thoughtfully and stepwise, making them understandable and never overwhelming or personal.

Then, not so long after Sam's father left, his fourth-grade class was learning about the mail: how to write letters with proper salutations like "Dear So-and-So" and "Sincerely, So-and-So" and how to prepare envelopes with addresses and return addresses in the right places. For practice, Sam's teacher asked each student to write a real letter to a real person who did not live at home. Sam sat at his desk and stared at his paper. He rolled his pencil in its pencil holder. He could not begin. After a time, Sam walked up between the rows of desks to where his teacher stood writing on the blackboard, her back to the class.

"Miss Leonard..." he started.

She turned around.

"I can't write the letter," Sam continued blankly.

"Why not?" she asked, leaning toward the boy, ready to get back to her task.

"I don't have anyone to write," Sam insisted, before he broke eye contact to study the chalk in her fingers and the powdery smudges on her roomy round-cut skirt.

"Surely you can think of someone," she pressed.

"I can't. There isn't anybody..." Sam insisted again. Rigidly.

Mrs. Leonard looked at Sam and then blew him away with nonchalance: "Why don't you write a letter to your dad?"

Sam stood there—stunned, shocked, breathless. Then, without a word, he walked back to his desk and wrote a letter to his cousin who lived in Texas.

In November, Sam's mother gave him a full-size Bible with a floppy black cover. They did go to church every Sunday, but Sam had never had his own Bible before. Unsure of what else to make of it, Sam took this to mean that, with his father gone, he was going to need all the help he could get. At night, he flipped and fanned his way through the flimsy see-through pages, and to his surprise he discovered that the Bible was more helpful than he expected. It went into some significant detail about topics that everyone else took great pains to avoid. Sex. Love. Marriage. Even divorce. When Sam came across passages that described people who divorced as adulterers, he read and reread those night after night, trying to make sense of the strange language and of his strange new life. One afternoon in the car, Sam worked up the courage to ask his mother a question. "Did Dad leave because he's an adulterer?" Sam inquired casually as he hunched down in his seat and forced himself to stare straight ahead. Sam's mother slowed the car like she was waiting for her son to continue, so he said, "You know, was there some other woman?"

Sam's mother put her foot back on the gas and exhaled quickly. "God, no," she scoffed. "No one would want him."

Sam did not read the Bible anymore after that.

That December, Sam thought Christmas would never come. Christmas was something so special, so magical—and so wonderfully scripted and ritualistic—that it, and now it alone, seemed untouched by his new circumstances. Santa Claus brought the presents and Santa Claus had not changed. On Christmas Eve, some time after going to bed, Sam needed something—water, maybe—so he tiptoed down the hallway toward the kitchen. When he closed in on the den, it took a moment to understand what he was seeing, but soon he recognized that his mother was wrapping and arranging presents that were supposed to be coming from the North Pole. Sam turned around and sneaked back up the hall, and as he crawled into bed, he realized that all of the men in his life were gone: his father, God, and Santa Claus.

* * *

Sam recalls these moments so vividly because they are what are sometimes called flashbulb memories. Flashbulb memories are recollections that feel illuminated and frozen in time, like snapshots in the mind. Harvard psychologists Roger Brown and James

Kulik introduced this term to the scientific community in a 1977 paper in which they suggested that when we find out about events that are shocking or significant, we permanently imprint those surprises in memory, like photographs. Prototypical flashbulb memories are those of iconic, culturally newsworthy moments, such as the way almost everyone can recall where they were and what they were doing on the morning of September 11, 2001. We probably all remember with great clarity and brightness how we found out that planes had crashed into the World Trade Center, as well as what we did just next.

While Brown and Kulik were interested in how we remember shocking public events, their findings revealed that the cultural and the personal intersect. In their survey of white and black Americans, equal numbers of respondents reported flashbulb memories for hearing about the assassination of President John F. Kennedy, while far more blacks than whites also reported such memories for learning about the assassinations of civil rights leaders Martin Luther King Jr. and Malcolm X. This underscores the fact that flashbulb memories are not simply a catalog of events that are objectively important or out of the ordinary. Most crucial is how relevant or consequential an event *feels* to the individual. That is, flashbulb memories are *emotional memories*, and such memories have long been known to carry special significance in our brains and in our lives. In fact, the power and permanence of emotional memories was one of the founding— and remains one of the most enduring—questions in the study of the mind.

In 1890, the father of American psychology, William James, wrote that some memories seem indelible because "an impression may be so exciting emotionally as almost to leave a scar upon the cerebral tissues." Though in the nineteenth century no one understood quite how this scarring might work, many of James's contemporaries were reaching similar conclusions. The French neurologist and founder of modern neurology, Jean-Martin

Charcot, puzzled over how memories of shocking events were not only persistent but could also be all-consuming, functioning as "parasites of the mind." In Austria, the neurologist and father of psychoanalysis, Sigmund Freud, similarly posed that his patients "suffer mainly from reminiscences," from memories of moments when they felt unbearable feelings such as fright, anxiety, shame, or pain. Back in France, pioneering psychologist Pierre Janet suggested that such "vehement emotions" caused patients to have "the evolution of their lives checked." Although much of what was first known about the force of emotional memories came from studies of stress and trauma in women's lives, two world wars soon brought male patients into the fold. American psychoanalyst Abram Kardiner's writings on the "neurosis of war" are considered by many to be the seminal work on post-traumatic stress, setting the stage for the study of combat stress or the impact that war has on the psyche. "It is not like the writing on a slate that can be erased, leaving the slate like it was before. Combat leaves a lasting impression on men's minds, changing them as radically as any crucial experience through which they live," wrote American psychiatrists Roy Grinker and John Spiegel in 1945.

From an evolutionary standpoint, it makes sense that we take special note of people, places, or situations that seem to threaten or benefit our survival; that there is enhanced memory for emotional experiences. Sometimes these emotional moments are especially happy ones, like sunny days spent riding the waves at the beach, or exciting ones, like watching crabs scamper around on the kitchen floor. Other times, they are distressing or frightening events, like watching a parent walk down the hallway and out of our lives. But while happy and exciting events enrich our experience of *being* alive, frightening events provide important information about *staying* alive, and so negative emotional memories tend to be more firmly installed in our minds. As psychology researcher Roy Baumeister summarizes in his often cited paper, "Bad Is Stronger than Good": At least in our minds, "bad emotions, bad parents, and bad feedback have more impact than good ones, and bad information is processed more thoroughly than good." This is because our brains are wired to keep us alive, not happy, and I doubt a single paper has been written about, nor a single therapy session devoted to, a client's being unable to forget an extraordinarily joyful time. It is our shockingly upsetting experiences that are most deeply etched in our minds, and only in the last few decades have we come to better understand how the brain makes it so.

In the chapters ahead, the region of the brain we will hear about again and again is the amygdala, or the part of the brain neuroscientist Joseph LeDoux calls the "hub in the wheel of fear." A small almond-shaped region deep in the brain, the amygdala is a complex structure with many functions, but overwhelming evidence suggests it plays a central role in managing danger. When our senses detect disturbances in the environment—any potential physical or social threat—the amygdala is alerted, and within milliseconds it reacts. The amygdala is, again according to LeDoux, "where trigger stimuli do their triggering."

One key response that the amygdala triggers is the activation of the HPA axis, or the chain in the neuroendocrine system that consists of the hypothalamus, the pituitary gland, and the adrenal glands. When the HPA axis is stimulated, the adrenal glands release epinephrine, norepinephrine, and cortisol, hormones once commonly called adrenaline because they are produced by the adrenal glands and now more popularly and descriptively known as stress hormones because they help us adapt to stress. In our bodies, stress hormones prepare us for fight or flight, and in our brains, they heighten arousal, attention, and memory. Stress hormones tell our brains to wake up and pay attention, and tell our bodies to get ready to take action. They also tell our brains to remember what we see.

Brain imaging studies show that when we look at intensely emotional material, such as slides of highly pleasant or unpleasant scenes, activity in the amygdala increases; and to some extent, the greater the activity in the amygdala, the better the recall is weeks later. Very low emotional arousal suggests there is nothing significant to pay special attention to, and so to protect our brains from overload, mundane events like showering or driving to work are not likely to be remembered in great detail or for very long. Our brains protect us from another sort of overload by sometimes failing to remember times when we are too emotionally aroused, especially those times that involve the utmost terror or helplessness. This is why victims of shark attacks or violent crimes, for example, may not remember such traumas at all; the events are too overwhelming to assimilate. Moderate stress, however, alerts us to threats in the environment that we perceive we can and should do something about. "There is nothing like a little stress to create strong, long-lasting memories of events," says neurobiologist James McGaugh.

Emotional learning is powerful and it needs to be efficient, too, because when it comes to survival, there isn't a lot of room for repeated trial and error. It is for this reason that the amygdala is "quick to learn and slow to forget," it is said. "Emotional memory," says LeDoux, "may be forever." Just as Sam did not need to see his father walk away with his suitcase more than once to remember it decades later, many of us needed to live through only one 9/11 to be haunted by that morning always. Emotional memories stand stronger and longer than everyday recollections, and their vividness makes them feel more real and more central to who we are than the piddling day-to-day. The problem is that when these remembrances are negative, harking back to Charcot, Freud, and Janet, our emotional memories can function as "malignant memories." They are bad memories that do bad things. The tyranny of the past rules the present and the future as these outsize, tenacious reminiscences take over our autobiographies, and even our lives. Although Sam surely went to birthday parties and rode his bike and ate ice cream and played at the park when he was in the fourth grade, he hardly remembers anything about that year other than the losses and the shocks.

* * *

After Sam's father left, shiny silver dead bolts appeared on the front and back doors of his house. His mother did not mention them but she had the keys, so—as with many other things—it went without saying: The locks had been installed so Sam's father could not return. In the months and years that followed, the dead bolts only served as reminders that not once did Sam's father ever even try to come home. He did call to come get a long wooden table he had bought when he was a bachelor, and although Sam and his mother cleared it off and got it ready to go, his dad never showed. Nor did he come get his slides of Coney Island or his stamp collection, though Sam did not lie on the floor and thumb through its pages on Saturdays anymore. Catching sight of the black leather-bound binder on the bookshelf made Sam feel embarrassed and exposed, like seeing an old teddy bear he felt he could no longer pick up.

Sam's father did not come back for Sam, either, although one time he took the boy to a matinee. Sam had never been picked up by his father in the driveway before—it was strange—and as he walked to the car, he squinted in the glare of the sun. He could not tell if it was the bright light or the fact that he was working very hard not to cry, but as Sam climbed into the passenger seat he could not unscrunch his eyebrows. He shifted around in his seat not knowing what to say, disturbed by the fact that he had lost control of his face. Sam cannot recall what movie the two saw and he hardly watched it as he sat there gripping the armrests, distracted by the fact that even in the dark theater, he could not unscrew his forehead. What Sam did not know is that those brow muscles are called Darwin's Grief Muscles because they betray confusion and sadness, even when we try to hide them. As trauma expert Bessel van der Kolk explains, "The body keeps the score," especially when we have feelings our conscious mind cannot or will not register.

Sam's parents officially divorced on Valentine's Day—yes, really—just over two years after his father left. Later Sam would learn that, after the judge ordered his father to pay child support, Sam's father grumbled to his mother on the way out of the courthouse that he would kill them all first. That evening, Sam's mother went straight from work to a bar to celebrate with a friend, while Sam kept busy with sixth-grade homework. Around eleven o'clock, she walked in through the back door and let her purse fall on the floor, instead of placing it on the counter as she usually did. Then she rushed to the kitchen and threw up in the sink.

Most children of divorce go from seeing a parent every day to seeing the now absent parent between four and fourteen days a month. About a quarter of kids have little or no contact with the noncustodial parent, usually their fathers, within three years, and that was the case for Sam. Like many children, Sam wished he could see his father more, and he told his best friend that maybe he would go live with him in the summer sometime, that his dad was lonely and wanted him to come. "What in the hell is *that* about?" his mother asked after hearing the news from the friend's mother. "Your dad isn't lonely and you're not going to live with him. You never even hear from him except for getting cards on holidays."

For Christmas and Valentine's Day, Sam's father tore a ten-dollar bill into two pieces and sent half to Sam and half to Sam's sister, each tucked into a generic store-bought card. Known more for his cynical wit than for his symbolic gestures, Sam's father probably thought he was being clever and it was, indeed, a clever illustration of the fact that Sam's and his sister's lives now felt torn in two and unusable. Worthless. Sam and his sister tossed the torn bills into the trash because they did not know what else to do with them.

Maybe Sam was angry or hurt about those cards, but all he remembers feeling is guilt: guilt because he never sent his father anything at all. Sam knew better than to ask his mother to buy stationery or presents intended for his dad, and besides, Sam no longer knew where his dad lived. Once, a nonprofit sent a membership card to Sam's house with his father's name printed on the front. Sam tucked it into his wallet and pretended—even to himself—it was an emergency contact card, a way of reaching his father if he needed him, until one of Sam's friends called bullshit: "My dad got one of those cards in the mail, too. That's junk mail!"

Sam's father made good on his promise, not of killing them but of not paying child support. His family stopped taking vacations to the beach. They stopped playing sports. They stopped being sure if they could buy clothes or stay in their house. Once when his mother sat in the car and cried over her tax bill, Sam offered bravely, "We could sell Dad's stamp collection..."

Her sobs became bitter, choking laughter. "That stamp collection isn't worth anything," she said through gravelly chuckles. Now Sam was the one who felt like crying.

Sam's father moved back to New York. Sam knew this because, inside the holiday cards he still received every year for a while, instead of half a ten-dollar bill was a New York Lottery scratch-off ticket. Virginia did not have the lottery yet, so in a way the tickets seemed exotic and exciting. Sam would hunt a penny out of a drawer and sit down somewhere in private, ready to scrape away the gray powdery goo. Each time he scratched and lost, he felt tricked.

CHAPTER 3

Secret

I'm seven years old, talking to myself, because I'm scared, and because I'm the only person who listens to me.

—Andre Agassi, *Open*

On July 15, 1976, the rural farm town of Chowchilla, California, made national news. It was the next-to-last day of summer school and a school bus was ferrying children home from school when its driver slowed for a white van stopped in the street. Two masked gunmen jumped out of the van, boarded the bus, and then drove away with twenty-six children between the ages of five and fourteen, along with their bus driver, a man named Ed Ray. Guns trained on the children, the masked men drove the bus down into a nearby gully, where the confused hostages were transferred to two windowless pitch-black vans. The children were driven around and around, with no explanation, for eleven hours. There was no food or water, and no bathrooms, yet no one panicked or became inconsolable. The children sat calmly—many in their own urine—and passed the time by singing, "If You're Happy and You Know It Clap Your Hands."

Deep into the night, the vans came to a stop. The masked

gunmen ordered the children off the bus and down into a "hole," which later only a few recognized to be an opening in the top of a moving truck that had been partially buried underground. Once inside, the children heard a heavy metal plate being dragged over the opening above, sealing the twenty-seven hostages within. Then came the sound of shoveling, and of dirt and stones raining down on the roof above. One hundred miles away, parents had long since noticed that the school bus had disappeared, and as the FBI and the media descended on Chowchilla, the twenty-six children and their bus driver were being buried alive.

A few kids cried and screamed, and the bus driver pleaded for the men to stop, but before long, all went mostly silent both inside and outside the truck. As it had been all along, the children's behavior remained quiet and directed. The students and their bus driver made use of the mattresses, the few flashlights, and the bit of food left for them in the van. The older students looked after the younger ones, as the children mostly slept and sat in the dark and waited until far into the next day for what would come next. What came next was that, heavy with dirt, the roof of the moving truck began to collapse. Spurred into action by this immediate, life-threatening emergency, the driver and some older kids stacked the mattresses high, and they found a way to move the metal plate and dig their way out. The children expected to be shot when they emerged from the truck, but instead they stumbled into nothingness in the middle of nowhere.

After finding help, the children were taken to a nearby prison, where they were given hamburgers, apple pie, and brief physical examinations. None of the students were shaking or screaming or falling apart, so the doctors declared that they were "all right." Only two kids connected the word *kidnapping* to the experience they had just lived through. According to Lenore Terr, a psychiatrist who later worked closely with the families, "Nobody else in the group had known what to call it."

* * *

That same summer on the East Coast, a six-year-old girl named Emily and her thirteen-year-old babysitter were spending a Sunday playing board games. Emily's neighborhood was an orderly grid of tree-lined streets, where large, old homes were set back tastefully from the sidewalks, and sidewalks were set back tastefully from the street. It was a neighborhood where no one said no to anyone; that was not neighborly. And certainly no child said no to an adult; that was not polite. So when the red-faced man from down the block pounded on Emily's front door while Emily's parents and her twin brothers were at a baseball game, the babysitter flung the door wide. And when the man pushed past both girls and charged into the kitchen looking first for Emily's father and then for something in the kitchen, both of them did their best to help.

Slurring his words, the man rifled through the cabinets demanding to know where the liquor was, yet Emily thought he was saying pickles. "Where are the pickles? I know your father has pickles! Where does your father keep his *goddamn pickles*?" the angry man yelled, more into the cabinets than at the uneasy girls shifting around nearby.

This was confusing. Pickles were kept in the refrigerator, not the cabinets. And it was Emily's mom who pulled out the pickles for sandwiches, not her dad. Emily looked in the refrigerator but there were no pickles that day. She told the man this—over and over—but he went on searching for pickles in all the wrong places, knocking boxes of macaroni and crackers on the floor.

This did not make sense.

When the angry man left, Emily and her babysitter went back to their board game. They acted as if nothing had happened because nothing *had* happened that they could explain.

When Emily's parents and the twins returned, the babysitter reported what she could, and now it was Emily's mom who looked angry. Emily's parents whispered forcefully to each other in the next room, using some words Emily did not understand. Her mom hissed the word "alcoholic." Her dad said "fucking New Jersey blue laws." The conversation ended with her mom saying in a strange tone: "Of course you're his first stop when he runs out on a Sunday..."

All Emily could piece together was this: There was something wrong with Emily's father, and some people—like their neighbor—might know about it.

* * *

Watching a man ransack your kitchen is surely not as terrifying as being snatched off your school bus at gunpoint. Yet as different as these two stories seem, both tell us something important about what many children—and even many adults—do when they are afraid: They tend to go on behaving as usual. This comes partly from a wish that *life* would go on behaving as usual, a wish that if we just keep acting normal then everything and everyone around us will go back to being normal, too. But this is also what our brains tell us to do.

Remember that when the amygdala detects a threat in the environment, it fires up a state of preparedness or a "readiness to behave." What it means to behave, however, depends on the situation. Maybe we get ready for a fight, or maybe we get ready for flight. Yet because children are often outmatched by bigger, stronger, faster adults, fight and flight can feel like options they do not have. This leaves children feeling helpless and vulnerable and, in that case, the best thing may be to take it easy, to make no sudden moves. Go along to get along. Be quiet in every way.

If the amygdala is the "hub in the wheel of fear," then the part of the brain called Broca's area is the hub in the wheel of speech. It takes what we are seeing and hearing and feeling and puts it into words; then it signals the motor cortex to produce those words. Research on the brain shows that, for some people, when there is greater activity in the amygdala there is less activity in Broca's area. In the face of terror, as the amygdala fires up, Broca's area quiets down and so does the individual. This is likely the neurological basis for being scared speechless, and there is clearly adaptive value in not drawing attention to yourself—say, by shrieking and letting a nearby lion know you are hiding terrified in the bushes. This is probably why one boy who was on the school bus that day in Chowchilla reported later that he had simply been "too scared to cry."

When the brain is overwhelmed with fright, the words do not come and cannot come, and this is especially true for experiences that are unusual or without familiar labels. From both Emily's story and the children of Chowchilla, it seems clear that often children are not only too scared to cry; they are too confused to cry as well. Even when Broca's area is active and ready to do its job, we cannot put experiences into words if we do not have the words to work with. Much of life is pattern recognition, as what we see links up with what we know. We call a banana a banana— and we know it is a fruit—because we learned that in preschool. A round orange object could be a different piece of fruit such as a tangerine, or it could be a basketball, depending on its size and on how it feels and smells. All day, every day, our ordinary moments link up with words and categories we already know. This is how we talk about what we see.

Sometimes, though, things happen and we do not have the words or categories to match them. We have experiences we cannot name, and naming can be especially difficult for children who have lived less of life and who have fewer labels at their disposal. In moments like these, children need others to help them articulate their reality. Otherwise, they are left with a sort of alexithymia, or the inability to put feelings and experiences into words. We are all alexithymic as infants—the root *in fans* means "not speaking"— and as we grow, we label our inner and outer world with help from those around. People in our lives say, "That's a car!" or "You're tired!" or "That hurt!" and we say, "Yes!" When complicated grown-up problems do not fit with the words that children have—when no one says, "That's an alcoholic!"—they are left with the silent awareness that something important and frightening, yet unspeakable, has gone on.

In her graphic memoir, *Fun Home*, Alison Bechdel details a camping trip she went on when she was ten years old, a weekend that was part of her origin story. While her mother stayed home, Bechdel was accompanied by her brothers, her father, and a young man who was one of her father's secret gay lovers. Also on this trip, Bechdel stumbled across pornography for the first time, held a gun for the first time, and saw a giant snake in a riverbed. Years later, she would find this diary entry from the trip: "Saw a snake. Had lunch." The rest of it went unsaid for more than a decade. "My feeble language skills simply could not bear the weight of such a laden experience," she rightly concluded about her ten-year-old self.

Just as the children of Chowchilla could not begin to understand where they were going when they were driving around in those vans, neither could Emily make sense of why a man would angrily search her kitchen for pickles. No one ever explained that the slurring man was saying "liquor"; nor did anyone know that Emily was so upset by the events of that day. The supernormal child may act as if she hardly notices anything wrong—and besides, she seems "all right." Yet when we cannot connect what we see or hear to something we have seen or heard before, or when words simply will not do an experience justice—"Trauma mocks language," says feminist scholar Leigh Gilmore, "and confronts it with its insufficiency"—we literally do not know how to think about it. The unlinkable is unthinkable, and all we can say to ourselves is, "There are no words. I don't know what to do with that. I don't know where to put that." Where we put moments like these is off in a separate part of the mind. It is the part of the mind where the unformulated is kept apart until it, eventually, begins to feel like a secret.

* * *

Weekends at Emily's house began normal enough. On Saturday mornings, she and her brothers lay on the carpet in front of cartoons and ate bowls of Cheerios as long as they could get away with it. Emily's mother headed out on errands and Emily's father cracked open a beer and headed out to the yard. A few hours and beer cans later, he would retreat inside and start pouring brown drinks out of a big glass jug. He stirred these drinks with his finger and then sucked his finger clean, as if he did not want to miss a drop.

When the glass jug came out, Emily's father put on music in the living room and looked around for a dance partner. As the youngest and the only girl, Emily was always chosen. It made her feel special, the way her dad picked her up and spun her around, at least until he squeezed her wrists too hard or swung her dangerously close to the furniture. When Emily's father started to draw the curtains and turn out the lights in the middle of the day, Emily's brothers got squirmy and difficult, almost like they *meant* to pick fights with their father. This would result in shouting at best, or spanking at worst, so Emily took another approach: She scurried to the piano and played her father's favorite song, "King of the Road." Emily could not understand why her brothers never learned to play along.

If the glass jug went empty, the King of the Road took Emily with him when he drove to the store with the big red circles on its sign. Emily hated these trips because this was the only time she was ever left in a car by herself.

"Don't leave me here, Daddy!" Emily pleaded as her father got out of the car in the parking lot. "I'm scared!"

Then a car door slam.

Emily crouched down on the plastic mat on the floorboard and kept herself busy, searching under the seats for stray pennies or half-eaten rolls of breath mints. Every so often, she looked up and out of the window, glancing anxiously at the door of the store. Like a dog spotting its owner, she perked up with relief and anticipation when she saw her dad walking her way, clutching a brown paper bag with a glass bottle peeking out. Sometimes Emily's mother got her alone and asked if her father had stopped by the store with the red circles. Emily knew she was supposed to tell her mother the truth but she also knew she was not supposed to tell her father's secrets. The red-circle store must be a secret because no one ever talked about what it was or explained why she was left alone in the car outside.

When Emily's father brought home a brand-new bottle of the brown stuff, Emily and her brothers were in a bind. If they stayed inside, they risked doing something wrong and being within reach. If they went outside, they risked doing something wrong and being out of reach. Like the time they told their dad they were going to play at the cul-de-sac. On that day, as Emily and her brothers played with the other kids, they forgot all about their dad, and maybe they forgot all about the time, too, until in the middle of a game of hide-and-seek that stretched across several backyards, there was commotion. Some older kids from the neighborhood pedaled frantically toward the game and called out to Emily and her brothers:

"Your dad is looking for you!"

"He's mad!"

"You'd better go home!"

"He's got his belt off!"

At first, Emily stayed crouched behind the boxwoods where she was hiding, hoping this was either a horribly on-target joke or a ploy to get her out of her hiding spot. Then she crept out from behind the shrubs and saw the fear in the other kids' eyes, and she and her brothers jumped on their bikes and pedaled standing up toward their house. As Emily strained against the hill up to her house, she heard one of the kids yell, "Your dad's an alcoholic!"

That word again.

When they made it home, Emily and her brothers jumped off their bikes, abandoning them on their sides, wheels spinning, as they ran toward the front door. They were not supposed to leave their bikes out like that but the longer they delayed, the worse it would be. When they rushed to their father, he pushed Emily and her brothers up the stairs into their parents' bedroom. Then they were lying on the bed side by side, screaming as the leather belt cracked down on them hard. Emily had been whipped enough times to be very, very good at avoiding it, but as careful as she tried to be, sometimes she would make a mistake and get the belt anyway. Still, she *had not* made a mistake that day; her father had. She had told him she was going to the cul-de-sac and he did not remember, and that is what stung the worst. As psychiatrist and Holocaust survivor Viktor Frankl wrote, "At such a moment, it is not the physical pain which hurts the most, and this applies to adults as much as to punished children; it is the mental agony caused by the injustice, the unreasonableness of it all."

Emily and her brothers spent the rest of the afternoon lying on the twin beds in the boys' room, moping about their backsides and about the unreasonableness of it all. They would have liked to have gone back outside with the other kids they heard shrieking in fun, but they were too afraid to anger their father again, and too embarrassed to show their tearstained faces.

"Is Daddy an alcoholic?" asked Emily.

"That's a bad word," one of her brothers shot back. "You shouldn't say that."

It would be two decades before Emily would piece together in therapy that, yes, her father had been an alcoholic all along. Until that time, she had no real way of understanding why her family was the way it was, or why her shoulders came up around her ears at the sight of a man taking off his belt. Well into adulthood, that jingling, snapping sound made her shiver. So did the sound of liquid pouring, the way it went *glub, glub, glub* out of a bottle made of glass.

* * *

One in four children lives with an alcoholic. Alcoholism is the most common illness a child is likely to see a parent suffer from, though most of these children do not know quite what it is they are seeing. Part of the trouble is that it is difficult to recognize an illness if you do not know what the symptoms are. So here is the list, according to the *Diagnostic and Statistical Manual of Mental Disorders*, fifth edition—commonly known as the DSM-5. An "alcohol use disorder"—the current medical term for alcoholism—is a pattern of use that meets two or more of the following criteria: often drinking more than was intended; unsuccessful efforts to cut down or quit drinking; spending a great deal of time obtaining, consuming, or recovering from alcohol; a strong desire or urge to drink; drinking that interferes with responsibilities at work or at home; interpersonal problems caused by drinking; giving up other activities to drink; using alcohol in dangerous situations such as driving; drinking continues despite health, occupational, or social problems caused by alcohol; tolerance to alcohol, or a need to drink more and more; withdrawal from alcohol, or physical discomfort when abstaining for long periods. To meet two or three of these criteria is to have a "mild" alcohol use disorder. Having four to five symptoms qualifies as a "moderate" case, and six or more symptoms suggests the disorder is "severe."

Drinking and even problem drinking can seem too commonplace to have serious consequences, yet when considering the years of life lost to ill health, disability, or early death, alcoholism is the second most burdensome mental disorder in the developed world, topped only by depression. Problem drinkers are likely to suffer from an array of related health problems, to lose their jobs and their relationships, and even to die an early death. But make no mistake: Those hurt most by alcoholism are not the problem drinkers, they are the children of problem drinkers. While alcoholism can cut an adult's life short, problem drinking in the home undermines child development from the start.

Children of alcoholics lead different lives from their friends, and they are likely to face multiple adversities at once. Mothers or fathers, or both, can be alcoholics, but because men are twice as likely to be problem drinkers as women, the most typical stressor children live with is violence, particularly directed toward the mother. An estimated 60 percent of domestic violence cases occur when a parent has been drinking, and 30 percent of child abuse cases involve a parent who is under the influence of alcohol. Even children who are never struck by a parent are still likely to be "hurt on the inside" in myriad ways. Compared with their peers, children of alcoholics are doubly at risk for verbal abuse, sexual abuse, emotional neglect, physical neglect, mental illness in the home, parental separation or divorce, economic hardship, and having a family member in jail. Because mothers tend to be the primary caretakers of children in both intact and divorced families, some research suggests that life at home may be especially difficult if the mother is an alcoholic. When mothers drink, children are less likely to be fed and cared for in even the most basic ways. When fathers drink, some mothers attempt to buffer their children by protecting them from the consequences or simply by limiting their exposure.

Ironically, one of the ways families try to limit their children's exposure to alcoholism is by not talking about it. When life feels very scary, parents, like their children, often go silent, too. They try to keep on behaving as usual as they hide their problems from friends and relatives, and even from themselves. In his memoir, *Not My Father's Son*, actor Alan Cumming writes about how his family responded to his alcoholic father: "We never actually addressed what was really going on: that we were living with a tyrant, someone who, I believe now, was mentally ill. As our silence grew, so did our denial." This is not unusual. According to educational materials from the Hazelden Foundation written especially for children, having a parent who is an alcoholic can be like having "an elephant in the living room": "People have to go through the living room many times a day and you watch as they walk through it very...carefully...around...the...ELEPHANT. No one ever says anything about the ELEPHANT. They avoid the swinging trunk and just walk around it. Since no one ever talks about the

ELEPHANT, you know that you're not supposed to talk about it either. And you don't."

Lots of children, not just children of alcoholics, grow up with elephants in their lives: physical abuse, mental illness, neglect, poverty, sexual abuse, abandonment, divorce, domestic violence. Whatever it is, most children are too scared and too confused to talk about it—and besides, they notice that others would prefer they didn't. Left alone with complicated grown-up problems, young minds draw their own conclusions about the world.

* * *

When the elephant came home from work in the evenings, he sat down in the living room and drank brown drink after brown drink. Emily liked to sit on the edges of the room, watching television from behind some drapes like a little mouse. The more Emily's father drank, the more her brothers wrestled on the floor during commercials. "Pipe down!" yelled Emily's father. "Go to bed!" he shouted when the family programming ended. "We're hungry!" the twins demanded. "It's not a school night! It's summer!" they stalled. When the elephant got out of his chair and charged the boys, this was Emily's cue to scurry off to bed.

From her room, Emily heard four-way shouting as bedtime came and went. Her brothers hurled refusals and challenges. Her mother pleaded for her father to let her handle the boys, or maybe even for him to stop drinking and go to bed himself. Many times, this worked. Sometimes, it did not. On this particular night, Emily heard the noises of a fight turning physical. Grunts and slaps. Boys crying. Her mother shrieking. As annoyed as she was afraid, Emily got out of bed and walked toward the noise, ready to perform. Upon entering the living room, she saw one brother standing on a chair with her mother blocking the way to him, fending off her husband by sticking out both arms and a leg. Her father leaned in toward mother and son, leading with his elbow, the back of his hand ready to follow with a good smack. From her father's other hand, the other twin was hanging heavy, dangling by his arm held hard and fast in his father's too-tight grip. Emily could see red finger marks where the brother had twisted and struggled and gained an inch or two.

When parents lose control, some children try to be heroes by taking charge themselves. Older children may try to reason with their parents, while the younger ones shift the focus to their own silly or bad behavior, as Emily's brothers did; or, like Emily, they distract their parents with seemingly innocent misdirection. Pretending to be half asleep and much confused, Emily asked for some juice and the action stopped. Her father dropped one brother and backed away from the other, and then he stomped upstairs and slammed his bedroom door. Emily's mom sent the brothers to bed. She poured Emily something to drink and sent her back to bed, too. When Emily heard her mother turn off the television, Emily turned toward the task of falling asleep. Asking for juice was an old trick.

The next morning, the twins had bruises and marks on their arms, so Emily was sent to swim team practice without them. She pedaled her bike down to the neighborhood pool and thought about what to say to her coach, wondering if he already knew her brothers were not coming, if maybe he knew about the night before. She disliked the idea that people might be whispering about her family but she also imagined—or perhaps wished—that the adults talked about her more than they did. The way the grown-ups always had details worked out in advance about car pools and swim schedules and block parties, Emily pictured organized community meetings, ones where the adults got together and sat in rows of chairs and talked thoughtfully about the kids. If not that, maybe at least there was a phone tree.

This was all but proven that summer day. Emily swam laps, same as always, but her team must have been moving slowly, because the coach gave them all a loud talking-to. Emily hung on to the concrete lip at the end of the swim lane and pressed the balls of her feet into the smooth tile wall as she listened to her coach yell to the group, "Stop thinking about everything and your brother and get your head in the pool!" Psychoanalyst Donald Winnicott suggests that, as children try to make sense of the world, one way this process goes wrong is through coincidences, as coincidences "lead to muddle." The coach's words that morning were one of those unlucky coincidences that fed a false worldview. To Emily, his words were meant just for her, and they felt like code. *We all know what goes on at your house. No one is going to talk about it. No one is going to do anything about it. Shut up and swim*, he was saying. *This is your lot.*

* * *

Emily did shut up and swim. In the years that followed, she swam her way to out-of-town swim meets on the weekend and then to a college far away from New Jersey. When faced with the college application prompt "Describe a challenge you have overcome," seventeen-year-old Emily had trouble thinking of one. She felt blank. Finally, she wrote about a state swim meet when she won a blue ribbon despite being quite ill. Not for a moment did Emily consider writing about her father's alcoholism, probably because she still did not have a word for what had been wrong with her father; nor did she know that what she had lived through was a bona fide adversity. In retrospect, though, Emily doubts she would have written about her father's drinking had she been able to. Alcoholism seemed a seedier challenge than what colleges were really looking for, she thought, and it was one for which, in her family, there had been no uplifting blue-ribbon triumph, the kind that everyone seemed to want.

Psychoanalyst Carl Jung said in his autobiography about his own secrets around growing up depressed and with a depressed mother, "It would never have occurred to me to speak of my experience openly," and so it was for Emily. Never once did Emily talk about her father's drinking with her friends at school, and not a single time did she mention it to her boyfriends, or even to a man she lived with for more than two years in her twenties. This was more automatic than it was intentional, as she almost never thought about her father's drinking, either. Her early experiences were there in her mind somewhere, though, and they influenced her. Such as when she noticed that one of the men she had dated smelled like her father—or more accurately, like whiskey; Emily did not date him for long. And when she opted to spend holidays at other people's houses, rather than return to her own. Once, when Emily brought her partner to meet her family, she reflexively found reasons for the two to stay with a friend across town, only once joining up with Emily's father, and for breakfast at that. Emily does not remember consciously deciding to stay away from her father, or plotting to meet him early in the morning before he would have started drinking. She had tiptoed around the elephant both in her living room and in her own mind for so long that, by adulthood, so much about Emily's life and about her decision making still simply, and literally, went without saying. Talking about her father's drinking just "never crossed my mind," Emily said.

This is how secrets—and those who keep them—can be quite misunderstood. Skeletons in the closet. The dirt swept under the rug. Where the bodies are buried. We think of skeletons and dirt and bodies as information we willfully, tactically hide from others, when sometimes, and maybe even usually, secrets are automatic and multidetermined. Fear leaves us speechless. The lack of labels and categories leaves us without words. Those around us hint, or insist, that some things are better left unsaid. Supernormals rarely set out to fool others, and in retrospect they often realize there was a great deal that they kept not only from other people but even from themselves. Dostoevsky makes this distinction when he says, "Every man has reminiscences which he would not tell to everyone but only to his friends. He has other matters in his mind which he would not reveal even to his friends, but only to himself, and that in secret. But there are other things which a man is afraid to tell even to himself, and every decent man has a number of such things stored away in his mind." The problem is that having many such things stored away in your mind may not feel all that decent, and it can produce a vague, unshakable sense not just that one has secrets but that one is living a lie.

Journalist Charles Blow recalls this feeling of lying in his memoir, when he reveals how he managed to go on behaving as usual in his home after he was sexually abused by a relative: "I had to resort to the most useful and dangerous lesson a damaged child ever learns—how to lie to himself...There is nowhere to hide in a small house. I had to make room within the rooms, a safe place midway in the mind, behind seeing and before knowing...That's what people in this town and in our family did with secrets. No matter what it was—not a word. No good could come from giving voice to vice." Blow could not be safe in his house, so he survived by finding a place in his mind where he was safe from the knowledge of what had happened to him. He says he learned to "lie to himself" but really what he articulates so beautifully is the muddle that exists, for children and for adults, as secrets and lies and not knowing become all jumbled up.

* * *

Back in California in 1976, the children from the bus kidnapping returned to school that autumn, and the majority showed not a dent in their academic performance. Unbeknownst to others, however, many began to fantasize about being heroes or, to be more exact, about being better heroes next time. They imagined scenarios of revenge or escape should they ever be confronted by kidnappers again. Some secretly prepared themselves, with exercise or even weaponry, to be more decisively triumphant in the future—that is, to summon the fight or flight they had not been able to muster right away on that summer day. Although inwardly, many of the children would view the kidnapping as the origin story of their lives, outwardly they preferred not to be reminded of or known for the incident. Later that year, one of the boys was recognized at Disneyland, and some curious parkgoers asked if he was a student from the bus. His reply?

"No, I don't live in Chowchilla."

CHAPTER 4

Fight

I like it when a flower or a little tuft of grass grows through a crack in the concrete. It's so fuckin' heroic.

—George Carlin

In 1955, on Kauai, Hawaii's "Garden Island," psychologists Emmy Werner and Ruth Smith inadvertently began what would become a groundbreaking and decades-long study of resilience. Their subjects were 698 infants—all of the babies who were born on the island that year. These infants were from Asian, Caucasian, and Polynesian families, many of whom were struggling with multiple adversities. Some lived in chronic poverty and were undereducated and underemployed. Alcoholism or mental illness ran through many of the homes. Werner and Smith hypothesized that the more difficulties these children were exposed to when they were young, the more problems of their own they would have as they grew. This was a commonsense proposition, to be sure, but it was also one that had not, by the 1950s, been empirically demonstrated in a large sample, much less from the cradle and then across time. To do so, these nearly seven hundred brand-new citizens of Kauai were followed, from birth into middle adulthood, by psychologists, pediatricians, public health professionals, and social workers.

Unfortunately, Werner and Smith were somewhat right. Two-thirds of the infants they labeled as "high-risk"—those who grew up alongside four or more adversities—had serious behavioral or learning problems by age ten. By age eighteen, they struggled with their own delinquency or mental illness, and many had become pregnant. What Werner and Smith did not expect, however, was that, despite their troubled beginnings, one-third of the high-risk children went on to become "competent, confident, and caring adults." They earned educations and held better jobs than their parents. They sidestepped the substance abuse or divorce or domestic violence they had once known, found supportive partners, and built loving families. They were, in Werner and Smith's words, "vulnerable, but invincible."

This startling discovery turned Werner and Smith's work on its head. What was intended to be an inquiry about the devastating impact of early adversity became a seminal work about the possibility of transcending it. How exactly had these vulnerable children managed to make themselves invincible, if they were indeed so? There is no formula, of course, but decades of further research—both in the Kauai sample and in other studies—point to adaptations and conditions that facilitate one's "overcoming the odds," the title of one of Werner and Smith's books on the topic. Perhaps most notably, when Werner and Smith asked these "vulnerable, but invincible" adults how, in retrospect, they understood their own unexpected success, the answer was not all that surprising: The majority reported that determination—a fighting spirit—was their most important asset.

* * *

Paul looks like a superhero. Or to be more precise, he looks like a superhero might appear on his day off. Behind his glasses, he is handsome in a boy-next-door kind of way, and right now he appears to be about that age superheroes always seem to be, somewhere between twenty-five and thirty-five. His muscles strain a bit against his T-shirt, not so much that his bulk seems strange or steroidal but enough to give the impression that, underneath his casual exterior, Paul is surprisingly strong. He comes across as squeaky-clean and friendly, but he is guarded, too. Paul seems like the kind of person who would fare well in an emergency, like he is fit to take on the world, and in a way he is.

Paul is a nuclear engineer and a young officer in the navy. He found his way to me after he read a book I wrote on the importance of one's twenties, on the value of making a bold and courageous start in adulthood. He felt validated by the notion that all the hard work he had put into his own twenties would pay off, but he had questions, too. He wondered sometimes if other people his age—especially those not living in barracks or on submarines—were free to enjoy their lives more. They traveled for pleasure, he imagined, and they spent time with their loved ones while he left his partner—a young artist with an alcoholic father—back home alone. He wondered how he could be there for the woman he loved and the country he loved at the same time. Perhaps like many others in service, Paul sometimes looked around and asked himself: "Why am I doing this?"

Why indeed.

This was a question Paul heard often, not only from himself but also from others. Many who questioned him wrongly envisioned the military as a gathering place for those with no other options, yet there was Paul, an excellent student who had lived a middle-class life. To many, his decision to be an engineer in the navy seemed curious, or at least one with a story behind it. When I posed his own question back to him—"Why are you doing this?"—Paul was ready with a response. It was succinct and clear, in that way that perhaps the military trains one to be, yet his answer was also notable for its candid self-awareness: "I really struggled in school growing up, and for years I was hunkered down in a sort of bunker in a lot of ways. But the navy is an environment where I have been able to stick my head above the parapet and thrive."

* * *

For Paul, the fifth grade had come too soon. He was skipping a year so, on that first day, his teacher said, "Class, this is Paul. He is joining us from the third grade. Please make him feel welcome." She might as well have placed a target on his back.

Paul was certainly an easy mark. Of all the kids in his class, he was the smartest but also the newest, the youngest, the skinniest, and the weakest. On his first day on the playground, when the class played Red Rover, Paul gave it his all as he ran toward the line of cheering and jeering classmates, only to be bounced back from their joined hands like a rock out of a slingshot. In a way, all of his school years would come to feel like that. Paul spent his days trying to break in somewhere only to have the other kids grasp each other tightly, like they would rather have their arms broken than be seen as the weak link, the ones who let Paul through. Outside of recess, kids turned their backs to him at the lunch table. They stepped on the backs of his shoes. They leaned in together and snickered behind their hands when he spoke. They spit in his seat and left mean notes on his desk.

When another new boy joined the class, for a short while Paul had a friend. Together they articulated the sort of social class system at work: The "upper" boys were the biggest and the most athletic ones, the boys whom everyone watched carefully and wanted to be; the "middle" boys had some assets but not quite the right ones, so they worked anxiously to align themselves with the boys above them; the "lower" boys, of course, were Paul and a couple of others who mostly stayed away from each other for fear of compounding their bad situation. With his new friend, life as a "lower" was tolerable for a while but only until one of the mean notes on his desk said this: "Sorry. Can't be friends anymore. I want to move up."

* * *

Some kids live with emotional or physical abuse at home, while others live with it at school, where it goes by the name of bullying. About one in three children are bullied, usually at school, by the age of eighteen, although what that bullying looks like varies widely. An estimated 25 percent of bullied children are the targets of verbal aggression; they are made fun of, insulted, or called names, or they have rumors spread about them. About 10 percent are bullied physically, by being pushed, shoved, tripped, spit upon, or the like. About 5 percent are ignored or excluded from activities, and another 5 percent have their physical safety threatened. And according to a 2011 study from the Pew Research Center, about 10 to 15 percent of teens reported being harassed via the Internet. Like Paul, most children who are bullied are targets of more than one kind of aggression.

To understand bullying and its impact is to understand the role of power: Bullies have more of it, while their targets have less. Contrary to the widespread notion that bullies are insecure outsiders, most have assets that are respected by their peers. Maybe they are physically large or are fast runners or skilled athletes, or perhaps they are popular or socially savvy. Bullies abuse whatever power they have to maintain their dominant position in the crowd. The targets of bullies, on the other hand, tend to be socially vulnerable, usually because they are different somehow. Maybe they are chosen, as Paul was, because they are younger or smaller or new to a class. Sometimes they are perceived as unattractive or unathletic. They may be disabled or economically disadvantaged, or they may be a member of an ethnic minority or identify as LGBTQ.

Although elementary school students do experiment with

bullying behaviors, the lion's share of bullying takes place in middle school. Bullying behavior spikes during transitions between grades or schools or during other times when social groups are disrupted. Boys and girls jockey anew for friends and invitations, and it is during this social free-for-all that various forms of aggression may be used to establish, or reestablish, the status quo.

When Paul moved on to middle school, most of his classmates moved along with him, as did his low status. More than ever, the boys scrambled for a place at the top of the social heap, or at least for a place as far from the bottom as possible. During school, kids pelted Paul with the bad words they were just learning—gay, stupid, weirdo, pussy, fag, loser, asshole, shithead, pencil dick—and after school they pelted him with rocks while he waited for his bus. Contrary to the old sticks-and-stones adage, the words did hurt—and in fact, recent research has found that social pain travels along the same pathways in the brain as does physical pain.

The imbalance of power is not only what makes bullying possible and intractable but also what makes it so harmful. Of course, some fighting and competition is common and even normal among kids, but those who experience repeated aggression at the hands of more powerful others feel more threatened, less in control, and more anxious and depressed than those who experience aggression at the hands of peers on their same level. Feeling helpless to change what is happening to them, the targets of bullying may live with chronic fear and dread, and the harm that this may cause is as varied as bullying itself. Many victims of bullying feel bad about themselves and feel isolated from others. Because bullying often—but not always—takes place at school, targets may perform poorly in their classes and have a negative view of education and teachers. They may suffer from physical ailments such as headaches, stomachaches, or sleeping problems, and report mental health problems such as depression, anxiety, and suicidal thoughts. These problems tend to be more severe if the youth is targeted once a week or more, and they may continue well into adulthood as the experience of powerlessness and victimization becomes woven into who they are, with depression or anxiety lasting for years or even decades after bullying subsides.

This might have been how it went for Paul were it not for one of the rocks hurled his way. When Paul came home with a bloodied eye that required stitches, his mother considered that perhaps he ought to beat a retreat; that maybe the family should move so he could go to another school: "*I feel bullied by those kids!*" Paul heard his mother cry to his father that night behind their closed bedroom door. Hearing those words and his mother's sobs, what struck Paul the most was the unfairness, the wrongness, of it all. Parents are not supposed to cry. Families are not supposed to move. People who do bad things are not supposed to get away with them. So in that moment, Paul decided to stay right where he was. He was going to find a way to fight back.

* * *

When faced with danger, our deepest instincts are to fight back or run away. This "fight-or-flight" response was so-named in 1915 by psychologist Walter Cannon, who observed in animals that, when threatened, the body mobilizes to defend itself or to flee. In Cannon's model, every living being's goal is to maintain homeostasis—another well-known word he coined—and, to do so, the brain coordinates bodily systems in order to ensure the stability of what, before him, French experimentalist Claude Bernard called the milieu interieur, or the internal environment.

Cannon's ideas have been refined over the years, but a century later we know that he was largely correct. Following disturbances in our environment, the brain and the body respond in an effort to make things right. The amygdala triggers the release of stress hormones, and as a result heart rate increases, focus narrows, digestion slows, and blood flows to our muscles for extra energy. These changes prepare us to react to stress—to do something about it—by either advancing or retreating, through fight or through flight.

When we think of the fight in fight or flight, we may imagine physically harming someone or something, and in the most primitive evolutionary sense, to fight is to punch a person who shoves us or to throw rocks at a bear that charges our way. In the modern world however, fighting back can take many forms. The word *aggression* is derived from the Latin *aggredere*, which can mean "to attack or assail," but it can also mean "to approach or attempt," or "to seize an opportunity." For the family hero, to fight often means to attack a problem. Rather than raging against another *person*, fighting the good fight is more often about battling back against a *situation*—poverty, discrimination, abuse, bullying, unfairness, abandonment—whatever the case may be.

Fueled by some original injustice, family heroes are not afraid to work long and hard without immediate rewards, even in the face of multiple setbacks. There is an unwillingness to be beaten, an impulse to fight for one's own survival and to better one's circumstances, an imperative to stand up for oneself and for what is right. In fact, they usually feel they have no choice. Failure is not an option, as they say, because neither is keeping on with life the way it is.

In my office, this is how family heroes describe themselves:

> I am a fighter.
> I am a survivor.
> I am determined.
> I am a scrapper.
> I am tough.
> I am strong.
> I never give up.
> I just keep going.
> I do what has to be done.
> I'm driven.
> I am a striver.
> I always find a way.

I pick myself up and brush myself off.
I do whatever I set my mind to.
Backed into a corner, I come out swinging.

Most family heroes do not literally become fighters, of course, and even Paul joined the military as an engineer, a problem solver. But no matter who or what they may look like on the outside, on the inside they see themselves as fighters at heart. Many draw strength from the stories not just of superheroes but of all sorts of fighters. Real-life heroes who can show them a way forward. Characters in books and movies and music that seem as powerful and as relentless as they may feel. Fictional assassins who know something about locking in on a target and having that killer instinct. Metaphorically speaking, they are hunters. They are stalkers. They are slayers. They are soldiers. Whatever the situation—or the inspiration—each day feels like a fight for survival, and scrappers that they are, family heroes use whatever strengths, whatever weapons, they have to prevail: smarts, sports, family, talent, work ethic, personality, even language.

Also once a student who, like Paul, felt young and out of place, Senator Elizabeth Warren describes in her memoir, titled *A Fighting Chance* no less, a Midwestern adolescence in which she learned to work with what she had: "I was only sixteen, but because I'd skipped a grade, I was now a senior in high school. The way I looked at it, I wasn't pretty and I didn't have the highest grades in my school. I didn't play a sport, couldn't sing, and didn't play a musical instrument. But I did have one talent. I could fight—not with my fists, but with my words. I was the anchor on the debate team."

And as millions of people know by now, Lin-Manuel Miranda, in his smash Broadway musical *Hamilton*, tells the story of Alexander Hamilton, who "wrote his way out" of poverty in the Caribbean and into becoming one of the nation's Founding Fathers.

Maybe fewer people, though, are aware that Hamilton's story is not entirely unlike that of Miranda, who wrote his way out of some tough times, too. As a child in Washington Heights, Miranda was picked on for his verbal skills: "I caught my first beatin' from the other kids when I was caught readin'," he raps on *The Hamilton Mixtape*. Miranda fought back against his troubles with his songwriting, winning a Pulitzer Prize, a MacArthur "Genius" Fellowship, two Grammy Awards, and three Tony Awards by the age of thirty-six. "It's up to me to draw blood with this pen, hit an artery," he raps some more. The pen, as they say, is mightier than the sword.

* * *

Paul returned to school with a bandage over his eye, and he began waging what he called an internal battle for self-respect. Much the way some kids have lucky socks they wear to soccer games, Paul started his day by rummaging through his dresser drawer, looking for his superhero T-shirts. He wore them in layers under other shirts and jackets, like armor, he said, and they protected him from feeling defenseless and alone. Days at school were long, and as he counted down the hours—"six more, five more, four more to go"—Paul practiced being strong, at least in his own mind. He memorized the periodic table. He solved word puzzles. He worked a Rubik's Cube. He changed his handwriting so it slanted to the left rather than to the right. Mind over matter, whatever it was, Paul was determined to make it so. Ever since the stitches, the kids no longer threw rocks at him, and the words and comments that came his way Paul deflected: "I refused to accept that what they said about me was true."

These might sound like imaginary victories, or mere wishful thinking, but researchers know that fighting back on the inside can be as important as what happens on the outside. One study examined the well-being of eighty-one adults who had been held

as political prisoners in East Germany and who had been subjected to mental and physical mistreatment including beatings,
threats, and being kept in the dark. Decades after their release,
about two-thirds of the prisoners had struggled—or were even
still struggling—with post-traumatic stress, while about one-third
of the prisoners had not. To understand why some prisoners fared
better than others, researchers looked at the type of treatment
they received, as well as the coping strategies they used while held
captive. More predictive of later suffering than how severe the
abuse was or whether the prisoners feared for their lives was the
extent to which they gave up on the inside. Those who felt mentally defeated—who felt like "nothing" or who quit caring about
what became of them—were more likely to struggle for years and
even decades after their release than those who secretly fought
back in their own minds. Even though these prisoners may have
appeared to others to have given up, complying with guards and
signing false confessions, on the inside they were prevailing in
ways that no one else could see. Secretly, they refused to believe
they would be defeated, and they imagined that, sooner or later,
they would triumph. What happened on the outside did not matter as, in their minds, they were unbeatable.

Maybe being strong on the inside should have been enough
for Paul, but as had been the case with some of the children
from Chowchilla, he wanted to be physically strong too. "Was I
going to be the kid everyone kept telling me I was, the kid who
got pushed around?" Paul remembers asking himself. "Or was
I going to be someone else?" Paul's father signed his son up for
judo, and soon the dojo was a place where he did get to be someone else. "I was the most aggressive person there," Paul recalled,
taking pride in the way he channeled the fighter within. He made
a point of explaining that judo is not a sport of kicking or punching; it is a martial art in which one pins or neutralizes the oppo-
nent. Each afternoon after school, Paul could win without anyone
getting hurt.

Such daily mastery experiences and physical activity likely protected Paul from depression and anxiety that can go along with bullying and other adversities, yet there was more to it than that. Rather than engaging in routine or maintenance exercise, Paul's workouts both in and out of judo were increasingly designed to push his own limits. On the weekends, Paul put on his superhero T-shirts and ran two miles, then four miles, then six, the pounding of his feet keeping time with the rhythm of his breath and with the intense, thumping music he listened to. Sometimes Paul pretended he was training for the apocalypse. Sometimes he pretended he was invincible.

As an adult, Paul did look pretty invincible, and I commented on how certain and unshakable he seemed, even as he spoke about some very painful times. "I can talk about it now," he said, suggesting that, at one time, he could not. So I wondered—and I asked him—back then, before he could talk about it and before he could draw on the strength of being a naval officer, how did he put one foot in front of another, day after day, as he walked to classes in the hallways at school and as he ran for miles on the streets of his town? How did he fight back for all those years?

At first, his answer was no surprise. His dad was in his corner, he emphasized; and to be sure, having good people who can compensate for what is bad in life can make all the difference. But then Paul said something else. He named—even owned—an emotion that is so often a part of the story, yet one that many family heroes feel ashamed of including. "I got angry," Paul added unabashedly, as a simple matter of fact. "I realized it was wrong what those kids were doing to my family and me, and it made me angry. And that anger became my fire and motivation."

* * *

Anger has a bad reputation. Both scientists and laypeople tend to think of emotions as positive or negative, and of the six universal emotions—happiness, sadness, fear, anger, disgust, and surprise—only happiness seems clearly positive, and the negative emotions seem to be, well, all the rest. As would be expected, positive emotions are viewed as desirable and negative emotions are seen as undesirable; positive feelings lift us up, it is thought, while negative feelings drag us down. From this perspective, an emotion like happiness is to be cultivated while those like fear and sadness and anger are to be eliminated or at least managed. Historically, anger has been viewed as an especially damaging emotion, and this take on getting angry is echoed in many ancient sayings, like this one purportedly by Seneca the Younger—"Anger is an acid that can do more harm to the vessel in which it is stored than to anything on which it is poured"—or this one widely attributed to Buddha—"You will not be punished for your anger, you will be punished by your anger."

More recently, however, rather than judging feelings as good or bad, some scientists have suggested that it makes more sense that each of the universal emotions has a uniquely important role to play. It seems reasonable that while happiness is an emotion that allows us to enjoy life when all is well, other emotions can help us adjust and survive when all is not. With this in mind, researchers have begun to appreciate anger as an emotion with enormous adaptive value. There are many reasons why we become angry, although most involve feeling wronged somehow. A strong feeling of displeasure, anger emerges when we feel thwarted, provoked, or aggrieved. Maybe something or someone we treasure has been taken away, or we are prevented from attaining an object or a goal we desire. Often, but not always, to feel angry is to perceive injustice, an unfairness that results from the misdeeds of others. Anger is a signal that something has gone wrong. Something hurts. There is a violation of what "ought to be."

One afternoon, not long after Paul and I talked about the role that anger had played in his fight against bullying, I had a session with a client in her forties who still struggled with the effects of childhood bullying. I asked her if, growing up, she ever got angry about what was happening to her. (This may be changing some but, historically, girls and women have been especially discouraged from expressing or displaying anger.) "No," she replied. "But I think it would have been better if I had." As Toni Morrison wrote in *The Bluest Eye*, "There is a sense of being in anger. A reality and presence. An awareness of worth."

* * *

Seneca and Buddha were right that just feeling angry is not necessarily beneficial, and, to be sure, chronic anger is hard on the body and mind. What can be useful about anger, though, is not the feeling itself but the action it inspires. Anger is where the fight in fight or flight comes from. An energizer and organizer, anger moves us to close the gap between what we want and what we have, or between the way things are and the way we think they should be. It compels us to resist the current state of affairs, rather than giving up or giving in. A powerful emotion capable of generating enormous forward momentum, anger propels us toward our goals and even over obstacles along the way. Aristotle was able to hold this more generous view of anger when he wrote, "The angry man is aiming at what he can attain." This sort of active, even tireless, striving is a hallmark of the superheroic and the supernormal, and it has long been recognized as one of the key ingredients of success.

In the 1800s, Sir Francis Galton collected biographical information on nearly a thousand celebrated statesmen, writers, scientists, poets, musicians, painters, poets, military commanders, and others, arguing that eminence was the product of the "triple event of ability combined with zeal and with capacity for hard labour." The fact that the word *ability* is given pride of place, as the first of the three events mentioned, is likely no accident. A cousin of Charles Darwin, Galton makes the aforementioned argument in his blockbuster book, *Hereditary Genius*, in which he asserts that intelligence and talent are largely inborn, passed down in great families.

By the 1900s, however, researchers questioned the primacy of innate abilities such as intelligence and began to pay increasing attention to the other factors that Galton put forth: zeal and hard work. Lewis Terman launched the Study of the Gifted, for example, and followed academically precocious children into adulthood, and what he found was that tenacity was more predictive of whether these children became accomplished in their fields than was their IQ. More of the same was reported by Catherine Cox, a psychologist and student of Terman's, who examined the lives of 301 geniuses and found that when intelligence was controlled for, lifetime achievement was dependent upon traits such as "persistence of motive and effort."

In the twenty-first century, many of us know of this stick-to-itiveness as "grit"—or "passion and perseverance," as researcher Angela Duckworth defines it. Multiple studies have shown that grit contributes to success in far-ranging areas including grade point average, educational attainment, teacher effectiveness, National Spelling Bee ranking, staying married over the long run, and—as in Paul's case—retention in the workplace and the military.

Yet, despite how common it now is to hear about the importance of grit, perseverance seems to be well understood while the passion behind it is less so. Passion—the "zeal" Galton pointed to, or the "motive" referenced by Cox—is the emotional component that propels it all. Each of us needs a reason to dig in and fight for what we want, especially when what we want will not come easily. Indeed, in a video produced by the navy about the challenges of Officer Candidate School, three graduates of the program begin the recording by pointing to the irreplaceable power of a deep-seated feeling. "If you don't have the passion," says one, "you're not going to make it." None of this is to say that anger is the only emotion that can fuel hard work, but it certainly seems to be one way to get there. Several studies have shown that, from infants as young as seven months to adults of all ages, when faced with frustrating, challenging tasks—such as accessing a withheld toy, opening a locked box with the wrong key, and working both solvable and unsolvable problems—it is those who get angry who persist.

Brain science supports this notion that anger can indeed be productive, particularly when it is coupled with goal-directed, forward-moving behavior. In fact, when channeled into active, healthy striving, anger is the brain's opposite of fear. Anger first springs from the reactive amygdala, but when we move from feeling emotions to acting purposefully on them, activity shifts to the prefrontal cortex, or the area of the brain where we plan and execute intentional behavior. The right prefrontal cortex manages our more pessimistic responses, and it is activated when we feel angry and *powerless*, when we sit where we are and stew. However, something different happens in the brain when we feel angry and *powerful*, when we move from the question of "What has been done to me?" and instead ask ourselves, "What am I going to do about it?"

In the words of William Arthur Ward, "It is wise to direct your anger toward problems, not people; to focus your energies on answers, not excuses." To benefit from the anger that we feel, we must move from being a victim to being an activist, at least on our own behalf. This redirection of energy from powerlessness toward purposeful activity has long been recognized as therapeutic for trauma and grief—"Work, work, work. This is the single most important goal of traumatized people throughout the world," wrote Richard Mollica, an expert on survivors of mass violence from around the world—and it is a maneuver that can even override the more emotional, uncontrolled, reckless forms of anger such as rage.

When we perceive there is something we can or should do to overcome the obstacles in our way, anger activates the left prefrontal cortex, or the side of the brain that manages our more empowered responses. The left prefrontal cortex is where we work toward goals, solve problems, and plan for and pursue the things we want. In this way, getting angry and taking action can be good for us as it moves brain activity to the side of the brain where we feel assertive, self-directed, and in control. It is here in the left pre-frontal cortex that anger can help us advance our agendas, feel more determined, and even feel more positive about the future.

In fact, although it has long been seen as a negative emotion, in action and in the brain, anger looks a lot like happiness, an emotion that also utilizes the left hemisphere. In a series of studies, research psychologists Jennifer Lerner and Dacher Keltner compared adults who were fearful, angry, or happy. In contrast with fearful adults, those who were angry or happy shared similarly optimistic predictions about their future, even about events that they may or may not be able to control, such as having a heart attack, finding a job, choosing a profession, or marrying well. Further work suggests that, although both happy and angry people tend to be optimistic, the optimism they experience is not quite the same. While happy people tend to believe good things will come their way, those who feel angry are more likely to believe that they will make good things happen for themselves. The optimism that angry people feel may be closer to having faith in one-self rather than having faith in the world, or so said researchers Jennifer Lerner and Larissa Tiedens; it produces "a bias toward seeing the self as powerful and capable."

There is also evidence that because anger makes our problems feel more manageable, it can actually help us feel less stressed. In another study by Jennifer Lerner and colleagues, ninety-two adults were faced with known stressors such as counting backward from 9,095 by 7s, counting backward from 6,233 by 13s, and mentally solving difficult math problems from the Wechsler Intelligence Test. To add to their frustration, participants were told of their mistakes as they made them, and they were pushed to work harder and faster or else, they were warned, they might fall behind others. While participants who became anxious or fearful as they worked through the problems had higher heart rates, blood pressure, and cortisol levels, those who became angry had lower levels of these same stress measures. There is a grounding self-assurance that can go along with feeling indignant. Sometimes, those who get angry feel stronger and more confident. They feel more equipped to move forward and right the wrongs of the world.

* * *

The military might seem like the last place Paul would choose to be after escaping the relentless hierarchy of his childhood but it was, in fact, the clear structure that appealed to him most. There he lived in a world where relationships felt orderly and fair rather than unpredictable and capricious, and where he was judged on the talents that he had. Looking back, Paul suspects he went into the navy because his strengths still felt somewhat tentative— "Having a lifestyle where I stayed physically active and mentally sharp was important or else I worried I'd relapse and end up like I used to be," Paul remembers—but far from going back to being a target for his peers, Paul emerged as a leader among them. The running, the coursework, the relentless physical training: Paul had been putting himself through those sorts of paces for years, and he had a lot of experience coping with stress. Now as an officer, Paul says, "I see myself as stronger and more capable than most people around me because of the treatment I lived through. I see myself as an optimist, not because I think bad things don't or won't happen but because I believe I can overcome whatever comes my way. I feel independent and confident. I feel tested. I feel brave."

Poet Dylan Thomas said, "There's only one thing that's worse than having an unhappy childhood, and that's having a too-happy childhood." I do not know if this is true or not, but I do know that, unlike Paul, too many family heroes feel lesser somehow because of the tough times they have seen, imagining they would certainly be better people if they had had stress-free lives. They look longingly at peers who seem uncomplicated and happy, imagining they are more desirable, more deserving, more attractive, more normal, more fit for life, more...everything. This is not necessarily the case.

While unrelenting, overwhelming stress is not good for us, to struggle is not all bad. Learning to cope with stress is a lot like exercise in that we become, as Paul said, stronger and more capable through exertion and practice. This is what child psychiatrist Michael Rutter called the "steeling effect," or the notion that exposure to some hardships steels us against the impact of future ones, and research psychologist Richard Dienstbier made a complementary argument with the "toughness model." In Dienstbier's view, if we experience the feeling of being under pressure, we become less frightened by our own physiological arousal, and we begin to see threats and problems as situations we can manage.

There is ample evidence that exposure to adversity can indeed make us hardier, that grappling with moderate levels of stress is even better for us than experiencing none at all. Experiments with young squirrel monkeys have shown that early exposure to brief stressors resulted in their being more resilient; compared with monkeys who had no previous exposure to stress, those who had been exposed to moderate stressors were more comfortable and less anxious in new situations, and they even had lower levels of cortisol.

Also, in a study of over five hundred Dartmouth students, about half of whom served in the Vietnam War, those who were exposed peripherally to combat showed greater gains in psychological health across adulthood than did veterans with direct exposure or no exposure at all. And in a multi-year study of a nationally representative sample of over two thousand adults, aged 18 to 101, research psychologist Mark Seery and his colleagues found that those who had experienced at least some adversity were both more successful and more satisfied with their lives than those who had experienced extremely high levels of hardship—and compared with those who had experienced very low levels of adversity.

These adults also coped better with more recent problems they encountered, leading the study's authors to conclude, in partial agreement with Nietzsche, that "in moderation, whatever does not kill us may indeed make us stronger."

* * *

"I guess my life since the bullying started could be considered one long fight," Paul told me. "I still fight a battle with myself to be the best I can be, and to prove to both myself and others that I can, and will, succeed in whatever way I choose. I have my degree. I have my rank. I have my hobbies. I have my friends. But the battle rages on. There is plenty more to achieve." That was, after all, why Paul had sought me out. Not because he felt his life was not going well but rather because he was determined to make it better all the time.

Like for many family heroes, Paul's next battle was to find a way to have love in his life, too. He worried that being in the military was incompatible with being there for his girlfriend, and he wanted to know how he could be a better partner. There were, of course, challenges ahead, logistical ones at least. Still, I reminded him that not only do determined problem solvers do well in the military, but they tend to do well in relationships as well. Being a fighter was who he was, and although that took Paul away from home a fair bit, it was also the reason he was working so hard to find a way to keep his relationship together.

Paul wondered if his girlfriend could understand the fighter in him—if she could love that about him—but maybe she already did. Tucked away in a drawer at the barracks, Paul kept a drawing of himself as a superhero. It was a charcoal sketch his girlfriend had done of him because that was how he seemed to her. Courageous. Strong. Unbeatable. On a mission.

CHAPTER 5

Flight

If one is lucky, a solitary fantasy can transform one million realities.
—Maya Angelou

When Mara was a newborn, her mother had an urge to throw her against the wall. She rocked her in a nursing chair each day and night, and all the while she stared at a spot across the room, a target where she imagined hurling her baby girl. One evening when she thought she could resist no more, she turned out the lights so she would not see the spot and wedged herself tightly in a corner, knees to her chest, squeezing Mara hard. This is how Mara's father found them, both wailing. Don't turn on the light, Mara's mother said, confessing everything between terrified sobs. Mara's father crouched in frozen fear as mother and baby screamed together and, before he could act, his wife's shrieks reached a piercing crescendo and the baby fell silent. Both parents thought Mara had died when in fact, she had fallen fast asleep. As if a switch inside her had simply turned off, she went from being a squirmy, squealing baby to a limp and quiet eight-pound source of warmth. That night, Mara's mother was hospitalized with what the doctors at first thought might be postpartum depression—except that after she came home and Mara went from being a baby to a toddler, it only got worse.

Once a busy caterer who loved to try out new dishes on her family and friends, Mara's mother became more irritable and unpredictable with each passing year, and Mara and her father never knew if dinner would be on the table or on the ceiling. More than once, Mara packed her child-size suitcase to run away, but because she was not allowed to leave the yard, she sat in the farthest corner of their large wooded lot and stared at the sky. It seemed so empty, it was like looking at nothing, except for the birds and the planes that flew whichever way they wanted. Watching them, Mara could sit out there for hours.

* * *

In response to fear, our brains are hardwired for fight or flight. Yet when fighting back is not an option and neither is physical flight, many family heroes stick around and comply with what the situation demands while, on the inside, they find ways to escape. Maybe they fall asleep when they become overwhelmed, or they flee without leaving the yard. Even when their bodies must stay put, they take their minds somewhere else. This is one of the key survival strategies of many family heroes: One way or another, they get away. They resist being defined or engulfed by whatever ails those near to them.

According to psychologists Susan Folkman and Richard Lazarus, there are two ways of coping with stress: problem-focused coping in which the individual works to fix the problem, and emotion-focused coping in which the individual manages his emotional response. Problem-focused coping and emotion-focused coping are somewhat akin to modern forms of fight or flight, and neither approach is inherently better than the other. Rather, much like the Serenity Prayer taught in Alcoholics Anonymous— *God grant me the serenity to accept the things I cannot change, the courage to change the things I can, and the wisdom to know the difference*—the art of adaptation is choosing the right way to cope at the right time. Many family heroes find ways to minimize the impact of their difficult surroundings, often first by trying to fight back, to change things somehow and improve their lot. If that does not work, they do not necessarily accept their situation but they accept that, at least in the moment, they cannot change it, and they distance themselves from the chaos around.

Distancing is a form of emotion-focused coping, one based on the recognition that while we may not be able to change the bad things that happen to us, we can change how much we pay attention to those bad things and how much we let them affect us. In psychology, the oldest and broadest term for such distancing is *dissociation*, a word that refers to a wide variety of strategies that allow us to disengage from our surroundings. The most extreme forms of dissociation are associated with post-traumatic stress disorder, and tend to be sensationalized and pathologized in books and movies. Maybe this was why, as an adult, Mara wondered what her lifelong tendency toward dissociation meant about her mental health. The most common forms of dissociation, however, are not necessarily sensational or problematic but are typically used as creative and temporary forms of coping. Listen to how, as a child, Maya Angelou minimized the impact of her time spent in Missouri, a place where she lived for many months and where she was chronically sexually abused by her mother's boyfriend: "In my mind, I only stayed in St. Louis a few weeks." Or hear how Angelou's brother, Bailey, handled his own childhood terrors: "He explained when we were smaller that when things were very bad his soul just crawled behind his heart and curled up and went to sleep. When he awoke, the fearful thing had gone away."

Knowing how and when to separate ourselves from our surroundings may sound sophisticated, but psychologist Harry Stack Sullivan argued that such distancing is "the most basic capacity of the human mind to protect its own stability," and its use can be seen even in very young infants. This is probably best illustrated in the "still-face" research designed by psychologist Edward Tronick. In these studies, a mother straps her months-old infant into a car seat and interacts with her baby normally for a moment or two. Then she looks away and turns back toward the infant with an expressionless face. This is disconcerting for the baby, who then attempts to engage her, usually first by smiling. When this fails and the mother maintains her stony expression as instructed, the baby escalates his attempts to bring her to life, squirming and flailing his arms and crying imploringly. When he smiles and then cries, the baby is using problem-focused coping—he is fighting back against her disengagement—as he tries to compel his mother to change her indifferent behavior toward him. When this is not successful, the baby switches strategies, looking away and withdrawing into himself, sucking on fingers or arms or toes. This is emotion-focused coping as the baby realizes that, without help from the mother, all he can do is soothe himself. The baby appears to give up looking for help or solutions on the outside, but he escapes on the inside in an attempt to save himself.

Holocaust survivor Viktor Frankl wrote that one of the most critical rules of self-preservation in concentration camps was this: "Do not be conspicuous." So it goes for children who live in homes where they fear for their safety, and even their lives. They may take great care to be quiet. They may play at being invisible by imagining themselves blending into the wallpaper or sinking into the floor. They may practice being immobile and unnoticeable like statues. Decades of research on family heroes shows that, when faced with chronic stress, good copers know how to retreat to safe places and how to take time away for themselves. Mental distancing is relied upon most heavily in infancy and early childhood and its use tends to decrease with age, perhaps as we have other options for physically, literally getting away. Infants can only look away and retreat into themselves while older children can withdraw to their rooms or other hiding places, where they can sleep or play or read rather than think about what is happening;

while there, they often snuggle up with and seek comfort from more predictable sources such as stuffed animals or pets.

Whether or not Mara could be conspicuous depended on whether or not her mother took her small white pills with the even smaller numbers stamped on them. Mara knew she had taken her medicine if her mother met Mara's bus after school. If she was there smiling and waving, then Mara could look forward to an afternoon of extravagant attention. Mara's mother could bake her daughter's favorite cakes and cookies for hours, and the girl's happiest moments were sitting on the counter next to the Mixmaster, licking batter off wooden spoons. On these days, Mara thought she had the best mother in the whole world, and on these days she did.

Sometimes, though, the big yellow bus rounded the corner and no one was there waiting. On those days, Mara waved a self-conscious good-bye to her bus driver and wondered if he knew what awaited her. On days like this, Mara made herself scarce without leaving the house. Her favorite escape was to her bedroom closet, where pillows and blankets lined the long shelf above the clothing rod. Stepping lightly on a small dresser, Mara hoisted herself high up into the top of her closet. It was there that she discovered what she called her "magic trick." She looked at a spot, like the hinge on the door or a spot on the ceiling, and closed one eye. Then she opened that eye and closed the other eye. Going back and forth, opening only one eye at a time, Mara realized that her eyes saw the hinge or the spot from slightly different angles; binocular vision worked by fixing both eyes on the same thing at the same time. Then, somehow, she trained her eyes or her brain not to do that. She realized that if she let the two images drift apart, the world became doubled and unfocused. By staring into the space between the two images, Mara found a way of looking right at something but not really seeing it at all.

The more she practiced her magic trick the easier it became, so easy that when Mara's mother's face changed from light to dark and she grabbed Mara's arms and would not let her go, Mara did not have to disappear by packing her little suitcase or retreating to her closet. By splitting her vision, Mara could slip into the space between what her right eye and left eye saw anytime she wanted. It made Mara feel untouchable, even when she was standing in front of her mother and the woman shook her as hard as she could.

* * *

In any given year, one in five adults struggle with some mental health condition, and one in twenty live with what are called serious mental illnesses. While there is no definitive list of mental disorders that qualify as "serious"—nor is there a group of mental disorders that are necessarily mild or insignificant—most psychologists would agree that schizophrenia and bipolar disorder are serious mental illnesses, and any number of psychological problems, from major depression to eating disorders to obsessive-compulsive disorder, can be considered serious mental illnesses if symptoms are severe enough to substantially interfere with everyday activities such as keeping a job, earning a living, maintaining relationships, running a household, or caring for oneself. Of course, in adulthood, one of life's everyday activities may be parenting. Though we may not think about mental health patients as parents, women with emotional disorders are just as likely as other women to be mothers, and up to 50 percent of women who live with a serious mental illness live with their children as well. Fathers with mental illness are neglected in the research, yet from the available data, it seems that men with emotional problems may be less likely than their peers to have children, or at least to live with their children, although of course many do.

By the time Mara was in elementary school, her mother was diagnosed with bipolar disorder, which is a mood disorder that affects nearly six million adult Americans—and therefore the day-to-day lives of millions of American children like Mara. Symptoms of bipolar disorder include emotional highs characterized by lack of sleep, limitless energy, and chaotic productivity followed inevitably by bottomless lows when sufferers may sleep or cry in despair for days or weeks at a time. As dramatic as the symptoms of bipolar disorder may be, witnessing the mental illness itself is likely to be only a small part of the stress children and families face. As their symptoms ebb and flow, parents with serious mental illnesses struggle to keep their jobs and pay their bills, and this makes it difficult to provide even the most basic necessities for their children. Parents with serious mental illnesses are more likely to be single parents, and on their own, their behavior may be too inconsistent for them to provide the structure children crave. Overwhelmed by their own symptoms and moods, parents like Mara's mother may be unable to notice or meet the emotional needs of their children. And because many mental illnesses are chronic and episodic, these stressors are likely to impact children not just once, but again and again across years.

Despite these challenges, parents with mental illness—like other parents—often find deep meaning in their roles as caregivers, and their love for their children and their desire to be good parents can be powerful incentives to do well. Children in these families tend to see their parents as good parents, viewing them more positively than do the parents themselves, as they look beyond their parents' illnesses and connect with the mothers and fathers inside. This benefits everyone, because even when caregivers struggle with emotional problems, children suffer less when they have warm and affectionate bonds with those they love. Just as having a serious mental illness does not automatically make one a bad parent, being the son or daughter of a parent with a serious mental illness does not necessarily mean a ruined life for the child. These children are at greater risk for emotional and behavioral problems of their own, yet studies of children and adolescents with parents who suffer from serious mental illness find that about one-third to one-half do well at school, at work, and in relationships, and are free of mental health problems themselves; they look and function like their peers.

How do they do it?

Some do what many children who live with adversity do: They find a way to get away.

* * *

Up in the protected space of Mara's shelf, there were stuffed animals and dot-to-dot books, but most treasured was a black, handheld transistor radio that she kept tucked among the pillows. When her mother cried the afternoon away, Mara sat up on her shelf and shoved the single cream-colored earbud into her ear. "I tried to get the sound as loud as I could," she recalled. "I didn't care about my hearing. I wished I was deaf so I would not hear." Mara rolled her finger along the plastic, toothed tuning dial on the radio, watching its little red needle move stiffly across the stations. Music and then static and then music and then static again. As she did this, Mara felt like she was fine-tuning her attention, and she blocked out the sounds of her mother in one ear by focusing on the music in the other.

One way we tune out of one part of life is by tuning into another. When we become absorbed in a single engrossing activity, we forget about our troubles, big and small. Listening intently to music. Losing ourselves in a book or a movie. Playing an instrument. Daydreaming and fantasy. Watching television. Throwing ourselves into a hobby or sport. These are just some of the ways in which we distance ourselves from the stress of everyday life by attending to something else, usually as a way of relaxing or of lessening the wear and tear of the world around. In his memoir, *Instrumental*, classical pianist James Rhodes remembers escaping the pain of childhood sexual abuse by getting away to play music: "The school had a couple of practice rooms with old, battered upright pianos in them. They were my salvation. Every spare moment I got I was in them." And in her memoir, *Life in Motion: An Unlikely Ballerina*, Misty Copeland, the first African American woman to become a principal dancer at American Ballet Theatre, remembers dance as a way of forgetting about the realities of her childhood: "Whenever I danced, whenever I created, my mind was clear. I didn't think about how I slept on the floor because I didn't have a bed, when my mother's new boyfriend might become my next stepfather, or if we would be able to dig up enough quarters to buy food."

Any absorbing activity involves a kind of selective attention—or selective *inattention*—a shifting of focus that allows us to narrow our experience and to shut out awareness of small stressors or even grievous misdeeds. While such activities may sound like escapism, the mind strays from the here and now as much as 50 percent of our waking hours, suggesting that these distancing maneuvers serve some important survival functions. Indeed, researchers have found that absorbing tasks and preoccupations can be quite positive: They reduce stress, preserve feelings of safety and control, restore a neutral mood after bad things happen, and sometimes result in the feeling of "flow."

Even when Mara was not on her shelf, she was an expert at focusing her attention on the thing of her choosing, seeming not to notice when her mother crashed, in one way or another. So the police saw one evening when they marched her mother in through the back door, after she had run her car into a telephone pole in a hypomanic speeding frenzy. Mara was eating a pizza in front of the television, listening to a game show with one ear and to the police with the other, never once looking their way. "My eyes were glued to the TV," Mara recalls now, "and I knew it must have seemed strange, but truly, I could not turn my head and look at them."

Like Mara, Jean Piaget—a Swiss philosopher and father of the field of cognitive development—grew up with a mother who was mentally ill. He coped with, and distanced himself from, her unpredictable moods by immersing himself in the orderly world of science. "One of the direct consequences of my mother's poor mental health," wrote Piaget, "was that I started to forego playing for serious work very early in childhood; this I did as much to imitate my father (a scholar of painstaking and critical mind who taught me the value of systematic work) as to take refuge in a private and nonfictitious world." At the age of seven, Piaget began studying nature. By ten, he had published an article on a rare sparrow in a magazine and was researching and classifying mollusks. By fifteen, he was a recognized malacologist, although the editors who received his work did not know the young scholar's age.

* * *

Mara's private world was not a scientific one. Her shelf was a fantastic place where she listened to music and let her mind wander at will. The term *mindwandering* may imply a lack of direction, but social scholars remind us that "not all minds that wander are lost." Mindwandering allows the self to move from one place to another—hopefully better—place, and this sort of mental mobility can set a trapped child like Mara free. As she listened to music, she pictured herself in far-off places, doing far-flung things. She got to live here, she got to live there, but when she was down off her shelf and her mind was not allowed to roam, she felt a sick sort of dread: "I had to be where I was," Mara recalls. "I had to be me."

When we are unable to transform reality, sometimes we cope by transforming it in our minds, becoming engrossed in daydreaming or fantasy, at least for a few moments or until another form of escape becomes possible. Many family heroes recall having rich fantasy lives as children. Daydreams of being an animal or a superhero are the most common, but the imaginings are as varied and diverse as children themselves. What these fantasies share is their ability to remove the child from a state of fear and helplessness and hopelessness, transporting her to a place where anything she can dream up is possible, even a happy life. After Eleanor Roosevelt's mother died and she was sent away from her father to live with an aunt, she said, "I wished to be left alone to live in a dreamworld in which I was the heroine and my father the hero. Into this world I withdrew as soon as I went to bed and as soon as I woke in the morning, and all the time I was walking or when anyone bored me."

An over-reliance on fantasy can be more delusional than productive, to be sure, but when used intentionally and flexibly, fantasy helps children—and adults—survive. In one study of abused children from Israel, the use of fantasy, in conjunction with other coping mechanisms, was found to be an important source of hope, one that predicted doing well in life fourteen years later. "I never knew whether I would live tomorrow, but when evening came, I used to stand near the window and imagine the lights of New York," one of the study's participants remembered about her childhood. "I sat for hours and imagined myself entering the great city." Similarly, Viktor Frankl described how, during the Holocaust, he and other prisoners found their own release by fleeing to an inner world where one could go anywhere, even back home: "In my mind I took bus rides, unlocked the front door of my apartment, answered my telephone, switched on the electric lights. Our thoughts often centered on such details, and these memories could move one to tears."

Fantasy comes more easily to children than to adults but, for all ages, one of the most accessible ways to become absorbed in a world other than one's own is through the portal of books. "Writers are often better therapists than we are," a supervisor once said to me, and many family heroes treat themselves by reading. "I suppose all fictional characters, especially in adventure or heroic fiction, at the end of the day are our dreams about ourselves," said graphic novelist Alan Moore. "And sometimes they can be really revealing." Sometimes family heroes identify with fellow fighters who help them feel strong, too, and other times they are drawn to characters who are powerful in other ways. So it was for writer Akhil Sharma who recalls, in his memoir *Family Life*, how he coped after his older brother was left paralyzed and brain-injured in a swimming pool accident, an event that devastated his family: "I was always lost in a book, whether I was actually reading or imagining myself as a character. I liked books where the hero was a young man, preferably under twenty-five, who had a magical power that he discovered over the course of the book. Vanishing into books, I felt held. I had always believed that I might possess supernatural powers, like flying or maybe seeing into the future."

What one reads depends on what one needs, and while some, like Jean Piaget, use books to stay connected with order and reality, Mara used books the same way she used music—as a way of being someone and somewhere else. The Boxcar Children were her first favorites, and she envied their adventures without parents. Mara pretended her closet shelf was her very own boxcar, and she relished spending time in a world that was the opposite of her own. "The kids had brothers and sisters to keep them company but they didn't have any parents to worry about. And they had their own space," she recalled. When Mara got hungry, she made like a Boxcar Child sneaking into town to steal food from a store as she tiptoed down the stairs and into the kitchen, where she quietly pocketed boxes of Jell-O gelatin from the pantry. Back in her closet, Mara licked her finger and dipped it in the sugary powder, again and again, until her finger turned red and she felt warm inside. The pillows on her shelf were often grainy, as if dirtied with sand, but no one could expect an old boxcar to be spick-and-span.

* * *

For Mara, middle school was a series of temporary escapes. Her closet shelf was not strong enough to hold her anymore so, like many family heroes as they age, Mara often found a way not to be home.

During the week, she busied herself with activities after school, and on the weekends she slept over at friends' houses. In the summers, she went away to camps—soccer camps, youth camps—for as long as her father would permit her to be away.

Some of her getaways were more planned than others. One afternoon, Mara had just hopped off the school bus and kicked off her shoes by the back door when she saw cookbooks strewn about, splayed open, all over the kitchen. For an instant her heart soared: It had been such a long time since her mother had made her favorites. Then Mara noticed that the pages were marked up with different-colored pens, and her mother was lying on the floor. There would be no baking today, her mother said warily. The cookbooks contained messages that she had worn herself out trying to decode.

Mara went into the bathroom and climbed out the window— the routineness with which she did so was lost on her at the time— and she walked barefoot some four blocks to a friend's house. Her friend's mother eyed her curiously when she opened the door and there stood Mara, uninvited and without anything on her feet. "It's freezing!" she exclaimed. "Where are your shoes?" Mara smiled and shrugged as she entered the front hall. Her silence was automatic. She and her friend passed the afternoon playing video games, and Mara relaxed into the feeling of being in a house where nothing strange or frightening might be about to happen. When enough time had gone by that she could smell dinner cooking, and she thought her dad might be home, Mara borrowed some sneakers and walked back toward her house.

At home, Mara often spent her evenings rearranging her bedroom furniture and imagining she lived in an apartment in a high-rise, far, far away. Her light switch, she pretended, was an intercom through which she spoke with an imaginary doorman. Eventually, she moved into the basement and pretended more of the same. It would be years still until Mara would be old enough to really leave home, but in her mind she was already gone.

* * *

By high school, Mara's favorite place to get away to was the public library. An institution known since ancient Egypt as the "healing-place of the soul," the library was where Mara went to recuperate from her life. In the center of the building, in a round skylighted atrium, stood a giant globe, probably twenty feet in diameter, which rotated slowly on its tilted axis. The library was built in a two-story circle around it, and Mara liked to climb the stairs to the second floor and look down at the blue-and-green swirls as they slowly made their way around. From up there, with its whispering sounds and uniform lighting, the library was like being off in space. When she was there, Mara felt as far away as she could get.

There was a table she liked up on the second floor where, just as she had once become absorbed in her radio and her books, Mara became immersed in her homework. Maybe like it had been for Piaget, it was an orderly world that Mara escaped to now, and she kept her mother out of her mind by staying occupied with tests and term papers and calculating her grade point average. Not surprisingly, Mara made straight A's.

Sometimes, to relax, she borrowed self-hypnosis tapes from the audiovisual section—those who are good at becoming absorbed in fantasies are usually quite skilled at self-hypnosis—and she pushed two square, padded, even-armed chairs together, making a little crib-like bed where she could curl up. Just as she had once trained her eyes to split her vision, Mara now trained her mind to do what the tapes said. One taught her to erase her thoughts like chalk on a chalkboard, and she would lie there, eyes closed, willing the eraser in her mind to be stronger and more persistent than the words that popped up in the blackness on the back of her eyelids. Her favorite tapes, though, helped her visualize who she might be one day; they were guided meditations in which she met up with her future self.

For many family heroes, the most wide-open place to escape to is the future. For the child with an average and expectable life, living in the present may represent being able to be carefree and spontaneous, while thinking about the future may feel scary and uncertain. For family heroes, however, rather than being afraid of change, what they fear most is that life will stay the same. In looking ahead, in being bold, they have nothing to lose.

In this way, some family heroes, like Mara, use fantasies about the future not just cathartically as a way of disengaging from the here and now but also proactively as a way of arming themselves for the there and then. And this is where emotion-focused coping can start to look a lot like problem-focused coping; where fight and flight begin to merge. Daring to have a vision of one's future self furthers achievement, and this sort of autobiographical planning may be especially important for the family hero. Studies of transcendent individuals, or those who overcome obstacles in their way, show that they tend to be self-determined, intentional, and future-oriented.

Up on her second-floor table, Mara pored over test prep books and college guides and maps of faraway places. She set her sights on a particular Ivy League school, not because she knew anyone who had been there but because she had heard of it and it sounded far away. The librarian printed out admissions information, and she toted those papers around in her backpack like a secret, elaborate getaway plan. A friend gave her a key chain with the school's logo on it and she held on to it for years, like a talisman. "He was the only person who knew about my dream and, when he gave me that key chain, it was like he gave me permission to take my dream seriously," Mara recalls. "Before that, I think it really was just a fantasy."

When we fantasize about future selves, the more concrete and actionable a vision the better—and sometimes, the family hero begins by setting her sights simply on some specific thing. A particular job. A faraway city. A quiet home. A safe relationship. An apartment with a doorman. A red car. A school that looks good. For actor Alan Cumming, it was a set of plates he bought at a country fair that allowed him to imagine one day being free of his father: "They were my ticket out," Cumming said of the treasured plates in his memoir, *Not My Father's Son*. "I would be eating off them in a place where there were buses and taxis and where I would never have to wait in a public place for hours, cold and damp, wondering if my father had concluded his liaison, and if or when he would come for me."

Ultimately, Mara's ticket out would be her hard work in school, but it was her key chain and her college guides, too. They were proof that life existed elsewhere, that there were other places that she could escape to once and for all. Set up at her table on the second floor, watching the world turn below, she did not yet know that she would grow to be an adult who would travel far and wide, and who would ultimately do exactly as she planned—attend that Ivy League school and live her life far away from where she sat. For now, it was enough to feel like she was above it all, in an otherworldly place, as she plotted her tomorrows and decided where on Earth she was going to go next.

CHAPTER 6

Vigilance

I've got second sight and amazing powers of observation.
　　　　　　　　—Roger Waters, "Nobody Home"

When Jessie was very young, she thought her older sister might be Rosemary's Baby. It was 1968. Roman Polanski's horror film was newly released and much-whispered-about among the adults, so what other way to understand Charley? Charley did like to pull up the neighbor's flowers, especially ones that seemed prized or carefully planted. She played mean tricks like putting buttermilk in Jessie's glass and watching her gag in surprised disgust. She pinched and twisted Jessie's skin to see what the welts would look like. And at night when they lay in their bed talking, Charley swore Jessie to secrecy and then whispered to her she was adopted. So convincing was she, Jessie looked through her mother's desk in an attempt to find the legal papers. Maybe that would explain why Jessie's mother did not protect her more.

Jessie was shy, and she was embarrassed by what Charley had done to the neighbor's flowers, but to play with their dog, she would summon the courage to walk next door and ring the doorbell. She loved to run around the fenced yard that seemed a world away from home, the dog chasing her and licking her face when she fell down. With the cool grass and the soft fur against her skin, Jessie felt carefree, like a child, something she never felt when she was with her sister. Once when these neighbors went on vacation for a week and boarded their dog, Charley delighted in convincing Jessie they were all dead and gone.

Maybe stunts like this were supposed to be childish pranks, and that is usually how Jessie's mother interpreted them. "Kids fight..." Jessie's mother would say vaguely rather than authoritatively, her words drifting off as if she did not know what to do about it or how to finish her sentence. But by the way Charley enjoyed tormenting her, Jessie sensed something more sinister. She sometimes wondered if Charley was a devil child.

* * *

When Jessie came home from elementary school, Charley was always already there. The middle school bus made its way through the neighborhood first, which meant that by the time Jessie walked through the front door each day, she felt like she was tiptoeing into someone else's home. Nearly six feet tall, Charley ruled the television, the food, the phone, and the house from where she sat in the center of the couch in the center of the den. If Jessie challenged her—"What happened to the potato chips?" or "I want to turn the channel"—then Charley would rise up off the couch and come after her—shoving her, hitting her, kicking her, or pulling her hair. Most days, Jessie just lay on the floor of the den, watching what Charley chose to watch on TV and eating bread and butter. She sometimes pretended—or felt like—she was a prisoner.

Of course there were times, even many times, when Jessie and Charley were good sisters. They shared meals and a bedroom and weekends and holidays, and Charley even stood up for Jessie if someone picked on her at the local ice rink. They united in the backseat singing silly songs during long car trips and had been raised to say "Good night, I love you" no matter what had happened during the day. That was the most confusing part. Jessie learned that you can never know what to expect from people, even people who say they love you. She learned that the good guys can be the bad guys, and that sometimes the bad guys live in your house.

One afternoon, Jessie balked at Charley's telling her she could not go play with the dog next door. She walked, and then ran, to the kitchen to call their mother at work, but the rotary phone that hung on the wall took so long to dial, Jessie could only stand there, desperate and determined, waiting for the seven numbers to click around. Click-click-click-click-click-click, click-click-click-click-click-click-click-click, click-click-click-click-click-click-click, click-click-click...

Before Jessie could get through all the clicks, Charley had the phone out of her hand, hitting her in the head with the receiver— *thud!*—before letting it drop with a loud crack on the linoleum floor. The phone was left dangling off the hook so, for the rest of the day, no one could call in or out.

"I'm telling Mom!" Jessie screamed as she tore off toward their bedroom, where, if she could beat her sister there even by seconds, she could slam and lock the door and wedge a chair underneath the knob, as she had done many times before. Charley pounded on the door and raged: "I'll kill you if you don't open the door! I'm going to go let that dog run away!"

Jessie paced small, frantic paths in the bedroom, listening for what was next. She heard Charley thunder down the hall, rifle the drawer in the bathroom, and then she was outside the door again, picking the lock with a bobby pin until *pop!*—the knob sprang unlocked. Jessie's heart raced as Charley threw her considerable weight against the now slightly open door. She watched the back of the chair and the doorknob give a little, and she pushed a small dresser in front of the door as well, her heart racing some more. Unable to get in, Charley moved on and Jessie's heart slowed a little as she sank down to the floor and put her back against the dresser that was against the door. She sat and stared for a while at the electrical outlets across the room. She appreciated the way they looked back at her like little faces, wide-eyed and mouths agape with horror, the only witnesses around.

Hours later, when Jessie heard the clack of her mother's heels just home from work, she pulled her dresser from the door and the chair out from under the knob. She marched into the kitchen and, in a flood of tears, told about the hitting and the phone and the chair and the dresser and her worries about the dog next door. Jessie's mother listened, but perhaps because she did not have enough money for a babysitter, she could not afford to acknowledge that Jessie was being abused: "Just go straight to your room after school, honey, and lock the door until I get home," she said. "Problem solved."

* * *

Home is the most dangerous place in America and, by many accounts, the sibling relationship is the most violent within those four walls. Aggression between siblings is believed to be the most common form of family violence, with violence between siblings more prevalent than spousal abuse and child abuse combined. National statistics are difficult to come by because sibling violence is rarely reported to authorities—and when it is it tends to be legally ignored as a family problem—but extensive survey data paint a disturbing picture.

Multiple large studies estimate that about one-third of children are hit, kicked, punched, bitten, or attacked by a brother or a sister in any given year. By the time they leave home, between one-half and three-quarters of young adults will have been the victim of physical aggression by a brother or a sister at least once. Though many of these acts are isolated slugs in a crowded backseat or the occasional kick over a toy, a concerning number of assaults are serious and even recurring, and they result in cuts, bruises, broken bones, and chipped teeth. This physical abuse is often accompanied by even more frequent emotional abuse: intimidation, ridicule, belittling, and threats toward pets and possessions. Between 3 and 14 percent of young adults report having been threatened by a sibling with a gun or a knife, and some of these aggressive siblings turn their rage against their parents as well. Findings like these have led researchers to conclude that "children are the most violent persons in American families."

Sibling violence may be pandemic but, ironically, its ubiquity only contributes to it being seen as harmless. Pervasive cultural stories reinforce the notion that fighting between siblings is, if unfortunate, likely inevitable. The myth of Romulus and Remus tells us that Rome was founded by Romulus after he killed his brother in an argument over land. In the first family of the so-called Abrahamic religions, Adam and Eve's older son, Cain, killed their younger son, Abel, in a jealous rage. Though certainly intended as cautionary, tales like these normalize family violence, suggesting that sibling rivalry and aggression are as ancient as civilization, as old as humankind.

The line between sibling rivalry and sibling abuse is admittedly a blurry one, and like Jessie's mother, many parents trivialize sibling violence as a normal part of childhood. "That's what kids do," some say, or "My brother used to hit me and I turned out all right." Perpetrators of violence are more likely to be older siblings and male siblings, a fact that is easy to shade as "boys will be boys." While sisters can be chronically and seriously abusive, and they may be genuinely terrifying and dangerous to a child like Jessie, girls are often not seen by adults as legitimate threats. Even brothers and sisters who are on the receiving end of aggression at the hands of siblings minimize their own experiences, preferring labels such as sibling *conflict* and *rivalry* rather than sibling *violence* or *abuse.*

Violence between siblings tends to be more frequent before adolescence but more extreme after adolescence. Aggression among young children is common and usually peaks before the teen years, as kids learn better strategies for handling frustration and as they become busy with friends and activities outside of the home. Because many warring brothers or sisters "grow out of it" and violence between young siblings may not leave permanent physical scars, parents often deny its significance. Nevertheless, aggression between young children can be frequent and can have long-lasting emotional effects; intersibling violence has been linked to subsequent school bullying, anxiety, depression, and dating and domestic violence. Violence that does continue into high school tends to be increasingly severe and injurious, as older children are bigger and stronger, and have access to more dangerous weapons.

At a time when nations are taking school bullying and violence so seriously, it is unclear why we dismiss aggression between siblings as unimportant. Children are more likely to be hit—once, and again and again—by a brother or a sister than by a peer. And unlike peers who may shift with grades and whims, the sibling relationship is for many years inescapable and, as in Jessie's case, can make home feel like a prison. Typically our only "cradle-to-grave" bond, brothers and sisters can be among the most influential—or damaging—figures in our lives. Parents may be our template for romantic relationships, but peers are often our template for social ones. Younger siblings already watch their older siblings more closely than they watch their parents, so what happens when a sibling is dangerous to boot?

* * *

"The best predictor of future behavior is past behavior," renowned psychoanalyst-turned-behaviorist Albert Ellis purportedly said. Children who grow up with stress and violence know this, and as a result they develop what are called "traumatic expectations," or the strong belief that more bad things are coming their way. They live moment-to-moment with what psychologist Jerome Kagan termed an "anxiety of premonitions." There is often, or even always, the free-floating feeling—the realistic fear—that something is about to go wrong. Consciously or unconsciously scanning the environment for danger, children like Jessie become keen observers of the world around. They pay exquisite attention to details and to the moods and behaviors of others and, because they cannot expect others to be there for them, they learn to watch out for themselves. They become vigilant.

In her vivid memoir, *The Glass Castle*, Jeannette Walls details life with an alcoholic father and a neglectful mother, a childhood that included being burned in a stove fire at age three and, not too many years later, fleeing a flophouse that was ablaze. "I lived in a world that at any moment could erupt into fire," she writes plainly. "It was the sort of knowledge that kept you on your toes." One part of the brain that keeps us on our toes—that keeps us vigilant—is the amygdala. The amygdala is hard at work not just during fight or flight but also in all of those moments that precede the need for fight or flight. It triggers a state of heightened arousal not only when there is clear and present danger but also in uncertain and *potentially* dangerous situations. In what, fittingly, is called the smoke detector principle, our amygdalae (and the defenses they trigger) err on the side of being overly sensitive and overly responsive; a false positive is preferable to a false negative. If you are Jeannette Walls, you need that fire alarm to ring out loud, and not when the whole house is on fire, but at the very first sign of smoke.

Our brains adapt to the lives we lead, and research suggests that chronic stress that repeatedly activates the amygdala creates long-lasting alterations, including heightened sensitivity to threat. These sorts of changes can be seen among soldiers who have returned from war. In one study, researchers used fMRI scans to compare activity in the amygdalae of two groups of soldiers. One group consisted of thirty-three soldiers who were deployed to Afghanistan, where their duties included combat patrols, land-mine removal, and transportation across enemy territory, and where they took enemy fire and saw seriously injured soldiers and civilians. The other group consisted of twenty-six soldiers who were never sent overseas. Before deployment, fMRI scans showed that both groups of soldiers exhibited the same level of activity in the amygdala in response to the photos of angry faces—a universal threat cue. After deployment, the group of soldiers that had been to the war zone had increased activity in the amygdala, now showing a greater response to angry faces compared with the group that never saw combat.

Of course, it is not just war that makes our brains more sensitive. There are different ways of living in fear every day, and abusive siblings, alcoholic parents, dangerous neighborhoods, and school bullies are but a few examples of the different sorts of minefields children pick their way through every single day. Not surprisingly, we see the same sort of brain changes found in soldiers among children who live with violence. One study examined twenty children who had been exposed to family violence and twenty-three who had not. Like soldiers who had returned from war, children who had been exposed to violence in the home showed greater activity in the amygdala in response to photos of angry faces than did the children who had not lived with violence in the home, and the degree of activation was positively correlated with the severity of the violence seen. And it is not just violence that sensitizes the amygdala. Children separated from their mothers, or reared in orphanages or by depressed mothers, for example, have all been found to have larger amygdalae than their peers, perhaps because they grow accustomed to looking out for themselves.

If the best defense is a good offense, it would follow that, in a dangerous world, it is beneficial not just to react to a threat, but also to be able to detect it. Early detection confers the advantage of time, allowing us to be proactive or to get in front of our problems. So many children and teens, and their amygdalae, become skilled not only at responding to danger but also at seeing it coming their way.

* * *

"Once you've been there long enough," one soldier said of the war zone, "you start to know: That ain't right. It's like when you walk down your block. You know your neighborhood. And you know when things are normal." What is normal for the family hero? Children who do not live in average, expectable environments but in violent or unpredictable ones become adept at spotting warning signs. Like soldiers in combat, they are especially attuned to details in their surroundings, particularly those that suggest something "ain't right." Noticing when the environment is awry is a power that many family heroes possess relative to their peers, and even relative to their own other abilities. Family heroes like Jessie describe a hypersensitivity to danger—almost a sixth sense about it—and, indeed, research studies about threat detection suggest just that.

Preschoolers from troubled families are already paying closer attention to certain details than are their peers. One study looked at fourteen preschoolers who attended a therapeutic school, each of whom had been mistreated in some way. Some of the children had been physically or sexually abused, and others had witnessed domestic violence or been neglected. These preschoolers completed the Wechsler Preschool and Primary Scale of Intelligence, also known as the WPPSI (pronounced *whip-see*). In this study, the overall IQ scores for the mistreated preschoolers were in the average range, suggesting that, in general, their intellectual abilities did not differ significantly from others their age. They did, however, perform better than same-aged peers on one subtest: Picture Completion. The Picture Completion subtest consists of drawn pictures of common objects or real-life situations that are missing something, like a door without a doorknob or a table without a leg. This subtest measures visual alertness and attention to detail, especially the ability to differentiate essential from nonessential details. Thirty percent of the mistreated preschoolers had Picture

Completion scores that were significantly higher than average, or more than one standard deviation above the mean. While 10 percent of the general population performs better on Picture Completion than on other WPPSI subtests, nearly every mistreated preschooler performed best on this subtest.

Because the major predators of human beings are other human beings, among the most relevant cues that something is wrong, or is about to be, are the expressions on the faces of those around us. Charles Darwin argued that emotions are universal and that our survival depends on reading and reacting to them. Further research, most notably by Paul Ekman and Carroll Izard, has suggested that each of the six emotions understood the world over—anger, disgust, fear, happiness, sadness, and surprise—requires specific movements of facial muscles. We are wired through evolution to be sensitive to these expressions, and some children may become especially so. Multiple studies show that mistreated children are skilled at spotting one emotion in particular: anger. If it is true that, as Proverbs 20:3 asserts, "any fool can start arguments; the honorable thing is to stay out of them," it often falls on the family hero to be honorable, or at least not to be foolish. Perhaps this is why they become so attuned to anger. Consider three studies that show what this looks like in a lab.

In the first study, twenty-four children aged eight through ten who had been physically abused were tested alongside twenty-three children of similar age who had not. Children viewed color pictures of faces that displayed anger, happiness, fear, or sadness, one at a time on a computer screen. Each picture was initially presented in an unfocused or "fuzzy" format that made the expression difficult to discern. Every three seconds, the picture of the face became more focused and the emotion became progressively easier to identify. After fourteen of these three-second intervals, the picture was entirely in focus. With each interval, children were asked to judge which emotion, if any, they could discern. The abused children identified angry expressions sooner, on the basis of less information, than did the children who were not abused. These abused children were, however, no quicker to recognize happiness or fear, and they were slower to recognize sadness.

In a related study, these same researchers presented ninety-five nine-year-olds—about half of whom had been physically abused and half of whom had not—with a series of photos of models' faces as their emotional expressions unfolded from neutral to happy, from neutral to sad, from neutral to angry, from neutral to afraid, or from neutral to surprised. Compared with their non-abused peers, abused children correctly identified anger earlier in the formation of the expression, when fewer facial musculature cues were available. The more hostility was reported in the home, the quicker the child was able to detect an angry expression. In terms of identifying the other emotions—happiness, sadness, fear, surprise—the abused children performed no differently than their peers.

A third study examined whether children who have been exposed to violence not only spot danger sooner, but also remain on alert longer. As measures of arousal, heart rate and skin conductance were measured in eleven abused and twenty-two non-abused four- and five-year-old children while they heard two unfamiliar adults—actors for the study—begin to argue in the next room. The interpersonal episode the children overheard had four phases: (1) neutral conversation, (2) intense angry speech, (3) an unresolved silent period, and (4) a resolution period during which both adults apologized. Both abused and nonabused children became emotionally aroused when the angry speech erupted, but while nonabused children returned to a baseline emotional state upon realizing the conversation did not pertain to them, abused children remained "on alert" in a state of anticipatory monitoring, even throughout the apology phase of the conversation.

Consider these words by Charles Darwin: "Pain or suffering

of any kind, if long continued, causes depression and lessens the power of action; yet it is well adapted to make a creature guard itself against any great or sudden evil." And that is what happens in the brains of many family heroes: They learn to guard themselves against whatever might come. To live with conflict or uncertainty or violence—especially violence that is unspoken or denied—is to learn that what people do is more important than what people say. As a result, the family hero may become a shrewd observer of the world around her. She lives in a state of automatic alertness, one that keeps her unconsciously and supremely attuned to subtle changes in the expressions and mannerisms of others. She is like a barometer, always gauging the moods of others in an effort to forecast their behavior. As Jessie said, "My sister was supposed to watch me after school but I was the one who ended up watching her. I watched her like my life depended on it."

* * *

By the time Jessie was in middle school, she felt like she used her brain more at home than she did at school. Monday through Friday she got off the bus, unlocked the front door, and began scanning for clues about the remainder of the day. With one quick glance in Charley's direction, Jessie sensed what would come next. Relaxed eye contact meant Charley was happy—or that she wanted something from Jessie—so it might be a day when the sisters would spend the afternoon in the kitchen scraping together the ingredients to make cookies or the money to order a pizza. Deliberate eye contact with flared nostrils meant Charley was hiding something or lying about something, and that left Jessie racking her brain about what might soon go wrong. A downcast gaze meant Charley was in a prickly state and so Jessie should lock herself in her room as her mother suggested.

Jessie passed many afternoons closed away in her bedroom, doing homework and reading books from school. It was then that she discovered Greek mythology, and Athena in particular, a helper of heroes and the goddess of wisdom and war. Jessie was fascinated by this female who ruled with brains rather than brawn; by a woman who recognized the power of being strategic. Jessie knew she would never be bigger or stronger than Charley, but maybe she could outthink her. Jessie was especially taken by the detail that Athena was often pictured with an owl perched on her arm. "Owls are wise. They can turn their heads to see in all directions, and they see well at night," Jessie says now. "I needed to be like that because it got to be that the nights were worse than the days."

Contrary to what her mother said, Jessie's problems were not solved when her mother came home from work in the evening. As Charley got older, fights became about skipping school or stealing money rather than about potato chips or television channels. Now Charley was quick to throw a glass to end a conversation she did not like, although she kept the violence just this side of egregious by fighting mostly with slaps and fists. If their mother confronted her about her empty wallet, in a flash Charley would now pound on her—not Jessie—backing her into her bedroom, where she would lock the door and pummel her in private. The dull thud of fists on flesh terrified Jessie and made her feel sick with guilt. Panicked with helplessness and responsibility, she screamed and cried from the other side of the door—"MOM! MOM ARE YOU OKAY? CHARLEY, STOP HITTING HER! STOP HITTING MOM! MOM, OPEN THE DOOR!"

When their mother threatened to call the police, Charley would spend the evening shut up in the bathroom, threatening to kill herself. Jessie never stood outside the door and yelled on these nights. She sat at the kitchen table and worked on her geometry proofs or she memorized countries and capitals for her world history class, thinking to herself, *Do it! Please do it!* Jessie sometimes thought about putting poison on Charley's toothbrush in a sort of self-defense but she did not know what kind of poison to get.

At night, Charley's mother slept with her purse under her pillow and Jessie slept with Charley. When Charley was in a good mood, the two girls talked and laughed in bed like good sisters, and this confused Jessie because it felt like protecting herself and betraying herself all at the same time. What Jessie did not know is that this is what unbroken prisoners do. They look for ways to enjoy themselves, even as they look for ways to survive or escape. When Charley was in a bad mood, she drew a line down the middle of the sheet with a marker and warned, "If you cross this line, I'll stab you with my scissors." Jessie learned to sleep on her side on the edge of the bed, always facing away from Charley with one leg hanging down toward the floor. Gripping the side of the bed with her leg kept her from rolling over in the night.

Jessie often worried that Charley would kill her—or her mother—before dawn, so she trained herself to stay awake by setting herself up in a battle against the digital alarm clock on her bedside table. Aiming to be the last person in the house to fall asleep, she willed herself to see the sequential numbers that only came around once per hour. First the goal was to make it until 10:11. Then 11:12. Then 12:34. She lay there and thought about being Athena, or Athena's owl, and by the end of middle school she could make it all the way to 1:23 or even 2:34 if she set her mind to it, which was the point. In the morning when the girls woke up, Charley acted as if nothing bad had happened—ever—and, though she must have, Jessie felt like she had never even closed her eyes.

* * *

Jessie began to feel like she was different from other people. Her home was different, she was certain, because when she tentatively shared details about her life with friends, she heard back quickly and casually, "Yeah my brother is a real pain, too," or "All my sister and I do is fight over makeup and stuff." With these responses, Jessie knew to say no more. But Jessie felt different on the inside as well. She felt like she moved through the world more strategically than her friends, and maybe she was right. "My life was like a chess game that I was always learning from and mastering," Jessie remembers. "If I do this, you do that; if you do that, I should do this." She became so accustomed to Charley's stealing her things that she developed a habit of taking mental pictures of rooms when she left them; if something was missing or disturbed when she returned, then Jessie noticed right away.

Most family heroes do not know about the amygdala and so they cannot explain their extraordinary nonverbal skills, or how they manage to stay alert all day, and sometimes even all night. They are as puzzled as anyone at their uncanny ability to know when something "ain't right," and to react automatically to cues that sometimes they do not even know they see. They themselves wonder how they are able to spot anger and danger before everyone else, and this leaves them with the strange, powerful, and heavy feeling that—sometimes, at least—they can see the future before it arrives.

Sometimes the only way of understanding their superperception comes in the form of a connection with characters that have similar gifts. Like Jessie with Athena and her owl, some family heroes find a kinship with those such as Superman because of his X-ray vision or Spider-Man with his spider-sense. Others feel an affinity with detectives like Sherlock Holmes—including none other than Stan Lee, the creator of Spider-Man—because they, too, use their powers of observation to spot clues and solve mysteries that elude everyone else. "When I was young, my favorite superhero was Sherlock Holmes," said Lee. "Sherlock Holmes was just a superior human being. So, to me, he was as super as any superhero."

Childhood adversity is often viewed simply as a factor that hampers development, and indeed many studies have found that chronic stress, especially in early life, interferes with attention, emotion, behavior, and health. But there is more to it than that.

One way that the family hero overcomes hardship is by developing specialized survival skills, ones that are relevant to her own world. In many ways, Jessie's vigilance served her well, even outside her house. In school, it simply looked like conscientiousness— a quality often associated with resilient children and teens. Jessie was a thoughtful and diligent student. Always on time to classes or appointments, Jessie was careful not to make mistakes or to make a misstep of any kind. She was skilled at reading the moods of her fellow students and teachers, then managing herself accordingly.

This made Jessie a favorite among teachers and friends, and she attached herself to people she could trust. One way Jessie lessened Charley's impact on her was by choosing safe places to be and safe people to be with. Studies of children, adults, and primates show us that low-power individuals watch others more than their high-power peers do—and they are more accurate in their judgments about them. The same can be said for family heroes like Jessie. "You had to be able to read people in my family to see when hell was about to break loose," Jessie said. "So I'm good at watching people carefully. I preempt the bad things. But I know a good thing when I see one, too. I mean, I know what isn't bad."

In their landmark study of hundreds of famous men and women, Goertzel and Goertzel concluded that success often came not from being in the right place at the right time, but from being able to *recognize* being in the right place at the right time. A sensitive amygdala helps us pay attention not only to danger but also to opportunity. Family heroes like Jessie scan their environments, looking for chances to be safe—and even happy—until escape becomes possible, and usually that escape comes from spotting a school or a person or a job that will take them somewhere else. Jessie did go somewhere else: first to college and business school, and then to a high-pressure career in business consulting. She thrived on managing unpredictability and crisis, and her assessment skills were preternaturally advanced. For her thirtieth birthday, Jessie had a small owl tattooed on her back.

* * *

The relationship between physiological arousal and performance is like an upside-down U. When we are not alert, we do not perform well; when we are too excited, we do not perform well, either. Most people excel when they are moderately aroused, when they feel a real but not overwhelming need to pay attention and do their best. Family heroes like Jessie feel as if they live their lives at the apex of that upside-down U, like they are surfing a wave that never terminates, one that requires finesse and focus and countless minute adjustments. Being able to do this—day after day and night after night—can feel as empowering as it does out of control. It can be as exhilarating as it is exhausting.

Prolonged stress not only keeps the amygdala activated, but also suppresses activity in the prefrontal cortex and the hippocampus, both parts of the brain that help us downshift our own arousal. The prefrontal cortex is the part of the brain that moderates fear, as it "talks back to" or reasons with the more emotional amygdala. The hippocampus is where we place learning in context, recognizing that what went on in the home may not go on elsewhere, that one bad person is not representative of all people, that that was then and this is now. If one's amygdala is extremely sensitive, the prefrontal cortex and the hippocampus may be less able to be effective. As a result, family heroes can feel locked in to their own hyperarousal, simply unable to make it stop. In this way, vigilance can persist for years, and even for a lifetime, after the original exposure to danger.

From an evolutionary perspective, there is value in generalizing danger; in not being naive in every new situation. Yet the overgeneralization of danger is problematic, too, as the family hero may take those "traumatic expectations" and her "anxiety of premonitions" everywhere she goes. This is the insidious nature of the mistreatment that many children experience, especially when it is at the hands of loved and trusted others. When bad things happen again and again, the brain learns that danger is not an unusual encounter but rather a way of life. Besides, it is difficult *not* to overgeneralize abuse at the hands of those who are supposed to care for you, no matter how infrequent it may be. If Jessie's own sister was willing to hurt her—and her mother failed to protect her—then why should she expect better from mere strangers or friends?

Vigilance helps us manage external difficulties yet, over time, it can take a toll on the brain and the body, leading to an array of inner difficulties: upset stomach and diarrhea, over- or undereating, immunosuppression, insomnia, lowered sex drive, heart disease, anxiety, depression, and—most simply—exhaustion. Even as an adult, Jessie felt chronically on guard, as if her mind never rested. She worked so hard that she forgot to eat, and she had little time for life outside her job. She had trouble relaxing when other people were around, and she sometimes wondered if her friendships were genuine or if she was just a reflexive handler of other people. Jessie felt distant from, and even a bit resentful toward, those who seemed carefree and careless, people who never would have dreamed of needing an owl tattoo.

Rather than watching the clock in an effort to stay awake like she used to, after long days at work Jessie now watched the clock desperate to nod off to sleep. "I haven't really slept in 20 years," said one Vietnam veteran in a book by Laurence Gonzales, aptly titled *Surviving Survival*. Jessie, too, felt as if she could not and did not sleep. She must have slept, of course, but her sense that somehow she hadn't may not have been entirely inaccurate. Not only do those who experience chronic stress have trouble falling asleep, but once they do, they often don't sleep as deeply, spending less time in what is called delta sleep. During those long nights, Jessie wondered if she would ever have a regular life or even a regular night's sleep, like the seemingly normal people all around her.

Because she was good at reading people, Jessie fell in love with a man who was rarely angry and prone to no sudden moves. When the pair went on trips together, Jessie felt liberated from her own vigilance. She noticed the sun on her skin and how her food tasted. She felt a playfulness that reminded her of falling down in the grass with the dog next door. Jessie rarely thought about growing up with Charley anymore, except when she saw electrical outlets and their horrified little faces, or when someone referenced *Rosemary's Baby*. Jessie's new home with her partner felt like a vacation home, a place where she could get away from who she used to need to be. Over time, she stopped feeling like a prisoner or a warrior or an owl, and she stopped taking mental pictures of rooms.

When Jessie had children, she made certain that they felt safe—with each other and in the world—and in a way this brought her vigilance back. She had only recently let go of making her way through the world as if her life depended on it, and now there were little lives that *did* depend on her. It seemed there was always something to do or someone to tend to, and she noticed and met every need almost without thinking. Spending her days and nights again at the top of that inverted U, she was a successful consultant, a hardworking partner, and an attentive mother, but sometimes she felt exhausted by the relentlessness of her own mind. Jessie sometimes considered what decades of stress had done to her; if a childhood with Charley would kill her in the end.

Jessie did finally feel that she could go to sleep at night, though she still slept on the very edge of the bed, with the owl on her back facing her husband and the door. Her husband sometimes remarked that, with the slightest sound, Jessie's eyes flicked open, and she spoke to him clearly and coherently as if she had just been lying there resting, as if she had never really been asleep at all.

CHAPTER 7

Superhuman

When I was at boarding school, sent away during the war as a little boy, I had a sense of imprisonment and powerlessness, and I longed for movement and power, ease of movement and superhuman power.

—Oliver Sacks, *On the Move*

No one knows I'm here," Elizabeth said. The no ones she was referring to turned out to be her fellow medical residents at the nearby university hospital where she was working toward a joint medical and law degree, the MD/JD. "People would see it as a weakness, you know, needing help from a shrink." That day, and all the days that would follow over a period of more than three years, Elizabeth cried almost every moment she was in my office. Her tears were the barely noticeable kind, sort of seeping from her eyes and collecting every few minutes at the overhang of her jawline, where she wiped them away with the backs of her hands. In all of the hours we spent together, Elizabeth never once reached for a tissue, as if she wanted to be as self-sufficient as possible.

"I came here because I think I'm not human. It's like I don't have feelings," Elizabeth confided early on.

I pointed out that her tears suggested otherwise.

"I don't know why I'm crying," she said, seeming embarrassed and disconcerted by this inability to control her tears. "I never cry outside of here."

Then, after many sessions, came this: "Last night I read this article online. It was called 'I Am Adam Lanza's Mother.' You know, Adam Lanza was the Sandy Hook shooter, and the article was written by this woman who wasn't really his mother but she felt like she could have been. Because her son was really out of control and it was all about how hard it is to be a parent of a kid like that, never knowing what he'll do next or, you know, how to handle him."

Elizabeth sniffed and wiped some tears away.

"And you know what I thought to myself when I read it?" she asked me quite directly. "That I am Adam Lanza's sister. I mean, my brother didn't shoot anybody, but he was just like the kid in this article. Why doesn't anybody ever write about that?"

* * *

Elizabeth's brother, Henry, was a special-needs child though no one knew quite what his special needs were or how to meet them. As long as Elizabeth could remember, her parents had driven her brother to specialists and hospitals, some hundreds of miles away, for a better diagnosis in the hope of a better treatment. Intermittent explosive disorder. Autism spectrum disorder. Sensory integration disorder. Pediatric bipolar disorder. Tourette's syndrome. With every new label there was hope that something might tame the wild tantrums in public and the violent outbursts at home that resulted in broken dishes and even broken bones.

Elizabeth's parents' efforts to help Henry were nothing less than valiant. Her mother gave up her career and dedicated nearly all of her waking hours—and many hours when she surely would have liked to have been sleeping—to Henry's care. On weekdays, she homeschooled him and accompanied him to a parade of appointments: speech therapy, social skills training, occupational therapy, physical therapy, tutoring, psychiatry, play therapy. On weekends, she traveled to conferences to hear the latest thinking on developmental disorders. Sometimes Elizabeth's mother and father fought about how to handle Henry; her father did not want the squeaky wheel to get all of the grease whereas her mother said she saw no other way. Henry's mother usually won.

As the family was busied with Henry's special needs, Elizabeth grew up with no memory of having even the most ordinary needs of her own. She was an easy baby, so much so it was thought she, too, might have some developmental difficulties, given the way she sat in a playpen for hours without crying or calling for anyone. It was only when a third child came along—a baby girl—that Elizabeth came to life. Elizabeth and her younger sister grew up side by side, playing and talking out of the way of their older brother. Elizabeth credited her sister with being the best part of her childhood, and now her closest friend, and it seems that was what her parents hoped for all along.

When a relative questioned Elizabeth's parents about why they had had a third child when they were so overextended with Henry, Elizabeth overheard this in quiet tones: Her sister had been born so Elizabeth would not be alone in caring for Henry when both parents were gone. Elizabeth and her sister were going to need to get Henry through adulthood together. Feeling protected and sacrificed at the same time, Elizabeth had always wanted to talk to her sister about what she heard but did not have the heart to tell her the news: that she had been born to serve.

Once when Elizabeth and her sister played too long outside, Elizabeth came in sick with heatstroke. "Mommmmmm!" she called out before collapsing on the bathroom floor. Her mother yelled back from upstairs as she managed one of Henry's fits: "I need you not to need me right now!" It is said that siblings find niches, different from one another, so as not to compete for the same resources or the same spot in the family. Elizabeth stripped to her underwear and splayed out on her stomach like a starfish, her torso and her cheek cooling on the tile floor. If Henry's niche was having special needs, then Elizabeth's niche would be having no needs at all.

* * *

There are countless ways to be a special-needs child. The term *special needs* is a shortened way of saying that one has special health care needs. It is an umbrella term intended to cover any chronic physical, developmental, behavioral, or emotional condition that requires medical, mental health, or educational services beyond those that are commonly a part of growing up. Such conditions most commonly include learning disabilities, attention-deficit/hyperactivity disorder, mood disorders such as depression and bipolar disorder, anxiety disorders, autism spectrum disorders, behavioral disorders, developmental disorders, arthritis or other joint problems, intellectual disabilities, cerebral palsy, speech problems, tic disorders, asthma, diabetes, severe allergies, seizure disorders, hearing or vision impairments, and brain injuries. This is a long list but not an exhaustive one. Any condition that necessitates special services would qualify. Many special-needs children meet criteria for more than one condition—or, like Elizabeth's brother, they struggle with behaviors and symptoms that do not fit neatly into a diagnostic box at all.

According to the National Survey of Children with Special Health Care Needs, a representative sampling of tens of thousands of households across the nation, about 13 to 20 percent of boys and girls under the age of eighteen—or between ten and fifteen million children—have special needs. While boys are somewhat more likely to have childhood health problems than girls, special-needs children are roughly equally likely to be found in all income brackets. Advances in medical treatments mean that countless children who might once have died from their conditions—or who might have been institutionalized because of them—now are more likely to live at home, where their parents attempt to meet their special needs. Most of these special-needs children share a house, or even a bedroom, with at least one sibling.

It is important to be clear that two-thirds of special-needs children are not impacted much by their conditions, and neither are their families; their special needs are few. But about one-third have conditions that greatly affect their day-to-day lives and those of their parents and their brothers and sisters. Kids who have special needs often cannot just be kids. They may be unable to run and play and learn alongside others their age. Finances and marriages may be strained under the weight of constant caregiving, and often parents must work less, or stop working, in order to give their children what they need. It may be difficult for families to enjoy good times together, or to go out in public without receiving pitying looks or sympathetic smiles. Additionally, these struggles are often not temporary: Many special-needs children have conditions that will stretch far into their adult years.

* * *

Although there are many ways to be a special-needs child, the so-called typically developing siblings of special-needs children sometimes look a lot alike, and they can be anything but typical. Aptly known to some as "supersiblings," these brothers and sisters may compensate for their loved ones' disordered development with their own precocious development. Younger siblings may act like older siblings and older siblings may take on the role of little parents as they step up and help out with cooking, chores, and childcare. Mature beyond their years, supersiblings are often recognized by others as "little adults" or "old souls." "What would we do without you?" parents say. When their special-needs siblings cannot be flexible, these siblings take the backseat in the car and in the home.

Because children with special needs are rising in number, the challenges their parents face are beginning to gain prominence—as seen in the op-ed "I Am Adam Lanza's Mother"—but the siblings of special-needs children are a largely unrecognized, underserved group. Compared with their brothers and sisters, supersiblings are overlooked not just in the home but in the research as well, and only very recently have clinicians and families begun to recognize that the siblings of special-needs children are a special population themselves.

There are special benefits and costs that go along with having a special-needs sibling. Growing up a few feet away from a loved one with a chronic illness or disability can offer unique opportunities for personal growth, and consequently many supersiblings become more responsible and competent than their peers. Living with a sibling who is different can foster tolerance, empathy, compassion, and patience. Knowing that someone you love may never be well—and may even die—puts other childhood problems in perspective. Their childhood experiences can result in distinct skills, and many supersiblings take their talents and strengths and become valedictorians, class presidents, physicians, community leaders, and sports heroes. Young golf great Jordan Spieth credits much of his maturity and groundedness to having a younger sister with a neurological disorder. She is, he says, "the best thing that ever happened to our family."

Elizabeth's story is only one story, of course, and it is one that can be more difficult to talk about. It is a story about how, even though boys and girls may love their special-needs siblings, life can be hard for them, too. Supersiblings like Elizabeth may worry about whether they themselves might one day have their brothers' or sisters' problems, or give birth to children who do. They may feel embarrassed about the ways that their special-needs siblings are conspicuously different, and then feel they have betrayed their siblings in their hearts and minds. They may feel resentful about unequal treatment in the family as their siblings receive praise for everyday tasks while their own outsize accomplishments are simply expected, and then feel bad about lapsing into petty jealousy. They may feel burdened by the prospect of having to care for their siblings one day, and then feel ashamed for being selfish. Supersiblings often keep these feelings to themselves, and about half struggle with their own problems, such as depression, anxiety, substance abuse, or eating disorders, at some time during their lives, although friends and family may never know it.

Growing up in England, world-renowned neurologist and author Oliver Sacks had a brother who was diagnosed with schizophrenia as a teen. In late adulthood, Sacks wrote openly about his childhood ambivalence: "I became terrified of him, for him. What would happen to Michael, and would something similar happen to me too?" Like many children who live with adversity, Sacks coped by distancing himself from the problems in his home: "I set up my own [science] lab in the house, and closed the doors, closed my ears, against Michael's madness. It was not that I was indifferent to Michael; I felt a passionate sympathy for him, but I had to keep a distance also, create my own world of science so that I would not be swept into the chaos, the madness, the seduction, of his."

Later, Sacks recognized that his relocation to practice medicine in the United States was a move "partly to get away from my tragic, hopeless, mismanaged brother." Becoming a neurologist was, he said, a way to understand and master the brain, the organ that had devastated his brother and his family. There was, however, no quick or simple resolution. Sacks struggled with a secret drug addiction for four years in his late twenties and early thirties, and decades later he wrote of guilt that would never leave him: "I could, I should, have been more loving, more supportive...and the shame of this—the feeling that I was a bad brother, not available to him when he was in such need—is still hot within me sixty years later."

When the world looks at supersiblings like Oliver Sacks, or like Elizabeth, it sees, from the outside, an apparently seamless adaptation to their special circumstances. What the world often does not see—or cannot see—is a complicated mix of love, hate, protectiveness, embarrassment, guilt, anger, resentment, frustration, fear, and exhaustion. Like their special-needs brothers and sisters, what many supersiblings yearn for most is the average and expectable. They, too, want a life that is all their own, unaffected by illness. They wish they could enjoy an everyday relationship with their brother or sister, one that allows for rivalry and name-calling. They long for permission to have ordinary feelings and needs and milestones of their own. They would like to just be normal and even flawed themselves, but too often these supersiblings feel they cannot be normal, they need to be supernormal. They cannot be human, they must be superhuman.

* * *

In 1969, when Oprah Winfrey was fifteen years old, a special guest speaker visited her high school. In an hour that would change her life, the Reverend Jesse Jackson delivered what Winfrey described as "the speech of a lifetime" in which he gave the students this challenge and solution to discrimination: "Excellence is the best deterrent to racism. Therefore, be excellent." That evening, Winfrey went home and made a poster of these ten words to live by, and the poster remained taped to her mirror through college.

Excellence, it turns out, is the best deterrent to any form of discrimination based on difference, and Elizabeth knew—it seems instinctively—that the best way to protect Henry, herself, and her family from sideways glances and unfair treatment was to excel. To err may be human, but Elizabeth was exceedingly careful never to make mistakes of any kind.

Henry could not be left home alone, and no babysitter could handle him, so wherever Elizabeth's mother went, Henry went, too. Henry hated errands, and the grocery store most of all, with its bright lights and cold temperatures. He had trouble controlling his eating, and because he could eat a box of Little Debbies or

Crunch Berries in one sitting, his mother was not supposed to buy them. Some kids might fuss or cry in the store for sugar cereals or sweet snacks, but Henry had what his doctors had begun to call, for lack of a better term, blind rages. He shook his mother's big, metal shopping cart with his arms and kicked her with his feet and, while most other shoppers pretended to casually look away, he hissed and spit at those who dared to stare. Once, a store manager asked them to leave: "What am I supposed to do with my child while I buy food for us to eat?" Elizabeth's mother asked imploringly in response as Elizabeth wished she might sink into the floor.

When Elizabeth was young and Henry misbehaved in the grocery store, she would sneak away to an empty aisle and, looking carefully in both directions, reach into her shirt and pull out a necklace she kept tucked there. Raising her arms high up above her head, she was Oh Mighty Isis, pretending to swirl the clouds as she took control of the world. By the time she was in middle school, she attempted to transform stares and glares from strangers by using the only real power she had: being very, very good. She ran and fetched items for her mother so they could move quickly and efficiently through the store. From the outside, Elizabeth and her mother might have looked like frantic contestants on some strange game show, but on the inside, they felt like they were running for their lives. To skip the candy in the checkout line, Elizabeth's mother diverted Henry to the car while Elizabeth stacked items on the conveyor belt in an orderly fashion—fruits with fruits, frozen foods with frozen foods, boxes with boxes, dairy with dairy—before she laid down her mother's credit card and her sister pushed the cart out to the parking lot. Elizabeth's mother might have had one very troubled child, but she had a model child, too.

Perhaps similarly to how Oprah Winfrey aimed to succeed as a black woman in a white man's world, Elizabeth felt she needed to be excellent, too. She had a vague and constant feeling that she had something to prove or offset. Day after day, school offered countless opportunities to do so. In the mornings, she walked quickly up the front stairs of the school and greeted her principal cheerfully—"Hi, Mrs. Miller!" She pretended not to notice Henry, who—now being "mainstreamed"—came out of the car like a giant piece of taffy, stretching and resisting against the guiding arms of his mother and the assistant principal. In the classroom, Elizabeth took comfort in the perfection of 100s, only to have Henry's shouts from the hallways sometimes pierce her world.

In one school talent show, Elizabeth hammered out a flawless minuet by Bach, and she did so with her cheeks flaming red, not because she was anxious about performing on stage but because she was angry. She heard Henry laugh out loud when she came on stage, and then Elizabeth's father ushered him out of the auditorium as she played. As she sat at the piano moving her fingers up and down the keys with poise, she also imagined herself screaming at her mother from the stage—"Couldn't he have stayed with a babysitter just *once*?" Later that night, when Elizabeth was sullen and she complained that Henry had ruined the night for her, her mother scolded her: "For God's sake, Elizabeth. You just had this great experience that Henry will never have. He can't control himself. You're lucky you can!"

* * *

Many family heroes seem to have some kind of secret weapon. "Lord yes, she had the stuff from the beginning," remembered an early teacher of novelist Alice Walker. "A lot of children passed my way, but Alice Walker was the smartest one I ever had." Or as biographer Carl Sandburg said about young Abraham Lincoln, who attended school only sparsely and sporadically: "Abe made books tell him more than they told other people." That secret weapon is not always book smarts, of course, and Andy Warhol remembered being noticed at a young age for his artistic skill: "The teachers liked me. They said something like I had natural talent. Or unnatural talent." Not every family hero will go on to be a famous novelist or artist or politician, and not every family hero need have some prodigious talent. A secret weapon that a great many do have, however, is a natural—or unnatural—ability to control themselves.

Self-control is the ability to direct one's own thoughts, feelings, and behavior, usually as a way to better adapt to the world. A sort of catchall word for how well we resist temptation, delay gratification, regulate our emotions, and work toward what we want, self-control is how we obey rules, follow directions, check emotions, cooperate with others, exercise consistently, eat healthily, keep promises, save money, get to work on time, and work hard. As noted by Sigmund Freud almost a hundred years ago, the ability of the individual to be in charge of herself—for reason to be stronger than passion, for the individual to bend to society, for the ego to be stronger than the id—has long been one of the hallmarks of civilization.

Now we know that self-control does not come from the ego per se; it comes from the prefrontal cortex. The human brain develops, and has evolved, from back to front and from bottom to top. The most primitive parts of the brain are buried deep at the bottom and the back of the brain, and these areas function automatically: The brain stem regulates heartbeat, breathing, and sleep without any effort on our part, for example, and the amygdala triggers fight-or-flight responses reflexively. The prefrontal cortex is literally and figuratively the most top and forward part of the brain. Located just behind the forehead, this is where our most advanced, forward thinking takes place. This is the part of the brain that provides "top-down" regulation of the amygdala, quieting our impulsive, emotional reactions and replacing those with conscious, intentional actions. The prefrontal cortex is where the executive functions reside, self-control being chief among them.

The most often cited illustration of self-control is the now famous "Marshmallow Test," developed by psychologist Walter

Mischel in the 1960s. In a classic set of studies, Mischel examined whether preschool children could resist eating one marshmallow right away in favor of waiting twenty minutes for the reward of getting to eat two. Not surprisingly, some gobbled up the single marshmallow in an instant, others tried to wait the twenty minutes but failed, and still others were able to hold out for the reward of two goodies. What was intended to be a snapshot of individual differences in children's ability to delay gratification became a long-running study of development, and over the years the predictive validity of the Marshmallow Test has turned out to be nothing less than astonishing. Those preschoolers who had enough self-control to wait for the reward of two marshmallows went on to have higher SAT scores, better coping skills, higher educational attainment, higher self-worth, and less drug use in adulthood.

In the decades that have passed since Mischel's preschoolers faced off with those marshmallows, other scientists have shown self-control to be pretty much all upside. In a 2012 meta-analysis that combined results from over one hundred studies and more than thirty thousand subjects, self-control was associated with better outcomes in school, work, love, and health. From early education through higher education, self-control means better attendance, more time spent studying, less time spent watching television, and higher grades and standardized test scores; self-control has even shown itself to be a better predictor of academic success than IQ.

Those with more self-control are at an advantage outside the classroom as well. They have better relationships and tend to be popular, at least in part because they are good at overriding their own desires and attending to the needs and wishes of others. Greater self-control is associated with better performance in sports, too, as it makes it possible for athletes to dedicate themselves to regular practice, and to keep calm and excel under pressure. And self-control helps us not only say yes to the work that is required in life but also to say no to destructive behaviors that might get in our way. As a result, those with greater self-control are less likely to struggle with impulse-control problems such as violence, anger, delinquency, and binge eating or drinking.

Self-control may even tell us something about why some who experience trauma go on to develop post-traumatic stress disorder (PTSD) while others do not. Brain imaging studies suggest that in the face of overwhelming experiences, those who develop PTSD show less activity and connectivity in the prefrontal cortex compared with those who have also experienced trauma but do not develop PTSD. This suggests that, at least in part, PTSD may be the result of inadequate "top-down" control of the amygdala, such that fight-or-flight reactions run amok. Indeed, one aspect of treatment for PTSD involves teaching greater control over one's thoughts, feelings, and behaviors. One of the defining features of PTSD is feeling overwhelmed and helpless as the result of trauma, and self-control allows us to feel in charge of ourselves and our lives even if we are unable to control some of the things that happen to us.

The predictive power of self-control is so strong that it is comparable to that of intelligence and socioeconomic status, yet, importantly, it is not the same as either of these. This means that self-control is a place of possibility, a way that even without being the smartest or the most privileged, the family hero still has an opportunity to excel. To be sure, as the study of Mischel's preschoolers suggests, some people start off with more self-control than others, and those who have more will likely do better in life. (Elizabeth's mother was partially right: Elizabeth was fortunate to have more self-control than her brother.) Self-control is not simply an inborn gift, however, available to the "haves" but out of reach of the "have-nots." Self-control can be built through practice and challenge, and those who battle adversity in their homes or neighborhoods are awash with practice and challenge. Every day there are opportunities to hold their tongues with troubled siblings, to choke back their tears in the presence of bullies, to tiptoe around the moods of an alcoholic, to avoid dangerous blocks on the walk home, and to work diligently toward the goal of getting out. Family heroes probably come into this world with at least their fair share of self-control—likely they would have passed the Marshmallow Test easily—yet one cannot underestimate the impact of being immersed in an environment where, day after day, one must continuously control how one thinks and feels and acts.

By adulthood, many family heroes attribute their survival and their success to their special ability to control their days and, therefore, their destinies. Indeed, those who transcend difficult circumstances often do so in part through self-control and self-direction. In the Kauai Longitudinal Study—the study in which a diverse cohort of infants in Hawaii were followed through midlife—the men and women who outperformed their disadvantaged beginnings were those who, by adolescence, believed in their own effectiveness, in their ability to overcome whatever obstacles lay ahead. In a different study, this one of nearly three thousand adults, aged twenty-five to seventy-four, a lack of parental support in childhood was associated with chronic mental and physical health conditions in adulthood, but it was those who felt in control of themselves and their lives who fared well.

Known for their amazing ability to put their executive functions to work, family heroes can be like "little executives" in their controlled and directed approach to life. They set goals and make posters for themselves—"Be excellent!"—and they do this knowing that being excellent comes not just from having some prodigious raw materials but also—or perhaps even more—from being willing and able to put those raw materials to work. Though Elizabeth never would have admitted it to others, she secretly felt something like omnipotent. She felt she could do anything she set her mind to as long as she chose wisely—which, of course, she typically did. "I don't understand failure," she said. "If you want to do something badly enough, you make it happen."

* * *

Because Elizabeth and her sister were "the lucky ones," they were not allowed to have complaints about their brother, nor did it seem they were allowed to have the whole range of human emotions. "In our family, it went beyond, 'If you can't say anything nice, don't say anything at all,'" Elizabeth recalls. "It was, 'If you can't feel anything nice, don't feel anything at all.'" Elizabeth was not sure what she felt anyway. As difficult as it is to have thoughts or feelings about a problem that no one wants to talk about, it is even more difficult to have thoughts or feelings about a problem no one *can* talk about because no one knows what it is. "Never having a clear diagnosis, it was hard to hold Henry accountable for anything," Elizabeth recalls. "Sometimes he would be just fine and then other times, watch out. But whatever it was, he couldn't help it, so I was told I could not have feelings about it."

Anger. Sadness. Fear. Those feelings were off limits. The sisters were told to be "better than that" and "above all that," so many hours at home were spent rising above being human. Like at the dinner table, when Henry taunted Elizabeth—"My classes are harder than yours, you know"—typical sibling rivalry might have resulted in some back-and-forth bickering that would have gradually ruined dinner for everyone. Instead, when Elizabeth said casually, playfully, "No, mine are harder, actually," dinner was ruined in an instant when Henry threw his plate at her. When Elizabeth dove down under the table and began to crawl out of the room, her mother commanded, "Get back up here! You're not going anywhere. You are going to sit right here and apologize to your brother."

Or like when, as teenagers, Henry charged Elizabeth with a butcher knife and her father called 911. After the police officers left with her brother in the backseat of their cruiser, Elizabeth and her sister collected the "sharps" in the house—the knives, the scissors, the screwdrivers—and hid them away in a shoe box. Later, on the solemn drive to the police station, Elizabeth's mother asked Elizabeth what she would like to do: "You could press charges but then he'll have a record... or we could put Henry in a hospital for a while..."

"If he goes to a hospital, will he ever be able to get a job?" Elizabeth asked, saddled with worry and responsibility for her brother's future.

"Yes, honey," Elizabeth's mother said. "No one will ever know."

"Then I guess he should go to a hospital," Elizabeth said.

Remembering that car ride years later, Elizabeth flashed a sardonic smile and quipped, "He wanted to murder me but I wasn't allowed to want to murder him."

* * *

By the time Elizabeth left for college, she was gifted at what trauma expert Bessel van der Kolk calls "dealing but not feeling." She took seven classes a semester, served as a residence adviser in the dorms, made the dean's list, and waited tables twenty hours a week. This might sound implausible or even impossible, but owing at least in part to her very capable prefrontal cortex, Elizabeth had always been able to do more than most others her age. Each semester, she needed special permission from a dean to take on her inordinately heavy load, and in this semiannual perfunctory meeting, her cheery disposition and color-coded planner spoke for themselves. No one knew, nor did Elizabeth herself think much of the fact, that she routinely drank as many as ten cups of coffee a day and slept as little as four or five hours a night. She often failed to notice when she was hungry.

Next she headed for law and medical school, where she played off her ready knowledge of the psychiatric drugs Henry had taken over the years, as well as her knowledge of the legal system: "How do you know all this stuff, Elizabeth?" her fellow students wanted to know. Elizabeth's achievements clearly differentiated her from her brother: If he was going to be stuck at home as a patient, then she was going to get somewhere as a doctor; if he was going to sit in the back of a police car, then she was going to have a law degree. Besides, as she watched her parents argue about the credit card debt that was piling up over Henry, Elizabeth now understood the full force of what she had once heard her mother confide to her aunt: One day, she and her sister were going to need to be able to support him. Elizabeth's family could not afford for her not to do well.

Yet as she excelled, Elizabeth instinctively knew to whisper about her accolades—summa cum laude, graduate school admission, selection as chief resident—or simply not to speak of them at all. She cringed when her accomplishments were mentioned in front of her brother, and the entire family took a collective, silent gasp when, in public, some well-meaning stranger inadvertently shone a light on the discrepancies between the siblings: "And what about you, young man? Are you in graduate school, too?" Elizabeth felt a heavy sense of culpability, that whatever was good for her was bad for her brother. She returned home less and less as the message she received from her parents shifted from "Your honor roll mention is upsetting your brother" to "Your existence is upsetting your brother."

Family heroes like Elizabeth live with an excruciating double bind: Their families need them to be well and do well, yet they are often left to feel bad about their own health and accomplishments. Their celebrations may be muted or nonexistent, and their achievements can be a source of pain or anger or sadness for those they have worked so hard to protect. While many family heroes do not feel entitled to their most primal human emotions, they may feel awash with a more sophisticated feeling: guilt. Guilt is a social, moral feeling that arises in the context of a relationship between two people. It surfaces when we feel we have behaved in ways that are damaging toward another, or when we see inequities in a group—especially in a group of family members. Guilt resides in the prefrontal cortex and is closely related to self-control—"I live in my goddamn prefrontal cortex!" Elizabeth would bemoan in sessions—and its evolutionary purpose is to promote fairness. Guilt prods us to even things out.

For most family heroes, though, life is not, and may never be, fair. Many live alongside brothers or sisters or mothers or fathers who struggle with problems they do not have and cannot fix. Though Elizabeth felt somehow responsible for Henry's unhappiness, she had done nothing wrong except get the longer end of the neurodevelopmental stick. The more she tried to "even things out" for her family by being good and helpful—by being supernormal and superhuman—the more she outstripped her brother and made him feel bad. Other than sabotaging her own success, which would only burden her parents more, there was nothing Elizabeth could do to make their lives more equitable.

Guilt is not adaptive when it cannot lead to some sort of repair, and indeed a meta-analysis that examined the results of over one hundred studies and more than twenty thousand subjects found that feeling responsible for events one cannot control is related to depression, a problem that Elizabeth was struggling with privately in therapy. "I don't feel like I am allowed to be really depressed or have a breakdown or anything because I'm the lucky one," she said. "But I don't feel like I am allowed to be happy, either."

When Elizabeth was set to graduate with her MD/JD, in lieu of gifts from her parents, she asked for one thing: that the day be about her. With some guilt, she requested that her mother and sister come alone, that Henry be left behind with her father, so she could enjoy her achievement. When the two women rang the bell at Elizabeth's apartment only just in time to dash to the ceremony, her mother reluctantly admitted that one of Henry's appointments that morning had run long. In a rare display of anger, Elizabeth shrieked, "I asked for *one thing* for graduation! I just wanted *one day* to be about me. You couldn't go *one day* without putting Henry first? He had to have an appointment *today?*"

"Henry is back in the hospital," her mother said icily.

Flooded with guilt, Elizabeth was trumped again.

"Just buck up and we'll have a good day," her mother continued. "That's what you always do. That's what you've always been so good at."

Unable to acknowledge her suffering, Elizabeth's parents simply could not afford—financially, logistically, or emotionally—to have more than one child with needs. Unable to understand her parents' bind, Elizabeth uncharacteristically pushed further for an explanation: "Why do you *always* put Henry ahead of me?" she shrieked some more.

After several rounds of denials, Elizabeth's mother said something that maybe she did not mean, or that maybe she did not mean to say: "You're an animal lover, Elizabeth," she exhaled, exasperated. "Let's say you have two little dogs. One dog is cute and cuddly and everybody runs over to it and wants to pet it and play with it. The other dog growls and snaps at people and no one wants to go near it. If you have to put one dog out on the street it's going to be the cute one because you know somebody is going to come along and pick it up."

CHAPTER 8

Orphan

It must be pure bliss to arrange the furniture just as one likes.
—Edith Wharton, *The House of Mirth*

Nadia seemed a bit older than she was, but a bit younger than she was, too. She seemed younger than her age because she smiled a lot and her toes turned in some when she sat. She seemed older than her years because, at twenty-six, she had met more adult milestones than many of her peers: She was a PhD candidate in art history and had now been married for more than a year. Dressed fashionably but casually in skinny green army pants and an off-the-shoulder shirt, Nadia was the kind of person who came across as effortlessly having it all. Looking at her, one would never guess that most of her friends had something that Nadia never would, or at least never would again: parents.

Nadia came to the United States when she was two years old. She does not know much about what happened before that time, but after that time, her upbringing had been an average and expectable one. She grew up in a happy home in Los Angeles—or to be more precise in a happy apartment, one that was just above the liquor store her parents owned. Life as she knew it changed forever, though, one afternoon during her first semester of college. It was 1997, and she returned to her dorm room, to these messages on her voice mail.

"Nadia, is it true?" asked one friend from back home.

"Are you all right?" said another.

"Oh my God, Nadia, call me..." pleaded her best friend of many years.

None of the messages were from her parents, so she called her best friend back.

"Nadia, oh my God, I'm so sorry!" she shrieked when she heard Nadia's voice.

"About what?"

"Oh my God, Nadia. Oh my God, Oh my God... you don't know?"

"Know what?"

"Somebody robbed your parents' store and..."

"Are they okay?"

"No! They... they died."

"Who died?" Nadia asked in disbelief. "The robbers?"

Her friend cried harder, having to say it: "Your mom and dad."

When Nadia came to my office, it had been eight years since she had received those calls. She thought not having parents would be easier by now, thought it should be easier by now—"People expect me to be over this, you know"—but there was always some new way of feeling left alone. Nadia was unprepared for how much, even as an adult, she still wished she had a mother and a father. "People are nice but it is not the same. I feel bad saying that but it's not," she cried. "Not having parents never stops sucking."

* * *

Most people recognize the death of a parent to be among the most fundamental tragedies of childhood. Few, though, realize how common it is. One in nine children will lose a parent to death before the age of twenty, which means that, in any given year, for every child diagnosed with cancer, thirty-five children will have a parent pass away.

Because it is an adversity that is difficult to keep secret, and one that typically carries no shame, much has been made of the fact that the death of a parent can be found in the biographies of many great men and women in history. In an often cited study published in 1978, psychologist Marvin Eisenstadt identified individuals whose accomplishments merited at least one column of space in the 1963 edition of Encyclopedia Britannica and the 1964 edition of Encyclopedia Americana. Of the 573 individuals he identified—from Homer to John F. Kennedy—nearly half had lost a parent by the age of twenty, a high percentage even for the times. Although Eisenstadt's data has not been updated since the middle of the twentieth century, the list of public figures who lost a parent early in life goes on: Supreme Court Justice Sonia Sotomayor; singers Barbra Streisand, Paul McCartney, Bono, and Madonna; actor Julia Roberts; New York City mayor Bill de Blasio; Speaker of the House Paul Ryan; and US president Bill Clinton, to name just a few.

As with other childhood adversities, the death of a parent can bring opportunities for personal growth. Eight out of ten children who lost a mother or father say they are more resilient than other people, and six out of ten say they are stronger because of their loss. Some feel like they have to be. Supreme Court Justice Sonia Sotomayor remembers being informed on the day of her father's death, "Sonia, you have to be a big girl now. Your mother's very upset; you can't cry anymore. You have to be strong for your mami." And in his autobiography, former president Bill Clinton points to the death of his father—the result of a car accident just before his birth—as the origin story of his life: "My father left me with the feeling that I had to live for two people, and that if I did it well enough, I could make up for the life he should have had."

Part of the heroic narrative has always been to take something bad and turn it into something good. But make no mistake: The fact that some—or even many—who suffer great losses go on to do great things does not mean that the death of a parent is a positive experience; nor does it lessen the magnitude of their grief. Nearly three-quarters of those whose parent died in childhood wish it had never happened and feel their lives would have been "much better" had they not. More than half of those who lost a parent at a young age say they would trade a year of their life for one more day with their mother or father. Yet they must learn to accept, even graciously, lives they never asked for. "I love the thing that I most wish had not happened," said Stephen Colbert about the death of his father and two brothers in a plane crash when Colbert was just ten years old. Good adaptation does not mean the absence of heartbreak.

Perhaps the most heart-wrenchingly honest description of the contradiction that one is left with when good things come out of bad things was expressed by Rabbi Harold Kushner, author of the timeless *When Bad Things Happen to Good People*, a book about the loss not of his parent but of his child: "I am a more sensitive person, a more effective pastor, a more sympathetic counselor because of Aaron's life and death than I ever would have been without it. And I would give up all of those gains in a second if I could have my son back. If I could choose, I would forego all the spiritual growth and depth which has come my way because of our experiences, and be what I was fifteen years ago, an average rabbi, an indifferent counselor, helping some people and unable to help others, and the father of a bright, happy boy. But I cannot choose."

* * *

A paper titled "The Painted Guinea Pig," published in 1976 in *The Psychoanalytic Study of the Child*, tells a story about how children struggle to comprehend loss. The loss, in this case, was the death of a pet in a kindergarten classroom, a guinea pig named Guinny.

The children are told quite plainly about the pet's passing—"Guinny died and he was buried in the park," the teacher said—but they struggled to understand it completely. After some time, the teacher brought in a new guinea pig for a pet, this one a different color. "Who painted him?" the children asked, unable to fully grasp that this new guinea pig was not Guinny; that Guinny was gone for good. Guinny was never coming back.

Nadia was no kindergartner but she was a young person who faced an unexpected, overwhelming loss, a loss she could not take in all at once. Unlike a very young child, she knew her parents were gone and were never coming back, but what this would mean for her life going forward could only be realized one new painful moment at a time. When she filled out forms and wrote "Deceased" in the blanks where her parents' names used to go. Or when she needed to register for classes and started to dial her mother for advice. Or when she visited her hometown and drove past her old home, the building now sold to another owner. Losing a parent is a cumulative stressor, too, because, even though it happens in an instant, it takes its toll bit by bit. It is not just the event itself that is devastating; it is how it changes one's life over time.

"Children mourn on a skateboard," the paper about the painted guinea pig also said, meaning that young people grieve in an active way, that their lives do not stop when a loved one dies. Rather, they have friends to see and things to do, and their sadness comes along for the ride. Nadia mourned on a skateboard, too, as she rode hers around her college campus. She never left school, not even for a single semester. Nadia's parents would have wanted it that way, and besides, where else would she go? What else would she do?

Continuity is incredibly important to any bereaved child, and perhaps nowhere could life be more continuous than college, a place where—no matter what is going on back home—meals keep being served in the dining halls and big lecture classes keep meeting and tests keep happening and football games keep roaring. Much of the time, Nadia was able to forget about her new reality altogether as she was surrounded by other young adults whose parents also were nowhere in sight. If she strayed too many blocks from school, however, the bookstores and coffee shops and tattoo parlors and pizza places gave way to neighborhoods with two-story shingled homes, lights ablaze and families inside. It was then that she was smacked with her own homelessness, that she remembered that outside of school she had no front door to walk into, and not even anyone who was thinking of her as she rolled along and her skateboard went click, click across the seams in the sidewalk. The sound seemed loud and lonely in the void.

There were other painful moments that caught her by surprise.

The May that Nadia was set to graduate, she stepped into a favorite café only to find every table occupied by women, young and old, dressed in spring colors and some holding flowers. It was Mother's Day, she realized, and for the previous few Nadia had done something special to remember her mom. While Nadia waited for her order, she watched the pairs of mothers and daughters like an anthropologist, an outsider wondering what it would be like to be sitting at a table with a mother, too. Maybe sadder than trying to figure out how to celebrate Mother's Day was her forgetting it was even coming.

And there was graduation. Nadia spent the day with her three best friends and their families. "Everyone was so great to me. It really was a happy day. A lot of celebrating. But it's the little things, you know? Whoever I was with, I was always the only one who wasn't in the family, so I'd wind up taking the family photos. And I'd look at them through the lens of the camera. There was a box around them, a group of people who came first for each other. Sometimes people picked up on that and they would make sure there was a picture with me in there, too, which was really nice," she recalled, "but I know they were just trying to make me feel better, like things weren't the way they were."

It was 2001, and Nadia felt twentysomething anomie in the marrow of her bones. With school no longer on it, the calendar had lost all meaning and rhythm, and there was always some new way of feeling alone. She felt adrift and apart, like there was no real reason to be anyone or anywhere in particular. No real reason to act one way over another. To Nadia, not having parents was like not having religion.

On the morning of September 11, Nadia was living in an apartment in San Francisco with four other girls, all of whom were asleep when the first plane struck the World Trade Center. It was not even six a.m. Moments after the second plane crash, their cell phones and their landline began to ring and ring, as parents called with directions and warnings. *Wake up. Turn on the TV. Stay home from work. No one knows what will happen next. Do not drive across the bridge today.* Like her roommates, Nadia spent the next days and weeks in a daze of disbelief and sadness, and of course she thought about the sons and daughters who lost mothers and fathers. Only later did she remember noticing that no one had called for her that morning. The whole world was coming apart and no one thought of Nadia. It hit her then, four years after her parents had died: Nadia was an orphan.

* * *

The essence of being an orphan is to be left without protection.

Commonly, we think of an orphan as being someone, like Nadia, whose parents have both died. This is the story of perhaps the world's most famous orphan, Little Orphan Annie, and indeed many of our most beloved fictional protagonists were orphaned in this way, too, carrying their lives and the story forward in classics such as *Jane Eyre, Oliver Twist, Anne of Green Gables, Tom Sawyer,* and *The House of Mirth,* as well as in blockbuster series such as Lord of the Rings, James Bond, Star Wars, and Harry Potter. And of course, many of the world's most popular superheroes were orphans, too. Like Nadia, Batman lost his parents in a robbery.

Yet there is more than one way to be an orphan, more than one way to lose a parent. According to the office of US Citizenship and Immigration Services, a child is an orphan if he or she has lost both parents for any reason: "A child may be considered an orphan because of the death or disappearance of, abandonment or desertion by, or separation or loss from, both parents." The United Nations goes further still, recognizing as an orphan a child who has lost even one parent, with a motherless child being a maternal orphan and a fatherless child being a paternal orphan. And contrary to the notion that real orphans must live in orphanages, the vast majority of children who have lost one or more parents live with surviving parents, grandparents, or other relatives. Many of the world's orphans do not look like Little Orphan Annie at all.

Were Marvin Eisenstadt, the psychologist who scoured encyclopedias for eminent individuals, to repeat his study today—and to be more inclusive in his definition of what it means to lose a mother or a father—his list would be far longer, and would include many other noteworthy figures such as Gerald Ford, John Lennon, Alex Rodriguez, Jon Stewart, LeBron James, Simone Biles, Shaquille O'Neal, Marilyn Monroe, Jay Z, Willie Nelson, and Barack Obama, each of whom was left as a child by one or both parents. Eisenstadt wrote that he chose his rather narrow view of orphanhood because information about death was more readily available and because "the effects should be more prominent and more easily noticed than other forms of loss." With the latter, I would have to disagree.

Remember Sam, the boy whose father left and sent him torn-up ten-dollar bills and lottery tickets? As an adult, Sam confided lifelong complicated feelings about a childhood friend whose father died and left him a hefty inheritance. "I am ashamed to say this but I have always envied him. People know his story and they feel bad for him. And I feel bad for him! It is really sad that his dad died. And unlucky. But he is fortunate in a way to have a story that people can understand and sympathize with. What's my story? That I have a deadbeat dad? My friend's dad did not want to leave his family and when he did he provided for them. Mine left me by choice and never looked back, never made sure that I was all right."

Sam continued.

"I confessed some of this to my wife before she was my wife, and what she said is probably why I married her. She said, 'You lost a dad, too.' And you know, I could not believe it. I did lose a dad, but honestly I'd never realized that until she said it. I mean, there was no funeral, no nothing. People just avoided the subject when I was young and by the time he did die—I was an adult, I hadn't seen him in twenty years—I didn't even care, which people did not understand, either. The way I felt was that I had already lost him a long time ago, but back then nobody seemed to notice."

Sam is describing what is called disenfranchised grief, or the sort of sorrow that follows from a loss that is not widely acknowledged. Though they may not typically be recognized as orphans, or even consciously think of themselves as such, those who have been abandoned by a parent also feel bereaved. They feel left alone and left behind, and deprived of the care and protection a mother or father might provide, though they may not feel entitled to their very real experience of loss. This is something that hip-hop artist Jay Z understood with his mega-hit "Hard Knock Life (Ghetto Anthem)," in which he raps over and alongside the theme song from the Broadway musical *Annie*: "I found the mirror between the two stories—that Annie's story was mine, and mine was hers. I felt like the chorus to that song perfectly captured what little kids in the ghetto felt every day: 'Stead of kisses, we get kicked.' We might not all have literally been orphans, but a whole generation of us had basically raised ourselves in the streets." Like Annie's story was Jay Z's story, it was Nadia's story and Sam's story, too. It is the story of every child who has lost a parent to death or divorce or mental illness or jail—or to anything—and has been left behind to fend for themselves.

* * *

Sociologist and psychotherapist Lillian Rubin, whose own father died when she was five years old, made a career out of studying children who transcended trauma. One thing she found was that those who triumph over hardship—who overcome a hard-knock life—do so, at least in part, because they have a quality she called "adoptability," or a knack for being taken in by others. When life is difficult at home, or parents are not there, many family heroes find surrogate parents or substitute caregivers to make up the difference. Sometimes they have some sort of talent in sports or school or the arts—or even more often they have the sort of personality—that gets the attention of family members, teachers, neighbors, or friends. This is important because one of the single best predictors of good adjustment after adversity is having external support, and being adoptable attracts the attention of those who might help. Resilient children and teens are skilled at what psychoanalyst Stuart Hauser called "recruiting relationships."

Think back to the decades-long study of the "vulnerable, but invincible" children of Kauai. Once grown, the children of Hawaii's Garden Island said they had done as well as they had largely because, on the inside, they were determined and in control—but on the outside, they had something else going for them, too. By and large, these successful children were, in Lillian Rubin's term, adoptable. They had, researchers said, "easy" temperaments and were "easy to deal with," and this helped them attract both kith and kin. As infants, they were described as "active," "affectionate," "cuddly," and "good-natured," and these desirable qualities elicited positive attention from those around them. These sociable babies who slept and ate well had more positive interactions with their mothers by age one and with other caregivers by age two. In middle childhood, they were not intellectually gifted at school, but they were good communicators and were skilled at getting along with others, and already they were building a network of supporters. In adolescence, they were outgoing when they needed to be; ultimately, the higher the number of adults with whom the child liked to associate, the more likely that he or she would make a successful transition into adulthood. Every single "vulnerable, but invincible" child could name at least one committed adult outside the home who cared.

Nadia had adoptability. Her story was certainly compelling, and what most impressed people about her was that, after her parents died, she never missed a beat. She was a success story and an inspiration and that was why others liked having her around, because she was not falling apart. Intuitively, Nadia knew what researchers do, too: that when bad things happen, those who hide their distress—who are agreeable—are perceived as more resilient than those who do not. So as she made her way through young adulthood, Nadia was taken in for holidays and brought along on vacations with other people's families. In return for these kindnesses, Nadia was careful to cause no trouble. She was quick to clear the table and to load or unload the dishwasher. She was, in her own words, "everyone's favorite houseguest."

Many family heroes feel like everyone's favorite houseguest.

When she was in college, paternal orphan and future poet and novelist Sylvia Plath worked summers to supplement her scholarships, many of which were supplied by wealthy benefactors. In the summer of 1952, Plath worked for a woman, Margaret Cantor, as a mother's helper. Hear how Mrs. Cantor described Plath in a report to the vocational office at her school: "Sylvia is an exceptionally fine girl. Her manners and deportment are beautiful. Her consistently sunny disposition and her ability to express herself in vivid language make her a most interesting and welcomed person."

But contrast this with what we routinely expect from children, and especially from children of our own. "What is the normal child like? Does he just eat and grow and smile sweetly?" asked psychoanalyst Donald Winnicott. "No, that is not what he is like. A normal child, if he has confidence in father and mother, pulls out all the stops. In the course of time, he tries out his power to disrupt, to destroy, to frighten, to wear down, to waste, to wangle, and to appropriate." Children like Sylvia Plath, or like Nadia, cannot have confidence in their mothers and fathers; nor can they be certain that their surrogates will keep them around. They know better than just to be normal children.

* * *

Let's be honest. Lillian Rubin's term *adoptability* is a misnomer. In truth, most orphans never are adopted, and neither are most family heroes. It is easy, or maybe convenient, to imagine that those like Nadia have a surrogate parent—maybe a grandmother or an aunt or a coach—who steps in and does the job that their mothers or fathers for whatever reason cannot. Sometimes this happens. Consider the story of Simone Biles, four-time Olympic gold medalist whom many consider to be the greatest female gymnast of all time. Born to a mother who was addicted to drugs and alcohol, and to a father who had abandoned the family, Biles spent her earliest years in and out of foster care. As a toddler, she went to live with her maternal grandparents, who adopted her soon after. They are, Biles makes clear, her parents; they are her mom and dad.

Most family heroes, however, are fostered by a variety of good people. They piece together parenting—a weekend with this friend, a holiday with that relative, a week on this couch, a word of encouragement from that teacher, some advice from this mentor, an opportunity from that neighbor—like bricolage. Scrappers that they are, family heroes fashion whole lives out of the bits and pieces of the lives of others. Wherever they go, they take care not to ask for too much or to get too comfortable because they are entitled to none of it. Paula McLain, whose memoir, *Like Family*, is about living with foster families, had this to say about growing up in other people's houses: "It's like a hotel because nothing belongs to you. It's all being lent, like library books: the bed, the toothbrush, the bathwater."

Robert Frost said, "Home is the place where, when you have to go there, they have to take you in." For Nadia, there was nowhere she had to go, and no one who had to welcome her. Because of this, she moved through the world differently from other people. Every moment of every day, she felt like an interloper, like she was expendable. Nothing would have hurt more than for someone to tell Nadia she was too much trouble, that she was inconvenient, and so, to protect herself, she made herself easy. Malleable and agreeable, she went along with whatever her host or her roommates wanted, never caring whether they stayed home or went out or ordered pizza or went to a movie. When some of the girls she lived with took long, poorly timed baths or ate other people's leftovers, Nadia wondered what it would be like to be so unconcerned.

"Orphans always make the best recruits," or so said Judi Dench as "M" in the James Bond movie *Skyfall*. With her icy, jaded remark, Dench captured something that researchers who credit resilient children with having a gift for "recruiting relationships" tend to miss: It is not always clear who is recruiting whom. The notion of recruiting relationships makes the family hero sound like a little Pied Piper, holding a flute and all the power, gathering a stream of followers in his wake with his magic tune. But being an orphan, even an adoptable one, is nothing like that. If anything, adoptable orphans are the ones who feel they must cheerfully follow behind others.

If the family hero is "vulnerable, but invincible," invincibility and strength are what we see while vulnerability and powerlessness are what she feels. To have power is to be in a position to help or harm ourselves or others. Those who have it control resources—material and otherwise—like money, affection, supplies, or decisions. Those who do not have it pay close attention to those who do. Two people in a relationship, or in the same household, have different experiences depending on how much power they have. One of the most poignant differences, at least to the powerless, is that those in power are free to be themselves. They can feel what they feel and want what they want. They can be spontaneous and make choices largely without fear. They can be consistent inside and out. The powerless find it prudent to hide their true feelings and wishes—especially if they are not happy, easy ones.

Little Orphan Annie herself sang that "you're never fully dressed without a smile." But smiling means different things for different people, depending in part on how much power they have. Research shows us that, for high-power individuals, smiles on their faces correspond with internal states of pleasure or happiness, while low-power individuals smile to make other people comfortable; there is no correlation between their smiles and how they really feel inside. For the powerful, smiling is authentic, while for the powerless, it is strategic or obligatory. Those high in power smile when they want to while those low in power smile when they need to.

Long before Edna St. Vincent Millay won the Pulitzer Prize for poetry in 1923, she and her mother and two sisters lived like four orphans. After Millay's father deserted the family, mother and daughters moved from home to home, nearly vagabonds were it not for extended family members who opened their doors. "The girls were now their mother's 'little women,'" wrote Millay's biographer, Nancy Milford. "She cautioned them again and again against being or causing anyone trouble. She told them to be tidy, clean and responsible, and they took her admonishments seriously. They were careful among their relatives, mostly aunts, not to reveal how they felt or what they in fact desired."

Differences in power make for a lopsided, complicated relationship between orphans and the world, and even between orphans and their benefactors, although the benefactors themselves may not realize it. While more powerful people move through their day thinking in terms of rewards—"What do I want and how can I get it?"—the less powerful are most mindful of punishments—"What am I afraid of and how can I avoid that?" What orphans are most afraid of is being cast out by whoever is currently allowing them in, so to stay in good favor, they feel obligated to smile and fulfill the needs of others. They earn their keep. They sing for their supper. They step and fetch. They go along to get along. The result is that, too often, family heroes feel like anything but heroes; they may feel like pets, trick ponies, maids, or even prostitutes, kept around as long as they cause no trouble and provide comfort or entertainment or a service of some kind.

This may sound harsh, but differences between the powerful and the powerless are not necessarily malicious ones. Often they are structural, automatic, sometimes inevitable differences, and excruciating all the same. To point out these differences may sound ungrateful—which is not fair because family heroes like Nadia are grateful—but that is the point. Part of the disenfranchised grief that many family heroes feel, but never reveal, is the unacknowledged loss of the full range of their feelings: They lose the luxury of being able to be unappreciative or difficult, even for a moment.

Actress Marilyn Monroe, born Norma Jean Mortenson in 1926, never knew her father. She was raised only briefly and intermittently by her mother, who was in and out of mental institutions—mostly in—due to what was probably schizophrenia. As a result, Monroe lived off and on in an orphanage, the Los Angeles Children's Home Society, and in between was sent to live as a boarder with families who were paid five dollars a week to keep her. "The families with whom I lived had one thing in common—a need for five dollars," Monroe recalled in her autobiography. "I was, also, an asset to have in the house. I was strong and healthy and able to do almost as much work as a grownup. And I had learned not to bother anyone by talking or crying... I learned also that the best way to keep out of trouble was by never complaining or asking for anything. Most of the families had children of their own, and I knew they always came first... Everybody had the drop on Norma Jean. If she didn't obey, back she went to the orphanage." Monroe never would shake this feeling of being vulnerable, of not truly mattering to someone, and she would spend her life, shortened by suicide, trying to be more than, as she put it, "a sort of stray ornament, like some stray cat, to invite in and forget about."

* * *

Nadia was one of the first of her friends to get married. Like many family heroes who feel like orphans in one way or another, what Nadia wanted most in the world was to come first for someone. She wanted to be on someone's mind. She wanted a family and the comfort of a home of her own. Nadia was quick to say that, since her parents died, many kind and generous people had cared about her and taken her in, but only in my office was she also able to say that it was not the same.

Whether or not to have a wedding had been difficult to decide. It often is. Weddings, like graduations and holidays, are social celebrations that tend to be driven by social norms. But family heroes do not have lives that fit the norm. What this means is that occasions that are supposed to be about communality can remind them of their differences. Days that are supposed to be happy can also be complicated.

For many family heroes, weddings force questions about what to do about a difficult parent or sibling, and too often arrangements feel dominated by the past rather than inspired by the future. Weddings are for people who have families, it seemed to Nadia, and she had trouble envisioning who would walk her down the aisle or who would sit watching from the front row. Weddings are for people who are *becoming* a family, her partner reminded her, and it was the twenty-first century: They could do this in any way they chose. They talked about going away on a trip to get married but Nadia's partner loved her, and he understood her, and he wanted her to let something be all about Nadia.

It was not always easy.

Nadia's best friend and maid of honor lived far away, so one Saturday, Nadia struck out alone in search of a wedding dress. At store after store, she tried on one after another, realizing in the process that she did not know anything about choosing a wedding dress, or which one looked best. She looked around and saw other young women there with their mothers, who helped their daughters pull big white dresses over their heads. When the stores began to close, Nadia came home in tears, and her partner said he would go shopping with her the next day. "You're not supposed to see my wedding dress!" Nadia protested. Another social norm. "That's dumb," he protested back. "This is about me and you, and I'm going with you." Nadia can still vividly recall the two of them smiling and laughing together in the fitting room, and deciding on a dress—it is one of Nadia's happiest flashbulb memories.

A few months later came another happy emotional memory. Nadia was putting on that same dress in a room down the hall from where the ceremony would soon take place. She heard the festive din of the many dozens of people who had come to be there with them—friends from college and childhood, relatives from far away, friends of her parents who were so happy to see that her life was turning out well. At first, Nadia thought she must be overhearing another event happening nearby: a cocktail party maybe? But then she realized that those were her wedding guests. It was stunning, she thought, that so many people had come all that way just for her.

* * *

Now that she was married, Nadia's memories of her parents were not fading as much as they were becoming outdated. She remembered quite clearly how her parents felt about her doing her homework or cleaning her room. It was difficult for her to imagine, however, what they might think of her life now or of the man she married. It had been easier almost to be without a mother when she was in her late teens or early twenties, when she and others her age were separating from their parents and making their own way in the world. Nadia had "mourned on a skateboard" and busied herself with young adult life, but now a grown woman, she was unprepared for how much she still longed for a mother.

She noticed herself watching older women and the things they did like tiny miracles. When her mother-in-law placed a wooden spoon across the top of a boiling pot of pasta, to keep the water from boiling over. Or when her boss at work said simply, offhandedly, "Don't drive in the snow, Nadia. It's not safe." Or when a woman on an airplane quieted a young mother's crying baby, holding the squirming bundle up to her shoulder: "You're good at that," the young woman said; "I've had a lot of practice," the woman said back generously, taking care not to undermine the new mother's confidence. Nadia felt like she was stealing moments of mothering like bread crumbs to nourish her—or maybe she was storing them up like acorns so she would know what to do when she became a mother herself.

Nadia suspected she came to therapy to be mothered in forty-five-minute increments. She needed an older woman to care for her, one she could learn from, but sometimes her sessions seemed as agonizing as they were helpful. One of the constraints of therapy is that there are start times and stop times, and bills in the mail. Perhaps unavoidably, it was a lot like being a houseguest again in a home where she wished she could live, with one important difference: She was able to tell me so. "I want a mother I don't have to schedule an appointment with," she sobbed. Some afternoons, when sessions were over, Nadia cried some more in her car, and I felt like crying, too. The one thing I did not do was try to talk Nadia out of her feelings. Yes, it was true that she had a partner and a therapist and friends and family members who cared, but it was also true that no one would ever be able to fill the void left by the death of her parents. No matter how many years had passed, she was entitled to her grief.

Before long, Nadia's thoughts turned from whether she could ever have a mother to whether she could ever be a mother. It was difficult, and sad, for her to imagine having a baby without her own parents there. Yet her mother and father had loved being parents, and one way she felt she could remember them and honor them was to be the kind of parent they had been for so many years. We took time to talk about the happy memories from Nadia's childhood: the chocolate candies her mother made for holidays, the science projects she had done with her dad, the books her mother used to read to her at bedtime, the homemade ginger ale she mixed up when Nadia wasn't well. Yes, it was true that Nadia's mother would not be there to help Nadia be a good mother, but she had already shown her how.

As they had done with the wedding, Nadia and her partner talked about creating their own family in their own way. Sometimes Nadia thought about adopting a child because she knew a lot about what it felt like to long for a home. She went online to research the process, and was soon clicking through the webpages of an agency. There were photos and short sentences about "Featured Children," each one dressed in their Sunday best and described as liking jokes or school or ice cream or biking. Their smiles were so big it hurt to look at them.

CHAPTER 9

Mask

The persona is a kind of mask, designed on the one hand to make a definite impression upon others, and, on the other, to conceal the true nature of the individual.

—Carl Jung, *Two Essays on Analytical Psychology*

Raised in the Midwest by a mother who detested boys and openly disliked him, Johnny Carson discovered magic as a way to entertain and please. Magic shows were his entrée into show business, helping him become a young master of performance and misdirection. Carson's thirty-year tenure as host of *The Tonight Show* made him one of the most beloved men in America, yet despite his exceptional popularity as the "King of Late Night," he was also one of the most private public figures in modern history. "Nobody knows Johnny," said Truman Capote.

The late critic Kenneth Tynan likely had it right when he said that, when talking with Johnny Carson, "you get the impression that you are addressing an elaborately wired security system." Like the sleight-of-hand tricks with which he began his career, Carson's public persona directed attention away from the real action, or Carson's inner world. Ed McMahon, Carson's sidekick on *The Tonight Show*, once observed that his boss "was comfortable in front of twenty million but just as uncomfortable in a gathering of twenty." Six nights a week in front of these twenty million people, he revealed himself through the medium and to the extent of his choosing. In his monologues and on the show, he controlled the conversation and he let the audience see what he wanted them to see.

Not surprisingly, Carson never wrote a memoir. In an attempt to peer through the "veil of secrecy surrounding Johnny Carson," documentary filmmaker Peter Jones gained access to Carson's personal and professional archives after his death. He was even granted interviews, many off the record, by those closest to him. "What surprised me," Jones said on National Public Radio, "was how little we could find about his interior life. I think there was Johnny Carson that America saw and then there was John William Carson that he kept to himself. Johnny Carson did not really exist anywhere else except in front of the camera."

* * *

Martha called her mother "the mamarazzi." That was because, as far back as she could remember, her mother had been chasing her with a camera. Martha in the bathtub. Martha sitting in a chair. Martha walking to the car. Martha in her panties. Even when Martha asked her not to take pictures, it seemed the woman would not stop or could not stop, yet often the photos were anything but candid. "Stand in front of an animal that has soft, pretty fur," Martha's mother said with disgust when the girl stretched up proudly in front of an elephant during a trip to the Bronx Zoo. "Nobody wants to see an animal with rough, dry-looking skin."

Martha's mother had three children by three different exhusbands, Martha being the one born to the wealthiest man and the only minor left in the home. Photos of her were valuable, it seemed, as a steady stream sent to her father on the Upper West Side kept the support payments flowing in return. Martha's father was not a hands-on parent, but he sent large checks to give his daughter (and consequently her mother) an extremely comfortable life. Yet to Martha's mother, their life together never seemed quite as comfortable as the one she imagined she ought to have been living. "He owes me," Martha's mother said one day, proudly modeling a new floor-length mink. "And you have to have money to get money."

When Martha was young, she used to like to watch her mother dress up for dates: the pearls, the heels, the smell of perfume. It all seemed so special and exciting; being a part of it, Martha felt special and excited, too. Once when her mother entertained a man in the living room of their large apartment, Martha sat in her nightgown at her mother's feet. She watched the woman flex her high-heeled foot and twist it around and around as she laughed and spoke. It seemed like such a glamorous gesture. When Martha was sent off to bed, she scurried away and tucked herself in, arranging her stuffed animals all around her. She imagined that, after she went to sleep, her mother and her mother's date might come in and see how cute she looked.

Once a pinchable, brown-haired Shirley Temple of a girl, by the time she hit puberty Martha was all teeth and bad haircut, her curls as unruly as her gangly arms and legs. "It was like my mom turned on me when I stopped being this cute little kid," Martha said, "when I wasn't an attractive accessory anymore. I could see it on her face every time she looked at me. It was like she hated me for not being whatever it was she wanted to see. When my dad got remarried, she told me it was because I wasn't as cute as I used to be."

Martha's mother controlled her daughter with cruelty, hoping to improve the girl's appearance with harsh words and ruthless comparisons. When Martha wore clothes that made her feel comfortable, her mother made her feel uncomfortable: "No one wants to see you without earrings!" she shrieked. When she left her naturally curly hair untended, her mother screeched some more: "You look like a goddamn hairball from the shower drain!"

Psychoanalyst Donald Winnicott said that "the precursor of

the mirror is the mother's face." What he meant by that is that long before babies and children try to figure out who they are and how they look by peering into a mirror, they are accustomed to seeing themselves reflected back in the expressions of their parents. Some children look into their mothers'—or fathers'—faces and see love or delight or acceptance. What Martha saw reflected back was displeasure, disappointment, and disgust.

By adolescence, when Martha saw herself in the mirror, she felt like she was looking at herself through the lens of her mother's camera. Trapped in her mother's perspective, she scanned herself for vulnerabilities and imperfections. In her closet, each item of clothing hung there as if with a tag that only she could see, labeled with her mother's favorable or unfavorable comments: "You need to wear bright colors like this" or "You look like a lesbian in that." So it was for every part of Martha's body, too, and any liking that Martha might have thought she had: Her mother's judgments were attached to every one. It seemed dangerous to have ideas of her own—and indeed, when Martha told stories about when she was young, they were more about her mother than herself.

Martha cannot remember much about what she thought or felt growing up, other than that when she left her bedroom, she felt anxious and self-conscious, afraid of running afoul of her mother's preferences. If she emerged without straightening her hair, her mother sometimes tried to yank her curls straight with a brush, which was painful and only made her hair puffy. "Your hair looks like a goddamn squirrel's tail!" her mother shrieked, before following up with projections. "No one is going to want to marry you like that!" Several times, the woman became so enraged that she hit Martha on the head with a hairbrush, hard enough to leave lumps. More than once, Martha fell over unconscious.

When Martha's father called to say he was having a baby with his new wife, Martha's mother kicked the metal trash can in the kitchen until it dented, and then she threw herself on the floor in a sobbing heap of self-pity. "We'll be all right, Mom. Dad won't forget about us," Martha reassured, crouching down to rub her mother's back. "But you won't straighten your hair!" her mother screeched in return as she kicked Martha away with her leg—weakly, pathetically—and looked up at her with a tearstained face and a hateful look of accusation.

* * *

Each year, about three to five million children are referred to Child Protective Services for suspected child abuse. Martha was not one of them. No one ever contacted anyone on Martha's behalf; nor would Martha have considered herself to be abused. To Martha, being hit with a hairbrush was serious but it had not been frequent enough to seem like abuse; being hit with criticism had been frequent but it did not seem serious enough to be harmful. "I was loved. I had a nice place to live. It wasn't like I had some dad who beat me with a belt or locked me in a closet," Martha was quick to say.

Because it takes place behind closed doors, and because definitions are imprecise, child abuse is vastly under-recognized, with an estimated 85 percent of cases being unreported. Physical abuse is nonaccidental injury to a child, usually as the result of slapping, punching, kicking, burning, pinching, biting, or hitting with an object. Because discipline and abuse are often confused for each other, violence toward a child that "leaves marks" tends to be seen as more serious, and as more likely to indicate abuse. Yet slapping a child, while certainly abusive, does not leave bruises, and parents who worry about appearances know better than to leave visible marks on their children. No one at school could see the lumps on Martha's head, but when she sat in class she could feel them.

Martha never imagined that she fit the profile for physical abuse when, in fact, the profile was not as clearly defined as she thought. Child maltreatment cuts across race and class, and girls are just as likely to be abused as boys. Hands and fists—not belts—are the weapons most frequently used. Fathers tend to be the offenders in the severest forms of abuse, especially those that lead to fatalities, but it is mothers—because they are likely to be primary caretakers or single parents—who are the most common perpetrators of child abuse, wielding whatever is close at hand such as wooden spoons or spatulas or hairbrushes. Being hit with a hairbrush may not seem as injurious as being hit with a belt, but the experience of being physically hurt by a parent is the same no matter what instrument is used, especially if the abuse happens repeatedly. All forms of physical abuse create stress in children's bodies and minds, heightening their risk for stress-related illnesses down the line.

If physical abuse is an assault on a child's body, then emotional abuse is an assault on a child's mind. In more extreme cases, emotional abuse may involve isolating or confining a child such as in a home or in a closet, as Martha mentioned, or exploiting or corrupting a child by exposing him to illegal or inappropriate behaviors. Most commonly, though, as in Martha's case, emotional abuse consists of verbally harming a child by rejecting, ignoring, belittling, shaming, ridiculing, or threatening her. Or, as Martha also experienced, emotional abuse may be as elusive as failing to recognize the child as a separate and inherently worthwhile person, conveying that her value only comes from meeting the needs of a mother or father; this sort of emotional abuse is also known as narcissistic parenting.

No physical contact is required for emotional abuse to occur, and because of this, it tends to be seen as less hurtful than other forms of child maltreatment. Yet some of the most poignant studies in the field of psychology have demonstrated that this is far from true. Psychoanalyst René Spitz rocked the psychoanalytic world when he observed—and filmed—infants in orphanages who were well fed and tended to medically but who outnumbered the nurses nearly ten to one. Deprived of love and attention, the orphans lay in their beds, grief-stricken, listless, and lifeless. "Give mother back to baby," Spitz famously concluded, nodding to the primary importance of the bond between parent and child.

And, in some of the best-known studies in the field of psychology, ones now widely considered unethical, researcher Harry Harlow separated rhesus monkeys from their mothers at birth. Isolated in their cages, the orphaned monkeys were able to choose between two mannequins meant to be surrogate mothers: One was a wire mannequin monkey covered in a soft cloth material and the other was a wire mannequin monkey without a soft covering who dispensed food. Other than when feeding, the baby monkeys frantically, desperately clung to the soft, cloth mother, craving comfort above all else.

Parental care is the core of safety in our first twenty years of life. It is one of the greatest assets a child can have, and one that carries enormous protective power. Caring parents not only shield us from hardship but also help us cope with the hard times that do inevitably come along. When a child lives with adversity— whatever it may be—the single greatest protective factor is a loving, close, warm relationship with a parent or caregiver. Emotional abuse is, therefore, doubly hard, as it both exposes the child to stress and, at the same time, robs her of her best chance of dealing with it. It is perhaps for this reason that multiple researchers have concluded that, rather than being less harmful than other childhood adversities, emotional abuse is *more* likely than other adversities to lead to negative physical and mental health outcomes such as heart disease and depression. Leonard Shengold went so far as to call emotional abuse "soul murder." The victims of soul murder may appear to go on living on the outside even as they are dying on the inside.

*　*　*

"There is no such thing as a baby," said Winnicott. "If you set out to describe a baby, you will find you are describing a baby and someone." With those words, Winnicott meant that every living thing has an environment, and that babies grow to be who they are in the context of who their parents are: young, old, rich, poor, experienced, inexperienced, healthy, unhealthy, warm, cold. Even a baby with an absent mother or father comes to be who she is in light of that absence: She is the baby—and then the child and the adult—whose someone is not there.

When a baby is born into an average and expectable environment, the environment accommodates the infant, at least for a while. "The good-enough mother," says Winnicott, "starts off with an almost complete adaptation to her infant's needs, and as time proceeds she adapts less and less completely, gradually." Babies cannot wait to eat or sleep, nor can they calm themselves down, so mothers—and fathers—race about with bottles and diapers and pacifiers until their babies get a little older, and then a little older still. As the baby becomes a child, he can put his needs aside for a minute or for an hour. He can bend himself to his parents and to the world. In normal development, over years and decades, parents' accommodations are fewer and farther between until both child and parent are adults and they enjoy a more even exchange. Perhaps one day the parent will become sick or reach old age and the adult child will be the one who does all of the accommodating.

When a child grows up in an environment that, for whatever reason, is not "good enough," it is the child who does most of the adapting. The son or daughter races about in service of the parent. She tiptoes through rooms where her father is drinking. He figures out his homework alone because his parents are tending to a chronically ill sibling. She feeds her brother and cleans the dishes when her mother sleeps all day in a darkened house. He skips lunch at school after his father loses his livelihood. Or, like Martha, she puts herself together in a way that will please and appease. Whatever the circumstance, the child senses that her caregivers cannot respond to what she wants or needs so, instead, she becomes gifted at responding to them. Because it is futile or even dangerous to have feelings and preferences of her own, she takes on the feelings and preferences of others.

For many family heroes, anticipating what others want—and giving it to them—feels almost like a special ability. "I figured out by age ten that I could be in any situation and survive, sometimes even flourish," said pianist James Rhodes in his memoir, *Instrumental*, "because I have the manipulative power of a superhero." Many describe themselves as chameleons who can blend in anywhere, or shape-shifters who can automatically size up any situation and fit themselves in with the world around them. This talent for changing color and form is in line with research that shows that those who respond well to adversity tend to be cognitively and emotionally flexible. They are able to "do whatever it takes," whatever "it" may be.

So it was for Martha, who became a quick-change artist, always at the ready to put on the mask or the costume or the behavior or the affect to suit any situation. It was almost unsettling, at least to her, the way that as soon as she saw someone, anyone—a friend on the street, a teacher in a class, a clerk in a store, a boyfriend of her mother's—Martha anticipated and became the person she thought they wanted her to be. She played the roles others expected her to play, a talent she took with her to a performing arts school, where, in high school, she took the train to study theater.

Being able to adapt to one's environment is, well, adaptive. We are wise to comply with the formal and informal rules of society, and at home we benefit from pleasing our parents. There are different social scripts to follow in different places, so we act one way at work or at school, another way when we are out with friends, and still another when we are at home with family. We adjust ourselves to the situation at hand. This goes too far, however, when the family hero gives up hope that anyone will ever adjust to her. Adaptation becomes, not just a social courtesy, but rather a way of life. Just as Martha saw herself through the lens of her mother's camera, the family hero may live almost entirely from the outside in. She is externally focused and reality-driven, and her life is organized around intuiting and meeting the expectations of others. Seemingly smart choices protect the self from attack because the family hero is never at odds with anyone—other than herself.

* * *

In his heartbreaking memoir, tennis champion Andre Agassi tells the story of being a child who lived at odds with himself. At the age of seven, he stood on a tennis court and hit thousands of balls a day. He played not against a person but against a ball machine he named "the Dragon," a machine rigged by his domineering and abusive father to send balls screaming toward his son's feet at a hundred miles per hour. A child who returns a million balls a year will go to Wimbledon and he will be unbeatable, was Agassi's father's thinking. "Never mind that I don't want to play Wimbledon. What I want isn't relevant," was young Andre's thinking, as was this: "I hate tennis, hate it with all my heart, and still I keep playing, keep hitting all morning, and all afternoon, because I have no choice. No matter how much I want to stop, I don't. I keep begging myself to stop, and I keep playing, and this gap, this contradiction between what I want to do and what I actually do, feels like the core of my life."

The contradiction that Agassi is describing is the split in the self that develops for some family heroes. When adaptation is a necessity, what we think does not match up with what we say, and what we want does not match up with what we do. Over time, feelings and actions drift farther and farther apart until there seems an unbridgeable distance between what is on the inside and what is on the outside, between what feels genuine and what other people see.

To Winnicott, being genuine comes from "being alone while someone else is present." It is acting spontaneously without always considering how others may react. It is "going on being," as Winnicott put it, no matter whom we might be around. When spontaneity is not safe and must be exchanged for strategy, however, life becomes calculated. The true self—a self that springs from what feels real on the inside—cannot develop, or must go undercover.

When this happens, what is left for all to see is what Winnicott called the false self. The false self is a defense, one whose function is to protect the true self as needed. Everyone has a false self, and at any given time one's false self lies somewhere along a continuum. At one end, it is nothing more than a socially appropriate, law-abiding, best-foot-forward version of oneself. On this end of the spectrum, the true self feels real and alive, yet it can be compliant when necessary. Farther down the line, however, the false self begins to take on a life of its own. It grabs the attention and praise of others, allowing the true self only a half-life or a secret life. Maybe this was how it was supposed to be for Andre Agassi, who said about his tennis career, "To the casual observer I've done something that seems like a desperate effort to stand out. But in fact I've rendered myself, my inner self, my true self, invisible. At least, that was the idea." Too often, though, as Agassi hints at, the cover-up goes awry. A strategy that was intended to be temporary goes on longer and longer, and eventually life begins to feel like a sham. "Life for me has always been fake it till you make it," Martha said. "Except the fake-it part just goes on forever."

Psychoanalyst Helene Deutsch called false selves at this far end of the spectrum "as-if personalities," because they are masters at acting as if they are whatever they need to be. Their lives, she wrote, are "like the performance of an actor who is technically well trained," and the most talented ones are very good at what they do. They appear entirely genuine, and no one would guess that the true self is not even on stage. In his memoir of an abusive and rebellious childhood, *This Boy's Life*, Tobias Wolff describes such a feeling after a conversation he had with a minister who attempted to reform him as a boy: "He had not 'reached me' at all, because I was not available to be reached. I was in hiding. I had left a dummy in my place to look sorry and make promises, but I was nowhere in the neighborhood."

For many family heroes, life can feel like a performance of one sort or another, one that is staged to delight—or at least to appease—the audience around. "If you cannot get rid of the family skeleton, you may as well make it dance," said playwright George Bernard Shaw—whose father was an alcoholic—making this arrangement sound more full of upside than it usually feels. Indeed, many on the world's stage—comedians, athletes, actors, politicians, artists, and more—stand there because they have been good at performing their whole lives. All the while, many have been hiding, not just in plain sight, but in the spotlight.

* * *

Martha's mother discouraged her daughter from going to college. These were her reasons, she said: "You don't need it." "If you're attractive enough, you'll always be taken care of." "You'll be in the money when your father dies." The truth, Martha suspected, was that her mother was afraid to be left alone, or worried she would have to move out of the apartment that Martha's father still paid for. Nonetheless, Martha postponed her studies and went to auditions in the city—some successful, many not—and she organized her life around the roles she needed to play. As long as there were rehearsals and performances and curtain calls, there were places Martha needed to go. There were people Martha needed to be.

Martha's longest-running gig, it seemed, was playing the part of her mother's cheerful companion. "I want people to know I'm available," her mother chimed as they headed out to cocktail parties or receptions. "And to see what I did!" On these occasions, Martha stood holding a glass of wine while she secretly dismissed—and maybe even hated—those who leaned in toward her false self with entertained and hungry smiles, captivated by her stories of the theater and by the sheen of her now perfectly straightened hair: the Martha show. Yet as much as Martha resented feeling unseen, even more terrifying was actually being seen. She bristled when she glimpsed the occasional other son or daughter, also masquerading as an enthusiastic "plus one"; she felt exposed, as she imagined that they might know something about how she really felt.

It must have been this part of Martha—the part that felt true and genuine—that surreptitiously filled out an application to study drama in college. Her mother was apoplectic, but to make it easier for Martha to go, her father bought the apartment they lived in and put it in Martha's name. "I don't know how you live with that woman," he said, denying his role in leaving her there.

It also must have been that true and genuine part of Martha who made an appointment to begin therapy the first week she arrived at school. She was noticeably witty and an excellent conversationalist, but she came across as extremely self-conscious and on guard, too, as if she was always waiting to do something wrong or for someone to become angry with her. Almost right away, something Martha said to me was this: "Please don't like me." She had come to therapy in the hope of getting to know who she was, and it would have been a crushing disappointment to find that I, too, was blinded by her charm; that I was only interested in "the Martha show." It took a lot of courage for Martha to tell me that, and we agreed that "the Martha show" was not the only performance we needed to steer clear of. We ran the risk of her playing the part of a good client, too, just pretending to make progress because that is what good clients do.

"It has not been pleasant as an adult to realize that dealing with my father's violence was the beginning of my studies of acting," said actor Alan Cumming. Nor was it pleasant for Martha to realize that her mother's physical and emotional abuse were behind what she was best at: playing a part. Said Winnicott, "In regard to actors, there are those who can be themselves and who also can act, whereas there are others who can only act, and who are completely at a loss when not in a role." Martha, it seemed, had become the latter, so now that she had some distance from her mother's anger and her hairbrush, she decided to figure out what it would mean to act like herself, to just be Martha.

* * *

Although she was quick to point out that she had not been locked in a closet growing up, Martha did have the feeling that a part of her—her true self—had never left her bedroom at home. She had kept herself hidden away and protected from being criticized and hurt, but she had never felt "seen" or "real." Maybe this was why, as Truman Capote had said about Johnny Carson, nobody knew Martha—not even the people she slept with, or maybe even loved.

Love requires desire, and some family heroes may have trouble knowing what they want. Chameleons and shape-shifters that they are, family heroes can find themselves in relationships—or in bed—with whoever desires them. Wanting and being wanted can become confused, a mix-up that is probably best summarized not by any famed psychoanalyst or theorist, but in a few lines of a song by Jane's Addiction that Martha liked: "Jane says, 'I've never been in love. I don't know what it is.' She only knows if someone wants her. 'I want them if they want me. I only know they want me.'"

Low self-esteem seems an easy explanation for such an approach to love and sex, but it is not that simple. Many family heroes feel good about who they are, even superior to others because of their special talent for managing people, and many are surrounded by suitors because of their personal gifts and social acumen. When it comes to relationships, however, they are not accustomed to making demands and so they may wind up with those who do not deserve them, or those who do not prove to be good matches. Accustomed to reflexively making life work, they make life work with whoever comes along.

As a girl, Martha saw herself through the lens of her mother's camera, and now as a woman, Martha saw herself through the eyes of whoever looked her way. She dressed and acted to suit other people, and maybe for this reason, she had relationships—seemingly successful ones—with a diverse set of people. Far from "going on being," as Winnicott put it, Martha could be different things to different people, depending on who she was around. Her relationships felt like performances, and she was so convincing it was disconcerting, even to herself.

"People don't know it, but I'm not actually participating in relationships a lot of the time," Martha confided. "There is this part of me that goes out into the world and succeeds. I am good at everything, and that includes being a friend or a girlfriend. I care about people when I'm with them and sometimes I even think I love them. But I almost feel like I am just good at doing what caring people do. Maybe that is why I can be in a relationship with someone and it can be really smooth but when it's over, it's over. It is like it never even happened, and maybe for me it never was happening. I know that sounds bad. But I feel like I did really care about the people I have been with, it is just that they didn't know that they were not actually in a relationship with me. I was never there."

* * *

Something shifted for Martha when Elizabeth Smart was rescued. After nine months of being held captive and sexually abused by a self-professed evangelical drifter, Smart was spotted, dressed head-to-toe in the garb provided by her kidnappers, walking down a street near Salt Lake City. According to reports in the newspaper, when Smart was approached and questioned by the police, she initially denied being the abducted girl, only eventually and reluctantly admitting, in the biblical parlance of her captors, "Thou sayest." In essence, all she could muster was "If you say so."

Quick to emphasize that she had, in no way, been through anything like Elizabeth Smart, Martha's eyes filled with tears when she spoke about what she read. "I understood exactly what she meant, though. You're scared long enough. You wear the clothes long enough. You act like you need to act. You talk how you need to talk. Eventually it takes you over. And even when you get the opportunity to break free—like I have now—you don't know how. You can't think for yourself. You can't speak for yourself. The words are gone."

It frightened Martha that she, too, felt she had lost the ability to think or speak for herself. She had ignored her own reactions and feelings for so long, she did not know what they were anymore.

She knew what to do when she was cramming lines for a part or placating her mother or pleasing a partner, but when faced with questions as mundane as "What do you want to do today?" or as personal as "Do you love me?" her mind went unsettlingly blank. When there wasn't something that she needed to do, she did not know what she wanted to do. She just knew at all times, in an instant, what someone else wanted or needed her to be.

Martha considered quitting acting but instead decided to take up improv, a kind of performing that forced her to work off-script and be spontaneous. For Martha, this sort of exercise was excruciating and terrifying, but fortunately it is for most other people as well. She froze in the first class and cried in the second, but by the third or fourth everyone was cheering her (and one another) on. "It's like group therapy," she said. "I know I have a hard time thinking for myself but it turns out I'm not the only one. Maybe there is hope for me after all."

Martha looked for flashes of genuineness offstage, too, and she began to write them down. She kept a notebook where she scribbled things she noticed she might like or feelings it seemed she felt. She even experimented with wearing her hair curly, which was more terrifying than it might sound. "I have a hard time trusting myself to identify what feels true about me, what my priorities are," Martha said. "Everything feels so risky." After some time, Martha began to come to sessions with new things she thought she might have discovered about herself. Some of them, she worried, seemed silly or childish even though they were not—"I feel like a kid, figuring out what colors or what foods I like." Other discoveries were anything but trivial—"I think I'm gay," Martha said one day with a nervous mix of tears and a smile. "But maybe you knew that all along."

(I did not.)

"I've been thinking that maybe my mom knew that all along," Martha continued. "Maybe that's why she was so afraid of me being who I was. Because I was nothing like her."

CHAPTER 10

Alien

Nobody realizes that some people expend tremendous energy merely to be normal.

—Albert Camus, *Notebooks*

Michelle was scared. The world did not look right to her, she said, and she often had the feeling she was not supposed to be in it. People in public spaces sometimes looked like actors in a play; in her Spinning class, the way women and men furiously cranked their pedals around and around, they looked ridiculous, like they were clowns riding bicycles in a circus. Either the world seemed unreal or she did—she was not sure which—and Michelle had stopped feeling like a person at all. Her existence seemed like a mistake somehow. Even when she was with close friends, she was frightened by how hard she had to work just to smile and seem happy. Sometimes she felt numb, like a zombie, like she was the walking dead.

Maybe that was why Michelle liked graveyards, why she took naps in a cemetery. There was a particular one she liked that she could walk to after work. It was nothing like those orderly ones that resembled golf courses with fake-looking flower bunches sticking up every few feet. This cemetery went way back to the 1800s and had a canopy of old trees and a low crumbly stone wall, seemingly held together by moss, that somehow managed to separate the cemetery from everything around it. Headstones of different heights and shapes stood, many at odd angles, among the crabgrass and clover. Some of them told stories. There were Civil War soldiers and widows. Babies who lived only a few months. Men who died from typhoid, and women who died in childbirth. If someone had come upon Michelle there, she might have said she liked the place because it was quiet, peaceful. But there were other quiet places she could have gone. Michelle retreated to the cemetery because it was comforting to be surrounded by those— or by the evidence of those—whose lives had also been difficult.

For Michelle, being among the living was disconcerting, and when she complained to a medical doctor about feeling cut off from her surroundings, she was evaluated for a seizure disorder. After a series of tests, including an EEG that involved strobe lights flashing in a dark room, only low blood pressure was uncovered. Michelle was told to eat more salt and drink more water. Her physician may not have recognized that while the feelings of disconnection Michelle was describing can be suggestive of seizures, they are also the common sequelae of trauma. And although we tend to think of low blood pressure as a healthy ideal, in some people it can go along with depression and anxiety.

As Michelle's doctor told her about the salt and the water, she sat there, on the examining table in her gown that gaped in the back, legs dangling down. She was too afraid to say out loud that he looked strange, like an academic caricature in a white jacket waving his arms as he spoke. Would he drag her down the hall to some locked ward? To keep her hold on reality, she gripped the squishy, cushioned edge of the table and did some mental white-knuckling as well, calmly stating in her mind, *I am sitting in this room. The doctor is talking. I am listening. Nothing strange is happening. I am not screaming out. I am not crazy*, though that last one she did not truly believe.

At nighttime, the possibility of insanity felt like a thief, like something that might creep into the dark corners of her apartment or her brain. She often stayed up into the early-morning hours, with all the lights and the television on, until her eyelids took over and closed on their own. She felt so very old and tired—she could not imagine going on much longer as things were—yet she was afraid to sleep for fear of not waking up. She was not afraid she might die in her sleep so much as she worried she would wake up to find that her mind was gone.

* * *

Michelle was fourteen when Coach Marc asked to hold her hand. She sat on the bench seat next to him in the cab of his pickup truck as they crackled down a gravel road, a horse trailer banging along in tow. "People like us understand what horses mean to each other," he said. "My wife complains about all the time I spend at the barn, but it takes time to raise polo ponies, and even longer to raise polo players—especially bratty female ones," Coach Marc rattled on as the truck and the trailer did, too. "Your parents don't get it, either," he tested. Michelle said nothing, and he went on. "Because if they did, they would pay for you to ride more," he added matter-of-factly, which surprised Michelle because she had thought their objections to her sport of choice were financial. No matter, though, because Michelle and Coach Marc had recently made a deal: She could ride at his barn all she liked if, in return, she exercised horses, mucked stalls, and polished tack. Michelle felt like the luckiest, most special girl in the world to be grooming for Coach Marc, but really, it was he who was grooming her.

As far back as Michelle could remember, she had longed to be like everyone else. In her town in rural Virginia, there were white kids and black kids, but very few who were something else. One day on the bus, an old woman had called Michelle a "Mongoloid," and after that Michelle tried to scoot as close as she could to the white girls, wearing the same kinds of jeans and doing the same sorts of activities when she could afford them. She begged her parents to let her take horseback riding lessons because, to her, nothing seemed more white and Virginian than that. Although Michelle may have started riding to be more popular with the girls, it was the ponies who liked her best of all. They welcomed and rewarded her daily, and she showed quick promise as a polo player.

Coach Marc's appreciation was more sparing and intermittent, and Michelle worked tirelessly for it. His begrudging mention of a college scholarship, or a promise to take her along to an out-of-town polo match, could sustain her for weeks, yet she could be crushed by his tirades when she made mistakes, like forgetting to close a gate at the barn. How could she be so ungrateful when he was giving her so many chances? he railed. In moments such as these, Coach Marc reminded Michelle she was nothing without him, and that if she was not careful she was going to lose it all.

That day in the truck, Coach Marc asked Michelle a simple question that bore an excruciating double bind: hold the hand of a grown man or say no to the person who could make her dreams come true. Coach Marc was from Argentina—where all the best polo players come from, he liked to remind her—and no one spoke back to him about anything. Michelle did not speak back to him about this, either. In response to his question, she stared straight ahead and said nothing—neither yes nor no. He reached for her hand anyway and pulled it onto the bench seat between them. His hand felt rough and big, a poor fit for her younger, smaller one. As Coach Marc rubbed the inside of her wrist with his strong thumb—pressing down way too hard—Michelle wanted to squirm and wrench herself away. Instead, she sat still like a statue, not knowing what else to do. As soon as they came to a stop at the barn, she hopped out of the truck relieved to get away, not realizing her troubles were not over.

By the time she was fifteen, Michelle thought she and Coach

Marc were having an "affair." Not because she wanted to be, or even understood what that meant, but because she did not know what else to call what went on between them. Coach Marc's demands had escalated bit by bit—Give me a hug, Let me kiss you, Let me lay on top of you—and it was the step-by-step process, not unlike that of breaking a pony, that made each new bind only a little worse than the one before. If only Michelle could make him understand: "I love you like a father, not like that," she begged and reasoned again and again. But Coach Marc could reason, too. "I do a lot for you," he reminded. "Show me you're grateful."

Michelle kept what was happening from everyone she knew, and even from herself: "He's South American," she rationalized. "Maybe this is normal there." The idea that Coach Marc was sexually abusing her never occurred to Michelle. She and Coach Marc never had sex and, besides, whatever was going on between them, Michelle felt more like an accomplice, albeit a conflicted one, than a victim. She was fifteen, not five, and she had never been held down or left in a battered heap. She made up excuses to spend more time at the barn, not less. Michelle did not know that, at her age, sexual activity—even when purportedly consensual—with an adult who was an authority figure was a crime in most states, including her own.

Michelle got that polo scholarship, and in return Coach Marc wanted Michelle's virginity before she left for college. Better to go to someone older and experienced, to someone who really loved her, Coach Marc reasoned again, than to some drunken fraternity boy. Coach Marc made a convincing case, but this was something Michelle was unwilling to do. When she refused long enough that she actually seemed to mean it, Coach Marc cut her down for being an ingrate, and threw her out of his barn for good. In fear of losing her college scholarship, Michelle went to her parents and told all. Unsure what to make of the "affair," they cautioned her not to mention it to anyone lest she be sued for slander.

* * *

Child sexual abuse is sexual assault against our most vulnerable citizens. Two-thirds of all sexual assaults reported to law enforcement are against minors under the age of eighteen. Across the life span, the single age with the greatest number of sexual assault victims is how old Michelle was when Coach Marc first asked to hold her hand: fourteen.

The precise prevalence of child sexual abuse is difficult to determine because of variations in screening methods and reluctance in reporting, but rigorous studies estimate that about 8 percent of boys and 25 percent of girls experience some form of inappropriate sexual activity before they turn eighteen. Most commonly, we think of sexual abuse as necessarily involving physical contact such as kissing, touching, or bodily penetration, but child sexual abuse occurs anytime a child is used for the sexual stimulation of someone else. This may include sex talk between an adult and a child, looking at children's naked bodies for pleasure, having children watch as adults masturbate, or viewing or producing pornography with a child. These activities may take place in person, over the phone, or online.

Michelle never imagined that her coach's actions toward her could be sexual abuse since that, she thought, was something that happened at the hands of a relative, or maybe something to fear from a stranger at the park. In fact, about 35 percent of children who are sexually abused are victimized by family members; and although children are often taught to beware of "Stranger Danger," only about 5 percent of victims are preyed upon by those they do not know, making this safety slogan incomplete at best. The majority of minors who are sexually abused—about 60 percent—are targeted by those in their social network, by familiar others exactly like Coach Marc. Most offenders are people whom children know and trust such as teachers, coaches, babysitters, neighbors, or clergy. Offenders are overwhelmingly, but not always, male.

Sexual abuse by a community member may sound somehow less egregious than sexual abuse within a family, but make no mistake: Its effects are just as serious and the betrayal is just as real. It can feel like a sort of "virtual incest," in that offenders may have been as loved or valued or trusted as a relative, and in some cases even more so. "I consider it incest," said one young athlete who was sexually abused by her coach, and who participated in research on the subject. "Because the time spent, the demands, the friendship, the opportunity...they are giving you something no one else can. They're brother, uncle, father...the child feels safe and will do anything. That's why it's incest."

Because the perpetrator is usually a familiar face, child sexual abuse tends to be a gradual form of exploitation rather than a single traumatic event. To prepare and entice the minor, offenders build intimacy and trust in a process widely known as grooming, yet typically experienced as a kind of seduction. This may begin, as it did for Michelle, with time spent alone when treats, secrets, and good times are shared, and the child receives attention and affection and praise she may not get from parents or friends. The child is made to feel special with statements of uniqueness like these: "You are my favorite" or "I have never told anyone this" or "You're the only one who understands me." Sometimes pie-in-the-sky promises, the kinds that children and teens are prone to believe—"You're going to be a star" or "We'll be together one day"—are made.

Transgressions are often incremental, beginning with seemingly harmless violations of personal space, such as sexualized comments or small touches. With each new request, the offender may ask for just a little bit more, using play and persuasion instead of force to get what he wants. Unwelcome advances may be explained away by the child or teen in order to hold on to the adult as a good figure in her life. Rather than believe that Coach Marc would exploit her, Michelle told herself that he was from another country and maybe, where he was from, this was how things were supposed to go.

Michelle did not go along with everything Coach Marc wanted but she agreed to enough that, ultimately, she blamed herself for all that went on. What Michelle did not know was that one-third of child sexual abuse cases involve what are called "compliant victims." They are children or teens who have seemingly voluntary sexual relationships with offenders. Yet, sexual activity with a person below the legal age of consent can never be consensual. Because children and teenagers can be easy to manipulate, and they are taught to obey adults and authority figures, they are not deemed as having the ability to provide consent for sexual activity before a certain age, even if the minor believes he or she can. This may seem problematic when sexual activity occurs between two minors, or between a sixteen-year-old and an eighteen-year-old, yet most experts agree that when at least one party is under eighteen and the age difference between those involved is more than five years—or the offender is in a position of authority—then a wrongdoing has most likely occurred.

Michelle's relationship with her coach met all of these criteria. The so-called affair began when Michelle was fourteen in a state where the age of consent was eighteen, and her coach was nearly forty years her senior and in a clear position of power. In very recent years, some explosive, overdue reporting on sexual abuse in sports—in swimming, bicycling, soccer, and gymnastics, for example—has emphasized not only how widespread the problem is but also how much it depends upon the unique position that coaches have, with direct access to their young athletes' bodies, minds, and futures. They have "near absolute power," said one man, a former soccer player and sexual abuse survivor interviewed in the *New York Times*. Coaches are, he said, "the gatekeepers of dreams."

To Michelle, Coach Marc was the gatekeeper of her dreams and more. "I thought I was going to college, and then I was going to South America to play with the best. I had posters on the wall. It was all I thought about. And I felt like by what I was doing with Coach Marc I was helping my family—my parents couldn't afford for me to play polo or go to college—but I also knew they would not approve of what was happening. I didn't want to be doing it but I knew if I'd stopped it I'd lose everything I had worked for. There was no good way out." Consider how this young athlete described the power her coach had over her: "I was totally dependent on him—he was God. From 15–19, he owned me basically." That could have been Michelle speaking.

* * *

Coach Marc may not have taken Michelle's virginity—or her love for polo—but what he did take were her feelings of normalcy. "His greatest legacy," she said, "was that he confused me about what was real or safe." With her scholarship, Michelle fled to college, but on the polo field and off she looked over her shoulder for Coach Marc. At matches, she scanned the parking lots for his truck, and as she walked to classes, she sometimes wondered if he might call her school and have her scholarship taken away.

When friends collected in apartments and swapped stories about relationships, Michelle warded off conversation about her sex life. "What was I supposed to talk about? The only experiences I had were things like hiding hickies from a fifty-year-old man," she said. To shut down questions, she told a few close friends something bad had happened with a boy back home—"I felt like I needed to tell them something they could understand, something that could stand in for what really happened"—but this only made her feel like a liar. "I'd always felt like I was lying about Coach Marc already, like I'd made a mountain out of a molehill, like I have no right to be so upset, so screwed up over what happened. Now here I was, being one of those people you hear about who lie about sexual assault." Michelle did not know it was common for family heroes to create "cover stories," or simpler, seemingly more understandable versions of their traumas.

Because her relationship and sexual experiences were not like those of other people, Michelle felt *she* was not like other people.

Even—sometimes especially—when she sat right next to her peers, it seemed that they lived on one planet and she on another. Michelle did not know that alienation, or a pervasive sense of disconnection from others, is one of the most common consequences not only of sexual abuse but also of any kind of adversity. When bad things happen, we become far removed from those who have not shared our hardships. Isolated and alone with our unusual circumstances, we feel unable to connect with everyday experiences and those who have them. For many family heroes, then, men and women going about their lives can be bustling, mystifying examples of what it must be like to want to do something, or to believe in the world.

No matter the adversity, or how exactly it is experienced, many family heroes feel different from other people. Sometimes the feeling comes from the inside—as in "I am abnormal"—and other times it comes from the outside—as in "My life is abnormal." Nadia, who lost her mother and father in a robbery, had this to say about her day-to-day: "In the years after my parents died, I craved normalcy so much. I just wanted people to look at me normally, to treat me the same. Instead I was taking care of other people and their reactions. How bad they felt for me. I didn't want this to change me and make me not normal. I wanted to be able to have a normal life. People tried to help and tell me there would be a new normal but I am not sure that life has ever felt normal since I lost my mom and dad."

For those like Michelle whose adversities are kept secret, there may be a sense that there is something wrong deep down inside them. The smiles and laughter of others serve almost as cruel reminders of the contrast between what family heroes may see and how they may feel:

> Different
> Crazy
> Damaged
> Alone

Worried

Exhausted

Helpless

Hopeless

Alert

Suspicious

Afraid

Guilty

Withdrawn

Judged

Hurt

Lonely

Empty

Suicidal

Perfectionistic

Angry

Old

Self-pitying

Closed off

Out of control

Depressed

Pitied

Stuck

Misunderstood

Ashamed

Agitated

Unable to concentrate

Stupid

By the time Michelle made it to my office, she was working for the government as a victim witness coordinator—a legal advocate for survivors of all sorts of crimes: "Justice was something I never got. After fifteen years, I'm still trying to right this wrong." Every day, Michelle was righting a lot of wrongs, and even though the work was very hard, her eyes lit up when she spoke about her clients, especially children and teens who bravely stood up against those who had hurt them. "One of my clients wore a Wonder Woman T-shirt to a police lineup today," she said, beaming with pride.

At work, Michelle was the one who was a hero to a lot of people, but she often described herself using the words above—especially *guilty* and *crazy*. "If people really knew about my life," she said early on in therapy, "they'd probably want me to find God or find, you know, a medication or something." In response to this, I asked Michelle—as I have asked so many family heroes before—if she ever thought of herself as resilient. Or strong. "Resilient people don't take naps in graveyards," she said with certainty. Then she added something I had heard many times before: "Strong people don't need therapy."

* * *

Perhaps the greatest tragedy for any person who is distressed, argued psychologist Edith Weisskopf-Joelson, is that he or she who suffers is "not only unhappy, but also ashamed of being unhappy." For Michelle, the fact that she was struggling with depression and anxiety only seemed to confirm—medically, officially—that she had been right all along: Something was wrong with her and she was not like other people. Michelle was having a hard time, to be sure, but she was far from alone.

Over half of Americans encounter some significant adversity in childhood, and about half of Americans meet the criteria for some mental health disorder in their lifetime, too. Although it may seem that those who struggle with their mental health cannot, by definition, be considered resilient, this is incorrect. According to the American Psychological Association, resilience is adapting well in the face of adversity, trauma, tragedy, or significant ongoing stressors. And there were many ways Michelle had adapted well. She had graduated from college with honors, and earned a master's degree in criminal justice. At work, she did a lot of good for a lot of people, and on the weekends she won award after award in polo.

On the outside Michelle was the picture of resilience, but on the inside she was suffering, as is often the case. The American Psychological Association makes it clear, as does much research, that "the road to resilience is likely to involve considerable emotional distress." Pain and struggle are almost always part of the untold story of the family hero. When I asked Michelle if she would think less of her clients if they, too, sought therapy—she often referred them to it, in fact—she answered, "No, of course not. But the people I work with, they've been through real traumas. What I went through is nothing compared to that."

The brain processes all threats in the same way: a snake, a gun, a drunk parent, a bear, an abuser's truck, the sound of a violent sibling's voice, a mother's menacing scowl. There are not different parts of the brain that react to different types of stressors. Rather, any experience that is perceived as a potential danger triggers the amygdala and throws us into fight or flight. When, for whatever reason, the amygdala is activated too often, however, or when it learns it is safer just to stay on high alert, we become overexposed to—poisoned by—our own stress hormones. This is how our lifesaving adaptations can make us sick.

As Robert Block, past president of the American Academy of Pediatrics, testified before a Senate subcommittee on children and families in 2011, childhood adversity "may be the leading cause of poor health among adults in the United States." We know this, in large part, because of the Adverse Childhood Experiences (ACE) Study, the landmark study that shocked the medical community not only with how common early adversity is for children but also with how harmful to our health it can be down the line. Unfortunately, one of the most consistent findings to come from the ACE data has been this: There is a dose-dependent, generally linear relationship between exposure to hardship in childhood and resulting health problems across the life span, from fatigue or ulcers or arthritis to the leading causes of death: heart disease, cancer, chronic lung disease, liver disease, and autoimmune diseases. The more hardships we endure in childhood, the more health problems we are likely to face in adulthood. A relatively recent discovery, this connection between childhood stress and adult health took so long to put together partly because common hardships tend to be kept secret, and also because there are "sleeper effects," or lags between early stressors and the impact they may have on our adult selves. Yet by now the relationship is indisputable, and looking back it can be seen in health data from adults dating to 1900.

Without a doubt, childhood adversity gets under our skin. Chronically stressed children show signs of chronic inflammation—an immune response and major risk factor for a wide range of diseases—even by adolescence. And hard times work their way even into our cells. Studies have shown that adults who grew up with chronic adversity have shorter telomeres, or the protective caps that sit on the ends of our strands of DNA. Telomeres naturally become shorter as we age, but they can also be shortened by stress. The problem is that as our telomeres wear down, we wear down; our cells age more quickly, and we do, too. Our chronological age and our biological age do not feel like they match, and perhaps for this reason it is not unusual for those who faced early chronic stress to say that, although they may look well on the outside, on the inside they feel a hundred years old. It can be difficult to imagine living a long and full life, and it is true: Childhood adversity can shorten the life span by up to twenty years.

The harmful effects to our bodies are not limited to organs such as our hearts and lungs but, rather, may be greatest when it comes to the most complex organ of all: the brain. The brain develops throughout childhood and well into our twenties, which means that early chronic stress can work its way into its architecture, becoming wired into who we are. This impacts our mental health—or what Block prefers to call "brain health"—and there is a clear connection between early adversity and brain health. It is estimated that childhood adversity is associated with one-third to one-half of all mental health disorders, with depression and anxiety being the most common among them. Other disorders can be the result of stress, too, of course, such as post-traumatic stress disorders, adjustment disorders, eating disorders, and sleep disorders. Indeed, the term *trauma spectrum disorders* has been used to describe these related, and often overlapping, conditions.

In the twentieth century, researchers looked for relationships between specific adversities and particular disorders: Did loss of a parent cause depression? Did sexual abuse lead to post-traumatic stress? Now, we know that there is no such thing as "child sexual abuse syndrome," in that there is no set way we can expect such a child to struggle, nor is there any one way we would expect the adult child of an alcoholic or the adult survivor of neglect to look. The effects of chronic stress in early life on mental health are cumulative—and nonspecific—so what matters is not the particular kind of adversity that one experiences so much as the amount of unmitigated stress over time.

Whether someone like Michelle will struggle in this way or that way, a little or a lot, or for a long while or a short while, is the result of a conversation between nature and nurture that takes place over time. Genetics, stress, and support in childhood—and genetics, stress, and support in adulthood—ultimately determine whether an individual struggles with mental health symptoms and, if so, what that struggle looks like and how long it might last.

* * *

Contrary to what Michelle thought, strong, resilient people do go to therapy. In fact, seeking support from others is part of what it means to "adapt well" after an adversity; it is part of *how* we reduce our stress. Sometimes family heroes seek help from friends or parents or teachers or lovers. Other times, especially when they feel cut off from those around them, a therapist or some other professional may seem like the safest place to start. For Michelle, therapy was where she learned that her affair with Coach Marc had been sexual abuse, and not really an affair at all. It was also where she stopped feeling ashamed of struggling with depression and anxiety, and treated these like the brain health problems they were.

Still, I wanted more for Michelle. According to trauma expert Bruce Perry, "The research on the most effective treatments to help child trauma victims might be accurately summed up this way: what works best is anything that increases the quality and number of relationships in the child's life." The same goes for adults. Michelle had horses, and one person whom she felt truly knew her and cared for her: "Thank you for being the first person to tell me I am strong and resilient," she said. But for Michelle to truly believe me, I felt she needed to hear those things from a second and a third and so on. I did not want to see Coach Marc rob her not only of her feelings of normalcy but also of her relationships.

Yet bad people were everywhere, it seemed to Michelle. She had seen them in her life, and she saw them at work every day as well. Besides, if there were good people out there, she was not so sure they would want her. "Why would anyone choose me when they could find someone normal?" Michelle asked. It seemed to her perfectly reasonable to assume that the world was populated with cheerful, uncomplicated people who had never known hard times. These were the kind of women and men people wanted, she was certain.

Michelle's belief was all but confirmed when a friend, who knew nothing of her history, told her he was dating, but would not marry, a young woman who had been sexually abused: "That's the worst problem to have," he said. "She would have too many issues to raise kids." This was a devastating blow. It was as if everything she suspected to be true—and maybe unconsciously hoped was not—had been unwittingly proven by a single, casual exchange.

As it often goes, what Michelle's friend said was, in fact, unin-

formed and *not* true. Sexual abuse, because it is so intimate and
abhorrent, does tend to be seen by many as the most damaging
of adversities, but the most recent research tells us there is no
hierarchy of trauma. When something bad happens—whether it
be sexual assault or physical abuse or a family splits apart or any
other adversity—how much this event affects us depends on many
different variables: how old we are when it happens, how long it
lasts, how much it changes our lives, how we cope at the time, how
others react when we tell them, what sources of support we have,
what other stressors we are managing, what other successes we
can point to, as well as the genetic material we bring to the situation. Comparing adversities leads nowhere.

* * *

After many years of listening to family heroes, I cannot help but
conclude—as has some research—there may be no more dangerous judgment about childhood adversity than the notion that one
is abnormal because of it. "Being a stand-up, productive, normalised member of society? Not so much," wrote James Rhodes in
his memoir of sexual abuse. Due to that belief, those like Michelle
deny themselves friendships and love, as well as full participation
in the world, when these are the very things that may help them
the most. They withdraw from people in one way or another, feeling uncomfortable in the company of others. Or they let people
who are not good to them into their lives, not because of some
sort of repetition compulsion, but because they feel unfamiliar
with or unworthy of anything more. Or they collapse with relief
into the arms of the so-called normal, only to find out later that
those with average and expectable lives have problems, too. All
too often, these are the ways that an unhappy childhood becomes
an unhappy adulthood, and then maybe an unhappy childhood
for someone else again.

Perhaps this is why sometimes I feel an almost desperate
urgency to get through to clients like Michelle, to convince them

that, contrary to everything they believe, they are not abnormal: They are supernormal. And family heroes are some of the most courageous and compassionate people—some of the best people— I have known, not in spite of the difficulties they have faced but because of them. I want to shake them or hug them and just make them understand right then and there: *You are good. You are normal. There is no normal.* Sigmund Freud himself said that normality was an "ideal fiction," and that "every normal person is only approximately normal." Or, if you prefer, take it from graphic novelist Alan Moore: "There's a notion I'd like to see buried: the ordinary person. Ridiculous. There is no ordinary person."

It would be nice to be able to say that with a couple of quotes like the ones above, or with a few well-timed, well-crafted interpretations of my own, I was able to free Michelle from the judgment that she was different and damaged, and soon thereafter she went on to have a collection of close and caring friends or lovers. But the conviction that one is not normal is not only one of the most destructive beliefs that those like Michelle carry with them, it is also one of the most intractable. Family heroes like Michelle will not be easily talked out of their suspicions, which are there to keep them safe. Besides, people imagine, it is my job as a therapist to understand different and damaged people, and to tell them that everything is going to be just fine. Surely I have lost my grip on normal myself, they may also imagine, being surrounded by so many people with problems. "Maybe I really am crazy," Michelle said to me one day, "but you just don't know it."

Michelle was not crazy. That I did know. And I knew that the majority of children and teens in this world—and in this country—encounter at least one adversity in early life, and that many overcome them, too, although not without their struggles and not without support. And I knew that caring relationships, good friends, loving partners are almost always what saves them in the end. I knew this because I had seen it happen again and again, and in later chapters we will read about those for whom it did.

Many, however, like Michelle, cannot imagine that they may ever have all that. So I am going to end this chapter by acknowledging the way many family heroes feel: that their experience of alienation may not be so neatly solved, and that they may never be so fortunate. Usually, though, a part of them hopes they are wrong and, just as an orphan collects scraps of parenting, those like Michelle collect tiny indicators that, one day, they too might be accepted and loved not just by those who do not really know them but, most of all, by those who do.

At an outdoor festival in our city, Michelle and I were introduced to each other by a shared acquaintance. Of course we already knew each other well, but only within the bounds of confidentiality, so we greeted each other with a handshake and a smile. Then I introduced Michelle to my family, standing there with me, which prompted a tearful next session in my office. "You're real!" Michelle exclaimed, seeming genuinely surprised. "It's almost like I didn't actually know that until I shook your hand...I can still remember how it felt. Your being a real person...it made everything you've said to me seem different...like you aren't just a doctor saying those things...like you are a person who really thinks that way. I couldn't believe you would talk to me, and be so friendly," Michelle cried, with heartbreaking tears. "I couldn't believe you would introduce me to your children."

In that moment, I wondered if maybe I had not done more to help Michelle with that handshake and introduction than I had in all of the hours we had spent together before. "Life itself," said psychoanalyst Karen Horney, "still remains a very effective therapist."

CHAPTER 11

Antihero

[Frankenstein was] made up of bad parts but was trying to do good.

—Johnny Cash

In 1962, Stan Lee, editor and chief artist for Marvel comics, upended the universe of superheroes and revolutionized the comic-book industry when he drew the very first Spider-Man. Unlike any superhero who had come before, Spider-Man was not a full-grown man who gallantly took on the world's problems with his strapping physique and a heart full of bravery. He was a teenager named Peter Parker who lived with his aunt and uncle and who had troubles of his own. Money was tight and he was picked on at school. He had girl problems. And the powers he did have—such as superstrength, the ability to crawl up walls, and a spider-sense for danger—were not derived from some great calling or cause but were the unwelcome result of a freak occurrence: being bitten by a radioactive spider.

Superman had been like a Greek god sent from the heavens and who only pretended to be the mere mortal Clark Kent, but Spider-Man brought superheroes down to earth. Despite the fact that his comic book series was called The Amazing Spider-Man,

Spider-Man felt far from amazing. Put most simply, "Clark Kent was a disguise...Peter Parker was a fact," said Marvel writer Len Wein.

Spider-Man is most often credited with being the first antiheroic superhero, although some would argue it was Batman, with his brooding manner and revenge as his raison d'être. But if an antihero is a protagonist who lacks the noble qualities of the hero, then it was Spider-Man who truly disrupted the image of the caped crusader. More an accidental and reluctant hero than a purposeful or enthusiastic one, not only was Spider-Man human, but he was a human with flaws and contradictions. Beset by insecurities and motivated by guilt rather than bravery, Spider-Man suspected he was secretly bad, or at least secretly not super. He was uneven and unsure, and for the first time the reader heard all about it.

For decades, the inner life of superheroes had been largely left out of the plot lines; suddenly this changed. With Spider-Man, Lee used the thought bubble liberally, showing the reader that Spider-Man's thoughts did not always match Spider-Man's deeds. In public, onlookers saw Spider-Man's bright costume and his amazing feats, but in private—though no one would have guessed it—Spider-Man was troubled by his dual existence and longed to be a normal teenager. In regard to this turn in comics, "maybe it was time," said artist Ramona Fradon. "You can't have those characters running around forever without beginning to wonder what they did in their off-hours."

Although Spider-Man was created almost on a whim and was intended to be a one-off, by the end of the twentieth century he had eclipsed Superman as the country's most popular comic-book hero. Superman may have been the prototype for the world's first superheroes, but Spider-Man became the new template for more realistic and relevant ones. When asked about his favorite superheroes, President Barack Obama said, "I was always into the Spider-Man/Batman model. The guys who have too many powers—like Superman—that always made me think they weren't really earning their superhero status. It's a little too easy. Whereas Spider-Man and Batman, they have some inner turmoil. They get knocked around a little bit." Readers everywhere identified with superheroes who struggled with problems on the inside even as they fought against different ones on the outside. Thus came a flood of characters—the Incredible Hulk, the Avengers, Daredevil, and, arguably, the majority of twenty-first-century incarnations of superheroes—who showed that being a superhero was more complicated than just good versus evil. Maybe these modern, relatable superheroes inhabited a space *between* good and evil. Like Spider-Man, they were too good to be villains but too bad to get to feel like heroes.

* * *

One of Vera's first memories was a sort of thought bubble. She was five years old when her kindergarten teacher complimented her for being happy and sweet, and inside she felt, but did not yet have the words to say, *You have no fucking idea*. What Vera's teacher had no fucking idea about was that things were not what they seemed. At school, Vera was a chatty child with ambiguously brown skin and a wide grin, but in the evenings she had little to smile about at the apartment she shared with her brother and her mother, a woman whose problems with drugs kept her from being the parent she might have meant to be.

Approximately two million children live with a parent who abuses drugs, placing them at a significantly increased risk for mistreatment. Having a mother who abuses substances is one of the five leading predictors of child maltreatment, and between one-third and two-thirds of reports to Child Protective Services involve substance use in the home. Because mothers or fathers who are addicts may be more preoccupied with drugs than with their children, neglect is the most common problem in houses where parents are users. Although neglect is at least as harmful to children as physical or sexual abuse, it tends to receive the least amount of attention from professionals.

The relationship between drug abuse and child maltreatment is often a straightforward one, put most simply by this woman, a former addict: "It's not bad people that become addicts and it's not bad people that don't care about their kids. It's just people that addiction has got the grip of and that is more powerful than anything, even the love that a parent would have for their children. It just overrules even that."

When parents are busy seeking or doing drugs, or when they are incapacitated from their use, their ability to care for their children is impaired. Money may be spent on drugs rather than on food or clothes, and parents may spend time in jail or in treatment centers. In homes where drug use is high, parental supervision tends to be low, and parents show less involvement with and less interest in their children. For these sons and daughters, the most basic needs—such as nutrition, hygiene, supervision, and attention—are often unmet, or they are needs that children must try to meet themselves.

* * *

For Vera, feeding herself was easy. Breakfast, she skipped. For lunch, she tucked a fruit roll-up in her backpack. For dinner, Vera usually cooked macaroni and cheese—the kind with the bright-orange powder—on the stove, boiling water on her own long before she probably ought to have been. "I made cereal if I was feeling lazy," Vera recalls, with no awareness that a child who opts for cereal when left to fend for herself is not being lazy.

Vera grew up in central Florida in a place that was about an hour too far from either coast to be pretty. It was hot and dusty, and her neighborhood consisted of some nondescript streets dotted with apartment buildings and corner stores and pastel-colored stucco bungalows. A nearby orange juice factory left the air smelling like burnt oranges. "That's what I remember about being at home," Vera recalls as an adult. "Oranges outside. Cigarettes and drugs inside. There was always the smell of something burning."

Vera's aunt worked at a Catholic school, which Vera was allowed to attend nearly for free. She was fortunate to be able to go there—people told her so all the time—but the contrast between school and home was painful, too. When mothers swept in before soccer games and brushed their daughters' hair into ponytails, Vera watched with envy and puzzlement; she felt proud about being able to do her own hair but also she wondered what it would feel like to have someone do it for her. When a girl told her mother she was hungry and, in a flash, the woman went out and was back with a sandwich from Arby's, Vera could hardly believe what she saw. Later that night, Vera asked her mother if they could get Arby's sometime. "We can't afford fast food," she barked.

Bounding into school each day, Vera seemed like a heroic child, gamely overcoming whatever her troubles were at home. But Vera did not feel so heroic. At school, her life looked good, but at home things were bad. On the outside, *she* looked good, but inside she felt bad. Maybe this was why she had always felt like a liar, even when she was not saying anything.

Vera's school uniform was a navy-blue smock-dress, so no one could tell that it was rarely washed, but what went under her uniform proved more difficult. She wore a cousin's old underwear, safety-pinning them where the elastic had long since given way, and when she walked to the front of Mass, she prayed to God they would not fall down around her ankles. Sometimes, when she picked through clothes left on the floor, there were bugs crawling in her dirty underwear, a sight and a memory that would make her feel unclean for the rest of her life. As an adolescent, Vera only had one bra, and between washings it became so brownish that she changed for gym class in the locker room as quickly as possible, as if she was trying to get away with something. Once Vera's gym teacher spotted her: "Tell your mother to wash your clothes!" the teacher boomed, her words reverberating off the rows of metal lockers.

Vera felt caught in a lie.

* * *

Still, every day, Vera put on her uniform and went to school, and there she amazed people. Despite her disadvantages, she did as well as or better than the other students in her grade and far better than her own brother, who went in and out of suspension at a different school—and then in and out of juvenile detention centers—while Vera sat obediently in class. She never caused trouble. She never *seemed* troubled. She exceeded expectations in every way, and no one, including Vera, knew quite how.

For reasons that are not entirely understood, on average girls are hardier than boys when subjected to developmental stress. One study—the largest and longest of its kind—looked at the birth certificates, household characteristics, kindergarten readiness, academic performance and attendance, school discipline, graduation rates, and criminal records in a sample of over one million schoolchildren born between 1992 and 2002 in Vera's home state of Florida, an ethnically and socioeconomically heterogeneous place. Researchers found that, in the face of family disadvantage, not only do girls outperform boys in school, but sisters also fare better than their brothers, despite being raised in the same homes.

This gender difference appears early in kindergarten, continues through elementary and middle school, and crystallizes into a sharp divide by high school. Some have suggested that perhaps girls are less negatively impacted by single-parent homes because absent parents tend to be fathers and the available parents tend to be mothers. Others point to the fact that girls tend to have less rowdy temperaments, and they are likely to act "in" rather than act "out"—to internalize their problems—and these are qualities that are rewarded by schools. In the media, more superheroes may be male than female, but in real life, for whatever reason, more girls than boys just seem bulletproof, somehow less affected by the quality of their neighborhoods and by the kind of parenting they receive. Or maybe, Vera thought, she was just better than her brother at hiding who she really was.

After school, Vera sometimes found her mother in the alley behind the neighborhood bar, where workers on breaks and the regulars on benders sat in discarded, half-broken chairs and smoked and drank. When Vera tried to lure her mother back to their apartment, she was swatted away like a mosquito.

"Why don't you just let 'er go live with her aunt?" asked a woman with a lazy eye and a gruff smoker's voice that made it unclear whether she was trying to get rid of Vera or save her from her situation.

"'Cause I don't like that bitch, that's why," Vera's mother slurred sharply, referring imprecisely, but most likely, to the aunt.

The adults chuckled as Vera shuffled back down the alley, making her way toward home.

Once Vera became so angry when her mother would not come, she told her she was running away, and she crouched for a long time behind some palmetto bushes just down the road. When she saw her mother coming her way, she stepped out elated—"Here I am!"—only to discover that her mother was not looking for her at all. She was on her way to get more cigarettes.

By the time she was in high school, once her homework was done, Vera would meet up with an older boy who lived down the way, and at night the two teenagers would smoke her mother's cigarettes, drink her beer, and have sex on her couch. Vera could not have explained why she did any of this, nor could she have explained why she scratched on her wrists with a serrated knife once and wore big Band-Aids to school, but she did remember wishing that someone—no, not someone, a teacher—might say something.

No one did.

* * *

It may not seem all that heroic of Vera to have been drinking and smoking and sneaking around, but it is not altogether surprising. Family heroes may seem superhuman, but they are not, and it is not uncommon for there to be a streak of rule-breaking or "delinquency" along the way. Although many family heroes must learn to be duplicitous, they are far from being malicious, and they tend to hurt or endanger themselves more than anyone else. Maybe they begin running with a troubled crowd, abusing substances that get in the way of their own success, walking away from good opportunities, or sleeping around indiscriminately. Supporters who had high hopes may shake their heads and sigh their sighs as they talk of squandered potential and unfulfilled promise. At least for a time, the family hero appears to have opted for self-destruction, but as is so often the case, things may not be what they seem.

In 1967, just a few years after Spider-Man landed on the pages of comic books, psychoanalyst Donald Winnicott presented a paper titled "Delinquency as a Sign of Hope." The thrust of this talk, given to professionals who worked in group homes for adjudicated youth, was that sometimes bad behavior—even unlawful behavior—is a healthy sign of life. It is a distress call, an "SOS" said Winnicott, and one that contains the wish that if one makes enough noise and waves her arms wildly enough, then a bystander might see her struggling and come to the rescue. Someone somewhere might save her from her bad situation and from her relentless adaptation to it. At least some of the time, delinquency indicates that there is hope that life could be different.

As far back as kindergarten and her memory of the thought bubble, Vera had kept quiet about what her life was really like. As she aged and came into contact with new people—new friends and teachers and coaches—there were also new possibilities that someone might intervene. Maybe this was why, for a brief time in high school, Vera let her troubles show. Maybe she was hoping that someone would notice when she let her grades slip or when she put her head down on her desk day after day. Once the police brought her home well after midnight, and when they rang the doorbell, no one was home. Sometimes this sort of SOS is effective and the family hero recruits real, all-in help, this time not by being charming or easygoing but by being alarming and difficult. Often, though, as with Vera, these less-than-endearing cries for help are unanswered, and the family hero learns to give up on other people. She realizes help is not coming so she goes back to saving herself.

*　*　*

In college, Vera was a poster child for diversity, and for overcoming adversity, too. A scholarship student, she appeared in a recruiting photo for her school and was in a special seminar for first-generation college students. When she made the dean's list, she was invited to the president's house for a reception. Each time she heard "You're amazing!"—which was often—she felt like that kindergartner again whose thought bubble still read, *You have no fucking idea.*

No one knew, or perhaps no one wanted to know, what went on for Vera when she was not smiling from a photograph or from the front row of class. Scholarships and financial aid made it possible for her to attend college, but they did little to help her live alongside her peers. When classmates went out to dinner and to bars, Vera begged off to study where there were free snacks. Once in a while she tagged along, stopping by the ATM, where she punched in a hundred-dollar deposit, slid an empty envelope into the machine, and withdrew twenty dollars right away; she was only stealing from herself, because the "error" would have to be repaid, but as she rejoined her friends, she felt like a criminal all the same. When Vera needed toilet paper for her bathroom, she stole it from the stalls in the academic buildings, tucking any spare roll she saw into her backpack. Vera thought about stripping in a bar, or selling her eggs, to earn extra income but she never went through with either one.

Vera's life had always felt like a lie, but now the more she had, the more her existence felt like thievery, too. If "to come by something honestly" means to inherit it from your parents, then Vera felt she had come by her life dishonestly, like she had stolen an existence not meant to be her own. It was not that her successes weren't real—she knew she had done the hard work herself—but she also knew that none of it had happened in the way people wanted to believe.

Like the campus that surrounded them, Vera's fellow students seemed so spiffy and manicured, they looked like characters on a movie set, like people whose clothes had never been dirty, people who had never stolen toilet paper or thought about selling themselves in some way or another. Vera wavered between thinking that they must live empty and frivolous lives, and suspecting that she was living a dark and ugly one. She was outperforming almost everyone she knew, but she could not shake the feeling that she would never be as good as those around her.

Vera bummed a cigarette from a young construction worker who was putting a new roof on her dorm. She liked the way his eyes narrowed a bit, like he enjoyed being in on something. Soon they were taking regular smoke breaks, and then they were having regular sex in a motel near the highway. Vera studied with her classmates in the evening, and then she left her dorm to meet a waiting car. The time they spent together was nothing special but it felt real: real time spent with a real person who had lived a real life with real problems. Just before the sun came up, she walked back in through the front door of her dorm, flashing her school ID card at the security guard who sat at the front desk. He was the only person who knew her secret, whatever it was.

After an hour or two of sleep, Vera plunked herself down in the front row of her large lecture class, notebook out and pen poised to write. Sore from having sex not long before, Vera felt the wood of the auditorium seat pressing up against her flesh, like the dull pain of digging one fingernail into the bed of another fingernail. It was a grounding, bodily reminder that the students who sat beside her and the professor who smiled at her did not really know who she was. Her double dealing made her feel superior, untouchable, and wretched.

One parents' weekend, knowing that Vera did not have a mother or father who would attend, the president of her college asked Vera to babysit her young son. "I can't believe the president actually knows who you are," her roommates said admiringly, although Vera felt quite sure that no one, especially the president, actually knew who she was. At the end of the weekend, the president thanked her for her help but forgot to pay her. Vera killed the woman off in her mind right there and then, and by that I mean she wrote her off as someone who only pretended to care. *No one would suspect it,* Vera thought, *but I'm a thief and a whore and a murderer, too.*

* * *

Vera wondered if, on top of all of the other bad things she imagined herself to be, she was an addict as well. After graduation, she found a job in New York City, where during the day she worked hard and, at night, she got high. After years of fighting against the way her life could have gone, she was so, so tired. Every minute of every day, she exceeded expectations, and she looked forward to the time each night when she could come home and close the door on the world. She took long pulls on cigarettes, marijuana joints, and bottles of cough syrup, and sinking into substance-induced sleep she wondered if, after years of defying the gravity that was her family, her genes would pull her down into addiction after all.

Substance use and abuse are moderately heritable, so because her mother was a drug abuser, Vera was at risk for similar troubles of her own. To be sure, the relationship between early adversity and substance abuse in adulthood is well documented, but the connection is more complicated than genes. The more adversities one faces in childhood, the greater the likelihood that by the teen years, one will engage in risky behaviors involving drugs, alcohol, and cigarettes—regardless of whether or not one's parents were themselves problem users. Living through even a single chronic stressor makes a person two to four times more likely to use and abuse substances as an adult, and those who live through multiple adversities are as much as ten times more likely than their peers to do so.

This linear relationship between early stress and later substance use holds across four generations dating back to 1900, and it can be seen in other primates too. Rhesus monkeys who are exposed during rearing to stress such as maternal separation and social isolation opt to drink more alcohol when given access—even to the point of intoxication—compared with monkeys who were not exposed to early distress. Taken together, researchers estimate that childhood adversity of any kind ultimately accounts for one-half to two-thirds of serious problems with substance use.

Rather than simple heredity, then, a more nuanced understanding of the relationship between early distress and later substance use must include self-medication. Throughout history, the principal use of drugs has been to relieve suffering, and this includes self-administered substances that lessen emotional pain. Emotions are signals to ourselves about our environments, and certainly the depression and anxiety and sleep problems and post-traumatic stress that often follow on the heels of childhood adversity are signals that something has gone wrong, that relief is needed.

If exposure to early adversity results in chronic stress, then the chronic use of substances can be one way to cope—a "special adaptation," it is said—albeit a rudimentary and counterproductive one. Substances from food to cigarettes to alcohol to cough syrup to marijuana to heroin have been shown to be neuroregulators, capable of changing our brains and our moods. "Fucking smoking," wrote James Rhodes in his memoir.

"These magical cylinders with the most extraordinary medicinal qualities offered me everything I felt I was missing." Some drugs calm us by quieting the amygdala while others soothe us by releasing neurotransmitters, such as dopamine or serotonin, that lessen our despair. But one hardly needs to be a scientist to be aware of the notion that drugs and alcohol can function as pain relievers. It is one that country music singers have been crooning about for decades: "If this bottle would just hold out 'til tomorrow," sang Dwight Yoakam in "It Won't Hurt," "I know that I'd have sorrow on the run."

Often, then, substance users like Vera are not seeking an emotional state they enjoy as much as they are looking to escape from feelings they do not enjoy. So it was for Robert Peace, a young man not unlike Vera whose story of moving from the streets of Newark to the Ivy League is told in *The Short and Tragic Life of Robert Peace*. Like Vera, Peace felt alienated from his fellow college students—"I just hate all these entitled motherfuckers!" he said in a rare complaint—and he often retreated from his rarefied surroundings and his job in the dining hall to his dorm room to get high: "It's like nothing matters, not even time, and for a couple hours I can just *be*."

Family heroes like Vera—and like Robert Peace—are often isolated and left alone with their problems, so they try to be self-sufficient. Masters of self-correcting, they may try to right their emotions through the use of substances. They suspect they cannot lean on others, so some may use substances as a crutch instead. When they feel there is no one to depend on, they may depend on food, cigarettes, alcohol, or other drugs. In an attempt to self-soothe, self-manage, and self-regulate, they self-medicate. "Every problem was once a solution," it is said.

Vera got a new job at a company where she would be drug-tested, so she quit using drugs the same way she had once picked her head up off her desk in high school and gotten back to work. She just did it. Without substances, she felt trapped, with no way out of the relentless adaptation that was her life. It was then that she began to be visited by thoughts of suicide, and it is estimated that two-thirds of suicide attempts can be attributed to adversity in childhood. But again, her tendency toward self-preservation was too reflexive; besides, she felt guilty about unpleasantly surprising those around her with the person she feared she really was, the person she feared she had always been: a girl who appeared good but was actually bad, the girl that people had no fucking idea about.

Vera also felt, perhaps incorrectly, that ending her life would not make much of an impact on the world, so it seemed like a strange thing to bother doing. Killing herself felt like going a step too far when, instead, she could just kill off the person she was pretending to be. Vera could stop being amazing. She could snatch defeat from the jaws of victory. She could move far, far away and become a heroin addict. It helped to know there was always that.

* * *

Vera had come a long way, both literally and figuratively, from her early life in landlocked, low-slung central Florida. Outside the window of the high-rise where she worked, there were buildings and bridges and water in every direction, not a palmetto bush in sight. She had a college degree and a white-collar job, and the only substance she leaned on now was the occasional glass of wine. Vera was a success, and she was often called upon to share some (usually heavily self-edited) version of her story with the Boys and Girls Club her company sponsored. Yet still, each time she entered a public restroom and saw a roll of toilet paper there for the taking, she was reminded of all the bad things she felt she had done. She had stolen. She had met men in hotel rooms. She had numbed herself with drugs. She had worn dirty clothes. She had felt anger, and even rage, toward people who had helped her.

Two weeks after 9/11, Vera needed to fly on a plane. On the way to the airport, she asked the taxi driver to stop so she could step into a store, where she bought a framed picture she did not even want. Vera carried the picture onto the aircraft so that, if the plane were hijacked, she could break the glass and have some kind of weapon. As she sat in her seat, her hands folded and her feet touching the picture stowed under the seat in front of her, she reflected on the fact that she was probably the only passenger there to have smuggled a weapon onto the aircraft. Vera wanted to be like other people who sat there and closed their eyes and sipped on their little plastic cups of soda, but although her intentions were good and even heroic, she felt locked into her role, always ready to do what it took to survive. "No way was I going to be trapped and defenseless," she recalled. "No way was I getting on that plane with nothing."

If a hero is someone who is admired for bravery or great achievements or good qualities, then Vera felt she did not qualify. Though she was often called courageous for all she had overcome, she did not feel particularly brave: "Is it brave to jump off a sinking ship and thrash your way through rough, shark-infested waters, or is it just the only thing to do?" she wondered out loud.

In 1997, Daniel Challener authored a book titled *Stories of Resilience in Childhood: The Narratives of Maya Angelou, Maxine Hong Kingston, Richard Rodrigues, John Edgar Wideman, and Tobias Wolff.* What is interesting is that, originally, the working title of the book was *The Autobiographies of Desperate Children.* Ultimately, Challener decided that *resilience* was a better descriptor for these men and women than *desperate,* and maybe it is. Maybe it is also true, however, that feeling desperate and being resilient are not such different constructs but are, in fact, often related. To Vera, though, being brave and being desperate must be two separate things, and this led to her most devastating misgiving about her own goodness: that whatever she had, she had obtained by any means necessary.

Maybe desperate was how Johnny Cash—the country music icon—felt for much of his life, too, or at least after his fourteen-year-old brother, Jack, was killed in an accident in a woodshop. Jack, "the golden child" of the family who, even from a young age, had plans to go into the ministry, had been out earning money for the family, while the younger Cash, who was then just twelve, was off fishing. All his life, Cash would feel guilty and despairing about being the son who lived, both because he adored his beloved brother and because he suspected he was not as good a person. Cash was not the only one who thought so: "Too bad it wasn't you instead of Jack," his father allegedly said after a night of drinking.

Not long after Jack's death, Cash saw the movie *Frankenstein*, a story that would become a lifelong favorite because he identified with the monster who was bad but who tried to be good. He saw the rest of his years as a battle between lightness and dark, between his brother's good influence and his own bad ways. "The Man in Black," as he was widely known to audiences, grieved all his life, which may have had something to do with his penchant for dark clothing—and for gospel music and pills. Sometimes Cash took pills to drive all night or stay up for shows, and other times he took them to change from feeling bad to feeling good. Whatever the case, it got to a point where, Cash said, "it felt barely human." Desperate to die, he crawled deep into a labyrinth of caves in Tennessee, a place he had been before and where, when the light gave out on his flashlight, he could perish in the dark. Instead, God saved him from killing himself, Cash felt, and now desperate to live, he found his way out. When he emerged from the cave, there was June Carter, a woman whose love saved him, too, standing there with food and drink and Cash's mother. Although the accuracy of this story has been disputed, if nothing else it was a personal parable for Cash, one he chose to tell in his autobiography.

Iraq War veteran Jessica Lynch was right when she said, "The truth is always more heroic than the hype." And the truth about family heroes is that they are not perfect. They are not saints or angels. We expect too much from our heroes, wanting their stories always to inspire and never to confound or disappoint. Family heroes may have some remarkable abilities, but they are human beings all the same, and rather than being immune to having problems of their own—such as with alcohol or drugs—they are at heightened risk for them, at least for a while. Maybe what is most extraordinary about family heroes is not that they never have their own difficulties but that they battle back against these as well.

Like Spider-Man—and like Johnny Cash—Vera never really felt amazing. She was as perplexed as anyone about how exactly she had managed to be the sole, sober success from her family. She occupied the strange position of being the highest-functioning member of her dysfunctional family yet also, to her knowledge, the one among her friends and colleagues with the most troubled background. Vera had once dreamed of having clean clothes and good food, and now that she did, she listened to her favorite song—any version of "Amazing Grace"—and dreamed of some sort of redemption, of finally getting to feel clean and good on the inside, too. Vera's challenge now was to forgive herself for the things she had done and for the person, at times, she had had to be. She felt ambivalent about her survival instincts—which, despite being deeply human and adaptive, can be at odds with the heroic ideal. Vera did not know that guilt, not only for being the one who survives but also for *how* one manages to do it, is often part of being a survivor.

This was something that Viktor Frankl understood, and was willing to say, in one of the most humble passages he wrote about the Holocaust: "On the average, only those prisoners could keep alive who, after years of tracking from camp to camp, had lost all scruples in their fight for existence; they were prepared to use every means, honest and otherwise, even brutal force, theft, and betrayal of their friends, in order to save themselves. We who have come back, by the aid of many lucky chances or miracles— whatever one may choose to call them—we know: the best of us did not return."

CHAPTER 12

Reboot

I come from nowhere.

—Andy Warhol

In the comic-book industry, a reboot is when writers rework a character from scratch or very nearly so. Origin stories are rewritten so that superheroes can have a fresh impetus. Time lines are revised so that characters can move into new eras. Continuity is broken so that caped crusaders can have the freedom to leap into different story lines. On the business side of things, reboots allow creators to produce new sorts of material, thus appealing to new generations of fans. On the narrative side of things, reboots make it possible for superheroes to have whole new lives.

Wonder Woman is probably the earliest well-known example of this revisionist history so commonly found in the superhero genre. Created in the 1940s by William Moulton Marston—a Harvard-educated psychologist who invented an early version of the polygraph—the original Wonder Woman was royalty among the Amazons of Paradise Island, a superhero whose superpower was a golden lasso that compelled others to tell the truth. In 1968, in the hope of broadening her appeal for a feminist audience, new writers gave Wonder Woman a new story: a reboot. No longer a warrior princess, Wonder Woman turned in her name, her costume, and her special powers and became Diana Prince—a modern woman who fought crime with karate and in pants.

Although it generated some new drama, the "Diana Prince era" angered old fans, too, including Gloria Steinem, who preferred the idea of a woman with superpowers. In 1973, Wonder Woman was rebooted again in The New Adventures of the Original Wonder Woman. Back were the superpowers and the costume, as well as her Amazonian roots, though when she was not saving others she disguised herself as everyday woman Ms. Prince. Most recently, in 2017, Wonder Woman was rebooted once more, this time as the sword-wielding heroine of a blockbuster Hollywood movie.

Family heroes often write their own reboots. Recall that for such heroes there are origin stories, and the quests for survival and triumph that follow come to define their lives. Every day, they put on their costumes and masks, and they use whatever powers they have to fight back against the dangers in their world. But just like superheroes on the pages of comic books, many find themselves battling the same perils year after year. It gets old, and exhausting, and many begin to wonder, *Is this ever going to change?* For family heroes, then, a reboot is the opportunity to take control of their origin stories and begin again so that they, like Wonder Woman, might get to have whole new lives.

* * *

Anton had it all worked out. Just the night before, he had organized into a playlist all the songs he could find about leaving, and as he pulled onto the highway they began to blare out of the windows of his car. The speed and momentum. The loud music as it blew through the wind. It all made Anton feel important some-how, or like something significant was happening. Which it was. Anton was doing it. He was getting away.

On his way out of town, Anton had passed by the bookstore where he used to look at travel guides. It was there he had cho-sen the Great Northwest as his destination, though he could not say why, other than maybe because it sounded like the opposite of where he was now: "the shitty fucking Southeast." He had driven past the mall, the one where, on a back-to-school shopping trip, he and his mother had trudged back and forth across the food court in the center to the four department stores, each of which had declined her different credit cards. He had seen the convenience store that refused to take their checks, and the gas station where his father once worked as a mechanic—and where Anton did, too, after he got his GED, and even after his father was caught stealing money from the register. On what seemed like every storefront, Anton had noticed a newspaper vending machine offering up newspapers, the ones that listed the arrest reports that sometimes included his father's name.

Anton was going to a place he had never been on a side of the country he had never seen, and that was the glorious point. At nineteen years old, Anton had long felt like a prisoner in his own life. In the mornings, he had gone to a dead-end job he knew he was lucky to have, one where he could not shake the feeling that people expected him to be stealing, too. In the afternoon, he went home to a run-down house where the sound of a ringing phone made his heart race: "Don't answer it," his mother said, expect-ing debt collectors on the other end. In the evening, Anton read until late in the night up in his attic room, where, in the wintertime when the lights went out, mice sometimes dropped from the raf-ters onto his bed. He would never forget the sound and sensation of them plopping down lightly near his feet.

Today, however, Anton was making a run for it. He felt like

he was breaking out of jail and leaving what felt like his criminal past behind when, really, it was his father who was the one behind bars.

* * *

"The world doesn't usually think about bank robbers as having children—though plenty must," said Del, the protagonist in Richard Ford's *Canada*, a boy whose father, like Anton's, was a thief. Plenty of bank robbers do indeed have children, as do plenty of violent offenders, drug offenders, sex offenders, and other adults who find themselves on the wrong side of the law. In fact, of the more than two million men and women who are incarcerated in the United States, over 50 percent are parents. According to a report by the Pew Charitable Trusts, almost three million children under the age of eighteen have a parent behind bars. That is 1 in every 28 children; just thirty years ago, it was 1 in every 125. Two-thirds of incarcerated adults are, like Anton's father, serving sentences for nonviolent crimes, such as drug offenses and crimes against property.

When parents break the law, their sons and daughters are often the unintended, and unrecognized, victims of their crimes. In the home, they are left with less money, food, structure, supervision, and security, and as teens they become more likely to drop out of school and to break the law themselves. In the body and the mind, there is more stress as children wonder: *When will I see my mom or dad again? Am I safe? What are people thinking about me? What will happen to my parent? What do I tell people about my parent? What will happen next? Is there enough money to buy food? Who is at the door? Who is on the phone?*

Incarceration has an impact on so many families that, in 2013, *Sesame Street* took up the topic on its show. In a video segment—and an accompanying online toolkit—adults, children, and puppets explain what incarceration is, as well as the sadness, loneliness, and embarrassment a child may feel when his mother or father is away in jail. In its way, *Sesame Street* was giving voice to the fact that losing a mother or a father to "the system" is a lot like losing a mother or father through abandonment or death. Yet because this loss is more stigmatized, there are fewer services and supports for these so-called orphans of justice, or the children who are left behind.

Mass incarceration has been called "one of the signature social changes that occurred in America in recent decades," so we are only beginning to understand what this means for the sons and daughters of the imprisoned, including those who, like Anton, are on the cusp of adulthood. Recent research suggests that children pay a steep penalty for their parents' time behind bars, even after their parents come home and even after these children grow up. In their twenties, adult children of incarcerated parents are more likely to be depressed, to abuse drugs and alcohol, and to be offenders themselves; they are 33 percent less likely to attain higher education, and they are less likely to earn as much money as their peers.

None of this was going to happen to Anton, though. He had a plan, which began with leaving the town where it seemed every street contained a bad memory. "I hadn't done anything personally to feel humiliated about except have parents," Ford's Del also said in *Canada*. Neither had Anton, but regardless, he wanted out. He was going to reboot his life.

* * *

A reboot might take place at any time, but the transition to adulthood is when life suddenly presents the greatest number of what have been called "second-chance opportunities." It is a developmental period of unparalleled possibility and change, a time of great reorganization when children become adults, students become workers, and sons and daughters become partners and parents. Many family heroes spend their child or teen years marking days off the calendar, scanning the environment for or fantasizing about their chance to get up and out. Then one day the supernormal teen becomes an adult, and life is no longer something that must be gotten through. For the first time, life is something that can be changed.

At the same time, adulthood can also be a time of increasing vulnerability, particularly for those who are on their own. Sons and daughters who receive little guidance or support from their parents may, at the age of eighteen, be left without even the few benefits they had before: public schools, teachers or coaches who care, reduced-fee lunches, after-school programs, foster care or other social services. The overwhelming uncertainty that is a part of modern young adulthood is difficult to navigate in the best of circumstances, not to mention for those whose parents are unable or unwilling to help them find their way. Cumulative disadvantage and strain may begin to exact their toll: Adulthood is when stress-related mental health problems, such as depression and anxiety, typically begin to emerge, and it is a time when many begin to use substances to cope.

Young adulthood is, therefore, an inflection point for many. It is a time when one's life can take a turn for the worse or for the better, a time when one good move—or a series of good moves—can redirect the life of the family hero. Often, it is the only thing that does. Numerous research studies have followed children who faced a wide range of adversities in early life—the Great Depression, violent neighborhoods, sexual abuse, foster care, teen parenthood, mentally ill parents, alcoholic parents, early delinquency—and while some of these children followed in the footsteps of their parents, or remained on the paths their childhoods set out for them, those who changed direction did so, in large part, because they were able to see and to seize a second chance at life.

How exactly do they do it?

There is no one way.

Decades ago, especially for women, marriage seemed the only way out of an unhappy childhood: "Marriage to Jim brought me escape at the time," said Marilyn Monroe about finding a husband at age sixteen. "It was that or my being sent off again to another foster home." Becoming a wife or a husband is certainly one way to leave home—and childhood—behind, but there are hazards, of course, in partnering young and fast as a means of running away. All too often, one difficult family situation is traded for another.

Today young women and men have far more options for starting anew, many of which we have heard about already. Some—like Emily or Martha or Michelle—use the talents they have, such as swimming or acting or polo, as their way of getting themselves to a better or safer place. Often, that better or safer place is college, as it was for Vera, who escaped drug abuse and neglect at home, and for Mara, whose dream-school key chain sustained her as she watched the globe in her public library turn around and around. Higher education can indeed be a key to a better life, a way to earn degrees or certifications that open new doors. There is also more to it than that. College is a place where, maybe for the first time, there are hot meals and clean beds and doctors, and it is a place where new friends, new mentors, and new ideas introduce the family hero to a whole new world.

Some find that whole new world not at school but by joining a religious organization or the Peace Corps or some other purposeful group. Others, like Paul, the boy who was bullied in school, discover new lives and new roles in the military, and recent research has found that those who have experienced hardship are more likely than their peers to enlist in the armed forces. Still others, like Anton, release themselves from the environmental traps that homes and hometowns can be simply by moving away. They "pull a geographic": They get in their cars, or on a bus or a plane, and just go.

* * *

As Anton made his way from east to west, for a while, he stopped as infrequently as he could. Each state looked much the same as the one before, so mostly he watched the odometer tick higher like progress. He took his first real detour off the highway and into St. Louis so he could pass ceremoniously through the "Gateway to the West," or the arch that, Anton discovered, did not seem much like a gateway at all. It was disappointing, but not so long after that Anton noticed the landscape began to change into sights he had never seen. He spent a whole day driving in one straight line through the flat, open prairies of Kansas, reading *Catcher in the Rye* propped open on his steering wheel, one eye on the road. At sunset, Anton saw the tall grasses glow red, an image he would never forget. It was the first truly beautiful bit of nature that Anton had ever beheld.

There would be more.

North and west of there, the sky was bigger and more open and Anton felt like he could breathe easier, like there was more air. He slowed down around Yellowstone National Park, which—with its mountains and bison and geysers and moose—Anton decided must be the most marvelous place on Earth. At night, he slept in his car in driveways that led up to empty vacation cabins, and during the day he sat for hours in steamy natural hot springs just outside the park. He gazed up at rocky slopes and at the pine trees that stood on them in swaths, so neat and orderly and all about the same size. From a distance, they looked like the tiny trees that architects use in models, and Anton felt like he had been plunked down in a whole other, more perfect world. He even saw a double rainbow.

If all that sounds too picturesque, consider that, on his way to the Great Northwest, most nights Anton slept in his car in truck stops where he had the benefit of streetlights and bathrooms. Other nights, he pulled far off on the shoulders of frontage roads and clutched a tire iron as he fell asleep in the backseat. Anton was willing to do almost anything to protect himself, to get some distance from the past.

* * *

If the essence of trauma is that "the past is always present"—that the events of yesterday are forever intruding on the thoughts of today—then one way to reduce the impact of childhood adversity is to keep the past and present as separate as possible. Some may do this simply by setting their minds to it, but this can be difficult, especially when the past is very powerful or very near. So many, like Anton, perform the ultimate act of compartmentalization: They put as many miles as they can between the past and the present by physically leaving the past behind.

Remember that one way family heroes may adapt to their circumstances at home is by distancing themselves from the bad things in their lives. They may hide out in their rooms, or stay late at school. Some keep busy with friends or hobbies or jobs. When adulthood offers fresh opportunities for separating themselves from the stressors around them, family heroes use those same instincts to move out of their houses or out of their towns. This might sound like escapism, but there is more to it than that.

In the brain, the amygdala has a job to do, as we know, and that job is to detect danger in the environment. If a threat is identified, the hippocampus and the prefrontal cortex work together to evaluate the amygdala's alarm, the hippocampus by placing experiences in context and the prefrontal cortex by appraising whether the danger is, in fact, as bad as it seems. When the brain is subjected to chronic stress, however, the amygdala can become too good at its job, and the hippocampus and the prefrontal cortex may become overloaded, impaired, or otherwise unable to discriminate well. When this happens, every loud noise must be a gun, every angry face must be mad at me, every ringing phone must have a bill collector on the other end, and this overgeneralization is how "the past is always present." From an evolutionary perspective, it makes sense to be conservative about danger—better safe than sorry, it seems—although for many, it is unclear where exactly safety lies.

"My boundary is the Mississippi," Anton said. For him, safety lay on the other side of the country. Without exactly knowing it, Anton was helping his brain by reducing the cues that set off his amygdala: the particular sound of the phone that rang at home, the corner store near his house that no longer took his family's checks, even the bookstore where he had drawn up his plan for a second chance. Now Anton's days were filled with new sights and new places and that suited him just fine.

By changing his surroundings, Anton was helping his brain to forget—or, more accurately, he was helping his brain fail to remember. The brain remembers best in context, because our senses trigger memories. If we want to fill out our memories about something, the more familiar sights, smells, sounds, tastes, and touches the better. This is why we remember more about being at a grandparent's house as a child when we visit that same house as an adult, or when we eat the treats Grandma used to bake or smell the cigars Grandpa used to smoke. And this is why, to facilitate recall, detectives take witnesses back to the scene of a crime.

Indeed, countless studies demonstrate we are better able to remember information if we return to the place where we learned it. A classic experiment conducted in the United Kingdom in the 1970s makes this point simply and well. In it, a group of deep-sea divers learned two lists of vocabulary words in two different environments; they learned one list of words on dry land and a different list of words underwater in their scuba gear. Afterward, the divers had better recall for words when they were tested in the environment in which they learned them. Words learned on land were remembered best on land, and words learned underwater were remembered best underwater.

Of course, memory is not entirely dependent on where we are, and changing locations or moving to a new place is not a magic eraser. If it were, then every soldier who comes home from war would return to baseline functioning—to his old self—as soon as he sits down in his living room. And we remember frequently used information, such as old addresses or our multiplication tables, no matter where we go. But context does matter, and the fewer cues and reminders we have, the less likely we are to feel that the past is right there with us. "Out of sight, out of mind," the old adage goes.

Yet remember what neuroscientist Joseph LeDoux suggested:

"Emotional memories may be forever." They are so powerful that we never really forget or "unlearn" them; we just crowd them out with new learning and new emotional memories. For the first months, and even years, that Anton lived out west, he was crowding out the past with new people and new places. To the brain, being somewhere new and different can feel like an emergency, albeit a good one. There are new streets to navigate, new stores to find, and new faces to remember. The brain is so busy getting to know its new surroundings it scarcely has time to think about its old ones.

New places and new experiences keep us from ruminating on—from accessing and rehearsing—our memories of old places and old experiences. To get your mind off one thing, you usually need to put it on another. Indeed, trauma research suggests that to keep unwanted thoughts at bay, it helps to engage in some sort of activity that requires mental work, whether that be solving crossword puzzles, playing tennis, cooking a meal, or working on a project. Activities that are too passive or too familiar only allow the mind to wander back to old places. "Memory lane was a sucker punch," said author Paula McLain, and Anton preferred never to walk that way again.

* * *

The true spirit of a reboot, of course, goes far beyond just changing one's circumstances; the intention, for most superheroes and most family heroes, is to change one's identity. It is an opportunity to start over not as the same person in a new place but as a new person altogether. To this end, many wake up in their new surroundings and experiment with who they are. They reinvent themselves again and again, trying to be this sort of person or that sort of worker. Some find power in symbolic gestures, such as by refashioning their lives with changes to their lifestyle or their appearance, or by getting rid of objects and possessions from the past that weigh them down. Others change who they are, quite literally, by changing their names.

Name changes can be found in the life stories of many of the self-determined—not just celebrities who want their monikers to be more appealing—from Bob Dylan to Bill de Blasio to Jon Stewart to Barack Obama, and usually they represent a break with the past as well as a sort of rebirth. Erik Erikson, the psychologist who popularized the concept of the identity crisis, or the search for self that takes place across adolescence and young adulthood, changed his own name—from Erik Homburger to Erik Erikson—to mean "Erik, son of himself." Said Marilyn Monroe about her name change from Norma Jean Mortenson: "I had to get born. And this time better than before."

Pop art hero Andy Warhol changed his name, too. Born Andrew Warhola, the son of Eastern European immigrants, Warhol grew up in poverty in a Pittsburgh ghetto. From an early age, he possessed a natural ability to draw, an inclination he may have inherited from his mother, an artistic woman who used to make tin flowers out of cut-up kitchen cans. Warhol's mother was a resourceful woman, too, and she sometimes mixed up a sort of pauper's tomato soup for the family—Heinz ketchup combined with water, salt, and pepper. Campbell's tomato soup, however, was her son's favorite—or so the story goes.

As a boy, Warhol was sickly and frail, but he was also a serious and determined student. "The way he fought out of his background through his art and his talent is extremely important," said one friend. "It explains him." According to biographer Victor Bokris, Warhol drew "compulsively, constantly, and amazingly," and his talents earned him a scholarship to art classes at the Carnegie Museum, a place where he glimpsed wealthy children and their families. "He never forgot what he saw," said another friend. When he wasn't drawing, Warhol liked to make collages out of pictures of heroes and celebrities he cut out of comic books and magazines. He dreamed of escaping one day to Hollywood or New York City, of leading a life like the ones he saw in newspapers and glossies.

At age twenty-one, Warhol did make his way to New York City, and it was there that he rebooted himself. The art world was a sophisticated and glamorous scene, a place where Warhol felt like an outsider—like he was from another planet, he said—because of his childhood and his accent. To fit in, he mimicked the behavior of those he saw, especially movie stars and the well-to-do. He told others of his background in bits and pieces, only some of which were true. "Never take Andy at face value," said art critic John Richardson at Warhol's funeral, a fitting suggestion about an artist who rose to prominence working at the intersection of identity, celebrity, and commercialism.

Although Warhol is the man who said that, in the future, everyone would be famous for fifteen minutes, he himself became a cultural icon whose own fame has lasted far longer than that. Among his masterpieces are silkscreen prints of images of other cultural icons—from Superman to Marilyn Monroe—works that suggest that who we are is, at least in part, a myth, something that can be copied and manufactured. And then, of course, there are his thirty-two paintings of Campbell's Soup cans, symbols for Warhol of loving comfort and also of something that could be bought at a store. In his life and work, Warhol advertised the notion that identity is something that is always being created and re-created, both from the inside out and from the outside in.

* * *

"Sometimes I wish I could reboot," said Sal, one of the protagonists in the science-fiction series TimeRiders. "Empty my head and start over." Getting busy with a new life out west did not exactly empty Anton's head but it did fill his mind with new things to think about. Enchanted by this feeling of newfound anonymity and possibility, for a while Anton moved again and again, spending some weeks here and some months there. He swelled with the power of being released from all that had come before, and with the potential to be someone else. Some things sound easier than they are, but moving somewhere new and forgetting the past—or forgetting to remember the past—can be easier than it sounds. For Anton, it was simpler than almost anything he had ever done. Anton had never lived in the present before—he had spent his childhood dreaming about a future somewhere else—and it did indeed feel like being reborn every single day.

Anton settled in a small town far up the coastal Northwest. Four days a week he worked as a mechanic, and the other three he marveled at what it felt like to wake up and decide who to be and what to do with his time. He rented a room in a second-floor apartment in an old house two streets over from the beach. There was an abandoned lot between his place and the water, so there he could sit on a long, wooden, rickety old balcony and look out across the weeds, watching the fog roll in and out. His first birthday out west—his first birthday of his new life—Anton lay on that balcony and read a book the whole day long. Two new friends pulled into the driveway and yelled from below—"Come out with us!"—but Anton stayed home with his book instead. He had never had a birthday without arguments or disappointments about what there had not been money to buy, and he was enjoying the gift of just being free.

Many years after Anton crossed the Mississippi and settled out west, Jaycee Dugard—the young woman who at the age of eleven was kidnapped on her way to a bus stop and then held captive in a backyard and sexually abused for eighteen years—would write two memoirs, the second titled *Freedom: My Book of Firsts*. In it, she recounts her first ride on an airplane, her first friends, her first trip to a mall, learning to drive, even being pulled over for the first time by the police. It is an endearing book about what it feels like to get to know the world for the first time as an adult, about what life is like when the ordinary is extraordinary. In one charming customer review on Amazon.com, a reader says this about the book: "It is a quick, easy read and perhaps a little boring. But, if anyone is entitled to be living a boring life with her animals, friends, and family, it is this woman."

I am not comparing Anton's early years to Dugard's, but maybe she would not mind my saying that the title and subtitle she chose capture perfectly what life after trauma is like for those who—in whatever way—manage to get away and start again. Freed at last from being tied to the problems of others, family heroes relish their many new experiences. As with many young adults, Anton's life was crowded with firsts—first jobs, first pets, first apartments, first girlfriends—but unlike many others his age, for him it was the seemingly mundane firsts, the average and expectable ones, that he would remember most.

Anton himself could have written a book about the wonders of opening a newspaper and not looking for his father's name, or going shopping without anxiety. He had certainly been to a mall before, but only now could he buy something in a store without worrying about whether his credit card might be declined. And when he was pulled over by the police for a routine traffic stop, like Dugard, he too panicked with the thought that he was doing something wrong. (Anton still sometimes felt like he might be caught stealing.) He felt a mix of relief and disbelief when he was allowed to drive on.

*   *   *

Anton's first love was a young woman, a waitress who was also in the process of rebooting herself. They lived together for a few years at Anton's place, where they played house as best as they could. Anton had never had sex before, and this made everything seem brand-new, even the old mattress on the floor where he and his girlfriend slept and made love, and the recycling bins in which they kept their clothes. Their lives were not fancy but debt collectors were not calling, and mice were not dropping down on Anton's bed.

Anton did not know much about cooking, nor did his girlfriend, but they made weekly trips to the grocery store, because they had the notion that was what people did. Neither had a comforting childhood favorite, like Warhol's tomato soup, but they tossed into their cart the few items they knew how to make, and some things they saw more experienced-looking shoppers buy. Standing in the checkout line, they could hardly believe their good fortune to have each other—and groceries—and it must have shown. As the two exited the store one Sunday, Anton rolled the cart along standing on its back, his girlfriend nearly skipping by his side. A smiling, middle-aged grocery clerk called after them, "Good luck, you kids!"

It felt like a good omen.

Anton's girlfriend was a good omen, or at least a good person in his life. When she looked at Anton, she saw neither a mechanic nor the son of a criminal: She saw things in Anton he had never even seen in himself. The way that he read, she encouraged him to go to school to be a teacher: "We'll do it together," she said, and for a while they did. Anton worked at a garage during the day and went to classes with her at night, but his girlfriend missed the big tips she used to make waiting tables in the evening. Soon he was the only one going to school, and not long after that she moved out to be with the manager at the restaurant where she worked. Anton was heartbroken, and he cried more over her than he ever had over anything else. He had let go of a lot in his life already, but he had never lost anything good before.

Anton took his teaching certification and rebooted himself once again, moving south to California. That was where he was, many years later, sitting at his kitchen table, working on his laptop and facing the window outside, when the telephone rang. It was a sunny day, but an unremarkable one, one he was in no way bound to remember until he answered the call, saying hello to what turned out to be a gruff and angry voice on the other end: a debt collector. His father had defaulted on a loan and had put Anton's name and Social Security number on the application, too. Just a moment earlier, Anton had sat as unbothered and unsuspecting as people who think they are safe tend to do. Then, suddenly, he was a kid again and his heart began to race.

Even the far side of the Mississippi, it turns out, was not far enough.

CHAPTER 13

Kryptonite

I was determined to get away, to be a person and not a charity or a problem. I knew I wasn't bad-looking and that I could pass.

—Nella Larsen, *Passing*

In 1989, playwright David Mamet published a book of essays titled *Some Freaks*. At the very end is a spare five-page composition, "Kryptonite," that makes an outsize claim: Superman is a sham. "Far from being invulnerable," Mamet argues about the Man of Steel, "Superman is the most vulnerable of beings because his childhood was destroyed."

Comic-book readers and nonreaders alike know Superman's origins. He was rocketed to Earth just moments before his home planet, Krypton, exploded. An orphan and an alien, he is a superman with superpowers but also one with an inalterable weakness: An ore called kryptonite, likely from a meteor from Krypton, can sap him of his superstrength. "And what is Kryptonite?" Mamet asks. "Kryptonite is all that remains of his childhood home. It is the remnants of that destroyed childhood home, and the fear of those remnants, which rule Superman's life." Because of this, Mamet concludes, "There is no hope for him but constant hiding, and prayer that his enemies will not learn his true identity. No amount of good works can protect him." Superman is doomed to, in Mamet's words, "adulation without intimacy."

Superman is faster than a speeding bullet yet he can never quite outrun his past.

With "Kryptonite," Mamet describes the lonely terror that resides not just in the heart of Superman but in the hearts of many family heroes as well. As much of their success has depended upon their rocketing themselves away from their untenable childhoods—separating themselves emotionally or physically from their early adversities—family heroes often live in fear of colliding with the past. Their kryptonite comes in the form of phone calls, traumatic reminders, chance encounters, family holidays, or other toxic intrusions that have the power to do them in. Of course, it is common for most adults to have trouble going home again, in one form or another, as they are irked by being treated like the children they once were or by being reminded of a more helpless time. For family heroes, though, the past can be triggering at best and annihilating at worst.

So, like Superman, some family heroes live in a vulnerable present. Feeling like aliens or orphans themselves, they may go through their days like outsiders in a world where they suspect they can never truly belong. They walk among friends and co-workers and even lovers who perhaps do not truly know them, or who may never be able to understand them. They build the best lives they can only to worry that good things will not last. Every day they wonder if today will be the day that a piece of the past will come back and ruin everything.

* * *

Calvin was, as far as he knew, the only person in law school who could sail through torts yet not point to every continent on the globe. This was because, before college, he had never been to school. Somewhere along the way, he settled on telling people he had been homeschooled as a child, but that was not really true, Calvin said, "because that would imply some schooling actually happened."

Calvin's father was a controlling and suspicious man who believed that popular culture would ruin his children. He saw it every day, he said, at the community college where he taught, and for this purported reason neither Calvin nor his sisters were allowed to attend school. Instead, they lived an isolated and rural existence in central California in a house with locks and bells on the doors so the children could be monitored with ease. They were left at home with a mother for whom English was a third language. None of the children knew what she thought about the rules her husband laid down because she said very little and spoke her mind not at all.

Calvin was one of the countless—or, more accurately, uncountable—adults who grew up with an adversity that could not be named. Although keeping a child isolated in his home is a form of emotional abuse, and not sending a child to school is a form of neglect, why a parent would impose such restrictions, or what exactly was the matter with Calvin's father, no one would ever quite know. As a result, there were no categories or statistics to help Calvin make sense of the life that he lived. Over time, though, Calvin read enough in books or saw enough on trips to stores to know that his family was not like other families. He knew that his life was, as he put it simply, "not normal."

More than anything else, Calvin wanted to be like other kids and go to school, and every August he begged. "You can't start school in the middle," went his father's annual retort. "You have no records so you don't exist." Calvin could read, though, and by the time he was a teen he was grading his father's students' papers. He knew a great deal about some subjects, such as government and US history, and nothing about others, like geography and algebra.

As Calvin got older, to keep a better eye on him, Calvin's father began to take him to work. Walking down the noisy halls with his father, Calvin stared at the students who moved loudly and unselfconsciously in powerful, carefree streams. Watching them, Calvin felt like a foreigner longing to defect. He imagined that, at any time, he might just fall in line with the students he saw, the very thing his father feared the most. When a banner appeared outside the college that said FIRST COURSE FREE!, Calvin convinced his father to let him sign up. Perhaps precisely because the class was free, or because his father worked at the school, there was little paperwork and not a single question about his previous schooling. Calvin had squeezed into school through a crack in the system, and soon under the watchful eye of his father he was taking more classes. The man did not know it, but Calvin was researching four-year universities and the emancipation process, too.

The public university system in California is a prestigious one, and Calvin set his mind on going there, because after a lifetime of not existing, to use his father's phrase, Calvin wanted a degree from a school that people would recognize. He wanted a pedigree. He wanted a name. By then, he was over eighteen but under twenty-four so—unless he got married or joined the armed forces—to receive tuition assistance he would need a letter from someone who could attest to his financial independence. Calvin knocked on the door of one of his community college professors. After years of secrecy, he was prepared to tell all.

"Can I close your door?" he asked on the threshold of this professor's office, his voice and hands shaking, rattled by what he had come to do. Once inside, Calvin began by spilling his father's strange objections to popular culture, and then he moved on to his desperate need for someone to vouch for him. Of course he would help, the professor agreed readily, so Calvin stopped short of confessing that he had never so much as seen the inside of a kindergarten. Being one or two smart moves away from a four-year university was no time to come clean about all that.

* * *

Calvin ran away to attend one of those big prestigious California universities he had dreamed of, and once there, he lived under an assumed identity, by which I mean he took cover beneath the assumptions that other people made about him. He rented a room in a house with other students, and he put his belongings away quickly, for he did not have many. Then he placed some posters on the walls of his room, like false advertisements for a heretofore typical life. Hoping to be caught in the act of doing something normal, Calvin sat intentionally but nonchalantly on the floor of the den and leafed through a magazine again and again, as his housemates came and went. He seemed so relaxed and cool no one would have guessed that, other than the siblings he had left back home, he had never had a friend before.

In college, Calvin did just as he had always dreamed. He fell in with the streams of students who wound their way around campus and with the clusters of coeds who formed study groups and service clubs. Calvin did not lie about his past so much as he left out the parts about his father and about school. No one would have guessed that Calvin had never taken the SAT or been on a school bus or learned his multiplication tables, and no would one have guessed that, because Calvin had betrayed him, his father had told him to never, ever come home again.

"I learned to dodge and deflect when people talked about television shows or birthday parties, things I never saw as a kid. A lot of other things just never came up. People take for granted that if you are where they are in life, then you've had the same life," Calvin said with an honest shrug. "Everybody assumed I was normal."

* * *

Calvin was doing what is called passing. He was allowing himself to be mistaken, if not for someone other than he was, then for someone who had lived a life different from the one he had lived. This particular meaning of the word *passing* emerged between the late 1800s and the early 1900s in reference to racial passing, most commonly when light-skinned blacks were able to pass for whites. Although passing happened every day, it was supposed to be hidden and it depended upon secrecy, so as a phenomenon it was taken up most candidly in film or fiction. James Weldon Johnson's *The Autobiography of an Ex-Colored Man* or Nella Larsen's *Passing*, for example, both tell the tales of racially ambiguous black folk who move to the big city, where they are able to pass for white. Once there, they make white friends, marry white spouses, and pray to have white children, lest their racial heritage be exposed. Immersed in white culture far away from the black communities and customs on which they were raised, for Johnson's and Larsen's protagonists there is no turning back. Indeed, historian Allyson Hobbs calls racial passing "a chosen exile" in that one separates oneself, usually willingly, from the only family and friends and land one knows, ultimately unable to go home again.

In the 1960s, sociologist Erving Goffman broadened the application of the term *passing*, defining it as the management of a dangerous identity of any kind, usually in order to avoid being discovered as different. The chronically ill may pass for being physically healthy to avoid special, and limiting, treatment at work. Criminal offenders may pass for those without police records to engineer a new start in a new place. The mentally ill may pass for being well to avoid discrimination. Gay men and women may pass for being straight so as to protect themselves from prejudice and violence.

For those with different or dangerous identities, Goffman recognized, there are no good choices. They may disclose their status and face the pubic consequences and social problems that follow, or they may keep their secrets and closely guard themselves and their personal information instead. "Because of the great rewards in being considered normal," Goffman wrote, "almost all persons who are in a position to pass will do so on some occasion."

At about the same time that Goffman was writing about managing different and dangerous identities, Holocaust survivors were struggling with how to handle their different and dangerous experiences as well. It may be difficult to imagine now, but in the decades just after World War II the full horrors of Nazi genocide were not widely understood and had not yet even been labeled "the Holocaust." As a result, refugees and survivors who arrived in the United States after Hitler's defeat—about 150,000 of them, mostly between the ages of fifteen and thirty-five—were unsure of how to talk about what they had endured and who around them might understand. Jews and survivors reported passing as the unaffected in order to sidestep painful memories and the uncomfortable reactions of others. "As far as they knew I came from France," said one woman who scarcely spoke of the war even with the man she would go on to marry.

Another young woman, who had a serial number tattooed on her arm at Auschwitz, told other young people she met it was her phone number. "Nobody talked about it" was the consensus, because all that had happened was too horrible, too sad, and too complicated, and because even those who did want to give voice to their own lives were often encouraged to keep quiet. In her memoir of girlhood during the Holocaust, *Still Alive*, survivor Ruth Klüger remembers being told by an aunt to erase what had happened "like chalk from a blackboard." It certainly was not as simple as that but as writer Eva Hoffman says, for many reasons and in many ways, "The survivors kept silent. They passed for normal."

Passing for normal is what some family heroes, like Calvin, do as well. The sons and daughters of alcoholics play in the neighborhood and act as if their mothers or fathers are just fine. The brothers and sisters of mentally ill siblings go to school and pretend all is well at home. Abused children change their clothes away from others so no one will see their bruises, and neglected ones do the same so no one will see their dirty undergarments. Teenagers who live in poverty and who have no money for lunch sit in the cafeteria and say they are just not hungry. One way or another, family heroes fall in with the unsuspecting, and it is easier than one might think. That was the thing about fortunate people, Calvin noticed: They assume that everyone they know is just like them.

Like the infamous "Don't Ask, Don't Tell" law, which prohibited openly gay men and women from serving in the military—and explicitly directed them to pass—passing of any kind requires, says psychoanalyst Kimberlyn Leary, "on the one side, a subject who doesn't tell and, on the other, an audience who fails to ask." And audiences generally fail to ask. Most likely this is because, to many, the very notion that differences or dangers are common and all around is inconceivable. Indeed, in the years after the Emancipation, so many light-skinned blacks were able to live among whites because, wrote historian Allyson Hobbs, "no one ever asked if [they] were black; the question was unthinkable."

Likewise, on the college campus where Calvin strolled from class to class and leapt from the dean's list to law school, it seemed unthinkable to those who knew him that he had grown up as strangely as he had. Of course he would never be quizzed about whether he had been to the third grade or had ever learned his continents; such inquiries would be as outlandish as Calvin's upbringing itself. No, Calvin was safe from being asked such things directly, and he could have prepared for questions like those anyway. What Calvin feared the most was what he could not see coming. He lived every day with the terror that, like a meteor spiked with kryptonite, one small piece of his past was going to come crashing into his present. Somehow, someway, someone was going to find him out.

* * *

In his memoir of drug addiction, recovery, and redemption, *Night of the Gun*, *New York Times* columnist David Carr ends his story this way: "I now inhabit a life I don't deserve, but we all walk this earth feeling we are frauds. The trick is to be grateful and hope the caper doesn't end soon." This was just how Calvin felt. There may have been no other student who was more thankful to be sitting in a lecture hall and sporting a law school T-shirt, like a highly visible identification card that proved he belonged. His casual dress in no way indicated that his day-to-day existence felt anything but relaxed.

Because Calvin was passing, there were, as Nella Larsen described in her novel of the same name, "perils, not known, or imagined, by others who had no such secrets to alarm or endanger them." For family heroes who pass, the past may be out of sight but it often is not out of mind. In fact, keeping secrets requires a great deal of mental work. Moment-to-moment, spontaneous thoughts and feelings must be suppressed, or at least edited to match what others expect to hear. Palatable life stories must be imagined, presented, and kept straight. Accidental encounters with the past must be avoided or diffused. Uncomfortable subjects must be dodged or subtly shifted. Sparse generalities must pass for adequate information. Every word and every action must be monitored and scrubbed of contradictions. Trading one kind of vigilance for another, Calvin had shifted from looking out for ways to escape his past to looking out for ways that his past might catch up to him. This meant that not only was his past different from that of those around him, but his present was, too.

Anyone who passes, wrote Goffman in *Stigma,* "must be alive to the social situation as a scanner of possibilities, and is therefore likely to be alienated from the simpler world in which those around him apparently dwell." Relationships must be deftly handled, as family heroes weigh the consequences of minute but consequential decisions: "to display or not display; to tell or not to tell; to let on or not to let on; to lie or not to lie; and in each case, to whom, how, when and where," as Goffman said. If that sounds exhausting, it is. Keeping secrets is cognitively and even physically taxing, chronically straining our bodies and minds. Calvin's past might not truly destroy him, as he sometimes feared—life is rarely that black-and-white—but like kryptonite, it zapped him of his strength when it felt too near.

No one knew how much Calvin did in secret. To speak to his mother and his sisters on the phone, he waited until his housemates were out so no one would hear if his father hung up on the call, or no one would see if Calvin became angry or began to cry. He checked and rechecked his bank account and his grade point average, terrified that one or both might fall below a workable number. He visited and revisited the financial aid office to renew and increase his loans and grants, which, as only students with loans and grants would understand, were never enough. He avoided students who hailed from his hometown, and he felt guilty about how much he hated them and their innocent but dangerous questions, like "Where did you go to high school?" When classmates went home for holidays, Calvin pretended to do the same but instead drove to the desert, where he camped out alone save for the coyotes that howled into the big open spaces at night. "Everyday life was so much work," Calvin recalls. "I just needed a break from being me."

Because they have secrets, family heroes who pass build their lives on top of lies of omission. They inhabit what feel like double, even triple, lives, with disconnects between who they used to be and who they are now, between where they came from and where they live today, between who they are at work and who they are at home, between who they are with family and who they are with friends, between what they say on the outside and what they feel on the inside. Many manage so much dissonance that nothing about their lives may ring true to themselves. "Have I made this all up?" they may wonder both about their successes and about the problems they fled. They may feel like fakes and impostors and cheats and pretenders, frauds who must be passing not only for people who have had normal and good lives but also for people who are normal and good themselves.

Passing may spare us the experience of being told we are bad, but it leaves us with the sneaking suspicion that we are doing something terribly wrong. To psychoanalyst Carl Jung, "every personal secret has the effect of sin or guilt" and, indeed, we tend to interpret secrets as inherently blameworthy. In one empirical study about how we think about our own secrets, participants were given ambiguous information about their performance on a task. Those who were required to conceal the information felt worse about how they did, and even about themselves, than did those who were instructed to tell another about how things had gone. That is, when we are not sure what to make of something that has happened in our lives, the very act of keeping it secret is seen as indicative of its badness, and of our own.

After graduation, when he applied for admission to the bar, Calvin was unsure of what exactly he was required to disclose. He had no criminal record, and no untreated mental disorders or substance abuse problems, but academic misconduct, false statements, and misrepresentation were frowned upon, too, and by his own estimation Calvin misrepresented himself almost every minute of every day.

* * *

A law degree might look like a flimsy piece of parchment, but to Calvin it was like a big piece of armor. It was a shiny shield that deflected questions about his past and protected him as he raced into the years ahead, changed cities, and was awarded a sought-after job as a public prosecutor. "Conversations only go so far back," he observed.

Calvin had won the battle for a bona fide existence, at least on paper. His résumé was impressive, and his assumed identity was too. More than ever, people assumed a great deal about who Calvin was. They took for granted that he was smart and hardworking, which was true, but Calvin was so successful that people also took for granted that he had had a charmed life, which was not true. This was a new bind for Calvin: As much as he had always wanted to be taken for normal, he resented being mistaken for *privileged*. Calvin had fought hard to be where he was, but strangely, where he was felt like nowhere. "It is like there is a box for people who are fortunate and successful, and there is a box for people who are unfortunate and unsuccessful, but there is no box for me. I don't fit anywhere."

This had been all but proven on one occasion in law school when Calvin divulged some of his background to a friend, a man who reacted with clumsy surprise. "Wow, I would not have been able to tell," he marveled, like there should have been some sort of sign. Then he looked for some tidy reason that Calvin's father had acted as he did: "Is he religious?" (No.) And he looked for a clear-cut, more identifiable adversity: "Did he sexually abuse you?" (No.) And he looked for a neat explanation for how Calvin had turned out as well as he had: "Did you have some great mentor or something?" (No.) Not wanting to be a puzzle or a rarity—and exhausted by the prospect of needing to help people understand how someone like Calvin could even come to be—he told few people about his life at all.

Calvin had come such a very long way, but he could not get away from how his life had begun. No matter how much he did with his present, he could not change his past. Because of this, he felt like an unwelcome outsider most of the time, and although that might sound like an insecurity that resided entirely within Calvin, those who pass know better. As someone who was passing for normal, Calvin was privy to the unkind things people said about those whose lives unfolded in ways that seemed other than average and expectable. He heard what his colleagues said about the criminals—and their "fucked-up families," as they were often called—whom they worked with every day. This is one of the most painful and alienating truths of someone who passes. "It is not that he must face prejudice against himself," wrote Goffman in *Stigma*, "but rather that he must face unwitting acceptance of himself by individuals who are prejudiced against persons of the kind he can be revealed to be." Or in Calvin's more accessible words: "People don't know it, but they insult you to your face."

* * *

"I am solitary," wrote psychoanalyst Carl Jung, "because I know things and I must hint at things which other people do not know, and usually do not even want to know." And with that, Jung puts forth what is perhaps passing's greatest burden of all: isolation. Without a doubt, distancing oneself from a difficult or dangerous past conveys many benefits, most notably a new life. As he once dreamed of doing, Calvin had stepped into the flow of people his age who were leading so-called normal lives. He was passing, and quite well. But to truly understand passing is to understand not just the exhaustion and the fear of being found out that results, but the loneliness, too. "Not close to a single soul," wrote Nella Larsen. "Never anyone to really talk to."

Calvin sometimes felt like the loneliest person in the world. He knew that sounded self-pitying or self-indulgent, and that it could not factually be correct, but he felt it all the same. He had the strange sense that, even after all this time, he had never once had a friend. Calvin did have friends, of course, and boyfriends and colleagues, too. "But they did not know my secrets," Calvin said, "so they never really knew that they never really knew me." Secrets separated him from everyone around so, no matter whom he was with, he felt surrounded by strangers. When others looked at Calvin, they saw a capable, affable, well-regarded professional, but like David Mamet wrote about Superman, Calvin felt doomed to "adulation without intimacy."

At the end of each day, Calvin went home to his apartment, where he could close the door on the rest of the world. In doing so, ironically, he was not as alone as he thought. In his memoir, Charles Blow remembers an abandoned house where he played after his sexual abuse, calling it his "Fortress of Solitude, like Superman's retreat... There in that house I stopped running from loneliness and embraced it. Loneliness became my truest and dearest friend, a friend who would shadow me for a lifetime." And in his memoir, President Barack Obama remembers solitude as "the safest place I knew."

Calvin kept his secrets and his distance to keep himself safe, too—to protect himself from losing friends and jobs—yet loneliness and isolation have their own ways of putting us at risk. One longitudinal study that followed a cohort of more than a thousand children from birth to young adulthood found that social isolation in early life was associated with poor health in one's twenties. And loneliness can be a chronic and cumulative stressor at any age, one that can raise blood pressure, elevate levels of stress hormones, increase symptoms of depression and thoughts of suicide, and compromise the immune system. Data from dozens of studies including hundreds of thousands of participants point to loneliness as a major risk factor for ill health and even death. Chronic isolation is deemed more harmful to our well-being than many well-known risk factors such as physical inactivity and obesity, and has been hailed as just as bad for our health as smoking. "One of the greatest diseases," said Mother Teresa, "is to be nobody to anybody."

Yet as Calvin described, combating loneliness is more complicated than just living with, or gathering with, other people. Loneliness is *perceived* social isolation from others, or the seeming unavailability of others, rather than objective social isolation. So many family heroes who pass feel disconnected from others even when—and sometimes *especially* when—they are surrounded by family and friends. They may feel most isolated sitting across the table from family members who have not been able to love or protect them. They may feel most lonely in a crowd of friends because it is there they are reminded that no one really knows who they are, that they are truly on their own.

"What I felt at almost every stage of my development was lonely," said Oprah Winfrey about her early life. "Not alone—because there were always people around—but I knew that my soul's survival depended on me. I felt I would have to fend for myself." Winfrey did indeed fend for herself, throughout a childhood and adolescence marked by sexual abuse and consequent promiscuity, by way of secrets and passing. After a teen pregnancy, Winfrey delivered a baby who died in the hospital, and recounting this, she said, "I went back to school and told no one. My fear was that if I were found out I would be expelled. So I carried the secret into my future, always afraid that if anyone discovered what happened, they, too, would expel me from their lives."

* * *

Calvin had a very different secret but one that he, too, once feared would result in his being expelled from school and from other people's lives. Now armed with two degrees—real achievements and true pieces of his identity that no one could take away—Calvin felt he could take more risks. He could try again to tell some people about his past. "It started with my friends. A fair number of them were gay," he said. "I was open about being gay long before I was open about the way I grew up. It seemed easier, like being gay was something people could understand. Not that being gay is easy, but that was the point. We could connect about feeling like outsiders, about feeling scared. I watched how people responded to that, to my being gay, and depending on how that went, I came out—to some people—about my other secrets. How my dad was, how I never went to school. A lot of them had big family problems or whatever too. Of course. I don't know why I thought I was the only one. I guess because I figured no one had a story quite like mine, which is probably true. But now I look around when I'm out in public—a restaurant, wherever—and I imagine how many people might be sitting there with secrets. I think it must be a lot."

Indeed, there were other people who could understand Calvin, but for so long he had not recognized them, for they were passing, too.

CHAPTER 14

Secret Society

Like burglars who secretly wish to be caught, we leave our fingerprints on broken locks, our voiceprints in bugged rooms, our footprints in the wet concrete.

—Ross Macdonald

Rachel wore a Batman ring. An artist and a hipster, she often fashioned surprising or incongruous clothing combinations, so it hardly stood out there on her pinkie, next to a small but sparkling engagement ring. Rachel had come to therapy because she had trouble trusting her fiancé's love for her. It was difficult to believe that he would not rather be—or that he would not be better off—with someone else. After talking about this obliquely for some time, Rachel got around to talking about the Batman ring, too. "Batman is my favorite superhero," she explained, "I think because he is like a detective. He has his forensic tools and he solves mysteries and catches the bad guys and calls the cops and nobody dies. That's why I'm such a fan, I think. Because I don't want to hurt anybody. I just want truth and justice, you know? That is one of the very first things I remember about being me."

Many years earlier, Rachel peered out from under the couch

in her parents' living room. It was large enough, and she was small enough, that she could lie there underneath it, her cheek resting on her outstretched arm. It was nighttime and she had crawled down the stairway and into the room where her mother and father sat on opposite sides of the room, drinking wine in recliner chairs and watching television late into the night. Rachel did this often, lying there unnoticed between them and watching television, too. The programs that played were too mature to be taken in whole but there were scenes, many of them confusing, that lodged themselves in her mind. A *Saturday Night Live* skit about Abraham Lincoln and something called an orgasm. A terrifying, grainy moment in a movie when army ants eat a person. A former child star she recognized but who was grown up now and showing her naked breasts. Much about Rachel's life was like that. The youngest of eight children, she was often exposed to things she was not old enough to understand.

Of all the surreptitious bits of television Rachel watched, one stayed with her above all others. It was an old *Columbo* episode, a detective show that was unfamiliar but clever and comforting. In the episode she saw, a man is murdered by being shut up inside a closet-size, walk-in safe. Knowing he will run out of air and die, the soon-to-be victim prepares a note identifying his killer, but since he cannot be sure of who will find his body (and the note), he hides the small piece of paper in a light fixture in the ceiling. Then, on the sides of black metal storage boxes that line the walls of the safe, he scratches a long arrow pointing upward toward the ceiling. Finally, he scrambles the boxes to obscure the arrow.

Rachel never forgot about the man in the safe; in fact, she thought about the *Columbo* episode often, which, to her, seemed a mystery in and of itself. More than two decades after she fit under the couch in her childhood home, and once Google made getting to the bottom of such things easier, Rachel located and rewatched the often remembered episode, which it turned out was called

"Try and Catch Me." Columbo, of course, does catch the killer. First, he notices the black paint under the victim's fingernails. Then he finds what appear to be random scratches on some of the metal boxes in the safe. Characteristically curious and befuddled, Columbo cannot quite let this strange situation go. Ultimately, he rearranges the metal boxes to reconfigure the arrow. He finds the note, and the killer is caught.

Crime writer P. D. James said, "What the detective story is about is not murder but the restoration of order." A restoration of order, it seemed, was what Rachel had been wishing for. "When I saw that *Columbo* episode as an adult, I realized that was how I had been feeling all these years," she recalled. "Like someone killed me, or something bad had happened at least, but I did not know who was in on it so this was not something I could tell just anyone. So I feel like there have always been these clues on me, like black paint under my fingernails. And I've been waiting for someone to notice them and connect them to what really happened. But most people don't notice the clues. And if they do, you never know whether they really want to get to the truth or whether they just want to cover it up."

So what were the clues on Rachel? What was the black paint under her fingernails? As an adult, one clue was the Batman ring on her finger, but as a child, Rachel would say it was tiptoeing down the stairs at night and falling asleep under the furniture in the den. As a teen, it might have been the way she began to dress in all black and hang out on the social fringes of her school. Or maybe it would have been the fact that she wrote sad poetry in a journal, a journal that once had a yellow cloth cover with tiny red flowers but that she had blackened over entirely with a permanent marker. The journal's title? *Black*.

In retrospect, these were some of the things that Rachel imagined a good detective like Columbo might have picked up on. Maybe he would have been bothered enough by Rachel's behavior, like he was by the fact that the man in the safe spent his last moments of life scratching on metal boxes, that he would be unable to rest until he understood what she was trying to say with her actions. When asked what she might have written on a note for Columbo to find, Rachel demurred. Later, she said it would have gone something like this: "When my parents aren't around, my brother makes me play 'the naked game.'"

* * *

Sibling sexual abuse is the most widespread form of sexual abuse within families—and the most neglected form, too. While most commonly occurring between an older brother and a younger sister, as it did for Rachel, any sibling configuration is possible, of course: Sisters abuse sisters; brothers abuse brothers; and sisters abuse brothers. Sometimes, there is a clear age and power difference between the offender and the victim, and sometimes the two siblings are very close in age. About half of adolescents who sexually assault another person, assault a sibling.

Though it can be difficult to distinguish from normal exploration or innocent sex play—or trivialized as a simple case of "Show me yours and I'll show you mine"—sibling sexual abuse is sexual behavior between two siblings that goes beyond age-appropriate curiosity and that, often, is not transitory. Typically seen as less taboo than sexual activity between an adult and a child, sibling sexual abuse is hardly less serious. In fact, because they often have regular unsupervised access to each other, sexual activity between siblings tends to be more physically intrusive, more likely to involve bodily penetration, more frequent and more long lasting than that between an adult and a child. It may occur regularly over a period of many years, as it did for Rachel, until one of the siblings ages out of the home.

The more intrusive and frequent sibling sexual abuse is, the more likely it is to have lasting effects, yet the impact on one's life is not predicted by the physicality of the abuse alone. Unwanted sexual attention from a brother or sister in the form of advances, stares, and exposure to pornography can be as damaging to a developing child as intercourse is. Yet perhaps what matters most is how one thinks about, or interprets, whatever it is that has happened. In one study of women who had experienced sibling sexual abuse as children, it was not the abuse itself that predicted depression and anxiety in adulthood, it was the beliefs one held about the sexual experiences that had occurred. Specifically, concluding that it is dangerous to let others get close, or that a normal life is not possible because of the abuse, was associated with worse outcomes in adulthood.

Many victims simply do not know what to think, partly because they are left alone to draw their own conclusions about what has transpired. Sibling sexual abuse is among the most unreported of all sex crimes, and for a multitude of reasons, victims rarely tell others about the abuse until many years later. Young children may not know what to say about what is happening between themselves and their siblings, or they may explicitly be told not to say anything at all. They may be uncomfortable with the sexual attention they receive, yet they may relish the special attention all the same, leaving them feeling confused. They simply may not know the behavior is wrong until they are older and the abuse has gone on for a time, leaving them feeling complicit. And sibling sexual abuse may take place in homes that shelter other problems, too, such as strained marriages or domestic violence, so boys and girls may worry about stressing their families even more.

Sadly, for those who do tell others about sibling sexual abuse, the responses they receive can be as hurtful and as harmful as the abuse itself. Failing to make it on his own as an adult, Rachel's brother decided to return home. In the years he had been away, his relationship with Rachel had already begun to take the typical turns for abused and abusive siblings as they age. Over holidays, they avoided eye contact with each other, and from the way her brother sidestepped her, Rachel sensed he felt sheepish and regretful about what he had done. The gifts he gave her at these same holidays seemed conciliatory yet manipulative, like the ones he used to give her sometimes when they played the naked game a lot, as if he was trying to make up for something he knew, then and now, was wrong. Despite these gestures, or maybe because of them, Rachel feared her brother's return to the upstairs hallway they shared. To protect herself, Rachel reluctantly told her mother the truth. Rachel's brother was sent to a therapist, and she was sent away to boarding school.

* * *

It is estimated that between 30 and 80 percent of those who have been sexually abused in childhood do not tell others about their experiences until many years after the violations occur, and most often not until adulthood. Like Rachel, family heroes may leave clues hoping that some caring or competent person will see the signs and want to get to the bottom of things. Or they may reluctantly, when they feel either safe enough, or endangered enough, come out with it once and for all. Whatever the case, disclosure rarely happens in a straightforward or timely way, and this is true not only for survivors of child sexual abuse but also for those who have lived with just about any childhood adversity. Family heroes keep secrets to keep themselves safe—it can be dangerous to share what one really knows or feels—but not talking about hardships can be dangerous, too.

Social psychologist James Pennebaker has spent his career studying the relationship between opening up and health. In one early and revealing study, he surveyed two hundred adults about their exposure to hardship in childhood and adulthood— including divorce, death of a close family member, sexual assault, physical assault, and "other traumas"—and also about the extent to which the participants had talked about these difficult events. Not surprisingly, some events were more likely to have been shared than others. Hardships that took place in adulthood as well as those that were difficult to hide or that carried little stigma, such as a parent's death, were more apt to have been talked over with family or friends. While participants who had shared their hard times generally fared well, those with an undisclosed adversity were more likely than the rest of the group to have experienced both minor and major health problems, from ulcers, flu, and headaches to cancer and high blood pressure. Most notably, it was not the type of adversity that predicted health problems; it was keeping one's troubles to oneself. That is, a death in the family that had not been talked about with others was just as harmful as was sexual abuse that had not been disclosed. From his work in this area, Pennebaker has concluded that "the act of not discussing or confiding the event with another may be more damaging than having experienced the event per se." Keeping secrets, it seems, may be bad for one's health.

These data may be concerning for the many, many family heroes who have a secret, but other work by Pennebaker suggests it is never too late to open up; that relief can come from talking about our darkest days even many years after those dark days have occurred. In one study, carried out in conjunction with the Dallas Memorial Center for Holocaust Studies, he interviewed Holocaust survivors whose average age was sixty-five. In the forty years that had passed since World War II, only about one-third had discussed their experiences in detail with others. The reasons for the other two-thirds' silence would sound familiar to family heroes everywhere: They were trying to move on and forget about the past, they felt no one would understand their unique experiences, they did not want to upset family and friends. Participants were nonetheless invited to discuss their time in concentration camps, labor camps, and ghettos in interviews that lasted between one and two hours. Those who were able to speak more freely about their experiences during the war showed improved health one year later. A similar study, this one conducted in cooperation with the Fortunoff Video Archive for Holocaust Testimonies at Yale, found that survivors who were willing and able to talk about the Holocaust, even though it was difficult, also reported better physical and mental health.

Of course, the notion that talking about what ails us can be curative, even years after the fact, did not originate with Pennebaker. It is the basis for the practice of confession in Christianity, and it is the foundation of psychotherapy. In the late nineteenth century, Sigmund Freud and his colleague Viennese internist Josef Breuer put forth their notion of the "talking cure." Together, the two men proposed that many emotional and bodily symptoms were caused by unexpressed memories, usually of disturbing events. If these memories were able to be talked about, the men suggested, then the feelings would be discharged, a catharsis would occur, and symptoms would lessen or disappear. More than a century later, dozens of different forms of empirically validated psychotherapy exist, but nearly all require that clients talk about their suffering to some extent. This has led some psychotherapy researchers to conclude that diverse bona fide psychotherapies are more alike than they are different; virtually all forms— from psychoanalytic psychotherapy to behavioral and cognitive therapies—are, in one way or another, talking cures.

* * *

Perhaps, then, confession is good for the soul, or at least it is good for your health. A meta-analysis of nearly 150 studies concluded that self-disclosure is beneficial—that much seems to be settled— but still no one knows exactly why. Freud's early supposition was that talking allowed for catharsis, or a release from the stress of suppressing memories and emotions, but research suggests there is more to it than that. Among the most supported theories is that what is actually most useful about telling our secrets goes further than simple stress release; putting our experiences into words helps us begin to make sense of our thoughts and feelings.

Remember, especially for children, secrets are often the product of moments when we say to ourselves, if we say anything at all, "There are no words. I don't know what to do with that. I don't know where to put that."

What does it mean, then, to take a feeling or an experience and, literally, "put it *into* words"? Words are labels and categories. They are boxes that organize the scattered contents of our minds. So when we talk about our experiences we are sorting them out, whether we intend to be or not, just by putting them into places where they might fit. We are able to say, "There are words. I do know what to do with that. I do know where to put that." The very act of doing so makes our most confusing or disturbing experiences more organized and understandable, and it makes them less scary and upsetting as well. Like P. D. James said about the detective story, putting feelings into words can be a restoration of order.

Brain imaging studies show that the very act of using words shifts the activity in the brain from the amygdala to the prefrontal cortex, from the seat of emotions to the executive functioning center. In one such study, participants were shown pictures of human faces with angry or fearful expressions, just the kind of stimuli that get the amygdala going. One group of participants were asked to match angry faces with angry faces or fearful faces with fearful faces, while the subjects in the other group were asked to choose words—such as *angry* or *afraid*—to label the faces they saw. For participants who labeled the faces with words, activity in the prefrontal cortex went up, while activity in the amygdala went down; participants who merely matched the faces saw no such shift. In similar research, participants were shown pictures known to elicit negative emotional reactions in the brain, such as images of sharks, snakes, spiders, guns, plane crashes, car accidents, or explosions. Some of the participants were asked simply to match the pictures—again, dogs to dogs, snakes to snakes—while others were asked to categorize each picture as either a natural or an artificial danger. While the matching condition elicited a strong response in the amygdala, the labeling condition saw less activity in the amygdala and more in the prefrontal cortex.

These studies suggest that words force a shift from the amygdala to the prefrontal cortex, so when we work with words, reason begins to supplant emotion. "A concept without a name is like a stray dog or a feral cat. To domesticate it, you have to call it something," wrote Holocaust survivor Ruth Klüger in her memoir *Still Alive*. Or, as is often said more colloquially, "Name it to tame it." Rachel was surprised to learn that there might be a different name for what her brother called "the naked game"—sibling sexual abuse—and she was even more surprised to find out how common it was. She read up on brothers and sisters who had been perpetrators and victims, and she saw similarities and differences between their experiences and her own. Ultimately, she decided on words of her choosing, and made sense of the experience in her own way.

"I have settled on a word for what my brother did," Rachel said. "The word *abuse* does not work for me personally because that sounds criminal and I do not think he was trying to be a criminal, or maybe I just don't like the idea that I'm a victim. I guess I did think those things when I was younger, and that was what the fondness for Batman and Columbo was about. I wanted truth and justice. But now I think of what happened as a mistake. It was misguided for my brother to think that what he was doing was not going to have a negative impact on me, and it was a mistake for me, although an innocent one, to have gone along as much as I did. So we both made mistakes. I can see that and I don't feel so confused anymore. My life makes sense."

Rachel went on, this time about what had brought her to therapy in the first place. "I used to have a hard time understanding how my fiancé could love me when I had all these bad things in my past, when I felt so crazy. But now I see that some parts of my life have been sad, not bad. I can see how the mistakes my brother and I made twisted things up for both of us but I don't feel crazy anymore. I can see why I have been depressed and angry, at times, but I don't feel crazy. I feel more normal than I ever have because I have talked about my secrets and I can finally understand them." As French writer Annie Ernaux says in her book *La Honte*, or *Shame*, "Perhaps the narrative, all narratives, render normal any act, including the most dramatic."

There is something special then—or at least especially useful—about putting our experiences into words. "Use your words!" we tell young children who are falling apart, and we tell them this because, through intuition or experience, we understand that words and sentences have the potential to create order, and to facilitate connection. By talking about our worst days with others, we might find out that our experiences are not as bad as we thought, and maybe we are not as bad as we thought, either. Our experiences can be understood, and we can, too.

* * *

In one telling study about the relationship between secrets and community, eighty-six students at Harvard recorded how they were feeling and what they were doing throughout the day and night for eleven days. Those who were keeping secrets felt less good about themselves overall, and felt more anxious and depressed, than did fellow students who were not. What lifted the mood of these students with secrets was spending time around school, whether studying or eating or just hanging out, with those like themselves—students who also had closely held secrets. Unfortunately, however, the students who kept secrets were more likely to spend time by themselves.

This is a problem because, although we imagine that the truly heroic need no one but themselves, social support is crucial—even a key difference between those who are and are not happy—and this may be especially true when life is at its most difficult. In one study of more than seven thousand adults who had experienced early adversities, those who had social support were less likely to struggle with anxiety and depression. And multiple meta-analyses including hundreds of studies and thousands of participants show that, in both children and adults, what predicts distress after adversity is not the severity of the event but how alone one feels afterward. Two of the most powerful predictors of being able to feel good in adulthood after early adversity, then, are sharing our secrets and having people in our lives who support us, and often these two things go hand in hand: Communication creates community. Sharing our secrets is one way that relationships become closer and more real, and we are most likely to confide in those whom we feel we can count on.

Research on revealing secrets shows that what those who open up want and need is a person who can be discreet, and who can be trusted not to judge or to respond with ignorance; if that person is able to provide further insight, all the better. For this reason, some family heroes, like Rachel, tell their secrets to "professional confidants," such as therapists or clergy. Others find belonging in support groups, such as Al-Anon meetings or therapy groups for those who share a particular experience or secret, which allow each group member to see that he or she is not the only one. Even more often, though, our first confidants—and our most important change agents—tend to be caring friends or supportive partners, laypeople who understand.

There are many people, and not just professionals, who can understand those like Rachel. She was part of an even larger community than she realized. Not only was she one of the roughly 20 percent of children who had been sexually assaulted, but also she was one of the majority of adults who have grown up alongside some early adversity, many of whom have kept secrets, too. Rachel's secrets left her feeling isolated when in fact she went about her day face-to-face and shoulder-to-shoulder with many, many others who shared, if not her specific experience of sibling sexual abuse, the experience of going about life with a secret. The power of finding these people cannot be overestimated.

Given this, it may seem that the way toward health and happiness and community for the family hero is to talk, talk, talk to as many people who will listen—but of course it is not that simple. While there are dangers in keeping our secrets to ourselves, the heroic child was correct all along to suspect that there are risks in telling them, too. Those who disclose may be blamed or shamed or rejected or refuted, or they may be discouraged from further honesty. Sharing our secrets can make us feel more connected or more isolated, safer or more endangered, depending on how others respond. This is what James Pennebaker called the "cruel paradox" of opening up.

Indeed, while many of Pennebaker's studies were conducted in laboratories where participants talked into tape recorders or to researchers who had been briefed on how to react, studies that have been carried out in the "real world" show more complicated results. Here are a few. Combat veterans who received negative reactions from family members and health care professionals when they spoke about their experiences at war were more likely to suffer from depression and PTSD compared with those who felt well received by their communities. For men and women who were HIV-positive, those who revealed their status had better physical health and greater overall well-being, but only insofar as their social groups were supportive. Women who were soon to have an abortion, and who received the full support of those they told, were less likely to become depressed after the procedure than women who received mixed reactions or who did not confide in anyone at all; the same went for women struggling with infertility. Gay men and women reported greater well-being on days they could talk openly about their sexual orientation, yet only if they felt understood by others. For peacekeepers in Somalia, stress levels were less related to whether or not they had seen combat than to how others handled their disclosures about what they had seen. Similarly, for sexual assault survivors and victims of violent crime, the negative reactions of others were more predictive of PTSD than were the characteristics of the assaults themselves. And while some find posting their secrets online to be freeing, others feel hurt and even devastated by negative comments and attacks. First disclosures can be especially important, as these often determine whether or when one might open up again. As John Steinbeck wrote, "A man who tells secrets or stories must think of who is hearing or reading, for a story has as many versions as it has readers."

* * *

"I am in an impossible position," Rachel explained. "I hold back from telling people 'my story' because I feel like my story can never be entirely mine. I feel like a character in my brother's story, because his story was always ahead of mine, and it had such a big impact on me. It's so unfair because I feel like if I tell people what my brother did, then I am letting his story be my story, and I am bringing the past into the present in a way that I would rather not. I feel like I am being punished for something that I didn't do. But if I don't come out with everything and tell people about my brother, then I feel like I am not telling the truth somehow, like I am some kind of liar. Or a fake. Then I get stuck with this feeling that if I was really and truly brave, then I would just tell everyone everything."

We live in what philosopher Chloe Taylor calls a "culture of confession." Every day, we are surrounded by examples— in memoirs, op-eds, and blogs, and on talk shows and reality shows—of those who have chosen to share their secrets with the world. For some, telling their stories loudly and proudly is liberating and empowering, and many family heroes have found solace and strength by way of reading the autobiographies of those who came before them. Speaking openly about issues that tend only to be whispered about can raise awareness and reduce stigma, and testimonials from real people can and do lead to real change. All around, we can see examples of those who have found meaning and salvation, who have transcended some of the darkest and most demeaning experiences, by using their words, and their voices, for good. Less visible, though, are those who make a different choice: those who decide not to share their secrets far and wide.

While it is correct that there are dangers in feeling silenced, it does not follow that the only way to live a brave or truthful life would be for Rachel to, as she said, "tell everyone everything." Early on, Rachel had said she wanted "truth and justice" in her life, yet somehow it felt neither fair, nor true, to be forever tied to the mistakes her brother made. Yet some, it seemed, demanded it. When Rachel waited some years to tell a friend about the sexual abuse in her past, the friend wondered why Rachel had not told her sooner, why she could not just be honest about who she was.

In one of his works, philosopher Jean-Paul Sartre writes about a person he calls the "champion of sincerity"—a man who insists that a gay male friend is acting in bad faith, that he is not being honest or authentic, when he prefers not to declare that he is a homosexual. Rachel's friend was taking a similar position in feeling dismayed and betrayed because Rachel had not confessed earlier to "who she was." But that is the problem, is it not?

As Sartre argues, maybe it is the "champion of sincerity" who is in the wrong, as he attempts to force his friend to reduce himself to a single category, even a stereotype. Sibling sexual assault was not "who Rachel was"; above all else, she yearned for the possibility of a life—and a self—that could be free of it. Yet, as for Sartre's "champion of sincerity," for Rachel's friend silence seemed suspect.

As Taylor, and other philosophers before her—including Sartre, and then Michel Foucault and Judith Butler—remind us, silence is complicated. Silence can reflect not having a voice, but it can also be an expression of freedom: freedom from opening ourselves up to more pain; freedom from being defined by one or two of our experiences, especially those that are not of our choosing. Just as words help us make sense of our experiences by putting them into categories and boxes, as people we look to make sense of the world by putting those around us into categories and boxes, too: male, female, black, white, gay, straight, abused, not abused. There is a certain freedom that comes with being undefined and uncategorized, or in not being entirely known by everyone. "You don't know me, anonymity insists. Now what?" says feminist scholar Leigh Gilmore in *The Limits of Autobiography*.

Many children keep secrets, at least in part, because they instinctively resist being known for the bad things that have happened to them. Remember the boy from the schoolbus in Chowchilla? By not wanting to tell everyone everything, Rachel was resisting being fixed to a particular story, too. Like many family heroes, she preferred not to be known for the misdeeds of others, or for something outside of herself and outside of her control. Rachel could not choose her brother but she could choose whether, how, when, and how much she talked about what he had done to her. Rachel knew she could not live a life in which her sexual abuse had never happened, but at least sometimes she wanted to enjoy a conversation or a meal or a relationship with someone for whom it never had happened: someone who did not know. Perhaps this sounds duplicitous—or not brave somehow—but maybe all Rachel wanted was to preserve the right to be among those who could, who had the privilege to, as the co-founder of *Essence* magazine Edward Lewis said, "define ourselves by the best that is in us, not the worst that has been done to us."

* * *

In one of his books, author David Wong—which it should be noted is a pseudonym—writes about a character who has this to say about keeping secrets: "There are two types of people on planet Earth: Batman and Iron Man. Batman has a secret identity, right? So Bruce Wayne has to walk around every second of every day knowing that if somebody finds out his secret, his family is dead, his friends are dead, everyone he loves gets tortured to death by costumed supervillains. And he has to live with the weight of that secret every day...But not Tony Stark, he's open about who he is. He tells the world he's Iron Man, he doesn't give a shit. He doesn't have that shadow hanging over him, he doesn't have to spend energy building up those walls of lies around himself. You're one or the other—either you're one of those people who has to hide your real self because it would ruin you if it came out, because of your secret fetishes or addictions or crimes, or you're not one of those people."

The notion that one must be Batman or Iron Man is an interesting idea, but a false choice, too, because there are more than two types of people in the world, and more than two types of superheroes. What Wong's character is really describing are the two ends of the spectrum in terms of keeping secrets: At one end are those who keep their secrets as if their lives depend on it, and at the other end are those who, as Rachel said, "tell everyone everything." But of course, there is a lot of room to move around in between. What many family heroes do—as is the case with the Justice League or the X-Men or the Avengers, the latter of whom "fight the foes no single superhero can withstand"—is share their secrets, and band together, with a trusted few.

By the time Rachel first saw *Columbo* from under the couch in her childhood home, she already sensed that she could not tell just anyone about "the naked game." So it goes for many family heroes who have something to say but who are unsure of whom to say it to. They want to be known but they intuit, or have already experienced, the "cruel paradox" of opening up. As a protective compromise, family heroes may leave clues, like black paint under their fingernails, for some caring or competent person to find. Maybe they drop tiny references to the adversities in their lives, like bread crumbs for a knowing friend or professional to follow; the misattuned will not pick up on the trail, and that is likely for the best. Or, early on in relationships, they may disclose smaller problems or less dangerous secrets like trial balloons, scrutinizing the responses they receive. And they pay close attention to what friends and acquaintances do and do not say. Rachel distrusted anyone who told insensitive sex jokes, or who gossiped or made judgments about people with family problems, and she stayed on the lookout for those who might be leaving clues behind, too. Sometimes, when creating community, "it takes one to know one."

In this way, and over time, Rachel traded her secret identity for a secret society of sorts. She cultivated a small group of confidants who knew her secrets and who felt a kinship around having lived with some of their own. She joined a support group for survivors of violence. She opened up to a friend whose father was schizophrenic. She reached out to another who had spent time in foster care. Her cousin began to talk to her about a shared relative who was a drug abuser. She was a member of a club that she had never asked to join, as they say, but still it was one in which she often found great solace.

In his work on trauma and community, sociologist Kai Erikson reminds us that adversity has the potential not only to disrupt our most meaningful bonds but also to create them. Trauma can forge community by fostering communality: relationships in which there is an extraordinarily deep sense of connection and understanding. In these kinds of friendships, people come together not because of shared hobbies or interests but because of shared life experiences—often quite intimate and profound ones. There is a special bond, such that all members can benefit from collective wisdom and protectiveness, and from the feeling of being stronger together.

After years of feeling like loners or outsiders, family heroes, like Rachel, who band together—in groups of twos or threes or fives—get to be less lonely and they get to be insiders. They create a community where they feel they can finally speak freely, and doing so calls into question one of the most damaging conclusions that can be drawn from sexual abuse, or from the alienation that may follow any adversity: that one is not normal. This was how it went for Rachel, not because she had a fiancé or even a therapist, but because she found friends.

"For a long time it was hard for me to understand why my fiancé would want to be with me. I didn't trust it. I felt like I was damaged because of my brother's mistakes, and when I was growing up my brother would say anything to have some kind of sexual contact with me. So I couldn't really accept it when my partner said he loved me or that I'm a good person," Rachel reflected. "Then I looked at my friends and realized that if one of my friends did to themselves what I used to do—disqualify themselves from being good or from having a normal life—I would never agree with that. So it forces me to rethink why that has to be true for me. Now I look at my friends and I can believe I'm normal because I can see they are, that I'm not a bad person because I can see they are not. I have always felt different, always an outsider, just wanting to be normal; now I realize that this is normal, or that I have a wider range of normal than some other people. Maybe there is no normal. Maybe most people, or a lot of people, have their thing. This does not have to ruin me. There is still time for me to have a normal life."

CHAPTER 15

Cape

The world is a dangerous place to live; not because of the people who are evil, but because of the people who don't do anything about it.

—Albert Einstein

The most iconic declaration in comic-book history is this: "With great power, there must also come great responsibility." Though a similar sentiment has been expressed by many others—Winston Churchill said, "Where there is great power there is great responsibility," and Franklin D. Roosevelt wrote on the eve of his death, "Great power involves great responsibility"—many know these words to be the moral revelation of Spider-Man. Gifted with special powers by way of a spider bite, teenage Peter Parker initially eschewed his unique abilities, and he was uninterested in using them for good. "I've got my own problems," he reasoned, and he did: bullying, money trouble, girl trouble, family strife. However, shortly after Spider-Man failed to stop an escaping thief because he felt it was not his duty, this same burglar killed his surrogate father, his beloved uncle Ben. On the last panel of the comic-book issue that tells this sad story, a grief-stricken and regretful Spider-Man walks down the road alone surrounded by the words of an omniscient narrator: "And a lean, silent figure slowly fades into the gathering darkness, aware at last that in this world, that with great power there must also come—great responsibility." It is in this moment that Peter Parker embraces his powers and his role as a superhero who has an obligation to do good.

A similar, though maybe less dramatic, transformation occurs for many family heroes. They may not have been bitten by spiders, but other events may leave them with strengths and competencies that, by adulthood, they feel compelled to put to use. Of course, like young Spider-Man, they too have their own problems. But also like young Spider-Man, they have been made keenly aware of injustice in the world, and so they become helpers or problem solvers at home or at work, often standing up for those who cannot stand up for themselves. In one way or another, they put on a cape and swoop in and save the day. To stand by and do nothing would be wrong; besides, helping other people is what they are good at. Likely, they have been doing it all their lives.

* * *

David's mother cried the night before she married his father, a man who was gone not long after David was born. "You are the best thing to come of that," David's mother often said to him. "You are the light of my life." This sentiment was expressed each night when David's mother tucked him into bed with hugs and kisses and, together, they sang "their song": "You Are My Sunshine." For a while, bedtime was a warm and happy time, and David thought his mother had the most beautiful voice in the whole world. "You should be a singer, Mommy," he encouraged her as she sat on the side of his small twin bed. When his mother said that her voice was not good enough for all that, David felt sad for her. And scared. He did not like to think of his mother as limited.

As David aged and listened more closely to the words of their song, he started to feel worried, and guilty, too: "You are my sunshine, my only sunshine. You make me happy when skies are gray. You'll never know, dear, how much I love you. Please don't take my sunshine away." And the second verse weighed on him the most: "The other night, dear, when I was sleeping, I dreamed I held you in my arms. But when I woke, dear, I was mistaken so I hung my head and cried." David got the feeling that he was the only good thing in his mother's life and that if he were not there, she would cry even more than usual.

* * *

In a given year, nearly 20 percent of adults suffer from depression, the most prevalent mental health disorder in the United States. Because it is so common, and even a household name, many do not recognize its invisible burden. Some illnesses, such as heart disease or cancer, do their greatest harm by shortening our life span, or how many years we live. Other disorders, however, shorten not our life span but our "health span," or how many years we live well. Depression is one of those illnesses. Because it is so widespread, and because it tends to be recurrent or chronic, according to research on the Global Burden of Disease (GBD), depression is the second leading cause of years lived with a disability (YLD)—or healthy years lost—in the world.

Depression affects both men and women, and it is especially common among women of childbearing and child-rearing age. This means, of course, that depression changes the lives not only of parents but also of their children, a reality that initially was uncovered somewhat by accident. In early research on the effects of parental mental illness on child development, researchers compared the well-being of children of parents who were diagnosed with schizophrenia with that of children whose parents were diagnosed with depression. The children of depressed parents were meant to be the comparison group, or control group. Of the two groups, the children of schizophrenics were expected to fare significantly worse, because schizophrenia was and is, undeniably, a mental illness with a more severe course. Surprisingly, researchers found that the two groups of children were equally impacted by their parents' mental health.

Parenting is one of the greatest challenges for individuals with mental illness, and this includes mothers and fathers with depression. Sustaining effort and warmth and support across years and even decades is difficult for many parents, and it can feel exponentially so for a caretaker who is depressed. We may think of depression as a disorder of tears and sadness, but the inability to experience positive emotions—the good things in life—is an equally distinctive feature, and one that is more difficult to hide. David did catch his mother crying sometimes, and she was often withdrawn or irritated, but most noticeable was that she rarely found pleasure in the day-to-day, or even in David's childhood milestones.

David felt responsible for his mother's happiness, however little of it there was, and to cheer her up, he made jokes at home and earned good grades at school, though even then her smiles did not last long. When David's mother noticed her son taking care of her feelings by complimenting her cooking, or thanking her for taking him somewhere fun even though she did not seem to enjoy it, she only became angry with herself. David suspected that, had it not been for him, his mother would have stopped doing anything at all. He had been saving his mother's life since the day he was born, and the older he got, the more true this became.

As adults, many children of depressed parents do fare well, but that does not mean that they do not struggle at times. In the longest-running such study to date, researchers followed children of depressed parents over a twenty-year period to the average age of thirty-five. In that time, children who grew up with depressed parents were more likely than their peers to be anxious in childhood, as they worried about their mothers or fathers, and about themselves. As these same children grew to be teenagers and young adults, they were three times more likely than others their age to be depressed, and twice as likely to be dependent on alcohol or drugs. By their mid-thirties, they were twice as likely as their peers to report a problem with their physical health, and five times as likely to have a heart problem specifically. And as they were growing up, 60 percent of these sons and daughters received no treatment—no support—of their own.

* * *

Many afternoons after school, David sat in the sparsely furnished waiting rooms of doctors' offices, waiting for his mother to emerge from behind closed doors. What kinds of doctors David's mother saw he did not know, but they were not doctors for children, it seemed, because none of them had toys or even *Highlights* magazines. David flipped through *New Yorker* magazines instead, looking for the drawn cartoons. Some he understood, and some he only pretended to understand. Either way, he made a point of chuckling at them when his mother emerged from the back hall of the doctor's office, red-faced and puffy-eyed, sometimes holding a small white piece of paper that meant a trip to the drugstore for a small brown bottle of pills. None of the doctors ever told David what was wrong with his mother, and none of them ever asked if maybe he wanted to come inside and see a doctor, too.

David's mother was what psychologists call the "identified patient" in the family, which meant she was the one with problems. David, of course, was the family hero, or the child who was tasked with saving the day. Family heroes love their parents, and are entirely dependent on them, so they work hard to make life better for their families in whatever way they can. At home, family heroes may look more like parents than children. They make sure their parents get off to work on time, or they take over the cooking and cleaning. They look after siblings and pets, and they are the family planners who remember doctors' appointments and trash days, or who give direction and advice to overwhelmed adults.

Family heroes make their parents feel better—and they make themselves feel better—by doing well. Like David as he laughed at sophisticated cartoons in the waiting rooms of doctors' offices, the most successful family heroes seem unaffected by, or even better off because of, the challenges that they face at home, and maybe in some ways they are. But because of this, it can be difficult to realize that sometimes these children need rescuing, too.

Maybe this was why, when David's mother took him along for long drives on the highway late at night—which she often did—he always imagined the same thing: that he was being taken to the hospital in an ambulance. He lay quiet and still in the far back of their station wagon, tucked into his sleeping bag, his head on a pillow, and as the car rolled along he watched the silhouettes of the tops of the trees speeding by outside. He relaxed into the feeling of weightlessness, the sensation of being whisked away and cared for; as long as the drive lasted, which sometimes could be as much as two hours, David pretended that he was being rushed to the emergency room. That may not sound like something that could go on for a long time, and there really wasn't a lot to it, but he stretched it out as long as he could. He imagined there was someone riding in the back with him—no one in particular, just some stranger—reassuring him that he was going to be all right, that he would get to the hospital in time. Eventually, though, David heard the sound of the blinker and felt the wagon make familiar turns, right and left and then right again, back toward David's house. David wasn't going to any hospital. No one was taking him to get any help.

* * *

David became a social worker, which is not altogether surprising. In a study of over fifteen hundred social workers, researcher Bruce Lackie found that, as children, over two-thirds functioned as the family heroes in their homes. Accustomed to succeeding at, and being valued for, taking care of others in difficult situations, as adults, many family heroes choose professions that are an extension of that role: medicine, nursing, psychology, teaching, psychiatry, social work, the ministry. So common is this trajectory that one book chapter devoted to the subject aptly features this title: "When the Family Hero Turns Pro."

Similarly, a small but consistent set of studies examining the influence of family history on educational and career choices has found that those in the helping professions often come from difficult backgrounds. In one study, 80 percent of social work students reported having an alcoholic parent, compared with 59 percent of business students; another similar inquiry found that while only about a quarter of business students reported alcohol abuse in the family of origin, nearly half of students of social work did. In other research, a wide range of early stressors—including substance abuse, physical, sexual, and emotional abuse, mental and physical illness, and violence in the home—were significantly more common in the histories of social work, guidance, and counseling students than in the backgrounds of students in seemingly less service-oriented fields, such as business and literature. Likely, there is more than a correlational relationship there, and many of those in helping professions confirm that their own experiences with early adversities did indeed influence their vocational choice.

David became a social worker not to help struggling adults—he had been doing that all his life—but to help their children, those who are often neglected in one way or another not only by their parents but also by the medical professionals all around. A moving, and rare, qualitative study reveals what the now grown children of mentally ill parents remember feeling and needing when they were young. Although some recall being relieved when their parents were looked after by someone other than themselves—"I appreciated it when my mother was taken care of in [the] hospital.

I knew that she ate, took her medicine, slept well and felt better"—
some of their most poignant memories were the pain of being left
to fend for themselves:

> "My parent came home [from the hospital] too
> early and no one wondered how we were going to
> manage everything."
> "I felt abandoned and lonely because no one
> explained what happened."
> "The [medical] staff never showed any concern
> for me or my siblings."
> "I wished I could have seen a social worker or
> a psychologist, someone who could have asked me
> about my reactions and explained my parent's illness
> to me."

David remembered feeling those things, too. As a child, he
accepted that his mother was too ill to care for him properly, and
it was only when he rode along in the back of her station wagon
that he let himself pretend that someone else would. It is for this
reason that David chose to work with children whose parents
were physically or mentally ill, or who were absent in one way or
another. One of his first young clients was an eight-year-old girl
whose mother died of cancer, and whose father was an uninvolved
parent who lived out of state. The girl was a family hero: a bright,
cheerful sprite who waited patiently while distant relatives and
teachers puzzled over whom she would live with and where she
would go. David met with her weekly at her school, and during
their time together she always chose to do the same thing: play
the board games Sorry! and Operation. As David sat on the floor
with her, they talked plainly about bad luck and illness, about the
facts that sometimes bad things happen for no good reason and
that sometimes doctors cannot save people. One afternoon, after

she left, David went into the bathroom and threw up. Working so closely with children in pain was not easy, but maybe better than most people, David knew how much they needed someone just like him. How then, he wondered, could he do anything else?

* * *

Psychologist and researcher Ervin Staub suggests a term for those like David: "heroic helpers." Heroic helpers see a need in the world and look for a way to meet it. They see a wrong in the world and feel a responsibility to right it. Unable to just stand by and do nothing while people are left alone with their problems, heroic helpers set their minds, and sometimes their career trajectories, to doing something about them. Matt Langdon, who directs the Hero Construction Company—which fosters the heroic impulse in children—puts it this way: "The opposite of a hero isn't a villain; it's a bystander."

In this way, maybe heroic helpers, or social workers like David, aren't so different from business students after all. David's decision to be a social worker was aligned with the age-old career advice to do what you are good at, and to do what moves you. And innovation and action in any field are almost always born out of problems that beg for solutions or needs in the community that are not being met.

Consider the story of Howard Schultz, the chairman of Starbucks. When Schultz was seven years old, his father broke his ankle and was unable to keep his job as a truck driver. Without his paycheck or access to insurance, Schultz's family fielded calls from debt collectors and borrowed money to pay hospital bills. Schultz lived out his boyhood in the projects in Brooklyn, where he watched his father move from one low-paying job to another. Then, as a young man, he saw his father die without a pension or any savings. Now Schultz is the head of one of the most recognizable brands in the world, and in addition to its coffee and its logo, Starbucks is well known for its mission to treat its employees with compassion and respect. One of its signature offerings is an extraordinarily generous and inclusive health care program, with benefits even for part-time workers. "I knew in my heart that if I was ever in a position where I could make a difference, I wouldn't leave people behind," Schultz said. "Although I didn't consciously plan it that way, Starbucks has become a living legacy of my dad."

Certainly there are a lot of ways to help people, to be a hero. Maybe heroes are military personnel and public servants who risk their lives to protect strangers. Or they are scientists who advance their fields through discovery. Or they are volunteers who do good not at work, but in their spare hours. Or they are underdogs who serve as role models, or whistleblowers who endanger themselves in the interests of others. Or they are leaders who guide us in difficult times. Or they are neighbors and relatives who care for those to whom they have no obligation. Or they are teachers who empower children with knowledge. Or they are writers who speak to others through words on a page. Or they are lawyers who stand with those who are vulnerable. Or they are ministers who inspire their congregations. Or they are businesspeople, like Howard Schultz, who create products or services or workplaces that people need. There are countless ways to make a difference in people's lives; what unites these heroic helpers is the ability, or the experience, to see that there is something in the world that needs to be done—and the audacity to step forward and try to do it.

There are as many paths to being a heroic helper as there are heroic helpers themselves, but one that Staub emphasizes, and knows a lot about personally, is what he calls "altruism born of suffering," or the tendency to transform pain into good works. In 1944, Staub was a six-year-old child in Budapest who, because of a man named Raoul Wallenberg, was spared the fate of nearly half a million Hungarian Jews, most of whom were sent to concentration and labor camps in Germany. Wallenberg was a Swedish businessman, diplomat, and humanitarian who, while stationed in Hungary, saved the lives of tens of thousands of men, women, and children—including Staub and his family—by granting them Swedish orders of protection and space in politically neutral "safe houses." When Hungary was liberated in 1945, about a hundred thousand Jews remained there, largely due to the efforts of Wallenberg, a heroic helper who reportedly died later in a Soviet prison.

In the research literature, family heroes like David have been called "parentified" and "burdened" and "hurried," and certainly many sons and daughters grow up too fast or carry far too heavy a load. Yet, without minimizing the pain and the danger in that, adversity does not have wholly negative effects, and less discussed is that difficult experiences can also be pathways to compassion and competence. A diverse set of studies has shown that those who have struggled—by way of war, natural disasters, terrorism, social marginalization, personal violence, or family strife, for example—are more likely to help others in need. According to Staub, they have a greater awareness of the problems that are all around them. They are more likely to be inclusive, or to see the similarities between their own struggles and those of other people, and to feel empathy for those in pain. And for those who have been able to overcome or transcend adversity, there is often a moral imperative to pass on what one knows, to help others do the same. A common motivation is one that David understood well: "I don't want other people to suffer the way that I did." This sentiment is the foundation for what renowned trauma researcher Judith Herman calls a "survivor mission."

"The great illusion of leadership," said theologian Henri Nouwen, "is to think that man can be led out of the desert by someone who has never been there." Family heroes have been there indeed. They found their way out of the desert that was mental illness or bullying or alcoholism or abuse, and many become effective, impassioned heroic helpers not in spite of their backgrounds but because of them. "The doctor is effective only when he himself is affected," wrote Carl Jung, a psychoanalyst whose mother, like David's, struggled with depression. Yet too many family heroes have a crisis of confidence and ask themselves, *Who am I to take on this work?* rather than *Who better than I to take on this work?*

* * *

As Spider-Man's Peter Parker often longed to be a normal teenager, David wondered sometimes what it would be like to be a normal adult, or at least what he perceived one to be. He watched with some envy as his friends pursued careers on a whim, or for the money. When the mother of one of his young clients, a woman who was incarcerated, was diagnosed with a terminal illness, David thought reflexively if not seriously about whether he ought to step forward to take her son in himself. *Oh, to be in marketing and to leave work at work*, he thought sometimes. David, like Spider-Man, imagined that maybe he would have been better off, maybe he would have been happier, with a life in which he had no real power to help people and therefore felt no responsibility to do so.

Maybe, and maybe not.

Family heroes tend to have good instincts, and whether they know it or not, by helping others they are helping themselves, too. In numerous studies, helping others has been linked to improved health and well-being, not just for those who receive the help, but also for those who do the good work. Here is just a sampling of what researchers have found. Adults who volunteer enjoy higher levels of happiness and satisfaction, and lower mortality rates, than those who do not give their time to others. When stressed, doing something for someone else has been shown to reduce one's heart rate and blood pressure. Doing work or having activities that feel meaningful and purposeful is a key predictor of physical health and emotional health, and to feeling satisfied with one's life. Actively caring for an ill spouse can lead to more positive feelings for the caregiver, and can reduce one's own risk of death. Widows who give tangible support to friends or neighbors or relatives recover from grief and depression faster than widows who do not. Cardiac patients who help new patients learn about and cope with their conditions enjoy a better recovery themselves, and being a volunteer has been associated with longer survival with HIV. Even participating in a research study can help us feel better, as was demonstrated by one study in which visually impaired adults who volunteered to be part of the development of a visual prosthesis (one that could not benefit them) reported feeling proud of themselves and uniquely valuable as a result. As one article summarizes, "it's good to be good."

What may be most surprising about being good or doing good, however, is not just that "it's good to be good" but also that the benefit of giving help may even outweigh that of receiving help. In a two-year study in which patients with multiple sclerosis provided social support to others with the disease, peer supporters were significantly more likely to feel a sense of self-confidence, autonomy, mastery, adaptability, personal growth, and purpose in life, and they were also less prone to feeling depressed and anxious. In terms of overall well-being, the helpers received nearly eight times the benefit of those who had received support. They felt their role as helpers had changed who they were and how they thought about the world, and they felt uniquely able to be of service because of their disease. In a similar study of more than one thousand churchgoers, giving help to others was associated with better mental health, even above and beyond whatever improvements came from receiving help. In a study of older adults, helping friends, relatives, or neighbors was found to reduce the risk of death by half, and providing emotional support to one's spouse reduced the risk of death by one-third, while receiving support from others had no such positive effect.

Many family heroes who choose to help others, either through work or volunteerism or in some other way, talk of the value of "turning a negative into a positive." This is a transformation that happens at many levels. When a painful experience becomes the impetus to do good works, we move from being a victim to being a hero. We get to feel competent and helpful rather than hapless and helpless. When we attend to the hardships of those around us, we forget for a time about our own problems and we even feel happier, too. When we reach out to those in need we enhance our feelings of connectedness to others as well as a connection to something outside of, and maybe bigger than, ourselves, thus lessening our experience of alienation. And when we engage with others in a meaningful way, we allow our days and our relationships to have weight and significance. We allow our lives to matter.

David had always known that he mattered to his mother, and as an adult he mattered to so many other people, too. He knew from experience that the kids he worked with needed him, and in fact they needed someone exactly like him: a person who truly understood their experience. His work was a calling, and he knew he made a difference every single day. Whether he might have been happier doing something else, had his life gone differently early on, was another question entirely. It was, David knew, one that could never be answered, but once in a while he thought about it anyway.

* * *

Family heroes are not comic-book characters, so whether "helping helps the helper" in the long run will depend on their doing something that ink-drawn superheroes almost never get to do, or maybe never need to do: take a day off. Remember that the one thief Peter Parker neglected to stop went on to kill his uncle—and of course we never see Wonder Woman or Batman take a vacation. When David went home at night, he was painfully aware that life did not stop for the kids he worked with just because it was six p.m.; in fact, for many of them, evenings and weekends were the most difficult and dangerous hours of the week. As long as he could remember, David had worried about what terrible fates might befall his clients—or his mother—when he was not around. But if they want to keep saving the day, family heroes need to be able to hang up the cape on a regular basis and save themselves, too.

With great power may come great responsibility, but good deeds still need to feel like a choice. Helping behavior that feels freely chosen is more likely to be effective—and rewarding—than are good deeds that do not. Yet for the superhero and for the family hero, choice is a tricky issue. Spider-Man did not choose to be bitten by a spider any more than David chose to be reared by a mother with depression: As adults, both figures were using the strengths gained from their experiences to respond to a calling that not everyone could hear, to do what they felt was important and right. For David, walking away from those who needed him was "not an option," but he was going to need to find choices where he could.

Family heroes may not get to choose their origin stories, but they do get to choose whether and how they help. Whether they devote their careers, or a tiny bit of their spare time, to using their powers for good, there are many different ways to be a heroic helper. Being a social worker was not the only way David could do good in the world, and this was something he was only beginning to think about: "I see how what I have been through and have decided to do with my life has made me a good person, and I have a very meaningful job. But sometimes I feel like growing up the way I did kept me from finding out who I am and what I was supposed to...I don't know. I just...I think I would have taken a different path in life if my mom had not been sick. A lot of things could be different. I don't know. Maybe I would have been living in Brazil studying hummingbirds."

Consider these words from a woman we have already met—Rachel—who, rather than pursuing a vocation related to the sibling sexual abuse she went through, became an artist because making art had always brought her joy, even when her home life was the most unhappy: "When people find out about my brother, they seem to want, or expect, me to have taken some redemptive path, to be a do-gooder in some way. But for me, the most healing thing I could do for myself was to allow myself to have a career and a life that was not about what happened with him. Maybe that is what I have to offer the world. Maybe how I help people is by showing them that it is fine to do that, too."

David was certain that social work was what he wanted to do—"I can still go to Brazil and learn about hummingbirds on vacation, or maybe I'll be a social worker in Brazil one day," he said—but he had trouble taking those vacations, and taking off the cape on nights and weekends, too. In his personal life, David often found himself in friendships and relationships with those who were struggling. This was a dilemma. He knew enough—from his job and from his own life—to recognize that most people are in the process of trying to overcome something. Yet it was also true that David was almost too comfortable with people in crisis, and he was frequently called upon to rescue friends and girlfriends who perhaps were not as resilient as he was. Some people might look at David and say he was addicted to stress, or to being in the helping role. Maybe. Or maybe being a heroic helper was all he knew, and it was difficult for him to imagine anything else.

When a woman he was dating overdosed on painkillers in what may have been suicide, David realized the danger he was putting himself in—and maybe others, too. If he wasn't careful, he could repeat his childhood by having a home and a life where he had to be the family hero once again. Only this time David would not be a child but, even more heartbreaking, there could be other children involved—his own. That woke him up. It was time to start believing in a home that was different from the one he grew up in, one where maybe everyone helps each other but no one needs saving. Perhaps famed graphic novelist Alan Moore was right when he said, "Part of the art of being a hero is knowing when you don't need to be one anymore."

CHAPTER 16

Avenger

The best revenge is to be unlike him who performed the injury.
—Marcus Aurelius

Jennifer became my client after she quit treatment with another therapist. Some might take this to be a bad sign, as if she was one of those clients who would never be satisfied or whose therapist could not do anything right. Perhaps. But it might also be true that, either consciously or unconsciously, Jennifer knew what she wanted from a therapist, and she also knew that, thus far, she had not gotten it. This, in fact, can be a very good sign.

Jennifer could point to the moment that her previous therapy ended, which was months before she actually stopped attending sessions. That defining moment took place when Jennifer told her therapist about a picnic she had attended with friends, many of whom had young children running about. Jennifer was a married woman in her thirties who was trying to decide whether she wanted to have children herself, a question she had never before felt "normal enough" to consider. At the picnic, Jennifer worried that the children there would intuit it somehow, that there was something wrong with her, that she was not fit to be around them. A few days later, Jennifer went to therapy and told her previous therapist, somewhat defensively, about her concerns: "I told her maybe I should have been somebody's second wife so I could have skipped all that," Jennifer remembered. "Looking back, I'm not sure why I said that or what I even meant by that second-wife comment. I guess I'll never know because she didn't ask me about it or challenge it in any way. She just nodded and I'm not sure if she seemed relieved I wasn't having kids, or I took it to mean she was relieved I wasn't having kids. Either way I felt like she let this view I had of myself stand, that I was not normal enough to have a family." Jennifer had been testing reality and testing her therapist, and her therapist failed.

After that session, Jennifer dutifully kept her appointments, although she began to take more notice in the parking lot of her therapist's car, the one outfitted with child-size booster seats. Now, it seemed to Jennifer, her therapist was the doctor, and she was the patient. Her therapist was sane, and Jennifer was crazy. Her therapist was normal, and Jennifer was not normal. Her therapist was a have, and Jennifer was a have-not.

Some time later, Jennifer gave the woman a fresh opportunity to take up her fears. She mentioned another social event, this one a kid-friendly work function when Jennifer noticed herself just feeling at ease, surprising herself by frolicking with the sons and daughters of colleagues. Someone even asked her to babysit. "Maybe I *could* be somebody's mother…" Jennifer said tentatively in her session, letting her thought trail off. Rather than seeing the hope that might have been budding within Jennifer, her therapist saw the contradiction: "I thought you didn't want to have children," she said.

"I kind of hated her for that," Jennifer recalled, "and I never went back to see her again. I didn't know it at the time, but now I realize I wanted her to doubt my fear that I could never be a parent. I guess it was a useful therapy in a way because I walked away thinking that I wasn't going to be sold short like that. It made me realize she was wrong about me. I was wrong about me."

* * *

Some say children are like little scientists. They are born with a drive to make sense of the world in order to adapt to it, and in the process they develop theories about how things work. Cars go zoom. Cats go meow. Stoves can be hot, but not all the time. When theories are proven again and again, they become beliefs that then can be resistant to change. Although much of what we think of as learning involves getting to know the material world— or how *things* work—children form theories and beliefs about how people work, too. Children who are abused learn that adults can be dangerous. Children of alcoholics learn that tempers may flare at any time. Those whose siblings have problems learn that babies can be born with devastating illnesses. Teens who are sexually abused conclude that relationships are not safe.

By the time they reach adulthood, children have made up their minds not only about the world but about themselves, too, at least for the time being. Some of the conclusions that family heroes reach—*I am a fighter, I am a self-starter, I have a responsibility to do good in the world*—allow them to fly higher than might have been expected, sometimes even far above their peers, while other conclusions set them apart in more painful ways. *I have a secret. I am different. I am bad. I am alone.*

One of the most common beliefs of this sort is one that Jennifer wrestled with: that they are not normal enough to have families of their own. Just as a child who is raised in poverty learns that warm coats and shiny toys are for other kids, those who go without love or protection learn that these are things other people get to have. "I'd not only never been in love, but I hadn't ever dreamed of it. It was something that existed for other people—people who had families and homes," said Marilyn Monroe in *My Story.*

Or they feel changed for the worse by their experiences, so much so they fear they are unlovable. Consider this passage by Elizabeth Smart from her memoir, also called *My Story*: "I couldn't help but stare at them. They seemed so happy. So in love. So normal," she recalled thinking in response to seeing an old, married couple walk hand in hand along a boardwalk as she trudged along with her captors. "I'm never going to have such happiness. I'll never have such a life. I'll never have a real husband. I'll never have any children of my own," Smart concluded at the time, yet years later this turned out not to be the case.

Monroe's and Smart's life stories are exceptional in many ways, but their conclusions about love and family are all too common. They are the same ones I hear from family heroes nearly every day. Love is for other people. Happy families are for other people. I'm too busy surviving to think about thriving. Indeed, some researchers argue that, from an evolutionary perspective, positive emotions such as love are somewhat "extravagant" because, although they contribute to our overall well-being and to our long-term fitness in terms of health and reproduction, they are not needed in the here and now of fight or flight. And extravagant is precisely how love and family can feel for many family heroes—like a luxury they may never know.

Here, for many family heroes, the resemblance to superheroes continues. Superheroes may defeat villains and save the world, yet most often they come home alone. Superman may be able to leap tall buildings in a single bound, but he cannot seem to find his way out of the love triangle among himself, Lois Lane, and his alter ego Clark Kent. Wonder Woman may have a Lasso of Truth but, like Superman, she cannot confess to being trapped in a three-way with Steve Trevor and her earthly identity Diana Prince. Batman cycles through many, many lovers but is perpetually unlucky in love. And in one of the most tragic story lines in comic-book history, Spider-Man accidentally kills the love of his life—Gwen Stacy—as he attempts to save her from a fall.

Once in a while, superheroes find lovers and partners—and even occasionally become married—but their happiness never seems to last for long. For one reason or another, most superheroes (or their writers) cannot figure out how to be who they are and have love at the same time. Their days and nights are too busy, too dangerous, and maybe even too unhealthy for partners, much less for children. This is a problem because if, as many have argued, close relationships are one of the key contributors to a good life, then—as researchers Christopher Peterson and Nansook Park note in *The Psychology of Superheroes*—"superheroes are anything but super in these terms."

* * *

Jennifer's father backhanded her mother so often that, all her life in her mind's eye, she could see that particular crab-colored pinky-red hue, the look of flesh that had been slapped hard. When she was a little girl, she could not understand why her parents had married each other, although to hear her mother tell it, "Everything was fine until we had you. The day you were born your father stopped getting his way." This was puzzling to Jennifer because all she had ever known was his getting almost nothing but his way. The family ate his favorite foods and watched his favorite television shows. They tiptoed around his early bedtimes and pretended not to be bothered when he banged out of the house for his early predawn shifts at work.

Later, Jennifer would come to understand that, after twenty years in the military, Jennifer's father was more of a confirmed bachelor than an eligible one when he met Jennifer's mother, a vision-impaired woman with a high school education. Jennifer's mother may have thought that being married was a bargain that would bring security, but Jennifer's father hated spending money he worked for on other people, so he often left his wife's and daughter's bills unpaid. Jennifer knew this because more than once she sat in the waiting room of her pediatrician's office while the receptionist explained that, unless Jennifer's mother had cash, the girl could not be seen. After Jennifer had braces put on her teeth, her orthodontist refused to take them off until he was paid in full, which for a long time he was not. When Jennifer got her first period and told her mother she needed sanitary pads, her mother shrieked in a panic, "We can't ask your father for any more money this week!"

During these years, Jennifer learned that doctors were for other people, safety was for other people, and happy families were for other people, too. Jennifer's father reminded his family that, whatever their privation, life for them was better than what he had endured in the military. Most days Jennifer's mother pretended this was true. Then, on one unusual afternoon, she declared she could not sit on a threadbare couch one more day, and with Jennifer's help she dragged the hulking piece of furniture through the family room and hoisted it off the railing of their back deck. When Jennifer saw it crash to the cement below with a thud, she felt hopeful, like something was going to change. When her father came home, he broke Jennifer's mother's arm, and now it was Jennifer who was shrieking in a panic, begging him to stop.

"Marriage is for better or worse," was all Jennifer's mother would say later.

*   *   *

In the United States, domestic violence—or what is more accurately known as intimate partner violence—is one of the most common forms of violent crime. An estimated two to four million women are the victims of domestic violence each year, and it is the leading cause of injury to women between the ages of fifteen and forty-four. About one-quarter to one-third of women who seek medical care at an emergency department are there because of intimate partner violence, although only about 5 percent of cases are identified as such.

Jennifer's father thought that home was a more fortunate place to be than the military, and in many ways it is or should be, but between 2001 and 2012, nearly double the number of women in the United States were killed by their husbands than troops were killed by war in Afghanistan or Iraq. As is the case with most adversities, domestic violence cuts across race, class, and socioeconomic lines, but women with disabilities, like Jennifer's mother, are especially vulnerable. The vast majority of women, disabled or not, say they feel unable to leave their abusers, at least in part because of money. They fear they would be unable to support themselves and their children so, often, they and their children stay put.

According to the National Survey of Children's Exposure to Violence, about 20 percent of youth—or about fifteen million children under the age of eighteen—will witness some form of intimate partner violence: pushing, slapping, hitting, punching, kicking, choking, stabbing, or even shooting. Males are the most common perpetrators of domestic violence, although females can be the aggressors, too. In families in which such violence occurs, the mean number of incidents is eleven, but the median number is three and the standard deviation is twenty-two. What this means is that while there are many, many homes in which violence takes place once or twice, there are also homes in which such aggression occurs dozens if not hundreds of times over the course of a child's life. Jennifer's house was one of the latter.

Children may be exposed to partner violence when they overhear physical fights from another part of the home, or they may see bruises or cuts or broken furniture after the fact, or a parent or sibling may confide in the child about what has gone on. Most often, however—an estimated 90 percent of the time—children who have been exposed to violence have directly witnessed one adult physically hurting another. And though these children have been called silent witnesses, they often are not so silent. About half of children exposed to partner violence report yelling at one of the adults involved in the hope of making it stop.

When those who witness domestic violence are not physically hurt—when they themselves are not the targets of violence—they may be thought of as spared from harm, or even as the fortunate ones in a family. Of course, children who grow up alongside violence feel neither spared nor fortunate. In fact, being close to violence leads to similar developmental consequences as being the victim of physical abuse, impacting the brain and the body in the same ways. Like children who live with any form of chronic adversity, those who live with domestic violence are more likely than their peers to suffer from stress-related illnesses such as depression, sleeping problems, substance abuse, and anxiety. For these reasons, simply growing up alongside domestic violence—if *simply* is the right word to use—is now recognized as a form of childhood maltreatment, an adversity in its own right.

More difficult to measure than levels of stress hormones or depression, however, is what chronic adversity—especially the sort that happens at the hands of trusted others—does to relationships. Human beings are social animals, and we come into this world wired to connect with, and to learn from, family and friends. Especially as children, our survival and pleasure depend on it. Yet when those who have a biological or moral imperative to love and protect us fail to do so, it is difficult to imagine that anyone else ever would. This undercuts not only our most basic feelings of trust but also our most ordinary hopes and dreams. Looking for love seems treacherous, or futile.

After many years of trying, what seemed futile to Jennifer was helping her mom. "I tried to save her but she wouldn't listen so I had to save myself," Jennifer said about leaving home to live with her grandparents. When Jennifer stormed out of the house one last time, and into the waiting car of a friend, her mother shouted after her, "You'll understand one day when you have children!"—as if Jennifer was going to make the same choices, as if her life was going to turn out just the same way.

* * *

The notion that history repeats itself is accepted as a truism. From what her mother said, Jennifer could expect to find herself similarly stuck one day, trapped in an unhappy marriage with a child she could not protect. Maybe—her mother seemed to be suggesting—she would even be a victim of domestic violence herself, or perhaps an abuser. It does seem to almost go without saying that children who are raised in unhappy families are in grave danger of becoming like the adults with whom they live. But maybe worse than its going without saying is that there are countless everyday expressions to remind us that this is supposedly true. The apple does not fall far from the tree. Like father, like son. Like mother, like daughter. You cannot be what you cannot see. Violence begets violence. Water seeks its level.

To be sure, children learn by observing others, and they often imitate what they see. Among the best-known studies of observational learning are the groundbreaking experiments by Albert Bandura, a psychology researcher at Stanford University, involving the Bobo doll. A Bobo doll is an adult-size blow-up doll in the shape of a bowling pin and usually painted to look like a clown; it is weighted on the bottom such that if it is knocked over it will bounce back up again. In 1961, Bandura tapped preschoolers at the Stanford University Nursery School, some of whom were shown an adult physically abusing the Bobo doll—punching it, hitting it in the face with a mallet, and kicking it high into the air. Later, when these same preschoolers were able to interact with the Bobo doll, those who had seen an adult beat it up were more likely to do the same. The Bobo doll study is iconic in that it famously supplied powerful data and imagery—photos of the adults and children beating up Bobo can be found in almost any introductory psychology text—to support the commonsense notion "monkey see, monkey do."

Bandura's seminal work provided the theoretical foundation for what is commonly known as the "cycle of violence," or the widely held view that those who are exposed to some sort of abuse will become abusers or victims themselves. The problem with the notion of the cycle of violence, or what is more formally known as the intergenerational transmission of abuse, is that it makes dysfunction sound like an infinite loop that one cannot get out of when, in fact, the evidence for the cycle of violence is rather sparse. Studies of the cycle of violence are rife with methodological problems, including being unable to rule out other contributing factors such as poverty or alcohol or education, and relying too heavily on extreme case studies or unusual clinical samples. In one review that examined every study of the intergenerational transmission of abuse published between 1975 and 2000, only ten out of two hundred studies were adequately designed to make statements about causality and only one used a nationally representative sample; from these data, authors concluded that the evidence for the cycle of violence was inconsistent at best. Similarly, a meta-analysis of intergenerational intimate partner violence conducted in the year 2000 concluded that a family history of violence had only a small to moderate effect on whether one would become involved in an abusive relationship in adulthood. Further studies conducted since the year 2000 have found the relationship between family violence in childhood and adulthood to be weak, except in the severest of cases.

What this means is that while a cycle of violence exists in some families, it does not exist in most. The majority of children exposed to violence will not themselves become involved in violent relationships, as too many other variables—individual strengths, positive aspects of their surroundings, other influential relationships—matter at least as much. Importantly, this holds true for other types of abuse as well—whether that abuse is physical, emotional, sexual, or related to alcohol or drugs—and for other adversities that many family heroes fear might be handed down from parent to child. Although some who are sexually abused in childhood will go on to become perpetrators, most will not. Parenting style has not been shown to be passed cleanly like a baton from generation to generation, and neither has divorce. Even for problems in which heredity is known to play a role—such as depression and alcoholism—it is estimated that genes are only responsible for about half of the variance in the outcomes; the rest can be attributed to other factors within the person and the environment.

Taken together, the evidence for the "cycle of" just about any kind of adversity discussed in these chapters is thin. It is far more accurate to say that what is passed down within a family or a community is a risk for such problems, but being at risk for something is not the same thing as being destined for—or doomed to—any particular outcome. Similarly, a family history of breast cancer or heart disease may increase by some margin the likelihood that we will experience similar health problems, but it in no way guarantees that we will suffer from these ills. In fact, awareness of the risks may even spur us toward making intentional, conscious, healthy, protective choices. A family history of unhappiness can do the same.

Consider this story, a parable that a minister shared with me as we talked about the phenomenon of the family hero. Two brothers are raised in a home in which the father is an abuser and an alcoholic. One brother grows up to be a heavy drinker and an absent parent, while the other becomes an abstinent man who cares deeply and gently for his partner and children. When asked by the minister how they think they came to be who they were, both brothers gave the same answer: "Given who my father was, how could I not?" Where some see the inevitability of sameness, others see an imperative to be different.

*   *   *

Children do learn a lot from their parents and from others in their social milieu, but observational learning goes beyond monkey see, money do. In 1963, Bandura conducted a follow-up study to his famous Bobo doll experiment in which preschoolers witnessed an adult being aggressive against the Bobo doll, only this time the aggression was rewarded with praise and treats in one condition of the experiment, while in another condition the aggression was reprimanded and punished. Preschoolers who saw that aggression led to bad things were less likely to copy what they saw than those who saw that aggression led to rewards. Though unfortunately lesser known than the original Bobo doll study, this experiment showed that even preschoolers pay attention not only to the actions of others but also to the consequences of those actions.

"A wise man learns from the mistakes of others," it is said. Although we tend to think of role models as those who show us the way forward, some of our most influential models serve as cautionary tales. We watch them go down paths that we decidedly do not follow. They are people we vow never to be. In one qualitative study of youth who had been exposed to domestic violence, some, like Jennifer, worried that they, too, would wind up trapped in unhappy relationships; yet even more said that they had learned from their parents' misdeeds. They paid close attention to how their suitors conducted themselves, choosing to stay far away from those who reminded them of a troubled mother or father. Because they did not take good relationships for granted, some even felt particularly poised to make careful choices.

"To see the parent is not to be the parent," wrote Leonard Shengold in *Soul Murder.* So it went for New York City mayor Bill de Blasio, a man whose father returned from World War II a hero, only to become a distant alcoholic, before ultimately committing suicide when de Blasio was eighteen. By his twenties, de Blasio had changed his last name to the family name on his mother's side. And though he said there was a time when he questioned his ability to have a family himself, he went on to become a man for whom his partner and children are central. Looking back, de Blasio credits his father for his military service and with teaching him some "very, very powerful personal lessons in terms of how to live life." From his father, Mr. de Blasio says, "I learned primarily negative lessons. I learned what not to do."

The power of doing things differently—of breaking the cycle, whatever that cycle is—cannot be overstated. And empowering was how it felt for Jennifer, who in adulthood went on to do just about everything differently than her parents had. She worked her way into a stable career, so that she would always be able to pay for the doctor or her toiletries or the things she needed. She chose a partner who was nothing like her father, and when they married they wrote their own vows, affirming their commitment but leaving out the words *for better or for worse*. "I heard those words as an excuse too many times," she said.

More haunting were the words Jennifer's mother shouted after her on the day she left home—"You'll understand when you have children!"—and this, Jennifer said, was what she feared most. "It is not that I don't want to forgive my parents. I do forgive them. And I feel compassion for them. But I don't want to understand them. To me, understanding them means excusing them. It means having a life so much like theirs that I might do the same things. Nothing is more terrifying than the thought that I would have worked so hard to get away from how I grew up but then just wind up turning out like them. If having a baby means that I have to be more understanding...then I cannot do it." When I suggested to Jennifer that, once she had children, rather than being more understanding of her parents, she might find she is even *less* understanding of the choices they made, she began to cry with relief.

* * *

"Whenever people ask me about having children or not having children, I never tell them what to do. I simply say, 'There is no experience like having children.' That's all. There is no substitute for it. You cannot do it with a friend. You cannot do it with a lover. If you want the experience of having complete responsibility for another human being, and to learn how to love and bond in the deepest way, then you should have children." These are the words of Morris Schwartz, the sociology professor who is the subject of the memoir by Mitch Albom, *Tuesdays with Morrie*. They are also the words I find myself wanting to say to every family hero who ponders having children of their own.

Having a child is a choice, and one sure way to do life differently than one's parents is never to become a mother or a father at all. Knowing all too well that marriage may not work, that childhood may not be happy, and that not all parents are up to the task, being a parent may seem especially risky to family heroes. Some decide not to have children because they are tired of taking care of others—"I just want finally to live for me," said one client of mine—and this is a good thing to know about yourself. But for Jennifer, there had been something melancholy about that solution, the one she had floated like a trial balloon in her previous therapy several years before. It had never been so much that she did not *want* children as much as she thought that, because of the way she was parented, she may not be fit to have them. Or she worried that by having children she might become trapped somehow in a life like her mother's, and the cycle of abuse and unhappiness would go around again.

What Jennifer could not quite see—or trust—was that having a family of one's own is as much an opportunity to break with the past as it is to repeat it. James Rhodes, the concert pianist who once never expected to become, in his words, "a stand-up, productive, normalised member of society," struggled with becoming a parent, too. Terrified that his child might suffer as he had—or because he had—Rhodes said he wished he could see it as simply as this: "That my son being born was the beginning of the end of my old life and the start of a new, much more fulfilling life." I am not saying it is simple for family heroes to have children—and to feel reborn in the process, too—but I am saying it is possible. It does happen.

To her surprise—and relief—this was the way it went for Jennifer, who, once her first child was born, did indeed feel like she woke up every day in a whole new world. The world itself had not changed, of course, which Jennifer remembered noting on her way home from the hospital. She watched with a curious detachment as the other cars sped by—racing people to work or restaurants or stores or homes—as if nothing was different when, for Jennifer, everything was. As she rode along in the backseat of the car next to her new baby, he looked at her with eyes as open, and as unconcerned with the past, as the sky.

People say that having children makes us tourists in our own cities, as we find ourselves visiting parks and museums and zoos that, before, we scarcely knew existed. As Jennifer's son—and then daughter—grew to be young children, she felt like a tourist in her very own life. It was not just that she went to new places, of course. Now Jennifer had new preoccupations, new priorities. She has a new role and a new identity, too. There were pleasures she had never known, like when her daughter returned from kindergarten with an "All About Me" worksheet on which in response to the prompt "I feel…" she wrote in her six-year-old scrawl, "peaceful at home." Seeing the world through the eyes of a happy child was something she had never done before.

"Avenger" might seem like a strange title for a chapter about having a family, but some family heroes out there, I think, may understand. Living well is the best revenge, as they say, and to some, having children is the ultimate act of living well. It can be the most personal way of fighting back, and of making things right. In an interview on National Public Radio, author Jonathan Safran Foer recalled how his grandmother, a Holocaust survivor, spoke about what having children and grandchildren meant to her: "She would say, 'like other people have diamonds and pearls, you're my diamonds and pearls. You're my revenge.' Her happiness… her definition of happiness was completely bound up in response to what had happened to her family. And, you know, her joy was her revenge."

Jennifer's children were her diamonds and pearls, too, and she treasured moments she once could not imagine would ever be hers. When her son brought her handfuls of rocks as if they were the most precious of gems, which, of course, they were. When she watched both children hop off the school bus and run headlong toward the house, in stark contrast with the way she had once run away from her own. When she heard them racing to the dinner table, excited with anticipation about whether any of their favorite foods might be served. "I don't remember having any favorite foods," Jennifer said, "much less having any hope that I might get them."

Research tells us that ordinary experiences make us happier as we age. This is perhaps nowhere more true than for the family hero, those for whom the ordinary can feel like something extraordinary. It feels luxurious simply to live in a home that feels like a safe place. It feels extravagant just to be able to meet our children's needs—and our own. The average and expectable can feel remarkable and surprising. To have love and a family can feel like justice one never expected to see.

"I never thought I would have a life like this," Jennifer said. "I never felt like I mattered to anybody when I was younger. Now when my kids come running to the door to greet me, or wave frantically from the window when I head off on the smallest errand, I matter so much it hurts. It's so wonderful it's terrifying." Jennifer had never had anything to lose before, and sometimes—maybe often—she feared her good fortune could not last. That she found profound joy and meaning and vulnerability in parenting was hardly unusual—it was just normal—and to her, that was the most remarkable part.

* * *

The way Jennifer lived now—in the present—it was sometimes as if her childhood had never happened at all. There were moments, of course, when she had to reckon with being motherless and fatherless all over again in brand-new ways. She felt sad for her children—and for herself—as she watched grandmas and grandpas swoop into town to hold new babies or to go to school for Grandparents Day or to give even the smallest advice. "I parent by Amazon," Jennifer said, meaning that most of what she knew about what sort of blanket or book or bike to buy for her children came from her own research and from the reviews that she read from other parents online.

She hid these moments from her son and her daughter, much as she had once hidden her troubles from her friends, and she cried in my office in anticipation of the day that they would have to know something about how she grew up. "I wish I could just never tell them. I don't want to lie to my kids but I don't want them to think about my parents when they look at me or try to understand me. Or when they try to understand themselves. I worked so hard to put all that behind me and to give them a different life. I don't want them to worry about me. I don't want to be some sad story. I just want to be their mom." All her life, Jennifer had looked at her mother and seen her predicament. She wanted to be different from her mother, not only by giving her children a home where they felt cared for and protected, but also by not having a predicament, a plight for them to see.

"Who are your parents?" Jennifer's eight-year-old son wanted to know as they ate dinner in a pizza parlor one night. He had drawn a family tree at school and could not quite figure out how his mother's family members fit together. Jennifer fumbled through an explanation about her mother and father, about how some people have problems that make it difficult for them to be good parents, to really enjoy being a parent like she enjoyed it, so she went to live with her grandparents, who could care for her like a mom or dad should. In a way, she had different parents at different times, Jennifer explained. A mom and a dad she lived with when she was young but, by now, she explained, her grandparents were her parents, too.

Her son blinked a time or two as she spoke and he listened. For what seemed like minutes, she looked into those same wide eyes she remembered from the car ride home from the hospital, only this time rather than being unconcerned with the past her son was having to take it all in.

Jennifer waited with shallow breaths for his reaction.

"I see you in a whole new light," he said finally and declaratively, which is precisely what Jennifer had feared all along.

Her heart sank. She was speechless.

"You're...you're human," he continued, his eyes now sparkling with something like delight. "You're like Cinderella."

Stunned and relieved, Jennifer smiled through tears. Her son did not see her as a sad story at all. To him, she was a real person who had had a painful beginning but found love and happiness in the end.

CHAPTER 17

Redemption

Love is the prerogative of the brave.

—Gandhi

In 1938—the same year that Superman debuted on the cover of his first comic book—Harvard physician and researcher Arlen Bock began what would become the longest-running study of well-being in history. He did so with the financial backing of a benefactor, dime store magnate William T. Grant, the Sam Walton of his day. Intended to be a revolutionary correction against the tendency in medical research to study sick people, the Study of Adult Development—or "the Grant Study" as, colloquially, it would forever be known—set out to better understand those who seemed destined to do well.

Subjects in the Grant Study were 268 Harvard students, carefully chosen because they were deemed to be intellectually, physically, and emotionally sound. Born toward the end of World War I, this was a group that grew up during the Roaring Twenties and were teenagers during the Great Depression. A sign of the times, the Grant subjects were white and male, and many, but not most, enjoyed privileged upbringings. Some were from families that had been in the United States for many generations while others were immigrants. Some were upper-class, yet nearly half received some form of financial aid. Half of the subjects' parents had no college degree, and many had seen hard times including poverty, alcoholism in the family, or the death of a parent. Yet one way or another, each of these men had made it to Harvard, and as a group they seemed likely to go on to lead successful lives. Many did.

Known to investigators only by code names and numbers, some became distinguished professionals such as senators or judges and, over time, a few of their identities have been made public. Ben Bradlee, the former executive editor of the *Washington Post*, opened his memoir with his experience of being a subject in the Grant Study, and President John F. Kennedy was revealed to be a Grant man, too. Pioneers it seemed, Bock and Grant had launched what, according to the *Harvard Crimson*, "might one day be one of Harvard's most important contributions to society, the analysis of the 'normal' person." Yet the analysis of the normal person was not quite what the study's founders were after. Both men were aiming to discover the secrets of what they called "superachievers."

While some studies in social science "go wide" by collecting a small amount of data from a large number of subjects, from the outset the Grant Study planned to go deep. In 1938, biological determinism ruled the day, and as it was for Superman, those who succeeded in life were thought to have done so because of some inborn superstrength or superintelligence or supersomething. For this reason, Bock and his colleagues—an internist, a psychologist, a physical anthropologist, a psychiatrist, a physiologist, a caseworker, and two secretaries—delved into their subjects' health with gusto. The Grant men sat for anthropological and intelligence testing. They ran on a treadmill in the Fatigue Lab. They took the Rorschach inkblot test and had their handwriting analyzed. They underwent the newfangled EEG. Their dietary habits were recorded, too, down to how much sugar they put in their morning coffee. Medical exams were so extensive, researchers made note of every physical attribute from brow ridges to organ functioning to "hanging length of [the] scrotum," a detail often cited to get the point across. Caseworkers made home visits, too, to gather the men's childhood and family histories, but it would be some years before such information would be of interest to researchers.

Along the way, psychology researcher George Vaillant signed on to the Grant Study, and over time he would become its longest-serving director as well as its resident narrator, weaving decades of data into books on the lives of the Grant men. The most recent, *Triumphs of Experience*, published in 2012, summarizes what exactly became of the men as they were followed from the age of nineteen into their nineties and counting. After Harvard, more than 80 percent served in World War II in the 1940s, and then most became married and started families. From the 1950s through the 1980s, their careers and their relationships advanced or, in some cases, retreated; in the 1990s and beyond came retirement and old age. Along the way, the physical exams continued, but the Grant men also regularly completed surveys and questionnaires. They underwent personality testing. They sat for interviews. Even their spouses and children were contacted.

Bock and Grant had conceived of the Grant Study in the hope of uncovering the secrets of superachievers, but of course research and lives are rarely so simple. Not one of the Grant men enjoyed a charmed life—everyone struggled in some form or another—and not one of those innate characteristics the researchers had been so keen to record predicted what came their way. Beyond a certain point—just a standard deviation above average, in fact—higher intelligence did not lead to more success; the men with IQs in the 110-to-115 range did as well at work as those with IQs above 150. It was alcoholism—not brow ridges or teaspoons of sugar—that broke up more families than anything else. And by age fifty, almost a third of the men had met the criteria for a mental disorder such as depression or anxiety at one time or another, a finding that baffled the study's founder: "They were normal when I picked them," Bock told Vaillant in the 1960s. There is no telling what Bock's reaction would have been had he lived to hear about Vaillant's most radical finding of all, revealed when the Grant men were in their nineties, when researchers had the benefit of their whole lives to work with. Vaillant declared that, by far, the most important influence on whether the Grant men's lives had turned out well was one the study's founders had really never considered at all: love.

Twenty years after the Grant Study recruited its first subjects, in a 1958 presidential address to the American Psychological Association, psychologist Harry Harlow lamented that "psychologists not only show no interest in the origin and development of love and affection, but they seem to be unaware of its very existence." So it was for the beginning of the Grant Study, but as the study reached its conclusion, researchers could hardly ignore the facts: Those who had had love in their lives flourished at home and at work while those who went without had not done so well. Sometimes the love that made the difference took the form of a good childhood: The men with the warmest childhoods, those in which they had felt loved and cared for by someone important, made 50 percent more money than those with the bleakest upbringings; they were more likely to feel satisfied with their lives in adulthood and to have other loving relationships, too.

But before we conclude that a good life depends on having good parents, it is important to note that Vaillant was clear that love can take many forms. What he saw in the Grant men's lives is that life-altering warmth and care can come from romantic partners, friends, teachers, grandparents, aunts, uncles, mentors, nurses, and siblings. Over 90 percent of those who were thriving at age sixty-five, for example, had been close to a brother or a sister when they were young. And quite poignantly, Vaillant saw that love can come from a source we just talked about in the previous chapter: children. "You know what I learned from my children? I learned love!" exclaimed one Grant man. "What it looks like is different for everybody," Vaillant concluded. "But love is love."

Of the longitudinal study, P. D. Scott said, "The follow-up is the great exposer of truth, the rock upon which fine theories are wrecked and upon which better ones can be built." The truth that the lives of the Grant men exposed is one that its founders surely never expected to find, and to be sure it wrecked their fine theory that well-being could be traced to a single biological variable such as brainwaves or intelligence. In retrospect, it seems almost naive to have set out on such a seemingly simplistic search, yet maybe Bock and Grant were not so naive after all; they were just looking in the wrong places. In the words of George Vaillant, the key to well-being in adulthood is not as complicated as one might expect: "The seventy-five years and twenty million dollars expended on the Grant Study points, at least to me, to a straightforward five-word conclusion: Happiness is love. Full stop."

* * *

The Grant Study's Harvard men may not be the most generalizable of samples, but Vaillant has a point. Many, many studies from around the world have suggested that relationships may be the most important source of meaning in our lives. And in study after study of resilience in particular, especially ones that look at lives across many years, love emerges as a powerful force for good. In the National Longitudinal Study of Adolescent Health, a study of more than twelve thousand individuals, what most protected at-risk teens from poor outcomes was feeling connected to a parent or a teacher or a mentor. In another longitudinal endeavor, this one a fourteen-year study of nearly seven hundred diverse youth and their families, it was parents, friends, teachers, mentors, relatives, and lovers who were the "lifelines" that saved those who found themselves swimming against the current. In more research, this tracing the lives of three hundred teenage mothers over seventeen years, the support of parents or significant others made it more likely for these young women to excel at school and in work. In a famed study of five hundred impoverished and delinquent urban youth, those who felt connected to work and love in adulthood were least likely to remain in the justice system. And in one study we have already heard about—the Kauai Study—only one in six of the struggling teens became struggling adults, with a good marriage to a stable and loving partner (or, in some cases, a good second marriage after an impulsive first one) being one of the most pivotal "second-chance opportunities" in adulthood. Part of the untold story of the family hero then is that, for many, love is the greatest reboot of all.

Not so many chapters ago, we saw how, often, family heroes find creative ways to start over in adulthood. They let themselves play with the notion, and with the reality, that life could be different than it used to be; that past does not have to be prologue. Many begin by changing their addresses or their occupations or their names, because family heroes tend to be independent problem solvers and those are the kind of solutions that can be worked out on one's own. Sometimes less well understood—at least for family heroes, that is—is how new relationships with others might help them begin again, too.

The connection between good relationships and a good life is one of the most consistent findings in social science research, yet if "happiness is love," as George Vaillant said, many family heroes struggle with the near-conviction that they may never have either. Love, you may recall, seems like it exists only for other people. It is a luxury, to be enjoyed by those who are thriving, but far out of reach of those who are just surviving. It is an extravagance that seems to have no place in fight or flight. Too often, family heroes may feel how Superman looked when he first appeared on that comic-book cover in 1938: Strong and tall, he is running fast and holding a big smashed-up green car high above his head while the bad guys scatter in all directions. Love, however, is nowhere in sight.

* * *

In 1958, the same year that psychologist Harry Harlow lamented that his colleagues seemed hardly to be aware of a thing called love, psychoanalyst John Bowlby published a paper, "The Nature of the Child's Tie to His Mother," to change all that. In those pages he put forth the beginnings of what would later be known as attachment theory, or the notion that babies are born to connect with those around them. According to Bowlby, love is hardly evolutionarily extravagant. It may *feel* extravagant to those who have been deprived of it, but to love and be loved is instinctual and innate and crucial to our survival. We come into the world crying and clinging to our caregivers—usually our mothers or fathers—and then smiling at them and following along behind them because it is adaptive. Whether we feel hunger or doubt on the inside or danger or cold from the outside, it is in the shelter of others where we find security and relief, whether we are infants or children or adults. "All of us, from cradle to grave, are happiest when life is organized as a series of excursions, long or short, from the secure base provided by our attachment figures," Bowlby said. Seeking closeness and love is a coping mechanism—perhaps the most adaptive one of all—and it is how we both survive and thrive.

Consider for a moment the story of Viola Davis, the Oscar-, Emmy-, and Tony-winning actor. Hers is a supernormal tale if there ever was one: "I consider myself a hero," Davis said in a 2016 interview with John Lahr in the *New Yorker*. "I don't have a cape, I don't have a golden lasso. I had a call to adventure, a call to live life bigger than myself." Davis grew up in extreme poverty with a father who was an alcoholic and who regularly beat Davis's mother. Davis and her sister routinely went without clean clothes or food—school lunch was their most reliable meal—and she carried a crochet needle in her coat pocket to protect herself from racial violence in her mostly white Rhode Island neighborhood. Because of their troubles at home, the girls were often in trouble at school, but Davis said there seemed nowhere they could turn for help: "It wasn't an option to out ourselves," she recalled.

To help themselves instead, Davis and her sister used make-believe and after-school activities to fight back against, and flee from, their circumstances: "We were like hunters," Davis said. "Even if we didn't really have any interest, we'd do it just to get out, just to channel ourselves into something." Ultimately, acting was both girls' way out and, in adulthood, Davis made her way to Juilliard, the New York stage, and Hollywood, places where she has won dozens of awards, more than a hundred nominations, and a star on the Walk of Fame.

Yet as Davis told Lahr, "The big 'Aha!' moment is that the trauma never goes away." By her mid-thirties, Davis had had only one romantic relationship, and this with a man who told her he loved her only one time. She tackled anxiety and low self-esteem in therapy, and this also turned out to be the place where she gathered the nerve to give love another try: "The moment I met my husband, all of it stopped. The worry, the anxiety. Everything." That might sound a little too easy, and maybe it does not always happen quite like that, but science is on Davis's side.

* * *

"We are the sum of all of the moments of our lives—all that is ours is in them," wrote Thomas Wolfe in *Look Homeward, Angel*. By now, it should be clear that repetitive, negative moments have an impact on our hearts and minds, and for all the same reasons, repetitive, positive moments do, too. Just as stressful experiences with others trigger the amygdala, boost stress hormones, and tax our brains and our bodies, soothing experiences with our loved ones have the opposite effect.

When we feel the support of a teacher or mentor, or we find comfort in the shelter of a caring parent or lover, or we take care of our children, or we enjoy a lighthearted moment with a friend, our amygdalae are quieted and our stress hormone levels are lowered. The reward systems in our brains are activated instead; we perceive that something good has happened and as a result we feel good all over. Physical intimacy—holding hands, touching, hugging, kissing, having sex—reduces stress hormones, too, and it boosts our levels of oxytocin and vasopressin, also known as the love hormones. Even just seeing photos of our loved ones calms us down, and our internal alarms are turned off.

Love does not just calm our brains, however. It changes them, and maybe faster and better than anything else. As love quiets the amygdala and reduces stress hormones, the brain becomes less concerned with fight or flight and is more open to newer, more expansive learning. Throughout life, the brain adapts and readapts to the world around, such that if the world changes, then the brain changes, too. This is neuroplasticity, and not only does this concept apply *to* love, but psychologist Louis Cozolino argues that "the greatest contributor to [neuroplasticity] *is* love." Just as birds learn their songs more quickly from other birds than from recordings, and children learn better from interactions with others than from videos, adults learn most effectively in relationships, too.

Over time, then, one moment at a time, feel-good experiences—whatever they are and whoever they come from—result in a host of benefits for the body and the brain: lower blood pressure, lower cardiovascular reactivity to stress, reduced risk of heart disease, improved immune functioning, decreased depression and anxiety, improved sleep, increased longevity, increased feelings of trust, enhanced openness, larger social networks, and better creative and cognitive functioning. If as Robert Block said in front of that Senate committee, childhood adversity "may be the leading cause of poor health among adults in the United States," our positive experiences with others in adulthood may be the leading cause of good health, and of happiness, too.

What all this means is that feeling good is more than just a break from feeling bad. Positive experiences are reparative, in that they are able to correct for negative experiences. Psychology researcher Barbara Fredrickson calls this the "undoing effect" that goes along with positive feelings and above all, with love. Love defies simple definition, to be sure, which is why theorists like Fredrickson tend to use the word almost as an umbrella term for the good feelings we experience—joy, gratitude, contentment, interest, hope, pride, amusement, inspiration, awe—in the context of a mutually caring relationship. Love, then, carries the double advantage of positivity plus connection, offsetting the harm of both stress and isolation. Acting something like a medicine, it downshifts our bodies and minds and it speeds our recovery from hard times. It may sound like the stuff of clichés to say that love heals, but love has a perhaps unequaled power to mend the strain and trauma that have come before.

* * *

Here I recognize that I have presented the reader with a conflict, and it is the same one that family heroes face every day. Many chapters ago, when we learned about origin stories, we learned that our brains are wired to keep us alive, not happy, and it is for this reason that "bad is stronger than good": "bad emotions, bad parents, and bad feedback have more impact than good ones, and bad information is processed more thoroughly than good," said researcher Roy Baumeister. This is why our most difficult moments tend to have an outsize effect on our autobiographies and our lives. Yet as we also just heard, love can be extraordinarily powerful, too.

For many family heroes, then, their greatest—and often last—battle is not one between good and bad out in the world; it is between good and bad on the inside, as our good and bad experiences vie for supremacy in our hearts and minds. This is not an easy battle—and it is one that our brains have not necessarily set us up to win—but it is one worth fighting nonetheless.

There are dangers, of course, and a lot of fears. I hear about them every day: People are too much work. I never know what they are going to want from me. I don't want to take on any new problems. Relationships are not worth the risk. It is not worth being scared all the time. It's not worth being stuck. It's not worth being controlled. It's not worth being hurt. I don't want to wind up like what I saw every day as a kid. I've spent my life trying to get away from that. I don't want to have to make someone else happy. I don't want to take care of anyone else. The world is not a good place. I've been through enough.

It is true that most family heroes have been through enough, and any new relationship carries the risk that they will be hurt again as they were before. Remember, home is the most dangerous place in America—and even outside the home, more of us are hurt in the contexts of relationships than anywhere else—and, for this reason, these can be the most difficult places to be brave. This was true for Helen, the first woman we met, who lost her brother and her father and who raced to her therapy session like a superhero: "I'd gone all around the world and fought for all kinds of justice but the most courageous thing I ever did was to come home and face my own problems. To love my mom even though her heart might always be too broken to really love me back. To face having a family of my own even though I knew I could lose them."

It takes courage to go beyond our own experiences, not just to try to live in places we may have never seen before, but to try to have the kind of relationships we may have never seen before.

It is daring to open ourselves up to other people even though we do not know how they are going to respond, and to stay open to the possibility that for every person who does not "get it" there is someone out there who does.

It is audacious to hope that we might have better lives than our parents not just at work but at home, too, or that we might be the first in our families to find love.

It is bold to believe that we are deserving of good treatment—not because we have done something good but simply because we are good—and that others might even give it to us.

It takes spirit to remember and be grateful for those who cared for us along the way, those who may not have been able to take our problems away but who mattered nonetheless.

Viola Davis was right that the trauma never goes away, but she was also correct that love can conquer fear. Hers is just one story, but it is a story I have heard countless times before, one that has been in these pages, in some form or another, all along. Here is some of what we have seen.

Having a good partner can be as powerful as having a bad parent. Sam, the man whose father left him with torn-up ten-dollar bills and lottery tickets, vowed never to get married, changing his mind only when he met a woman who understood his grief, and his determination not to get divorced himself: "You lost a dad, too," she said. Sam never forgot his painful memories, of course, but his new memories are what matter now. "My wife is the best thing that ever happened to me," he says with a lightheartedness he never expected to know. "Sometimes it feels like she's the only thing that ever happened to me."

Giving someone a good childhood can be even better than receiving one. Just as "helping helps the helper," getting to be the good person in someone's life—in our children's lives—can reward us beyond all measure, even leave us with a sense of wonder and awe. "I used to think because of the way I grew up I was less cut out than other people to be a parent. Now I think I may actually be more cut out for it than other people," says Jennifer about her experience of treasuring being a mother. "In the smallest ways, every day, I cannot believe this is my life."

Good people are almost always a part of the story, even if they can only play supporting roles. Elizabeth, the doctor who felt she needed to be a supersibling for her brother, says her most important "cradle-to-grave" relationship has been with her sister: "We have a bond that a lot of siblings—or spouses—don't have. We'll be taking care of my brother as long as we live so, in a lot of ways, she's my life partner." And for Anton, the man who left home to reboot himself, his relationship with his first girlfriend did not last but her effect on him did: "How we lived changed what I thought was possible in life. I saw I could be loved, and be happy. How she looked at me changed how I saw myself, and it changed what I became."

Love is not confined to the home. When Calvin, the man who had not been permitted to go to school as a child, looks back on the good people in his life, he remembers the teacher whose letter made it possible for him to go off to a four-year college: "For him, it was a small thing to do, but that letter got me out of the captivity that was my life. He may not have loved me or hardly even known me but he changed everything for me. I will always love him for that, and I wrote him a letter a few years ago telling him so." According to trauma expert Bessel van der Kolk, healing from trauma is "as much about remembering how we survived as it is about what is broken." Often it is about remembering who out there in the world helped us survive, too.

There is a difference between vigilance and fear. It takes courage—but some self-awareness and watchfulness, as well—to choose relationships that will not hurt us more. Paul, the navy officer, credits his father with encouraging him not only to stand up for himself but also to pick his battles: "I am probably more guarded than some people—I choose my friends carefully—but I decided I was not going to let bullying shut me off from the whole world." Jessie, the woman with the owl tattoo, was careful to find a spouse with whom she slept more soundly than she had ever thought possible, and David, the social worker who wore a cape for his depressed mother, is on the lookout for a partner he does not need to save.

Community is where we find strength in numbers. Martha, the actress who fled the mamarazzi, now surrounds herself with those who do not need her to smile for the cameras—or live her life—in any particular way: "I'm not sure if dating women will always be what I want to do, but I am enjoying it now so I am listening to that." And for Rachel, who wore the Batman ring, the support that mattered most came from her friends. Sibling sexual abuse and her self-doubts loomed so large that no one person—not a therapist and not her partner—could overcome them. "I didn't want to feel normal or valuable because my fiancé loved me," she reflected. "That's too much pressure on him and on our relationship. I think it is more realistic for love to come from a lot of different people anyway."

And for some a reparative relationship is first found in therapy: "Psychoanalysis is in essence a cure through love," said Sigmund Freud. Michelle, the woman who had been abused by her coach, felt loved in therapy, yet she had trouble believing that someone who was not a professional could care for her as well. "Thank you for being the first person to tell me I was resilient and strong," she said. "If I'd had someone to talk to fifteen years ago, if someone had validated what I said, I might have had a relationship by now." But Michelle's life is not over, and maybe—if she decides she wants to—she still will.

Of course, there is no one way this story needs to go, no one place that our good experiences need to come from. Just as the brain does not know the difference between different types of adversity or stress—there is no hierarchy of trauma—it does not discriminate among different types of positivity and connection, either—there is no hierarchy of love. "Love is love," as Vaillant said.

* * *

"I had a weak father, domineering mother, contemptuous teachers, sadistic sergeants, destructive male friendships, emasculating girlfriends, a wonderful wife, and three terrific children. Where did I go right?" said Pulitzer Prize–winning cartoonist and satirist Jules Feiffer. With these words, Feiffer describes just how different our relationships—and our lives—can be in adulthood, if we dare. And it points to a second, related conclusion that George Vaillant drew from his many decades of work with the Grant men, one that I wish family heroes everywhere could hear: In the long run, what goes right matters more than what goes wrong.

In the Grant Study, Vaillant saw that—over time—the quality of one's childhood had less influence on one's life than we might expect. He found early adversities, such as health troubles or family dysfunction or economic hardships, to be poor predictors of the future. Even the death of a parent foretold little by age fifty, and by age eighty those who had lost a parent as children were as happy and healthy as those whose parents had seen their sons become adults. In both work and love, Vaillant found, it was the Grant men's successes, and not their failures, that most influenced their lives to come. Across the years, he said, it was the love they had, not the love they did not have, that mattered most.

Learning (or relearning) to love and be loved in adulthood is possible, and though it may seem somehow less desirable than always having been able to rely upon others, this sort of pathologizing is unfounded and unfair: Research shows that those who find their way into stable, satisfying relationships in adulthood can do just fine, and often as well as those who enjoyed them all along. Adult relationships are our second, third, tenth, and twentieth chances at love. For each of us, every new encounter is an opportunity to rework not just our relationships but our brains and our lives as well.

What this means is that it is never too late for one good person—or for a collection of good people—to change our lives for the better one moment, one day, one year at a time. Perhaps most often, new beginnings come from new people we meet in adulthood, but other times we reconnect with, or maybe just remember, family and friends who cared for us along the way. We have learned about the "sleeper effects" of childhood adversity— the reality that chronic stress can accumulate over time and cause problems in adulthood—and there are positive sleeper effects as well. Positive experiences can pile up, too, and then suddenly, or not so suddenly, the good outnumbers or outweighs the bad.

For those who have difficulty imagining that this could happen for you, take heart. If nothing else, time is your friend. This is because of what psychology researcher Laura Carstensen calls the "positivity effect," or the finding that, as we get older, the good gains strength on its own. We spend less time remembering bad experiences and bad people. We have more control over our lives, and we tend to set them up so that we have more meaningful and positive interactions than negative or trivial ones. We have more control over our emotions, too, so we respond less strongly to the difficult moments that do come our way. Our faith in others tends to become stronger as we move across adulthood, and so do our relationships. Overall, in the second half of life, we pay more attention to what went right rather than what went wrong.

Admittedly, most of the stories we have read about in these pages have been about men or women in the beginning or the middle of their lives. That is when family heroes tend to be in the most pain, when they stand at the place where the accumulated stress of childhood and the staggering uncertainty of the future meet. As Carstensen would predict, older adults do not come to my office so often to talk about what went wrong in childhood, and when it does come up, they tend to emphasize what went well. "A lot of things happened when I was young that were terrible, and I have accepted that I may never completely understand them," said one client of mine in her sixties. "But that was a long time ago. By now I figure I have had more years of happiness than unhappiness. I choose to focus on that." Bad may be stronger than good especially when we are young and first learning the ways and the dangers of the world, but as life goes on better days can prevail. Just as the arc of history bends toward justice, the arc of a life bends toward goodness.

CHAPTER 18

Never-Ending

Real life is messy, inconsistent, and it's seldom when anything ever really gets resolved. It's taken me a long time to realize that.
—Alan Moore, *Watchmen*

In 2013, PBS aired the first epic documentary of the comic-book genre, *Superheroes: A Never-Ending Battle*. Its title highlights the fact that Superman, Batman, Wonder Woman, Spider-Man—and other such protagonists—still fight on in the twenty-first century much as they did when they were first imagined decades ago. The relentless, unfinished nature of these stories is, in part, what resonates with family heroes, most of whom intuit there are no neat endings in store for them, either. As much as Jennifer's son, the boy who saw his mother as Cinderella, wanted to believe that the hard part was over, that now she was living the happily-ever-after, the battle between good and bad will likely go on for her, and for all of us, in one way or another, as long as we live.

If it helps, bring these words along.

Own the fighter within. Be empowered by your ability to be strong and to bound over obstacles in your way. There is no need to feel bad about the times you have been angry, to feel ashamed for refusing to accept things the way they are. This is how family heroes survive and strive but, remember, you need to find ways to create some peace for yourself, too.

Find someone to tell your secrets to. If that person says the wrong thing, try someone else. And soon. This will get easier, and your story will become more organized and understandable with every telling. It will probably become shorter as well.

Even—and especially—if you were not taken good care of as a child, take good care of yourself as an adult. Find a physician and get a physical once a year. Tell him or her that you have a history of childhood adversity, because he or she will not know it just by looking at you. Sleep eight hours a night. Eat well. Play well. Exercise well. Work well, which includes taking time off. Start now. The good does not win out in the end if your life is cut short because of chronic stress.

If you think you may be living with depression or anxiety or insomnia or some other stress-related illness, treat it like the brain health problem that it is. Find a therapist, or tell your regular doctor. Remember that to struggle does not disqualify you from being a resilient person or a good person, and neither does sometimes feeling like an antihero. If, however, you are leaning on substances to cope, try leaning on people instead. They are better for you.

So are yoga and meditation, but these are not the only ways to reduce your stress. Clear your mind of painful thoughts and feelings by becoming absorbed in what feels natural to you: Reading. Podcasts. Biking. Knitting. Running. Nature. Movies. Mental distancing is a power all its own.

And physical distancing is just fine, too. Some hurtful relationships may improve with time, but many will not. If it would be helpful to you to make amends with someone who has hurt you, give it a try. If it will only bring you more heartbreak, you have permission to stay away. Avoid relatives, partners—or bosses—who are retraumatizing.

It is wise to protect yourself from dangerous people—but be

sure your armor is not too tight to let love in. Help the good people in your life have more of a presence than the bad. Write out a list of those you feel grateful for, and maybe some heartfelt letters, too. Put pictures and reminders of those who have mattered out where you can see them every day. Fight for their importance—in your life, in your brain—just as maybe they once fought for yours.

Make something of your present so your past does not loom so large. As you go along, resist the temptation to compare your hardships or triumphs to those of others. We all have different definitions of success and adversity, and of ordinary and normal, too.

Find people to love and to love you back, and remember they may come from all backgrounds. There is no need to pick sides in life, to restrict yourself to those who have suffered as you have; a diversity of perspectives enriches us all. Nor is it fair to assume that those who have had average, expectable upbringings are better suited for living than you are. This simply is not so.

If you have children, be the parent you wish you had. Create the home you always wanted. Yet resist the impulse to protect your children from every hurt, as well as the urge to toughen them up. Life will send its slings and arrows, and when it does: Listen. Validate. Name. Empathize. Problem solve. Love. You know what to do. All the things you may wish someone had done for you.

And as often as you can, be good to yourself, and to those you encounter. It may not be true that everyone you meet is fighting a hard battle but, as we know by now, a great many people are.

NOTES

pg. xiii: **"the most basic of all human needs"**: Ralph Nichols, "The Struggle to Be Human," Keynote Address at the First Annual Convention of the International Listening Association, Atlanta, GA, February 17, 1980, https://www.listen.org/resources/Nichols%20 Struggle%20to%20be%20Human.pdf.

pg. xiii: **"bell hooks"**: bell hooks, *Talking Back: Thinking Feminist, Thinking Black* (Boston: South End Press, 1999), 9.

CHAPTER 1: SUPERNORMAL

pg. 1:   **There is no greater agony**: Although the exact source of this quote is unclear, it is widely attributed to Maya Angelou.

pg. 4:   **what is called a family hero**: The concept of the family hero is often discussed as one of the roles that children may play in families in which a mother or a father is an alcoholic. Yet, family heroes are found not only in the homes of alcoholics but also in almost any family in which, for whatever reason, a parent or a child needs saving. See, Sharon Wegscheider-Cruse, *Another Chance: Hope and Health for the Alcoholic Family* (Palo Alto, CA: Science Behavior Books, 1989); see also Geraldine J. Glover, "The Hero Child in the Alcoholic Home: Recommendations for Counselors," *School Counselor* 41, no. 3 (1994): 185–190; Barbara L. Wood, *Children of Alcoholism: The Struggle for Self and Intimacy in Adult Life* (New York: New York University Press, 1987); Peter M. Vernig, "Family Roles in Homes with Alcohol-Dependent Parents: An Evidence-Based Review," *Substance Use and Misuse* 46, no. 4 (2011): 535–542.

pg. 4:   **ask yourself the following**: This informal quiz is adapted from https:/acestoohigh .com/got-your-ace-score. Note that the ACE quiz does not include bullying in its list of adversities, nor does it include problems with siblings. These experiences are addressed in this book due to their importance and prevalence

pg. 5:   **under the umbrella of childhood adversity**: Throughout this book, when discussing hardship, I prefer the term *adversity* to the word *trauma*, as adversity is generally defined as a situation that is statistically associated with difficulty or risk, yet it still evokes the possibility that the situation can be gotten over or at least grappled with. *Trauma*, on the other hand, from the Greek word for "wound," seems just to imply damage.

pg. 5:   **75 percent of children and teens are exposed**: Centers for Disease Control and Prevention, "Adverse Childhood Experiences Reported by Adults—Five States,

2009," *Morbidity and Mortality Weekly Report* 59, no. 49 (2010): 1609–1613, http://www
.cdc.gov/mmwr/preview/mmwrhtml/mm5949a1.htm#tab2; Ronald A. Cohen et al.,
"Early Life Stress and Adult Emotional Experience: An International Perspective,"
International Journal of Psychiatry in Medicine 36, no. 1 (2006): 35–52; Maxia Dong et al.,
"The Interrelatedness of Multiple Forms of Childhood Abuse, Neglect, and Household
Dysfunction," *Child Abuse and Neglect* 28, no. 7 (2004): 771–784; Vincent J. Felitti et al.,
"Relationship of Childhood Abuse and Household Dysfunction to Many of the Lead-
ing Causes of Death in Adults: The Adverse Childhood Experiences (ACE) Study,"
American Journal of Preventive Medicine 14, no. 4 (1998): 245–258; David Finkelhor et al.,
"The Victimization of Children and Youth: A Comprehensive, National Survey,"
Child Maltreatment 10, no. 1 (2005): 5– 25; David Finkelhor et al., "Prevalence of Child-
hood Exposure to Violence, Crime, and Abuse: Results from the National Survey of
Children's Exposure to Violence," *JAMA Pediatrics* 169, no. 8 (2015): 746–754; Ruth
Gilbert et al., "Burden and Consequences of Child Maltreatment in High-Income
Countries," *Lancet* 373, no. 9657 (2009): 68–81; Jennifer S. Middlebrooks and Natalie
C. Audage, "The Effects of Childhood Stress on Health Across the Lifespan," Centers
for Disease Control and Prevention, National Center for Injury Prevention and Control,
accessed September 1, 2016, http://health-equity.pitt.edu/932/1/Childhood_Stress
.pdf; Heather A. Turner, David Finkelhor, and Richard Ormrod, "Poly-Victimization
in a National Sample of Children and Youth," *American Journal of Preventive Medicine* 38,
no. 3 (2010): 323–330.

pg. 6:   ***Cradles of Eminence:*** Victor Goertzel and Mildred George Goertzel, *Cradles of
Eminence: A Provocative Study of the Childhoods of Over 400 Famous Twentieth-Century Men and
Women* (New York: Little, Brown, 1962); Victor Goertzel et al., *Cradles of Eminence: Child-
hoods of More than Seven Hundred Famous Men and Women* (Scottsdale, AZ: Great Potential
Press, 2004).

pg. 7:   **Only fifty-eight, or less than 15 percent:** Victor Goertzel and Mildred George
Goertzel, *Cradles of Eminence: A Provocative Study of the Childhoods of Over 400 Famous
Twentieth-Century Men and Women* (New York: Little, Brown, 1962); Victor Goertzel et al.,
Cradles of Eminence: Childhoods of More than Seven Hundred Famous Men and Women (Scotts-
dale, AZ: Great Potential Press, 2004).

pg. 7:   **"The 'normal man'":** Victor Goertzel et al., *Cradles of Eminence: Childhoods of More than
Seven Hundred Famous Men and Women* (Scottsdale, AZ: Great Potential Press, 2004), 133.

pg. 7:   **"The habits of a vigorous mind":** *Letters of Mrs. Adams: The Wife of John Adams* (Boston: Wilkins, Carter, 1848), 111.

pg. 7:   **Sigmund Freud is probably best known:** Josef Breuer and Sigmund Freud, *Studies
in Hysteria* (Boston: Beacon Press, 1950).

pg. 7:   **"Everywhere I go I find":** As quoted in Anaïs Nin, *In Favor of the Sensitive Man, and
Other Essays* (San Diego: Harcourt Brace, 1976), 14; this caption is also attributed to
Freud on a wall of the Freud Museum in Vienna.

pg. 7:   **"As the twig is bent, so is the tree inclined":** Alexander Pope, *Moral Essays*, epis.
i, line 149.

pg. 8:   **those who showed few signs of trouble:** Norman Garmezy, "The Study of Competence in Children at Risk for Severe Psychopathology," in *The Child in His Family*. Vol.
3, *Children at Psychiatric Risk*, eds. Elwyn J. Anthony and C. Koupernik (New York: Wiley,
1974), 77–97; Norman Garmezy, "Stress, Competence, and Development: Continuities
in the Study of Schizophrenic Adults, Children Vulnerable to Psychopathology, and
the Search for Stress-Resistant Children," *American Journal of Orthopsychiatry* 57, no. 2
(1987): 159–174; Norman Garmezy, "Vulnerability Research and the Issue of Primary
Prevention," *American Journal of Orthopsychiatry* 41, no. 1 (1971): 101–116; Ann S. Masten
and Auke Tellegen, "Resilience in Developmental Psychopathology: Contributions of
the Project Competence Longitudinal Study," *Development and Psychopathology* 24, no. 2
(2012): 345–361.

pg. 8: **similarly unaffected by poverty or deprivation:** Michael Rutter, "Maternal Deprivation, 1972–1978: New Findings, New Concepts, New Approaches," *Child Development* 50, no. 2 (1979): 283–305; Michael Rutter, "Protective Factors in Children's Responses to Stress and Disadvantage," *Annals of the Academy of Medicine, Singapore* 8, no. 3 (1979): 324–338.

pg. 8: **seemed to rise above childhood disadvantage and family discord:** Emmy E. Werner and Ruth S. Smith, *Vulnerable but Invincible: A Study of Resilient Children* (New York: McGraw-Hill, 1982).

pg. 8: **program that identified children who handled hardship well:** Lois B. Murphy and Alice E. Moriarty, *Vulnerability, Coping and Growth from Infancy to Adolescence* (Oxford, UK: Yale University Press, 1976).

pg. 8: **"steeling effect":** Manfred Bleuler, *The Schizophrenic Disorders: Long-Term Patient and Family Studies* (New Haven, CT: Yale University Press, 1978).

pg. 8: **"One would have thought that the picture":** Elwyn J. Anthony and Bertram J. Cohler, eds., *The Invulnerable Child* (New York: Guilford, 1987); see p. ix.

pg. 8: **"keepers of the dream":** Norman Garmezy, "Vulnerability Research and the Issue of Primary Prevention," *American Journal of Orthopsychiatry* 41, no. 1 (1971): 101–116; see p. 114.

pg. 9: **"Superkids":** Stephen E. Buggie, "Superkids of the Ghetto," *Contemporary Psychology* 40, no. 12 (1995): 1164–1165; Carol Kauffman et al., "Superkids: Competent Children of Psychotic Mothers," *American Journal of Psychiatry* 136, no. 11 (1979): 1398–1402; Maya Pines, "Superkids," *Psychology Today* 12, no. 8 (1979): 53.

pg. 9: **"Invulnerable":** Elwyn J. Anthony, "The Syndrome of the Psychologically Invulnerable Child," in *The Child in His Family*. Vol. 3, *Children at Psychiatric Risk*, eds. Elwyn J. Anthony and C. Koupernik (New York: Wiley, 1974), 529–544; Elwyn J. Anthony and Bertram J. Cohler, eds., *The Invulnerable Child* (New York: Guilford, 1987); Norman Garmezy, "Vulnerability Research and the Issue of Primary Prevention," *American Journal of Orthopsychiatry* 41, no. 1 (1971): 101–116; Maya Pines, "In Praise of 'Invulnerables,'" *APA Monitor* (December 1975), 7.

pg. 9: **"Invincible":** Emmy E. Werner and Ruth S. Smith, *Vulnerable but Invincible: A Longitudinal Study of Resilient Children and Youth* (New York: Adams, Bannister, Cox, 1982).

pg. 9: **"Children of steel":** Elwyn J. Anthony, "A New Scientific Region to Explore," in *The Child in His Family*. Vol. 4, *Vulnerable Children*, eds. Elwyn J. Anthony and C. Koupernik (New York: Wiley, 1978), 3–16.

pg. 9: **"Supernormal":** Elwyn J. Anthony, "Risk, Vulnerability, and Resilience: An Overview," in *The Invulnerable Child*, eds. Elwyn J. Anthony and Bertram J. Cohler (New York: Guilford, 1987), 3–48; quoted on p. 41.

pg. 9: **"The invulnerable children!":** Julius Segal and Herbert C. Yahraes, *Child's Journey* (New York: McGraw-Hill, 1978), 297.

pg. 9: **"resilience" research was born:** For reviews, see Vicki S. Helgeson, Kerry A. Reynolds, and Patricia L. Tomich, "A Meta-Analytic Review of Benefit Finding and Growth," *Journal of Consulting and Clinical Psychology* 74, no. 5 (2006): 797–816; Stephen Joseph and P. Alex Linley, "Positive Adjustment to Threatening Events: An Organismic Valuing Theory of Growth Through Adversity," *Review of General Psychology* 9, no. 3 (2005): 262–280; Stephen J. Lepore and Tracey A. Revenson, "Resilience and Posttraumatic Growth: Recovery, Resistance, and Reconfiguration," in *Handbook of Posttraumatic Growth: Research and Practice*, eds. Lawrence G. Calhoun and Richard G. Tedeschi (New York: Lawrence Erlbaum Associates, 2006), 24–46; P. Alex Linley and Stephen Joseph, "Positive Change Following Trauma and Adversity: A Review," *Journal of Traumatic Stress* 17, no. 1 (2004): 11–21; Ann S. Masten, "Resilience in Children Threatened by Extreme Adversity: Frameworks for Research, Practice, and Translational Synergy," *Development and Psychopathology* 23, no. 2 (2011): 493–506; David A. Meyerson et al., "Posttraumatic Growth Among Children and Adolescents:

A Systematic Review," *Clinical Psychology Review* 31, no. 6 (2011): 949–964; Mark D. Seery, E. Alison Holman, and Roxane Cohen Silver, "Whatever Does Not Kill Us: Cumulative Lifetime Adversity, Vulnerability, and Resilience," *Journal of Personality and Social Psychology* 99, no. 6 (2010): 1025–1041; B. W. Smith et al., "Resilience as the Ability to Bounce Back from Stress: A Neglected Personal Resource?" *Journal of Positive Psychology* 5, no. 3 (2010): 166–176; Richard G. Tedeschi and Lawrence G.Calhoun, "Posttraumatic Growth: Conceptual Foundations and Empirical Evidence," Psychological Inquiry 15, no. 1 (2004): 1–18; Richard G. Tedeschi and Lawrence G. Calhoun, "The Posttraumatic Growth Inventory: Measuring the Positive Legacy of Trauma," *Journal of Traumatic Stress* 9, no. 3 (1996): 455–471; Richard G. Tedeschi, Crystal L. Park, and Lawrence G. Calhoun, eds., *Posttraumatic Growth: Positive Changes in the Aftermath of Crisis* (Mahwah, NJ: Lawrence Erlbaum Associates, 1998).

pg. 9:   **no simple answers have been found:** Dante Cicchetti and Jennifer A. Blender, "A Multiple-Levels-of-Analysis Perspective on Resilience," *Annals of the New York Academy of Sciences* 1094, no. 1 (2006): 248–258; Suniya S. Luthar, Dante Cicchetti, and Bronwyn Becker, "The Construct of Resilience: A Critical Evaluation and Guidelines for Future Work," *Child Development* 71, no. 3 (2000): 543–562; Suniya S. Luthar, Jeanette A. Sawyer, and Pamela J. Brown, "Conceptual Issues in Studies of Resilience: Past, Present, and Future Research," *Annals of the New York Academy of Sciences* 1094 (2006): 105–115.

pg. 9:   **long list of purported assets:** For a summary of the "short list," see Margaret O'Dougherty Wright, Ann S. Masten, and Angela J. Narayan, "Resilience Processes in Development: Four Waves of Research on Positive Adaptations in the Context of Adversity," in *Handbook of Resilience in Children*, eds. Sam Goldstein and Robert B. Brooks (New York: Springer, 2012), 21; see also Suniya S. Luthar, ed., *Resilience and Vulnerability: Adaptation in the Context of Childhood Adversities* (New York: Cambridge University Press, 2003); Suniya S. Luthar, "Resilience in Development: A Synthesis of Research Across Five Decades," in *Developmental Psychopathology: Risk, Disorder, and Adaptation*, vol. 3, 2nd ed., eds. Dante Cicchetti and Donald J. Cohen (Hoboken, NJ: Wiley, 2006), 739–795; Suniya S. Luthar, Dante Cicchetti, and Bronwyn Becker, "The Construct of Resilience: A Critical Evaluation and Guidelines for Future Work," *Child Development* 71, no. 3 (2000): 543–562; Ann S. Masten, "Ordinary Magic: Resilience Processes in Development," *American Psychologist* 56, no. 3 (2001): 227–238; Ann S. Masten and Jelena Obradović, "Competence and Resilience in Development," *Annals of the New York Academy of Sciences* 1094, no. 1 (2006): 13–27; Ann S. Masten and Jenifer L. Powell, "A Resilience Framework for Research, Policy, and Practice," in *Resilience and Vulnerability: Adaptation in the Context of Childhood Adversities*, ed. Suniya S. Luthar (New York: Cambridge University Press, 2003), table on p. 13; Jennifer R. Riley and Ann S. Masten, "Resilience in Context," in *Resilience in Children, Families, and Communities: Linking Context to Practice and Policy*, eds. Ray D. Peters, Bonnie Leadbeater, and Robert J. McMahon (New York: Springer, 2005), 13–25; Michael Rutter, "Resilience Reconsidered: Conceptual Considerations, Empirical Findings, and Policy Implications," in *Handbook of Early Childhood Intervention*, 2nd ed., eds. Jack P. Shonkoff and Samuel J. Meisels (New York: Cambridge University Press, 2000), 651–682; also see Chris R. Brewin, Bernice Andrews, and John D. Valentine, "Meta-Analysis of Risk Factors for Posttraumatic Stress Disorder in Trauma-Exposed Adults," *Journal of Consulting and Clinical Psychology* 68, no. 5 (2000): 748–766; Ann S. Masten, Karin M. Best, and Norman Garmezy, "Resilience and Development: Contributions from the Study of Children Who Overcome Adversity," *Development and Psychopathology* 2, no. 4 (1990): 425–444; Ann S. Masten et al., "Competence in the Context of Adversity: Pathways to Resilience and Maladaptation from Childhood to Late Adolescence," *Development and Psychopathology* 11, no. 1 (1999): 143–169; Michael Rutter, "Maternal Deprivation,

1972–1978: New Findings, New Concepts, New Approaches," *Child Development* 50, no. 2 (1979): 283–305; Michael Rutter, "Protective Factors in Children's Responses to Stress and Disadvantage," *Annals of the Academy of Medicine, Singapore* 8, no. 3 (1979): 324–338; Emmy E. Werner, "Resilience in Development," *Current Directions in Psychological Science* 4, no. 3 (1995): 81–85.

pg. 10:   **many had help from what was good about their environments:** Dante Cicchetti and Jennifer A. Blender, "A Multiple-Levels-of-Analysis Perspective on Resilience," *Annals of the New York Academy of Sciences* 1094, no. 1 (2006): 248–258; Suniya S. Luthar, Dante Cicchetti, and Bronwyn Becker, "The Construct of Resilience: A Critical Evaluation and Guidelines for Future Work," *Child Development* 71, no. 3 (2000): 543–562; Ella Vanderbilt-Adriance and Daniel S. Shaw, "Conceptualizing and Re-Evaluating Resilience Across Levels of Risk, Time, and Domains of Competence," *Clinical Child and Family Psychology Review* 11, no. 1–2 (2008): 30–58; see also Urie Bronfenbrenner, *The Ecology of Human Development: Experiments by Nature and Design* (Cambridge, MA: Harvard University Press, 1979).

pg. 10:   **"power of the ordinary":** Ann S. Masten, "Ordinary Magic: Resilience Processes in Development," *American Psychologist* 56, no. 3 (2001): 235.

pg. 10:   **goes in and out of view:** Byron Egeland, Elizabeth Carlson, and L. Alan Sroufe, "Resilience as Process," *Development and Psychopathology* 5, no. 4 (1993): 517–528; Edmund W. Gordon and Lauren Dohee Song, "Variations in the Experience of Resilience," in *Educational Resilience in Inner-City America: Challenges and Prospects*, eds. Margaret C. Wang and Edmund W. Gordon (New York: Routledge, 1994): 27–43; Howard A. Liddle, "Contextualizing Resiliency," in *Educational Resilience in Inner-City America: Challenges and Prospects*, eds. Margaret C. Wang and Edmund W. Gordon (New York: Routledge, 1994): 167–178; Suniya S. Luthar, Dante Cicchetti, and Bronwyn Becker, "The Construct of Resilience: A Critical Evaluation and Guidelines for Future Work," *Child Development* 71, no. 3 (2000): 543–562; Jennifer R. Riley and Ann S. Masten, "Resilience in Context," in *Resilience in Children, Families, and Communities: Linking Context to Practice and Policy*, eds. Ray D. Peters, Bonnie Leadbeater, and Robert J. McMahon (New York: Springer, 2005), 13–25; John E. Schulenberg, Arnold J. Sameroff, and Dante Cicchetti, "The Transition to Adulthood as a Critical Juncture in the Course of Psychopathology and Mental Health," *Development and Psychopathology* 16 (2004): 799–806; Ella Vanderbilt-Adriance and Daniel S. Shaw, "Conceptualizing and Re-Evaluating Resilience Across Levels of Risk, Time, and Domains of Competence," *Clinical Child and Family Psychology Review* 11, no. 1–2 (2008): 30–58; Tuppett M. Yates, B. Egeland, and Alan Sroufe, "Rethinking Resilience," in *Resilience and Vulnerability: Adaptation in the Context of Childhood Adversities*, ed. Suniya S. Luthar (New York: Cambridge University Press, 2003), 243–266.

pg. 10:   **"observable track record":** Ann S. Masten and Jenifer L. Powell, "A Resilience Framework for Research, Policy, and Practice," in *Resilience and Vulnerability: Adaptation in the Context of Childhood Adversities*, ed. Suniya S. Luthar (New York: Cambridge University Press, 2003), 1–25; see quote on p. 6.

pg. 10:   **difficulties tough to spot:** Robert F. Anda et al., "The Enduring Effects of Abuse and Related Adverse Experiences in Childhood," *European Archives of Psychiatry and Clinical Neuroscience* 256, no. 3 (2006): 174–186; Joan Kaufman et al., "Problems Defining Resiliency: Illustrations from the Study of Maltreated Children," *Development and Psychopathology* 6, no. 1 (1994): 215–229; Julien Worland et al., "St. Louis Risk Research Project: Comprehensive Progress Report of Experimental Studies," in *Children at Risk for Schizophrenia: A Longitudinal Perspective*, eds. Norman F. Watt et al. (New York: Cambridge University Press, 1984), 105–147.

pg. 10:   **struggling covertly:** Kara Coombes and Ruth Anderson, "The Impact of Family of Origin on Social Workers from Alcoholic Families," *Clinical Social Work Journal* 28, no. 3 (2000): 281–302; Suniya S. Luthar, "Resilience in Development: A Synthesis of Research Across Five Decades," in *Developmental Psychopathology: Risk, Disorder, and Adaptation*, Vol. 3, 2nd ed., eds. Dante Cicchetti and Donald J. Cohen (Hoboken, NJ: Wiley, 2006), 739–795; Suniya S. Luthar, "Vulnerability and Resilience: A Study of High-Risk Adolescents," *Child Development* 62, no. 3 (1991): 600–616; Suniya S. Luthar, Dante Cicchetti, and Bronwyn Becker, "The Construct of Resilience: A Critical Evaluation and Guidelines for Future Work," *Child Development* 71, no. 3 (2000): 543–562; Ella Vanderbilt-Adriance and Daniel S. Shaw, "Conceptualizing and Re-Evaluating Resilience Across Levels of Risk, Time, and Domains of Competence," *Clinical Child and Family Psychology Review* 11, no. 1–2 (2008): 30–58.

pg. 11: **"average, expectable" environment:** Heinz Hartmann, *Ego Psychology and the Problem of Adaptation* (New York: International Universities Press, 1939).

pg. 11: **"good-enough":** Donald Winnicott, "Transitional Objects and Transitional Phenomena: A Study of the First Not-Me Possession," *International Journal of Psychoanalysis* 34 (1953): 89–97.

pg. 11: **a home—or a school or a neighborhood—where there is enough:** National Institute of Mental Health, "The Numbers Count: Mental Disorders in America," accessed August 29, 2016, http://www.lb7.uscourts.gov/documents/12-cv-1072url2 .pdf; US National Library of Medicine and the National Institute of Mental Health (2009) list these characteristics of good parenting: providing safety, affection, discipline, listening to the child, spending time with the child, monitoring his or her activities, and being a good role model.

pg. 11: **moderate, age-appropriate challenges are good for us:** Bruce S. McEwen, "Stressed or Stressed Out: What Is the Difference?" *Journal of Psychiatry and Neuroscience* 30, no. 5 (2005): 315–318.

pg. 11: **"above-average environmental burdens":** Heinz Hartmann, *Ego Psychology and the Problem of Adaptation* (New York: International Universities Press, 1939): 71.

pg. 11: **2010 report from the Centers for Disease Control and Prevention:** Centers for Disease Control and Prevention, "Adverse Childhood Experiences Reported by Adults—Five States, 2009," *Morbidity and Mortality Weekly Report* 59, no. 49 (2010): 1609–1613, http://www.cdc.gov/mmwr/preview/mmwrhtml/mm5949a1.htm#tab2; for similar but different estimations, see also Maxia Dong et al., "The Interrelatedness of Multiple Forms of Childhood Abuse, Neglect, and Household Dysfunction," *Child Abuse and Neglect* 28, no. 7 (2004): 771–784; Vincent J. Felitti et al., "Relationship of Childhood Abuse and Household Dysfunction to Many of the Leading Causes of Death in Adults: The Adverse Childhood Experiences (ACE) Study," *American Journal of Preventive Medicine* 14, no. 4 (1998): 245–258; Jennifer S. Middlebrooks and Natalie C. Audage, "The Effects of Childhood Stress on Health Across the Lifespan," Centers for Disease Control and Prevention, National Center for Injury Prevention and Control, accessed September 1, 2016, http://health-equity.pitt.edu/932/1/Childhood_Stress.pdf.

pg. 12: **financial hardship:** Paula S. Nurius, Edwina Uehara, and Douglas F. Zatzick, "Intersection of Stress, Social Disadvantage, and Life Course Processes: Reframing Trauma and Mental Health," *American Journal of Psychiatric Rehabilitation* 16, no. 2 (2013): 91–114.

pg. 12: **Adverse Childhood Experiences (ACE) Study:** Vincent J. Felitti et al., "Relationship of Childhood Abuse and Household Dysfunction to Many of the Leading Causes of Death in Adults: The Adverse Childhood Experiences (ACE) Study," *American Journal of Preventive Medicine* 14, no. 4 (1998): 245–258.

pg. 12: **adversity has a way of piling up:** Margaret O'Dougherty Wright, Ann S. Masten, and Angela J. Narayan, "Resilience Processes in Development: Four Waves of Research on Positive Adaptations in the Context of Adversity," in *Handbook of Resilience in Children*, eds. Sam Goldstein and Robert B. Brooks (New York: Springer, 2012), 17.

pg. 12: **"adversity package":** B. B. Robbie Rossman, "Time Heals All: How Much and for Whom?" *Journal of Emotional Abuse* 2, no. 1 (2000): 31–50.

pg. 12: **2004 study that examined the interrelatedness of hardships:** Maxia Dong et al., "The Interrelatedness of Multiple Forms of Childhood Abuse, Neglect, and House-hold Dysfunction," *Child Abuse and Neglect* 28, no. 7 (2004): 771–784.

pg. 12: **"shock traumas":** Ernst Kris, "The Recovery of Childhood Memories in Psycho-analysis," *The Psychoanalytic Study of the Child* 11 (1956): 54–88.

pg. 12: **"strain traumas":** Psychoanalysts and other clinicians have long recognized the addi-tive impact of seemingly small stressors. In 1895, Sigmund Freud wrote about "partial traumas," explaining that different distressing experiences "belong together in so far as they are components of a single story of suffering." See Josef Breuer and Sigmund Freud (1893–1895), *Studies on Hysteria, Standard Edition* 2 (London: Hogarth, 1955), 6; Henry Krystal and John H. Krystal, *Integration and Self-Healing: Affect, Trauma, Alexithymia* (New York: Routledge, 2009), 141. And in 1986, James Anthony told of "microdisasters"—the tiny tragedies that blew into the lives of some children every day at home. See E. James Anthony, "Terrorizing Attacks on Children by Psychotic Parents," *Journal of the American Academy of Child Psychiatry* 25, no. 3 (1986): 326–335.

pg. 12: **"cumulative traumas":** M. Masud Kahn, "The Concept of Cumulative Trauma," *The Psychoanalytic Study of the Child* 18 (1962): 286–306.

pg. 12: **"only cumulatively and in retrospect":** M. Masud Kahn, "The Concept of Cumulative Trauma," *Psychoanalytic Study of the Child* 18 (1963): 286–306; quote on p. 291.

pg. 12: **daily lives of children, and on developing bodies and brains:** Danya Gla-ser, "Child Abuse and Neglect and the Brain—A Review," *Journal of Child Psychology and Psychiatry* 41, no. 1 (2000): 97–116; Jennifer S. Middlebrooks and Natalie C. Audage, "The Effects of Childhood Stress on Health Across the Lifespan," Centers for Disease Control and Prevention, National Center for Injury Prevention and Control, accessed September 1, 2016, http://health-equity.pitt.edu/932/1/Childhood_Stress.pdf; Jack P. Shonkoff, W. Thomas Boyce, and Bruce S. McEwen, "Neuroscience, Molecular Biol-ogy, and the Childhood Roots of Health Disparities: Building a New Framework for Health Promotion and Disease Prevention," *Journal of the American Medical Association* 301, no. 21 (2009): 2252–2259; Jack P. Shonkoff et al., "The Lifelong Effects of Early Childhood Adversity and Toxic Stress," *Pediatrics* 129, no. 1 (2012): e232–e246; R. Jay Turner and Donald A. Lloyd, "Lifetime Traumas and Mental Health: The Significance of Cumulative Adversity," *Journal of Health and Social Behavior* 36, no. 4 (1995): 360–376; Bessel A. van der Kolk, "The Psychobiology and Psychopharmacology of PTSD," *Human Psychopharmacology: Clinical and Experimental* 16, no. S1 (2001): S49–S64.

pg. 12: **Difficult experiences get under our skin:** Jack P. Shonkoff et al., "The Lifelong Effects of Early Childhood Adversity and Toxic Stress," *Pediatrics* 129, no. 1 (2012): e232–e246.

pg. 12: **toxic stress, or chronic stress:** According to Richard Lazarus, "stress arises when individuals perceive they cannot adequately cope with the demands being made on them or with threats to their well-being." See Richard Lazarus, *Psychological Stress and the Coping Process* (New York: McGraw-Hill, 1966). Scientists and clinicians alike recognize there are three types of stress: positive, tolerable, and toxic. Positive stress is what we might think of as the average and expectable challenges that go along with life, such as when a child or adolescent faces a first day of school or performs in his piano recital or begins her first part-time job. Tolerable stresses go beyond the average and expectable, and are upsetting, short-lived experiences such as the untimely death of a loved one, a car accident, or a serious injury. Moments of positive and tolerable stress do pass and, with enough care from adults and buffering from the environment, children can emerge from these stronger and more capable than before. In contrast with positive or tolerable stress, however, toxic stress does not pass. It is prolonged, frequent strain, especially without adequate support from the environment. See Jennifer S. Middlebrooks and Natalie C. Audage, "The Effects of Childhood Stress on Health Across the Lifespan," Centers for Disease Control and Prevention, National Center for Injury Prevention and Control, accessed September 1, 2016, http://health-equity.pitt.edu/932/1/Child hood_Stress.pdf; Bridget M. Kuehn, "AAP: Toxic Stress Threatens Kids' Long-Term Health," *Journal of the American Medical Association* 312, no. 6 (2014): 585–586; Jack P. Shonkoff et al., "The Lifelong Effects of Early Childhood Adversity and Toxic Stress," *Pediatrics* 129, no. 1 (2012): e232–e246.

pg. 13: **hits, big and small, add up:** Steven P. Broglio et al., "Cumulative Head Impact Burden in High School Football," *Journal of Neurotrauma* 28, no. 10 (2011): 2069–2078; Philip H. Montenigro et al., "Cumulative Head Impact Exposure Predicts Later-Life Depression, Apathy, Executive Dysfunction, and Cognitive Impairment in Former High School and College Football Players," *Journal of Neurotrauma* 34, no. 2 (2017): 328–340.

pg. 13: **"may be the leading cause of poor health":** "Breaking the Silence on Child Abuse: Protection, Prevention, Intervention, and Deterrence," Testimony of Robert W. Block on Behalf of the American Academy of Pediatrics Before the Senate Health, Education, Labor and Pensions Committee Hearing, December 13, 2011, accessed September 2, 2016, http://www.help.senate.gov/hearings/breaking-the-silence-on-child -abuse-protection-prevention-intervention-and-deterrence.

pg. 13: **from ulcers and depression to cancer and autoimmune diseases:** Corina Benjet, Guilherme Borges, and Maria Elena Medina-Mora, "Chronic Childhood Adversity and Onset of Psychopathology During Three Life Stages: Childhood, Adolescence and Adulthood," *Journal of Psychiatric Research* 44, no. 11 (2010): 732–740; Vincent J. Felitti et al., "Relationship of Childhood Abuse and Household Dysfunction to Many of the Leading Causes of Death in Adults: The Adverse Childhood Experiences (ACE) Study," *American Journal of Preventive Medicine* 14, no. 4 (1998): 245–258; Norman Garmezy, Ann S. Masten, and Auke Tellegen, "The Study of Stress and Competence in Children: A Building Block for Developmental Psychopathology," *Child Development* 55, no. 1 (1984): 97–111; Richard S. Lazarus and Susan Folkman, *Stress, Appraisal, and Coping* (New York: Springer Publishing Company, 1984).

pg. 13: **"Why Succeeding Against the Odds Can Make You Sick":** James Hamblin, "Why Succeeding Against the Odds Can Make You Sick," *New York Times,* January 27, 2017, accessed February 26, 2017, https://www.nytimes.com/2017/01/27/opinion/ sunday/why-succeeding-against-the-odds-can-make-you-sick.html; see also Gene H. Brody et al., "Is Resilience Only Skin Deep? Rural African Americans' Socioeconomic Status–Related Risk and Competence in Preadolescence and Psychological Adjustment and Allostatic Load at Age 19," *Psychological Science* 24, no. 7 (2013): 1285–1293; Gene H. Brody et al., "Resilience in Adolescence, Health, and Psychosocial Outcomes," *Pediatrics* 138, no. 6 (2016): e20161042; Gregory E. Miller, Edith Chen, and Gene H. Brody, "Can Upward Mobility Cost You Your Health?" *New York Times,* January 4, 2014, accessed February 26, 2017, https://opinionator.blogs.nytimes.com/2014/01/04/can-upward -mobility-cost-you-your-health; Gregory E. Miller et al., "Viral Challenge Reveals Further Evidence of Skin-Deep Resilience in African Americans from Disadvantaged Backgrounds," *Health Psychology* 35, no. 11 (2016): 1225–1234; Mahasin S. Mujahid, "Socioeconomic Position, John Henryism, and Incidence of Acute Myocardial Infarction in Finnish Men," *Social Science and Medicine* 173 (2017): 54–62.

pg. 13: **resilience may be only skin-deep:** Gene H. Brody et al., "Is Resilience Only Skin Deep? Rural African Americans' Socioeconomic Status–Related Risk and Competence in Preadolescence and Psychological Adjustment and Allostatic Load at Age 19," *Psychological Science* 24, no. 7 (2013): 1285–1293; Gregory E. Miller et al., "Viral Challenge Reveals Further Evidence of Skin-Deep Resilience in African Americans from Disadvantaged Backgrounds," *Health Psychology* 35, no. 11 (2016): 1225–1234.

pg. 14: **The world's first superhero—Superman:** Laurence Maslon and Michael Kantor, *Superheroes!: Capes, Cowls, and the Creation of Comic Book Culture* (New York: Crown Archetype, 2013), 30–34.

pg. 14: **"faster than a speeding bullet":** The opening to Superman's 1940s radio adventures varied over time; for a summary, see Steven Younis, *The Superman Homepage*, accessed February 26, 2017, http://www.supermanhomepage.com.

CHAPTER 2: ORIGIN STORY

pg. 17: **"I don't really miss God":** Hole, "Gutless," by Courtney Love and Eric Erlandson, in *Live Through This*, DGC Records, 1994, accessed February 27, 2017, https://genius .com/Hole-gutless-lyrics.

pg. 18: **"a change occurs which alters":** D. W. Winnicott, "Delinquency as a Sign of Hope" (talk given to the Borstal Assistant Governors' Conference, King Alfred's College, Winchester, April 1967), accessed December 31, 2015, http://goo.gl/oTIIU7.

pg. 18: **"My seven-year-old world humpty-dumptied":** Maya Angelou, *I Know Why the Caged Bird Sings* (New York: Random House, 2009), 53.

pg. 19: **"No one hired a skywriter":** Shawn Carter, *Jay-Z Decoded* (New York: Spiegel and Grau, 2010), 12.

pg. 19: **One-third of marriages end:** D'Vera Cohn, "At Long Last, Divorce," Washington, DC: Pew Research Center, June 4, 2010, accessed December 20, 2015, http://www.pewresearch.org/2010/06/04/at-long-last-divorce; Centers for Disease Control and Prevention, "Divorce Rates by State: 1990, 1995, and 1999–2011," National Vital Statistics System, 2013, accessed December 30, 2015, http://www.cdc.gov/nchs/data/dvs/divorce_rates_90_95_99-11.pdf.

pg. 19: **the most common adversity:** Emmy E. Werner and Ruth S. Smith, *Overcoming the Odds: High Risk Children from Birth to Adulthood* (Ithaca, NY: Cornell University Press, 1992), 198.

pg. 20: **the first no-fault divorce law:** See, for a legal overview of no-fault divorce, Herma Hill Kay, "Equality and Difference: A Perspective on No-Fault Divorce and Its Aftermath," *University of Cincinnati Law Review* 56 (1987): 1, accessed December 31, 2015, http://scholarship.law.berkeley.edu/facpubs/1220.

pg. 20: **emotional or behavioral difficulties:** See, for a review, E. Mavis Hetherington and Anne Mitchell Elmore, "Risk and Resilience in Children Coping with Their Parents' Divorce and Remarriage," in *Resilience and Vulnerability: Adaptation in the Context of Childhood Adversities*, ed. Sonya S. Luthar (New York: Cambridge University Press, 2003), 182–212.

pg. 20: **75 to 80 percent appear to do just fine:** See, for a review, E. Mavis Hetherington and Anne Mitchell Elmore, "Risk and Resilience in Children Coping with Their Parents' Divorce and Remarriage," in *Resilience and Vulnerability: Adaptation in the Context of Childhood Adversities*, ed. Sonya S. Luthar (New York: Cambridge University Press, 2003), 182–212.

pg. 20: **not the same thing as the absence of distress:** See, for reviews, Joan B. Kelly and Robert E. Emery, "Children's Adjustment Following Divorce: Risk and Resilience Perspectives," *Family Relations* 52, no. 4 (2003): 352–363; Lisa Laumann-Billings and Robert E. Emery, "Distress Among Young Adults from Divorced Families," *Journal of Family Psychology* 14, no. 4 (2000): 671–687.

pg. 21: **"separate pathology from pain":** Tamar Lewin, "Poll Says Even Quiet Divorces Affect Children's Path," *New York Times*, November 5, 2005, accessed January 22, 2017, http://www.nytimes.com/2005/11/05/us/poll-says-even-quiet-divorces-affect-childrens -paths.html?_r=0.

pg. 21: **"resilient but not invulnerable":** See, for reviews, Joan B. Kelly and Robert E. Emery, "Children's Adjustment Following Divorce: Risk and Resilience Perspectives," *Family Relations* 52, no. 4 (2003): 352–362; Lisa Laumann-Billings and Robert E. Emery, "Distress Among Young Adults from Divorced Families," *Journal of Family Psychology* 14, no. 4 (2000): 671–687.

pg. 21: **unspoken struggles that are not revealed for years:** See, for reviews, E. Mavis Hetherington and John Kelly, *For Better or for Worse: Divorce Reconsidered* (New York: Norton,

2003); Lisa Laumann-Billings and Robert E. Emery, "Distress Among Young Adults from Divorced Families," *Journal of Family Psychology* 14, no. 4 (2000): 671–687; Judith S. Wallerstein, Julia Lewis, and Sandra Blakeslee, *The Unexpected Legacy of Divorce: A 25 Year Landmark Study* (New York: Hyperion, 2001).

pg. 21:   **"divorce is a cumulative experience":** Judith S. Wallerstein, Julia Lewis, and Sandra Blakeslee, *The Unexpected Legacy of Divorce: A 25 Year Landmark Study* (New York: Hyperion, 2001), 298.

pg. 21:   **research by Robert Emery and colleagues:** Joan B. Kelly and Robert E. Emery, "Children's Adjustment Following Divorce: Risk and Resilience Perspectives," *Family Relations* 52, no. 4 (2003): 352–362; Lisa Laumann-Billings and Robert E. Emery, "Distress Among Young Adults from Divorced Families," *Journal of Family Psychology* 14, no. 4 (2000): 671–687.

pg. 21:   **"filter of divorce":** Lisa Laumann-Billings and Robert E. Emery, "Distress Among Young Adults from Divorced Families," *Journal of Family Psychology* 14, no. 4 (2000): 671–687.

pg. 22:   **Three-quarters of children of divorce:** Lisa Laumann-Billings and Robert E. Emery, "Distress Among Young Adults from Divorced Families," *Journal of Family Psychology* 14, no. 4 (2000): 671–687.

pg. 22:   **childhoods were cut short:** Lisa Laumann-Billings and Robert E. Emery, "Distress Among Young Adults from Divorced Families," *Journal of Family Psychology* 14, no. 4 (2000): 671–687.

pg. 22:   **lost the ability to play:** Judith S. Wallerstein, Julia Lewis, and Sandra Blakeslee, *The Unexpected Legacy of Divorce: A 25 Year Landmark Study* (New York: Hyperion, 2001).

pg. 22:   **"My father died, we moved inland":** Paul Alexander, *Rough Magic: A Biography of Sylvia Plath* (New York: Da Capo Press, 2003).

pg. 23:   **"most people prefer the certainty of misery":** Virginia Satir, *The Satir Model: Family Therapy and Beyond* (Palo Alto, CA: Science and Behavior Books, 1991).

pg. 24:   **parents and parenting deteriorate:** E. Mavis Hetherington, "Coping with Family Transitions: Winners, Losers, and Survivors," *Child Development* 60, no. 1 (1989): 1–14; E. Mavis Hetherington, "An Overview of the Virginia Longitudinal Study of Divorce and Remarriage with a Focus on Early Adolescence," *Journal of Family Psychology* 7, no. 1 (1993): 39–56; E. Mavis Hetherington and John Kelly, *For Better or for Worse: Divorce Reconsidered* (New York: Norton, 2003); see, for reviews, Joan B. Kelly and Robert E. Emery, "Children's Adjustment Following Divorce: Risk and Resilience Perspectives," *Family Relations* 52, no. 4 (2003): 352–362.

pg. 24:   **other than where they were raised:** D'Vera Cohn and Rich Morin, "American Mobility: Who Moves? Who Stays Put? Where's Home?" *Social and Demographic Trends Report* (Washington, DC: Pew Research Center, December 17, 2008), accessed December 30, 2015, http://www.pewsocialtrends.org/2008/12/17/who-moves-who-stays-put-wheres-home.

pg. 24:   **have only one person:** Miller McPherson, Lynn Smith-Lovin, and Matthew E. Brashears, "Social Isolation in America: Changes in Core Discussion Networks over Two Decades," *American Sociological Review* 71, no. 3 (2006): 353–375; see also the classic, groundbreaking book on this topic, Claude S. Fischer, *To Dwell Among Friends: Personal Networks in Town and City* (Chicago: University of Chicago Press, 1982).

pg. 24:   **shoulders for their parents to cry on:** E. Mavis Hetherington, "Should We Stay Together for the Sake of the Children?" in *Coping with Divorce, Single Parenting, and Re-Marriage,* ed. E. Mavis Hetherington (Mahwah, NJ: Erlbaum, 1999), 93–116.

pg. 24:   **child support they are due:** Timothy S. Grall, "Custodial Mothers and Fathers and Their Child Support: 2011," *Current Population Reports* no. P60-246 (Washington, DC: US Census Bureau, October 2013), accessed January 1, 2016, http://www.census.gov/prod/2013pubs/p60-246.pdf.

pg. 24:   **support is especially unlikely to be paid:** Timothy S. Grall, "Custodial Mothers and Fathers and Their Child Support: 2011," *Current Population Reports* no. P60-246 (Washington, DC: US Census Bureau, October 2013), accessed January 1, 2016, http://www.census.gov/prod/2013pubs/p60-246.pdf.

pg. 25: **struggle to stay in the middle class:** Elizabeth Warren and Amelia Warren Tyagi, *The Two-Income Trap: Why Middle-Class Mothers and Fathers Are Going Broke* (New York: Basic Books, 2003).

pg. 25: **one-third of single-parent families:** Timothy S. Grall, "Custodial Mothers and Fathers and Their Child Support: 2011," *Current Population Reports* no. P60-246 (Washington, DC: US Census Bureau, 2013), accessed January 1, 2016, http://www.census.gov/prod/2013pubs/p60-246.pdf.

pg. 25: **they and their children are especially at risk:** Lenore J. Weitzman, *The Divorce Revolution: The Unexpected Social and Economic Consequences for Women and Children in America* (New York: Free Press, 1985), 16–41.

pg. 25: **"Having a child":** Elizabeth Warren and Amelia Warren Tyagi, *The Two-Income Trap: Why Middle-Class Mothers and Fathers Are Going Broke* (New York: Basic Books, 2003).

pg. 25: **"I know the day I grew up":** Elizabeth Warren, *A Fighting Chance* (New York: Metropolitan Books, 2014).

pg. 25: **"only between parents and children":** Adam Phillips and Barbara Taylor, *On Kindness* (New York: Farrar, Straus and Giroux, 2009).

pg. 25: **number of high-quality relationships:** Michael Rutter, "Resilience in the Face of Adversity: Protective Factors and Resistance to Psychiatric Disorder," *British Journal of Psychiatry* 147, no. 6 (1985): 598–611.

pg. 26: **"Even a good divorce":** Tamar Lewin, "Poll Says Even Quiet Divorces Affect Children's Path," *New York Times*, November 5, 2005, accessed January 22, 2017, http://www.nytimes.com/2005/11/05/us/poll-says-even-quiet-divorces-affect-childrens-paths.html?_r=0; Elizabeth Marquardt, *Between Two Worlds: The Inner Lives of Children of Divorce* (New York: Three Rivers Press, 2005).

pg. 26: **"the right thing for my family":** Lisa Laumann-Billings and Robert E. Emery, "Distress Among Young Adults from Divorced Families," *Journal of Family Psychology* 14, no. 4 (2000): 671–687.

pg. 26: **talked to them about divorce:** Judy Dunn et al., "Family Lives and Friendships: The Perspectives of Children In Step-, Single-Parent, and Nonstep Families," *Journal of Family Psychology* 15, no. 2 (2001): 272–287.

pg. 28: **flashbulb memories:** Roger Brown and James Kulik, "Flashbulb Memories," *Cognition* 5, no. 1 (1977): 73–99.

pg. 28: **snapshots in the mind:** Studies examining flashbulb memories have found that highly emotional events *feel* as if they are remembered more vividly and in greater detail, though these details may not always be correct; see, for reviews, Elizabeth A. Phelps, "Emotion and Cognition: Insights from Studies of the Human Amygdala," *Annual Review of Psychology* 57 (2006): 27–53; Olivier Luminet and Antonietta Curci, *Flashbulb Memories: New Issues and New Perspectives* (New York: Psychology Press, 2008).

pg. 29: **"leave a scar upon the cerebral tissues":** William James, *The Principles of Psychology* (New York: Holt, 1890), 670.

pg. 30: **"parasites of the mind":** Jean Martin Charcot, "Lessons on the Illnesses of the Nervous System Held at the Salpetriere," vol. 3, A. Delahaye and E. Lecrosnie, Paris: *Progrès Medical* 3 (1887).

pg. 30: **"suffer mainly from reminiscences":** Josef Breuer and Sigmund Freud, *Studies in Hysteria* (Boston: Beacon Press, 1950).

pg. 30: **moments when they felt unbearable feelings:** Sigmund Freud, "On the Psychical Mechanism of Hysterical Phenomena" (lecture presented at a meeting of the Wiener medizinische club, January 11, 1893), in *Standard Edition of the Complete Psychological Works of Sigmund Freud* 3 (London: Hogarth Press, 1962), 281–387.

pg. 30: **"the evolution of their lives checked":** Pierre Janet, *Psychological Healing: A Historical and Clinical Study*, vols. 1–2, trans. C. Paul and E. Paul (New York: Macmillan, 1925; original work published 1919), 660.

pg. 30: **"neurosis of war":** Abram Kardiner, *The Traumatic Neuroses of War* (Mansfield Centre, CT: Martino, 2012).

pg. 30: **"It is not like the writing on a slate":** Roy R. Grinker and John P. Spiegel, *War Neuroses* (Philadelphia: Blakiston, 1945).

pg. 30: **"Bad Is Stronger than Good":** Roy F. Baumeister et al., "Bad Is Stronger than Good," *Review of General Psychology* 5, no. 4 (2001): 323–370.

pg. 31: **"hub in the wheel of fear":** Joseph E. LeDoux, *The Emotional Brain: The Mysterious Underpinnings of Emotional Life* (New York: Simon and Schuster, 1996), 168.

pg. 31: **it plays a central role in managing danger:** Jacek Debiec and Joseph E. LeDoux, "The Amygdala and the Neural Pathways of Fear," in *Post-Traumatic Stress Disorder: Basic Science and Clinical Practice*, eds. Joseph E. LeDoux, Terrence Keane, and Peter Shiromani (New York: Humana, 2009), 23–38; Elizabeth A. Phelps, "Emotion and Cognition: Insights from Studies of the Human Amygdala," *Annual Review of Psychology* 57 (2006): 27–53.

pg. 31: **the amygdala is alerted:** Louis Cozolino, *The Neuroscience of Human Relationships: Attachment and the Developing Social Brain*, 2nd ed. (New York: Norton, 2014), 401–404.

pg. 31: **"where trigger stimuli do their triggering":** Joseph E. LeDoux, *The Emotional Brain: The Mysterious Underpinnings of Emotional Life* (New York: Simon and Schuster, 1996), 168–169.

pg. 31: **the activation of the HPA axis:** The hypothalamus secretes corticotropin-releasing hormone (CRH). CRH then stimulates the pituitary gland, which releases adrenocorticotropic hormone (ACTH). ACTH acts on the adrenal glands, which, in turn, produce epinephrine, norepinephrine, and cortisol.

pg. 31: **stress hormones prepare us:** Joseph E. LeDoux, *The Emotional Brain: The Mysterious Underpinnings of Emotional Life* (New York: Simon and Schuster, 1996), 206; James L. McGaugh, "The Amygdala Modulates the Consolidation of Memories of Emotionally Arousing Experiences," *Annual Review of Neuroscience* 27 (2004): 1–28; see, for reviews, James L. McGaugh, *Memory and Emotion: The Making of Lasting Memories* (New York: Columbia University Press, 2003); James L. McGaugh, "Memory: A Century of Consolidation," *Science* 287, no. 5451 (2000): 248–251.

pg. 32: **activity in the amygdala increases:** See, for a review of studies of classical conditioning, James L. McGaugh, "The Amygdala Modulates the Consolidation of Memories of Emotionally Arousing Experiences," *Annual Review of Neuroscience* 27 (2004): 1–28; James L. McGaugh, *Memory and Emotion: The Making of Lasting Memories* (New York: Columbia University Press, 2003); Donald G. Rainnie and Kerry J. Ressler, "Physiology of the Amygdala: Implications for PTSD," in *Post-Traumatic Stress Disorder: Basic Science and Clinical Practice*, eds. Joseph E. LeDoux, Terrence Keane, and Peter Shiromani (New York: Humana, 2009), 39–78.

pg. 32: **victims of shark attacks or violent crimes:** It is theorized that the hippocampus is adversely affected by stress that is too intense or prolonged; Joseph E. LeDoux, *The Emotional Brain: The Mysterious Underpinnings of Emotional Life* (New York: Simon and Schuster, 1996), 243–244.

pg. 32: **"There is nothing like a little stress":** James L. McGaugh, *Memory and Emotion: The Making of Lasting Memories* (New York: Columbia University Press, 2003), 111.

pg. 32: **"quick to learn and slow to forget":** Louis Cozolino, *The Neuroscience of Human Relationships: Attachment and the Developing Social Brain*, 2nd ed. (New York: Norton, 2014), 403.

pg. 32: **"may be forever":** Joseph E. LeDoux, *The Emotional Brain: The Mysterious Underpinnings of Emotional Life* (New York: Simon and Schuster, 1996), 145.

pg. 32: **"malignant memories":** Eitan D. Schwarz and Janice M. Kowalski, "Malignant Memories: PTSD in Children and Adults After a School Shooting," *Journal of the American Academy of Child and Adolescent Psychiatry* 30, no. 6 (1991): 936–944.

pg. 32: **tyranny of the past:** Bessel A. van der Kolk, Alexander C. McFarlane, and Lars Weisæth, *Traumatic Stress: The Effects of Overwhelming Experience on Mind, Body, and Society* (New York: Guilford, 2007), 3–23.

pg. 33:   **Darwin's Grief Muscles:** Leanne ten Brinke, Stephen Porter, and Alysha Baker, "Darwin the Detective: Observable Facial Muscle Contractions Reveal Emotional High-Stakes Lies," *Evolution and Human Behavior* 33, no. 4 (2012): 411–416.

pg. 33:   **"The body keeps the score":** Bessel A. van der Kolk, *The Body Keeps the Score: Brain, Mind, and Body in the Healing of Trauma* (New York: Penguin, 2014).

pg. 34:   **between four and fourteen days a month:** Joan B. Kelly and Robert E. Emery, "Children's Adjustment Following Divorce: Risk and Resilience Perspectives," *Family Relations* 52, no. 4 (2003): 352–362.

pg. 34:   **little or no contact with the noncustodial parent:** E. Mavis Hetherington and John Kelly, *For Better or for Worse: Divorce Reconsidered* (New York: Norton, 2003); Joan B. Kelly and Robert E. Emery, "Children's Adjustment Following Divorce: Risk and Resilience Perspectives," *Family Relations* 52, no. 4 (2003): 352–362.

pg. 34:   **wished he could see his father more:** William V. Fabricius and Jeff A. Hall, "Young Adults' Perspectives on Divorce Living Arrangements," *Family Court Review* 38, no. 4 (2000): 446–461.

CHAPTER 3: SECRET

pg. 36:   **"I'm seven years old":** Andre Agassi, *Open: An Autobiography* (New York: Vintage, 2010), 27.

pg. 36:   **made national news:** This account is drawn from Lenore Terr, *Too Scared to Cry: Psychic Trauma in Childhood* (New York: Basic Books, 2008).

pg. 37:   **"Nobody else in the group":** Lenore Terr, *Too Scared to Cry: Psychic Trauma in Childhood* (New York: Basic Books, 2008), 20.

pg. 39:   **"readiness to behave":** Kristine Erickson, Wayne Drevets, and Jay Schulkin, "Glucocorticoid Regulation of Diverse Cognitive Functions in Normal and Pathological Emotional States," *Neuroscience and Biobehavioral Reviews* 27, no. 3 (2003): 233–246.

pg. 39:   **best thing may be:** This is called the freeze reaction; Jeffrey A. Gray, *The Psychology of Fear and Stress*, 2nd ed. (New York: Cambridge University Press, 1988).

pg. 39:   **"hub in the wheel of fear":** Joseph E. LeDoux, *The Emotional Brain: The Mysterious Underpinnings of Emotional Life* (New York: Simon and Schuster, 1996), 168.

pg. 39:   **puts it into words:** Adeen Flinker et al., "Redefining the Role of Broca's Area in Speech," *Proceedings of the National Academy of Sciences* 112, no. 9 (2015): 2871–2875.

pg. 40:   **less activity in Broca's area:** Alastair M. Hull, "Neuroimaging Findings in Post-Traumatic Stress Disorder Systematic Review," *British Journal of Psychiatry* 181, no. 2 (2002): 102–110; Scott L. Rauch et al., "A Symptom Provocation Study of Posttraumatic Stress Disorder Using Positron Emission Tomography and Script-Driven Imagery," *Archives of General Psychiatry* 53, no. 5 (1996): 380–387; Lisa M. Shin et al., "A Positron Emission Tomographic Study of Symptom Provocation in PTSD," *Annals of the New York Academy of Sciences* 821, no. 1 (1997): 521–523; Lisa M. Shin et al., "Visual Imagery and Perception in Posttraumatic Stress Disorder: A Positron Emission Tomographic Investigation," *Archives of General Psychiatry* 54, no. 3 (1997): 233–241; Bessel A. van der Kolk, "The Psychobiology and Psychopharmacology of PTSD," *Human Psychopharmacology: Clinical and Experimental* 16, no. S1 (2001): S49–S64.

pg. 40:   **"too scared to cry":** Lenore Terr, *Too Scared to Cry: Psychic Trauma in Childhood* (New York: Basic Books, 2008).

pg. 40:   **pattern recognition:** Joseph E. LeDoux, *The Emotional Brain: The Mysterious Underpinnings of Emotional Life* (New York: Simon and Schuster, 1996), 280.

pg. 41:   **"My feeble language skills":** Alison Bechdel, *Fun Home: A Family Tragicomic* (Boston: Harcourt, 2007), 143.

pg. 41:   **"Trauma mocks language":** Leigh Gilmore, *The Limits of Autobiography: Trauma and Testimony* (Ithaca, NY: Cornell University Press, 2001), 6.

pg. 44: **"At such a moment":** Viktor E. Frankl, *Man's Search for Meaning: An Introduction to Logo-therapy* (Boston: Beacon, 2006), 24.

pg. 44: **One in four children:** Bridget F. Grant, "Estimates of US Children Exposed to Alcohol Abuse and Dependence in the Family," *American Journal of Public Health* 90, no. 1 (2000): 112.

pg. 45: **DSM-5:** American Psychiatric Association, *Diagnostic and Statistical Manual of Mental Disorders*, 5th ed. (DSM-5; Washington, DC: American Psychiatric Publications, 2013).

pg. 45: **topped only by depression:** Christopher Murray and Alan D. Lopez, "Alternative Projections of Mortality and Disability by Cause 1990–2020: Global Burden of Disease Study," *Lancet* 349, no. 9064 (1997): 1498–1504.

pg. 45: **likely to face multiple adversities:** Robert F. Anda et al., "Adverse Childhood Experiences, Alcoholic Parents, and Later Risk of Alcoholism and Depression," *Psychiatric Services* 53, no. 8 (2002): 1001–1009; Shanta R. Dube et al., "Growing Up with Parental Alcohol Abuse: Exposure to Childhood Abuse, Neglect, and Household Dysfunction," *Child Abuse and Neglect* 25, no. 12 (2001): 1627–1640; Christine Walsh, Harriet L. MacMillan, and Ellen Jamieson, "The Relationship Between Parental Substance Abuse and Child Maltreatment: Findings from the Ontario Health Supplement," *Child Abuse and Neglect* 27, no. 12 (2003): 1409–1425.

pg. 45: **men are twice as likely:** National Institute on Alcohol Abuse and Alcoholism, "Alcohol Facts and Statistics," National Institutes of Health, US Department of Health and Human Services, accessed February 14, 2016, http://www.niaaa.nih.gov/alcohol-health/overview-alcohol-consumption/alcohol-facts-and-statistics.

pg. 46: **most typical stressor:** Shanta R. Dube et al., "Growing Up with Parental Alcohol Abuse: Exposure to Childhood Abuse, Neglect, and Household Dysfunction," *Child Abuse and Neglect* 25, no. 12 (2001): 1627–1640; Robert F. Anda et al., "Adverse Childhood Experiences, Alcoholic Parents, and Later Risk of Alcoholism and Depression," *Psychiatric Services* 53, no. 8 (2002): 1001–1009.

pg. 46: **when a parent has been drinking:** James J. Collins and Pamela Messerschmidt, "Epidemiology of Alcohol-Related Violence," *Alcohol Health Research World* 17, no. 2 (1993): 93–100; National Institute on Alcohol Abuse and Alcoholism and Cygnus Corporation, *Ninth Special Report to the US Congress on Alcohol and Health* (Rockville, MD: US Department of Health and Human Services, Public Health Service, National Institutes of Health, 1997), 97–4017.

pg. 46: **"hurt on the inside":** Ann Laybourn, Jane Brown, and Malcolm Hill, *Hurting on the Inside: Children's Experiences of Parental Alcohol Misuse* (Aldershot, Hants, UK: Avebury, 1996).

pg. 46: **doubly at risk:** Robert F. Anda et al., "Adverse Childhood Experiences, Alcoholic Parents, and Later Risk of Alcoholism and Depression," *Psychiatric Services* 53, no. 8 (2002): 1001–1009; Shanta R. Dube et al., "Growing Up with Parental Alcohol Abuse: Exposure to Childhood Abuse, Neglect, and Household Dysfunction," *Child Abuse and Neglect* 25, no. 12 (2001): 1627–1640; Christine Walsh, Harriet L. MacMillan, and Ellen Jamieson, "The Relationship Between Parental Substance Abuse and Child Maltreatment: Findings from the Ontario Health Supplement," *Child Abuse and Neglect* 27, no. 12 (2003): 1409–1425.

pg. 46: **mother is an alcoholic:** Mogens Nygaard Christoffersen and Keith Soothill, "The Long-Term Consequences of Parental Alcohol Abuse: A Cohort Study of Children in Denmark," *Journal of Substance Abuse Treatment* 25, no. 2 (2003): 107–116; Shanta R. Dube et al., "Growing Up with Parental Alcohol Abuse: Exposure to Childhood Abuse, Neglect, and Household Dysfunction," *Child Abuse and Neglect* 25, no. 12 (2001): 1627–1640.

pg. 46: **When mothers drink:** Robert F. Anda et al., "Adverse Childhood Experiences, Alcoholic Parents, and Later Risk of Alcoholism and Depression," *Psychiatric Services* 53, no. 8 (2002): 1001–1009.

pg. 46: **When fathers drink:** Richard Berlin and Ruth B. Davis, "Children from Alcoholic Families: Vulnerability and Resilience," in *The Child in Our Times: Studies in the Development of Resiliency*, eds. Timothy F. Dugan and Robert Coles (New York: Brunner/Mazel,

1989), 81–105; Joan McCord, "Identifying Developmental Paradigms Leading to Alcoholism," *Journal of Studies on Alcohol and Drugs* 49, no. 4 (1988): 357–362.

pg. 46: **"We never actually addressed":** Alan Cumming, *Not My Father's Son: A Family Memoir* (Edinburgh: Canongate, 2014), 148.

pg. 46: **materials from the Hazelden Foundation:** Jill M. Hastings and Marion H. Typpo, *An Elephant in the Living Room* (Minneapolis: CompCare, 1984).

pg. 48: **distract their parents:** Deborah B. Jacobvitz and Nell F. Bush, "Reconstructions of Family Relationships: Parent–Child Alliances, Personal Distress, and Self-Esteem," *Developmental Psychology* 32, no. 4 (1996): 732–743.

pg. 49: **"lead to muddle":** Donald W. Winnicott, "Ego Distortion in Terms of True and False Self (1960)," in *The Maturational Processes and the Facilitating Environment: Studies in the Theory of Emotional Development,* ed. Donald W. Winnicott (London: Karnac Books, 1965), 140–152.

pg. 49: **"It would never have occurred to me":** Carl Jung, *Memories, Dreams, Reflections* (New York: Vintage, 1989), 41.

pg. 50: **secrets are automatic and multidetermined:** Stephen P. Hinshaw, "Parental Mental Disorder and Children's Functioning: Silence and Communication, Stigma and Resilience," *Journal of Clinical Child and Adolescent Psychology* 33, no. 2 (2004): 400–411.

pg. 50: **"Every man has reminiscences":** Fyodor Dostoevsky, *Notes from the Underground,* trans. Constance Garnett, eds. Charles Guignon and Kevin Aho (Indianapolis: Hackett, 2009).

pg. 51: **"I had to resort to":** Charles M. Blow, *Fire Shut Up in My Bones: A Memoir* (Boston: Houghton Mifflin Harcourt, 2014), 113.

pg. 51: **majority showed not a dent:** Lenore Terr, *Too Scared to Cry: Psychic Trauma in Childhood* (New York: Basic Books, 1990), 189–206.

pg. 51: **being better heroes:** Lenore Terr, *Too Scared to Cry: Psychic Trauma in Childhood* (New York: Basic Books, 1990), 189–206.

pg. 51: **"No, I don't live in Chowchilla":** Lenore Terr, *Too Scared to Cry: Psychic Trauma in Childhood* (New York: Basic Books, 1990), 112.

Chapter 4: Fight

pg. 52: **"I like it when a flower or a little tuft of grass":** Although the exact source of this quote is unclear, it is widely attributed to George Carlin.

pg. 52: **from birth into middle adulthood:** Assessed at ages one, two, ten, eighteen, thirty-two, and forty thus far, with a follow-up planned for the mid-fifites; Emmy E. Werner and Ruth S. Smith, *Journeys from Childhood to Midlife: Risk, Resilience, and Recovery* (Ithaca, NY: Cornell University Press, 2001).

pg. 53: **"competent, confident, and caring adults":** Emmy E. Werner, "Resilience in Development," *Current Directions in Psychological Science* 4, no. 3 (1995): 81–85.

pg. 53: **"vulnerable, but invincible":** Emmy E. Werner and Ruth S. Smith, *Vulnerable but Invincible: A Study of Resilient Children and Youth* (New York: McGraw-Hill, 1982).

pg. 53: **most important asset:** Emmy E. Werner and Ruth S. Smith, *Journeys from Childhood to Midlife: Risk, Resilience, and Recovery* (Ithaca, NY: Cornell University Press, 2001), 69.

pg. 56: **where it goes by the name of bullying:** Dan Olweus, *Aggression in the Schools: Bullies and Whipping Boys* (Oxford, UK: Hemisphere, 1978); Dan Olweus, Shane Jimerson, Susan Swearer, and Dorothy Espelage, "Understanding and Researching Bullying," in *Handbook of Bullying in Schools: An International Perspective,* eds. Shane R. Jimerson, Susan M. Swearer, and Dorothy L. Espelage (New York: Routledge, 2010), 9–34; for an overview, see a report by the CDC: R. Matthew Gladden et al., "Bullying Surveillance Among Youths: Uniform Definitions for Public Health and Recommended Data Elements, Version 1.0," Atlanta, GA: National Center for Injury Prevention and Control, Centers for Disease Control and

Prevention and US Department of Education (2014), accessed August 1, 2016, http://www.cdc.gov/violenceprevention/pdf/bullying-definitions-final-a.pdf.

pg. 56: **one in three children are bullied:** "Student Reports of Bullying and Cyber-Bullying: Results from the 2011 School Crime Supplement to the National Crime Victimization Survey," National Center for Education Statistics and Bureau of Justice Statistics, US Department of Education, Washington, DC (August 2013), accessed August 1, 2016, http://nces.ed.gov/pubs2013/2013329.pdf.

pg. 56: **what that bullying looks like varies:** Susan Swearer et al., "Assessment of Bullying/Victimization: The Problem of Comparability Across Studies and Across Methods," in *Handbook of Bullying in Schools: An International Perspective*, eds. Shane R. Jimerson, Susan M. Swearer, and Dorothy L. Espelage (New York: Routledge, 2010), 305–327.

pg. 56: **An estimated 25 percent:** Simone Robers, Jana Kemp, and Jennifer Truman, "Indicators of School Crime and Safety: 2012," National Center for Education Statistics, US Department of Education, and Bureau of Justice Statistics, Office of Justice Programs, US Department of Justice, Washington, DC (2013), accessed August 1, 2016, http://nces.ed.gov/pubs2013/2013036.pdf.

pg. 56: **via the Internet:** Amanda Lenhart et al., "Teens, Kindness and Cruelty on Social Network Sites: How American Teens Navigate the New World of 'Digital Citizenship,'" Pew Research Center's Internet and American Life Project, Washington, DC (2011), last updated November 9, 2011, http://www.pewinternet.org/Reports/2011/Teens-and-social-media.aspx.

pg. 56: **role of power:** Jaana Juvonen, Sandra Graham, and Mark A. Schuster, "Bullying Among Young Adolescents: The Strong, the Weak, and the Troubled," *Pediatrics* 112, no. 6 (2003): 1231–1237; Tracy Vaillancourt et al., "The Relationship Between Power and Bullying Behavior," in *Handbook of Bullying in Schools: An International Perspective*, eds. Shane R. Jimerson, Susan M. Swearer, and Dorothy L. Espelage (New York: Routledge, 2010), 211–222.

pg. 56: **socially vulnerable:** Nancy G. Guerra, Kirk R. Williams, and Shelly Sadek, "Understanding Bullying and Victimization During Childhood and Adolescence: A Mixed Methods Study," *Child Development* 82, no. 1 (2011): 295–310.

pg. 57: **social groups are disrupted:** Anthony D. Pellegrini et al., "Bullying and Social Status During School Transitions," in *Handbook of Bullying in Schools: An International Perspective*, eds. Shane R. Jimerson, Susan M. Swearer, and Dorothy L. Espelage (New York: Routledge, 2010), 199–210.

pg. 57: **establish, or reestablish, the status quo:** Anthony D. Pellegrini et al., "Bullying and Social Status During School Transitions," in *Handbook of Bullying in Schools: An International Perspective*, eds. Shane R. Jimerson, Susan M. Swearer, and Dorothy L. Espelage (New York: Routledge, 2010), 199–210.

pg. 57: **pathways in the brain:** Naomi I. Eisenberger, "The Pain of Social Disconnection: Examining the Shared Neural Underpinnings of Physical and Social Pain," *Nature Reviews Neuroscience* 13, no. 6 (2012): 421–434; Naomi I. Eisenberger and Matthew D. Lieberman, "Why Rejection Hurts: A Common Neural Alarm System for Physical and Social Pain," *Trends in Cognitive Sciences* 8, no. 7 (2004): 294–300; Naomi I. Eisenberger, Matthew D. Lieberman, K. D. Williams, and J. P. Forgas, "Why It Hurts to Be Left Out: The Neurocognitive Overlap Between Physical and Social Pain," *The Social Outcast: Ostracism, Social Exclusion, Rejection, and Bullying*, eds. Kipling Williams and Joseph Paul Forgas (New York: Psychology Press, 2005), 109–130.

pg. 57: **at the hands of more powerful:** Simon C. Hunter, James M. E. Boyle, and David Warden, "Perceptions and Correlates of Peer-Victimization and Bullying," *British Journal of Educational Psychology* 77, no. 4 (2007): 797–810.

pg. 57: **once a week or more:** Mona E. Solberg and Dan Olweus, "Prevalence Estimation of School Bullying with the Olweus Bully/Victim Questionnaire," *Aggressive Behavior* 29, no. 3 (2003): 239–268.

pg. 57: **may continue well into adulthood:** Louise Arseneault, Lucy Bowes, and Sania Shakoor, "Bullying Victimization in Youths and Mental Health Problems: 'Much Ado About Nothing'?" *Psychological Medicine* 40, no. 5 (2010): 717–729; David P. Farrington et al., "Bullying Perpetration and Victimization as Predictors of Delinquency and Depression in the Pittsburgh Youth Study," *Journal of Aggression, Conflict, and Peace Research* 3, no. 2 (2011): 74–81.

pg. 58: **depression or anxiety lasting for years:** Lucy Bowes et al., "Peer Victimisation During Adolescence and Its Impact on Depression in Early Adulthood: Prospective Cohort Study in the United Kingdom," *BMJ* 350 (2015): h2469; Gemma L. Gladstone, Gordon B. Parker, and Gin S. Malhi, "Do Bullied Children Become Anxious and Depressed Adults?: A Cross-Sectional Investigation of the Correlates of Bullying and Anxious Depression," *Journal of Nervous and Mental Disease* 194, no. 3 (2006): 201–208; Maria M. Ttofi et al., "Do the Victims of School Bullies Tend to Become Depressed Later in Life? A Systematic Review and Meta-Analysis of Longitudinal Studies," *Journal of Aggression, Conflict and Peace Research* 3, no. 2 (2011): 63–73.

pg. 58: **"fight-or-flight" response:** Walter B. Cannon, *Bodily Changes in Pain, Hunger, Fear and Rage* (New York: D. Appleton and Company, 1915).

pg. 58: **the milieu interieur:** Charles M. Gross, "Claude Bernard and the Constancy of the Internal Environment," *Neuroscientist* 4, no. 5 (1998): 380–385.

pg. 60: **"I was only sixteen":** Elizabeth Warren, *A Fighting Chance* (New York: Metropolitan Books, 2014), 11.

pg. 60: **"wrote his way out":** Lin-Manuel Miranda, *Hamilton: An American Musical*, New York, 2015; see also Ron Chernow, *Alexander Hamilton* (New York: Penguin, 2004).

pg. 61: **"I caught my first beatin' ":** Nas, Dave East, Lin-Manuel Miranda, and Aloe Blacc, "Wrote My Way Out," *The Hamilton Mixtape* (New York: Atlantic Records, 2016); see also "Wrote My Way Out Lyrics," *Genius*, accessed January 23, 2017, https://genius.com/Nas-dave-east-lin-manuel-miranda-and-aloe-blacc-wrote-my-way-out-lyrics.

pg. 61: **"It's up to me":** Nas, Dave East, Lin-Manuel Miranda, and Aloe Blacc, "Wrote My Way Out," *The Hamilton Mixtape* (New York: Atlantic Records, 2016); see also "Wrote My Way Out Lyrics," *Genius*, accessed January 23, 2017, https://genius.com/Nas-dave-east-lin-manuel-miranda-and-aloe-blacc-wrote-my-way-out-lyrics.

pg. 61: **mightier than the sword:** Edward Bulwer-Lytton, *Richelieu; Or the Conspiracy: A Play, in Five Acts* (London: Saunders and Otley, Conduit Street, 1839), 39, line 308, accessed December 8, 2016, https://archive.org/stream/richelieuorconsp00lyttiala#page/38/mode/2up.

pg. 62: **political prisoners in East Germany:** Anke Ehlers et al., "Predicting Response to Exposure Treatment in PTSD: The Role of Mental Defeat and Alienation," *Journal of Traumatic Stress* 11, no. 3 (1998): 457–471.

pg. 63: **mastery experiences and physical activity:** Kate Hefferon and Nanette Mutrie, "Physical Activity as a 'Stellar' Positive Psychology Intervention," in *The Oxford Handbook of Exercise Psychology*, ed. Edmund O. Acevedo (New York: Oxford University Press, 2012), 117–130.

pg. 63: **designed to push his own limits:** See, for a discussion of the benefits of physical challenges, Steven M. Southwick and Dennis S. Charney, *Resilience: The Science of Mastering Life's Greatest Challenges* (New York: Cambridge University Press, 2012), 136.

pg. 63: **emotions as positive or negative:** David Watson, Lee A. Clark, and Auke Tellegen, "Development and Validation of Brief Measures of Positive and Negative Affect: The PA–NAS Scales," *Journal of Personality and Social Psychology* 54, no. 6 (1988): 1063–1070; David Watson and Auke Tellegen, "Toward a Consensual Structure of Mood," *Psychological Bulletin* 98, no. 2 (1985): 219–235.

pg. 64: **negative feelings drag us down:** Joseph P. Forgas, "Affective Influences on Attitudes and Judgments," in *Handbook of Affective Sciences*, eds. Richard J. Davidson, Klaus R. Scherer, and H. Hill Goldsmith (New York: Oxford University Press, 2003), 596–618.

pg. 64:   **especially damaging emotion:** David Watson et al., "The Two General Activation Systems of Affect: Structural Findings, Evolutionary Considerations, and Psychobiological Evidence," *Journal of Personality and Social Psychology* 76, no. 5 (1999): 820–838.

pg. 64:   **uniquely important role to play:** Joseph J. Campos, "When the Negative Becomes Positive and the Reverse: Comments on Lazarus's Critique of Positive Psychology," *Psychological Inquiry* 14, no. 2 (2003): 110–172.

pg. 64:   **emotions can help us adjust and survive:** Joseph J. Campos, Rosemary G. Campos, and Karen C. Barrett, "Emergent Themes in the Study of Emotional Development and Emotion Regulation," *Developmental Psychology* 25, no. 3 (1989): 394–402; Richard S. Lazarus, "Does the Positive Psychology Movement Have Legs?" *Psychological Inquiry* 14, no. 2 (2003): 93–109.

pg. 64:   **enormous adaptive value:** See, for review, Jennifer S. Lerner and Larissa Z. Tiedens, "Portrait of the Angry Decision Maker: How Appraisal Tendencies Shape Anger's Influence on Cognition," *Journal of Behavioral Decision Making* 19, no. 2 (2006): 115–137.

pg. 64:   **many reasons why we become angry:** Leonard Berkowitz and Eddie Harmon-Jones, "Toward an Understanding of the Determinants of Anger," *Emotion* 4, no. 2 (2004): 107–130; Phillip Shaver et al., "Emotion Knowledge: Further Exploration of a Prototype Approach," *Journal of Personality and Social Psychology* 52, no. 6 (1987): 1061–1086.

pg. 64:   **taken away, or we are prevented:** Charles S. Carver and Eddie Harmon-Jones, "Anger Is an Approach-Related Affect: Evidence and Implications," *Psychological Bulletin* 135, no. 2 (2009): 183–204; John Dollard et al., *Frustration and Anger* (New Haven, CT: Yale University Press, 1939).

pg. 64:   **to perceive injustice:** James R. Averill, "Studies on Anger and Aggression: Implications for Theories of Emotion," *American Psychologist* 38, no. 11 (1983): 1145–1160; Nico H. Frijda, *The Emotions* (New York: Cambridge University Press, 1986).

pg. 64:   **"ought to be":** Nico H. Frijda, *The Emotions* (New York: Cambridge University Press, 1986), 198–199; Andrew Ortony, Gerald L. Clore, and Allan Collins, *The Cognitive Structure of Emotions* (New York: Cambridge University Press, 1988), 152–153.

pg. 65:   **girls and women:** Judith V. Jordan, "Relational Resilience in Girls," in *Handbook of Resilience in Children*, eds. Sam Goldstein and Robert B. Brooks (New York: Springer, 2012), 73–86.

pg. 65:   **"There is a sense of being":** Toni Morrison, *The Bluest Eye* (New York: Vintage International, 2007), 48.

pg. 65:   **moves us to close the gap:** Nico H. Frijda, Peter Kuipers, and Elisabeth Ter Schure, "Relations Among Emotion, Appraisal, and Emotional Action Readiness," *Journal of Personality and Social Psychology* 57, no. 2 (1989): 212–228.

pg. 65:   **compels us to resist:** Joseph J. Campos, Rosemary G. Campos, and Karen C. Barrett, "Emergent Themes in the Study of Emotional Development and Emotion Regulation," *Developmental Psychology* 25, no. 3 (1989): 394–402; Charles S. Carver and Eddie Harmon-Jones, "Anger Is an Approach-Related Affect: Evidence and Implications," *Psychological Bulletin* 135, no. 2 (2009): 183–204; Robert C. Solomon, *A Passion for Justice: Emotions and the Origins of the Social Contract* (Reading, MA: Addison-Wesley Publishing Company, 1990).

pg. 65:   **propels us toward our goals:** Charles S. Carver and Eddie Harmon-Jones, "Anger Is an Approach-Related Affect: Evidence and Implications," *Psychological Bulletin* 135, no. 2 (2009): 183–204.

pg. 65:   **"The angry man is aiming":** Aristotle, *Rhetoric*, trans. H. Lawson-Tancred (New York: Oxford University Press, 1991), 146.

pg. 65:   **active, even tireless, striving:** Rudolf H. Moos and Jeanne A. Schaefer, "Coping Resources and Processes: Current Concepts and Measures," in *Handbook of Stress: Theoretical and Clinical Aspects*, 2nd ed., eds. Leo Goldberger and Shlomo Breznitz (New York: Free Press, 1993), 234–257; Karen Reivich et al., "From Helplessness to Optimism:

The Role of Resilience in Treating and Preventing Depression in Youth," in *Handbook of Resilience in Children*, eds. Sam Goldstein and Robert B. Brooks (New York: Springer, 2013), 201–214; Jeanne A. Schaefer and Rudolf H. Moos, "The Context for Posttraumatic Growth: Life Crises, Individual and Social Resources, and Coping," in *Posttraumatic Growth: Positive Changes in the Aftermath of Crisis*, eds. Richard G. Tedeschi, Crystal L. Park, and Lawrence G. Calhoun (Mahwah, NJ: Lawrence Erlbaum Associates, 1998), 99–124; Sandra L. Schneider, "In Search of Realistic Optimism: Meaning, Knowledge, and Warm Fuzziness," *American Psychologist* 56, no. 3 (2001): 250–263.

pg. 65:   **"triple event":** Francis Galton, *Hereditary Genius: An Inquiry into Its Laws and Consequences* (London: Macmillan, 1892), 38.

pg. 66:   **tenacity was more predictive:** Lewis Madison Terman and Melita H. Oden, *The Gifted Child Grows Up: Twenty-Five Years' Follow-Up of a Superior Group* (Oxford, UK: Stanford University Press, 1947).

pg. 66:   **"persistence of motive and effort":** Catharine M. Cox, *Genetic Studies of Genius*. Vol. 2, *The Early Mental Traits of Three Hundred Geniuses* (Stanford, CA: Stanford University Press, 1926), 218.

pg. 66:   **stick-to-itiveness as "grit":** Angela L. Duckworth, Patrick D. Quinn, and Martin E. P. Seligman, "Positive Predictors of Teacher Effectiveness," *Journal of Positive Psychology* 4, no. 6 (2009): 540–547; Angela L. Duckworth et al., "Deliberate Practice Spells Success: Why Grittier Competitors Triumph at the National Spelling Bee," *Social Psychological and Personality Science* 2, no. 2 (2011): 174–181; Angela L. Duckworth et al., "Grit: Perseverance and Passion for Long-Term Goals," *Journal of Personality and Social Psychology* 92, no. 6 (2007): 1087–1101; Lauren Eskreis-Winkler et al., "The Grit Effect: Predicting Retention in the Military, the Workplace, School and Marriage," *Frontiers in Psychology* 5, no. 36 (2014): 1–12.

pg. 66:   **passion behind it is less so:** In her "Grit Scale," Duckworth equates passion with a "consistency of interests," or the ability to stay with one thing over the long haul, measuring this by reverse-scoring items such as "I become interested in new pursuits every few months" and "My interests change from year to year." Consistency certainly seems like an important aspect of grit but it is not passion. See Angela L. Duckworth et al., "Grit: Perseverance and Passion for Long-Term Goals," *Journal of Personality and Social Psychology* 92, no. 6 (2007): 1087–1101.

pg. 66:   **video produced by the navy:** US Navy, *Faces of Officer Candidate School (OCS)*, video, accessed August 1, 2016, http://www.ocs.navy.mil/OCS_video.html; Naval Service Training Command, *Faces of OCS Update*, video, June 15, 2012, https://www.youtube.com/watch?v=dEPQSK5r3ms.

pg. 67:   **those who get angry who persist:** Joseph J. Campos, Rosemary G. Campos, and Karen C. Barrett, "Emergent Themes in the Study of Emotional Development and Emotion Regulation," *Developmental Psychology* 25, no. 3 (1989): 394–402; Tracy A. Dennis et al., "The Functional Organization of Preschool-Age Children's Emotion Expressions and Actions in Challenging Situations," *Emotion* 9, no. 4 (2009): 520–530; Jie He, Qinmei Xu, and Kathryn Amey Degnan, "Anger Expression and Persistence in Young Children," *Social Development* 21, no. 2 (2012): 343–353; Joan A. Kearney, "Early Reactions to Frustration: Developmental Trends in Anger, Individual Response Styles, and Caregiving Risk Implications in Infancy," *Journal of Child and Adolescent Psychiatric Nursing* 17, no. 3 (2004): 105–112; Heather C. Lench and Linda J. Levine, "Goals and Responses to Failure: Knowing When to Hold Them and When to Fold Them," *Motivation and Emotion* 32, no. 2 (2008): 127–140; Mario Mikulincer, "Reactance and Helplessness Following Exposure to Unsolvable Problems: The Effects of Attributional Style," *Journal of Personality and Social Psychology* 54, no. 4 (1988): 679–686.

pg. 67:   **channeled into active, healthy striving:** Eddie Harmon-Jones, "On the Relationship of Frontal Brain Activity and Anger: Examining the Role of Attitude Toward Anger," *Cognition and Emotion* 18, no. 3 (2004): 337–361; Eddie Harmon-Jones and

Jonathan Sigelman, "State Anger and Prefrontal Brain Activity: Evidence That Insult-Related Relative Left-Prefrontal Activation Is Associated with Experienced Anger and Aggression," *Journal of Personality and Social Psychology* 80, no. 5 (2001): 797–803.

pg. 67: **"It is wise to direct your anger":** Although the exact source of this quote is unclear, it is widely attributed to William Arthur Ward.

pg. 67: **"Work, work, work":** Richard F. Mollica, *Healing Invisible Wounds: Paths to Hope and Recovery in a Violent World* (Nashville: Vanderbilt University Press, 2008), 170.

pg. 67: **maneuver that can even override:** Jaak Panksepp and Margaret R. Zellner, "Towards a Neurobiologically Based Unified Theory of Aggression," *Revue Internationale de Psychologie Sociale* 17, no. 2 (2004): 37–61; Rebecca L. Shiner, Ann S. Masten, and Jennifer M. Roberts, "Childhood Personality Foreshadows Adult Personality and Life Outcomes Two Decades Later," *Journal of Personality* 71, no. 6 (2003): 1145–1170.

pg. 67: **anger activates the left prefrontal cortex:** Henk Aarts et al., "The Art of Anger: Reward Context Turns Avoidance Responses to Anger-Related Objects into Approach," *Psychological Science* 21, no. 10 (2010): 1406–1410; Charles S. Carver and Eddie Harmon-Jones, "Anger Is an Approach-Related Affect: Evidence and Implications," *Psychological Bulletin* 135, no. 2 (2009): 183–204; Jaak Panksepp and Margaret R. Zellner, "Towards a Neurobiologically Based Unified Theory of Aggression," *Revue Internationale de Psychologie Sociale* 17, no. 2 (2004): 37–61.

pg. 68: **we feel assertive, self-directed, and in control:** Richard J. Davidson, "What Does the Prefrontal Cortex 'Do' in Affect: Perspectives on Frontal EEG Asymmetry Research," *Biological Psychology* 67, no. 1 (2004): 219–234.

pg. 68: **here in the left prefrontal cortex that anger can help:** Jennifer S. Lerner and Larissa Z. Tiedens, "Portrait of the Angry Decision Maker: How Appraisal Tendencies Shape Anger's Influence on Cognition," *Journal of Behavioral Decision Making* 19, no. 2 (2006): 115–137.

pg. 68: **in the brain, anger looks a lot like happiness:** Charles S. Carver and Eddie Harmon-Jones, "Anger Is an Approach-Related Affect: Evidence and Implications," *Psychological Bulletin* 135, no. 2 (2009): 183–204.

pg. 68: **fearful, angry, or happy:** Jennifer S. Lerner and Dacher Keltner, "Fear, Anger, and Risk," *Journal of Personality and Social Psychology* 81, no. 1 (2001): 146–159.

pg. 68: **"a bias toward seeing the self":** Jennifer S. Lerner and Larissa Z. Tiedens, "Portrait of the Angry Decision Maker: How Appraisal Tendencies Shape Anger's Influence on Cognition," *Journal of Behavioral Decision Making* 19, no. 2 (2006): 125; see also Carroll E. Izard, *The Psychology of Emotions* (New York: Plenum Press, 1991).

pg. 68: **another study by Jennifer Lerner and colleagues:** Jennifer S. Lerner et al., "Facial Expressions of Emotion Reveal Neuroendocrine and Cardiovascular Stress Responses," *Biological Psychiatry* 61, no. 2 (2007): 253–260.

pg. 69: **more equipped to move forward:** Phillip Shaver et al., "Emotion Knowledge: Further Exploration of a Prototype Approach," *Journal of Personality and Social Psychology* 52, no. 6 (1987): 1061–1086.

pg. 69: **"There's only one thing":** Paul Ferris, *Dylan Thomas: A Biography* (London: Hodder and Stoughton, 1977), 49.

pg. 70: **"steeling effect":** Michael Rutter, "Implications of Resilience Concepts for Scientific Understanding," *Annals of the New York Academy of Sciences* 1094, no. 1 (2006): 1–12; Michael Rutter, "Resilience as a Dynamic Concept," *Development and Psychopathology* 24, no. 2 (2012): 335–344; Michael Rutter, "Stress, Coping and Development: Some Issues and Some Questions," *Journal of Child Psychology and Psychiatry* 22, no. 4 (1981): 323–356; see also Donald Meichenbaum, "Stress Inoculation Training: A Twenty Year Update" in *Principles and Practices of Stress Management*, 2nd ed., eds. Robert L. Woolfolk and Paul M. Lehrer (New York: Guilford Press, 1993), 373–406.

pg. 70: **"toughness model":** Richard A. Dienstbier, "Arousal and Physiological Toughness: Implications for Mental and Physical Health," *Psychological Review* 96, no. 1 (1989):

84–100; Richard A. Dienstbier and Lisa M. Pytlik Zillig, "Toughness," in *Handbook of Positive Psychology*, eds. C. R. Snyder and Shane J. Lopez (New York: Oxford University Press, 2002), 515–527.

pg. 70: **adversity can indeed make us hardier:** Megan R. Gunnar et al., "Moderate Versus Severe Early Life Stress: Associations with Stress Reactivity and Regulation in 10-12-Year-Old Children," *Psychoneuroendocrinology* 34, no. 1 (2009): 62–75; Mark D. Seery et al., "An Upside to Adversity? Moderate Cumulative Lifetime Adversity Is Associated with Resilient Responses in the Face of Controlled Stressors," *Psychological Science* 24, no. 7 (2013): 1181–1189.

pg. 70: **early exposure to brief stressors:** Karen J. Parker et al., "Prospective Investigation of Stress Inoculation in Young Monkeys," *Archives of General Psychiatry* 61, no. 9 (2004): 933–941.

pg. 70: **exposed peripherally to combat showed greater gains:** Paula P. Schnurr, Stanley D. Rosenberg, and Matthew J. Friedman, "Change in MMPI Scores from College to Adulthood as a Function of Military Service," *Journal of Abnormal Psychology* 102, no. 2 (1993): 288–296.

pg. 71: **"in moderation, whatever does not kill us":** Mark D. Seery, E. Alison Holman, and Roxane Cohen Silver, "Whatever Does Not Kill Us: Cumulative Lifetime Adversity, Vulnerability, and Resilience," *Journal of Personality and Social Psychology* 99, no. 6 (2010): 1025–1041; see also Mark D. Seery, "Resilience: A Silver Lining to Experiencing Adverse Life Events?" *Current Directions in Psychological Science* 20, no. 6 (2011): 390–394.

CHAPTER 5: FLIGHT

pg. 72: **"If one is lucky":** Although the exact source of this quote is unclear, it is widely attributed to Maya Angelou.

pg. 73: **resist being defined or engulfed:** Elwyn James Anthony, "The Mutative Impact of Serious Mental and Physical Illness in a Parent on Family Life," in *The Child in His Family*, eds. Elwyn James Anthony and C. Koupernik (New York: John Wiley and Sons, 1970), 131–163; Elwyn James Anthony, "The Syndrome of the Psychologically Invulnerable Child," in *The Child in His Family*, eds. Elwyn James Anthony and C. Koupernik (New York: John Wiley and Sons, 1974), 529–545; W. R. Beardslee and M. A. Podorefsky, "Resilient Adolescents Whose Parents Have Serious Affective and Other Psychiatric Disorders: Importance of Self-Understanding and Relationships," *American Journal of Psychiatry* 145, no. 1 (1988): 63–69; Manfred Bleuler, "The Offspring of Schizophrenics," *Schizophrenia Bulletin* 1, no. 8 (1974): 93–107; L. Fisher et al., "Competent Children at Risk: A Study of Well-Functioning Offspring of Disturbed Parents," in *The Invulnerable Child*, eds. Elwyn James Anthony and Bertram J. Cohler (New York: Guilford Press, 1987), 211; Elaine Mordoch and Wendy A. Hall, "Children's Perceptions of Living with a Parent with a Mental Illness: Finding the Rhythm and Maintaining the Frame," *Qualitative Health Research* 18, no. 8 (2008): 1127–1144.

pg. 73: **two ways of coping with stress:** Susan Folkman and Richard S. Lazarus, "Coping and Emotion," in *Psychological and Biological Approaches to Emotion*, eds. Nancy L. Stein, Bennett Leventhal, and Thomas R. Trabasso (Hillsdale, NJ: Lawrence Erlbaum Associates, 1990), 313–332; Susan Folkman and Richard S. Lazarus, "Coping as a Mediator of Emotion," *Journal of Personality and Social Psychology* 54, no. 3 (1988): 466; Richard S. Lazarus and Susan Folkman, *Stress, Appraisal, and Coping* (New York: Springer Publishing Company, 1984).

pg. 74: **distance themselves from the chaos:** Maryann Amodeo and Mary Elizabeth Collins, "Using a Positive Youth Development Approach in Addressing Problem-Oriented Youth Behavior," *Family in Society: The Journal of Contemporary Social Services* 88, no. 1 (2007): 75–85; Jessica M. Fear et al., "Parental Depression and Interparental Conflict:

Children and Adolescents' Self-Blame and Coping Responses," *Journal of Family Psychology* 23, no. 5 (2009): 762–766; Adela M. Langrock et al., "Coping with the Stress of Parental Depression: Parents' Reports of Children's Coping, Emotional, and Behavioral Problems," *Journal of Clinical Child and Adolescent Psychology* 31 (2002): 312–324.

pg. 74:   **creative and temporary forms of coping:** For reviews, see Adela M. Langrock, Bruce E. Compas, Gary Keller, Mary Jane Merchant, and Mary Ellen Copeland, "Coping with the Stress of Parental Depression: Parents' Reports of Children's Coping, Emotional, and Behavioral Problems," *Journal of Clinical Child and Adolescent Psychology* 31, no. 3 (2002): 312–324; Richard Berlin, Ruth B. Davis, and Alan Orenstein, "Adaptive and Reactive Distancing Among Adolescents from Alcoholic Families," *Adolescence* 23, no. 91 (1988): 577–584; Philip M. Bromberg, "Something Wicked This Way Comes: Trauma, Dissociation, and Conflict: The Space Where Psychoanalysis, Cognitive Science, and Neuroscience Overlap," *Psychoanalytic Psychology* 20, no. 3 (2003): 558–574; Judith Butler, *Precarious Life: The Powers of Mourning and Violence* (New York: Verso, 2006); Constance J. Dalenberg and Kelsey Paulson, "The Case for the Study of 'Normal' Dissociation Processes," in *Dissociation and the Dissociative Disorders: DSM-V and Beyond*, eds. Paul F. Dell and John A. O'Neil (New York: Routledge, 2009), 145–154; Onno van der Hart and Rutger Horst, "The Dissociation Theory of Pierre Janet," *Journal of Traumatic Stress* 2, no. 4 (1989): 397–412.

pg. 74:   **"In my mind":** Maya Angelou, *I Know Why the Caged Bird Sings* (New York: Random House, 2015), 69.

pg. 74:   **"He explained":** Maya Angelou, *I Know Why the Caged Bird Sings* (New York: Random House, 2015), 93.

pg. 74:   **"the most basic capacity":** Harry Stack Sullivan, *The Interpersonal Theory of Psychiatry* (New York: Norton, 1953), 215–216.

pg. 75:   **"still-face" research:** Edward Z. Tronick, "Emotions and Emotional Communication in Infants," *American Psychologist* 44, no. 2 (1989): 112–119.

pg. 75:   **he escapes on the inside:** Judith Lewis Herman, *Trauma and Recovery* (New York: Basic Books, 1997), 42.

pg. 75:   **"Do not be conspicuous":** Viktor E. Frankl, *Man's Search for Meaning: An Introduction to Logotherapy* (Boston: Beacon, 2006), 51.

pg. 75:   **Decades of research on resilient children:** Judy Garber and Stephanie Little, "Predictors of Competence Among Offspring of Depressed Mothers," *Journal of Adolescent Research* 14, no. 1 (1999): 44–71; Lois B. Murphy and Alice E. Moriarty, *Vulnerability, Coping and Growth from Infancy to Adolescence* (Oxford, UK: Yale University Press, 1976).

pg. 75:   **Mental distancing is relied upon:** Eve M. Bernstein and Frank W. Putnam, "Development, Reliability, and Validity of a Dissociation Scale," *Journal of Nervous and Mental Disease* 174, no. 12 (1986): 727–735; Frank W. Putnam, *Dissociation in Children and Adolescents: A Developmental Perspective* (New York: Guilford Press, 1997).

pg. 76:   **seek comfort from more predictable sources:** Elaine Mordoch and Wendy A. Hall, "Children's Perceptions of Living with a Parent with a Mental Illness: Finding the Rhythm and Maintaining the Frame," *Qualitative Health Research* 18, no. 8 (2008): 1127–1144.

pg. 77:   **one in five adults struggle:** National Alliance on Mental Illness, "Mental Health Conditions," accessed January 29, 2017, https://www.nami.org/Learn-More/Mental-Health-Conditions.

pg. 77:   **just as likely as other women to be mothers:** Joanne Nicholson and Kathleen Biebel, "Commentary on 'Community Mental Health Care for Women with Severe Mental Illness Who Are Parents'—The Tragedy of Missed Opportunities: What Providers Can Do," *Community Mental Health Journal* 38 no. 2 (2002): 167–172.

pg. 77:   **live with their children as well:** Carol T. Mowbray et al., "Life Circumstances of Mothers with Serious Mental Illnesses," *Psychiatric Rehabilitation Journal* 25, no. 2 (2001): 114–123.

pg. 77: **men with emotional problems:** Stephen P. Hinshaw, *The Years of Silence Are Past: My Father's Life with Bipolar Disorder* (Cambridge, UK: Cambridge University Press, 2002); Andrea Reupert and Darryl Maybery, "Fathers' Experience of Parenting with a Mental Illness," *Families in Society: The Journal of Contemporary Social Services* 90, no. 1 (2009): 61–68; Thomas H. Styron et al., "Fathers with Serious Mental Illnesses: A Neglected Group," *Psychiatric Rehabilitation Journal* 25, no. 3 (2002): 215–222.

pg. 77: **nearly six million adult Americans:** National Institute of Mental Health, "The Numbers Count: Mental Disorders in America," October 1, 2013, accessed January 29, 2017, http://www.lb7.uscourts.gov/documents/12-cv-1072url2.pdf.

pg. 77: **millions of American children:** Sherryl H. Goodman and H. Elizabeth Brumley, "Schizophrenic and Depressed Mothers: Relational Deficits in Parenting," *Developmental Psychology* 26, no. 1 (1990): 31–39; Daphna Oyserman et al., "Parenting Among Mothers with a Serious Mental Illness," *American Journal of Orthopsychiatry* 70, no. 3 (2000): 296–315.

pg. 78: **only a small part of the stress:** Meenakshi Venkataraman, "Parenting Among Mothers with Bipolar Disorder: Children's Perspectives," *Journal of Family Social Work* 14, no. 2 (2011): 93–108.

pg. 78: **more likely to be single parents:** Carol T. Mowbray, Daphna Oyserman, and Deborah Bybee, "Mothers with Serious Mental Illness," *New Directions for Mental Health Services* 88 (2000): 73–91.

pg. 78: **their behavior may be too inconsistent:** Meenakshi Venkataraman and Barry J. Ackerson, "Parenting Among Mothers with Bipolar Disorder: Strengths, Challenges, and Service Needs," *Journal of Family Social Work* 11, no. 4 (2008): 389–408.

pg. 78: **likely to impact children not just once:** Constance Hammen and Patricia A. Brennan, "Severity, Chronicity, and Timing of Maternal Depression and Risk for Adolescent Offspring Diagnoses in a Community Sample," *Archives of General Psychiatry* 60, no. 3 (2003): 253–258; Daphna Oyserman et al., "Parenting Among Mothers with a Serious Mental Illness," *American Journal of Orthopsychiatry* 70, no. 3 (2000): 296–315.

pg. 78: **find deep meaning in their roles as caregivers:** Barry J. Ackerson, "Parents with Serious and Persistent Mental Illness: Issues in Assessment and Services," *Social Work* 48, no. 2 (2003): 187–194; Phyllis Montgomery et al., "Keeping Close: Mothering with Serious Mental Illness," *Journal of Advanced Nursing* 54, no. 1 (2006): 20–28; Carol T. Mowbray et al., "Life Circumstances of Mothers with Serious Mental Illnesses," *Psychiatric Rehabilitation Journal* 25, no. 2 (2001): 114–123; Thomas H. Styron et al., "Fathers with Serious Mental Illnesses: A Neglected Group," *Psychiatric Rehabilitation Journal* 25, no. 3 (2002): 215–222.

pg. 78: **tend to see their parents as good parents:** Meenakshi Venkataraman, "Parenting Among Mothers with Bipolar Disorder: Children's Perspectives," *Journal of Family Social Work* 14, no. 2 (2011): 93–108.

pg. 78: **children suffer less:** Elaine Mordoch and Wendy A. Hall, "Children's Perceptions of Living with a Parent with a Mental Illness: Finding the Rhythm and Maintaining the Frame," *Qualitative Health Research* 18, no. 8 (2008): 1127–1144.

pg. 78: **greater risk for emotional and behavioral problems:** For a review, see William R. Beardselee, Eve M. Versage, and Tracy Gladstone, "Children of Affectively Ill Parents: A Review of the Past 10 Years," *Journal of the American Academy of Child and Adolescent Psychiatry* 37, no. 11 (1998): 1134–1141; Arin M. Connell and Sherryl H. Goodman, "The Association Between Psychopathology in Fathers Versus Mothers and Children's Internalizing and Externalizing Behavior Problems: A Meta-Analysis," *Psychological Bulletin* 128, no. 5 (2002): 746–773.

pg. 79: **they look and function like their peers:** Manfred Bleuler, "The Offspring of Schizophrenics," *Schizophrenia Bulletin* 1, no. 8 (1974): 93–107; L. Fisher et al., "Competent Children at Risk: A Study of Well-Functioning Offspring of Disturbed Parents," in *The Invulnerable Child*, eds. Elwyn James Anthony and Bertram J. Cohler (New York:

Guilford Press, 1987), 211; Judy Garber and Stephanie Little, "Predictors of Competence Among Offspring of Depressed Mothers," *Journal of Adolescent Research* 14, no. 1 (1999): 44–71; Norman Garmezy, Ann S. Masten, and Auke Tellegen, "The Study of Stress and Competence in Children: A Building Block for Developmental Psychopathology," *Child Development* 55, no. 1 (1984): 97–111; Carol T. Mowbray et al., "Children of Mothers Diagnosed with Serious Mental Illness: Patterns and Predictors of Service Use," *Mental Health Services Research* 6, no. 3 (2004): 167–183; David G. Scherer et al., "Relation Between Children's Perceptions of Maternal Mental Illness and Children's Psychological Adjustment," *Journal of Clinical Child Psychology* 25, no. 2 (1996): 156–169.

pg. 79:   **"The school had a couple of practice rooms":** James Rhodes, *Instrumental: A Memoir of Madness, Medication, and Music* (Edinburgh: Canongate, 2015), 39.

pg. 80:   **"Whenever I danced":** Misty Copeland, *Life in Motion: An Unlikely Ballerina* (New York: Touchstone, 2014), 24–25.

pg. 80:   **selective *inattention*:** Harry Stack Sullivan, *Clinical Studies in Psychiatry* (New York: Norton, 1956).

pg. 80:   **50 percent of our waking hours:** See, for reviews, Matthew A. Killingsworth and Daniel T. Gilbert, "A Wandering Mind Is an Unhappy Mind," *Science* 330, no. 6006 (2010): 932–932; E. C. Klinger, "Thought Flow: Properties and Mechanisms Underlying Shifts in Content," in *At Play in the Fields of Consciousness: Essays in the Honour of Jerome L. Singer*, eds. J. A. Singer and P. Salovey (Mahwah, NJ: Erlbaum, 1999), 29–50; Benjamin W. Mooneyham and Jonathan W. Schooler, "The Costs and Benefits of Mind-Wandering: A Review," *Canadian Journal of Experimental Psychology* 67, no. 1 (2013): 11–18; Jonathan Smallwood and Jessica A. Andrews-Hanna, "Not All Minds That Wander Are Lost: The Importance of a Balanced Perspective on the Mind-Wandering State," *Frontiers in Psychology* 4, no. 441 (2013): 1–6.

pg. 80:   **serve some important survival functions:** Judith Butler, *Precarious Life: The Powers of Mourning and Violence* (New York: Verso, 2006); Jonathan W. Schooler et al., "Meta-Awareness, Perceptual Decoupling and the Wandering Mind," *Trends in Cognitive Sciences* 15, no. 7 (2011): 319–326; Jerome L. Singer, *The Inner World of Daydreaming* (New York: Harper and Row, 1975).

pg. 80:   **preoccupations can be quite positive:** Ralph Erber and Abraham Tesser, "Task Effort and the Regulation of Mood: The Absorption Hypothesis," *Journal of Experimental Social Psychology* 28, no. 4 (1992): 339–359.

pg. 80:   **feeling of "flow":** Mihaly Csikszentmihalyi, *Finding Flow: The Psychology of Engagement with Everyday Life* (New York: Basic Books, 1997).

pg. 81:   **"One of the direct consequences":** Jean Piaget, "Autobiography," in *A History of Psychology in Autobiography (Vol. 4)*, eds. Herbert S. Langfeld, Edwin G. Boring, Heinz Werner, and Robert M. Yerkes (Oxford, UK: Clark University Press), 237. Also quoted in Elwyn James Anthony, "Children at High Risk of Psychosis Growing Up Successfully," in *The Invulnerable Child*, eds. Elwyn James Anthony and Bertram J. Cohler (New York: Guilford Press, 1987), 161.

pg. 81:   **By fifteen, he was a recognized malacologist:** Elwyn James Anthony, "Children at High Risk of Psychosis Growing Up Successfully," in *The Invulnerable Child*, eds. Elwyn James Anthony and Bertram J. Cohler (New York: Guilford Press, 1987), 162.

pg. 81:   **"not all minds that wander are lost":** Jonathan Smallwood and Jessica A. Andrews-Hanna, "Not All Minds That Wander Are Lost: The Importance of a Balanced Perspective on the Mind-Wandering State," *Frontiers in Psychology* 4, no. 441 (2013): 1–6.

pg. 81:   **becoming engrossed in daydreaming or fantasy:** I use the terms *mindwandering*, *daydreaming*, and *fantasy* interchangeably, although some scholars would argue these are different constructs.

pg. 81:   **Daydreams of being an animal or a superhero:** Bruce D. Perry, "The Neurodevelopmental Impact of Violence in Childhood," *Textbook of Child and Adolescent Forensic*

Psychiatry, eds. D. Schetky and E. P. Benedek (Washington, DC: American Psychiatric Press, 2001), 221–238; Elwyn James Anthony, "Risk, Vulnerability, and Resilience: An Overview," in *The Invulnerable Child*, eds. Elwyn James Anthony and Bertram J. Cohler (New York: Guilford Press, 1987), 45.

pg. 82:   **"I wished to be left alone":** Victor Goertzel and Mildred George Goertzel, *Cradles of Eminence: Childhoods of More than Seven Hundred Famous Men and Women* (Scottsdale, AZ: Great Potential Press, 2004), 76; Eleanor Roosevelt, *This Is My Story* (New York: Harper, 1937), 21.

pg. 82:   **study of abused children from Israel:** Hanita Zimrin, "A Profile of Survival," *Child Abuse and Neglect* 10, no. 3 (1986): 339–349.

pg. 82:   **"I never knew whether I would live":** Hanita Zimrin, "A Profile of Survival," *Child Abuse and Neglect* 10, no. 3 (1986): 346.

pg. 82:   **"In my mind I took bus rides":** Viktor E. Frankl, *Man's Search for Meaning: An Introduction to Logotherapy* (Boston: Beacon, 2006), 39.

pg. 82:   **through the portal of books:** Kara Coombes and Ruth Anderson, "The Impact of Family of Origin on Social Workers from Alcoholic Families," *Clinical Social Work Journal* 28, no. 3 (2000): 281–302.

pg. 82:   **"I suppose all fictional characters":** Although the original source of this quote is unclear, it is widely attributed to Alan Moore.

pg. 83:   **"I was always lost in a book":** Akhil Sharma, *Family Life: A Novel* (New York: W. W. Norton & Company, 2014), 150.

pg. 83:   **found a way not to be home:** Elaine Mordoch and Wendy A. Hall, "Children's Perceptions of Living with a Parent with a Mental Illness: Finding the Rhythm and Maintaining the Frame," *Qualitative Health Research* 18, no. 8 (2008): 1127–1144.

pg. 84:   **silence was automatic:** Stephen P. Hinshaw, "Parental Mental Disorder and Children's Functioning: Silence and Communication, Stigma and Resilience," *Journal of Clinical Child and Adolescent Psychology* 33, no. 2 (2004): 400–411.

pg. 85:   **"healing-place of the soul":** Frieda Weise, "Being There: The Library as Place," *Journal of the Medical Library Association* 92, no. 1 (2004), 6–13.

pg. 85:   **usually quite skilled at self-hypnosis:** Auke Tellegen and Gilbert Atkinson, "Openness to Absorbing and Self-Altering Experiences ('Absorption'), A Trait Related to Hypnotic Susceptibility," *Journal of Abnormal Psychology* 83, no. 3 (1974): 268–277.

pg. 86:   **rather than being afraid of change:** Victor Goertzel and Mildred George Goertzel, *Cradles of Eminence: Childhoods of More than Seven Hundred Famous Men and Women* (Scottsdale, AZ: Great Potential Press, 2004), 80.

pg. 86:   **vision of one's future self furthers achievement:** Benjamin Baird, Jonathan Smallwood, and Jonathan W. Schooler, "Back to the Future: Autobiographical Planning and the Functionality of Mind-Wandering," *Consciousness and Cognition* 20, no. 4 (2011): 1604–1611; Angeliki Leondari, Efi Syngollitou, and Grigoris Kiosseoglou, "Academic Achievement, Motivation and Future Selves," *Educational Studies* 24, no. 2 (1998): 153–163; Benjamin W. Mooneyham and Jonathan W. Schooler, "The Costs and Benefits of Mind-Wandering: A Review," *Canadian Journal of Experimental Psychology* 67, no. 1 (2013): 11–18; E. Paul Torrance, "The Beyonders in a Thirty Year Longitudinal Study of Creative Achievement," *Roeper Review* 15, no. 3 (1993): 131–135; E. Paul Torrance, "The Importance of Falling in Love with 'Something,'" *Creative Child and Adult Quarterly* 8, no. 2 (1983): 72–78.

pg. 86:   **autobiographical planning:** Jerome L. Singer, *The Inner World of Daydreaming* (New York: Harper and Row, 1975).

pg. 86:   **self-determined, intentional, and future-oriented:** Thomas S. Bateman and Christine Porath, "Transcendent Behavior," in *Positive Organizational Scholarship: Foundations of a New Discipline*, eds. Kim Cameron, Jane Dutton, and Robert Quinn (San Francisco: Berrett-Koehler Publishers, 2003), 122–137.

pg. 87:   **"They were my ticket out":** Alan Cumming, *Not My Father's Son: A Family Memoir* (Edinburgh: Canongate, 2014), 72.

CHAPTER 6: VIGILANCE

pg. 88: **"I've got second sight":** Pink Floyd, "Nobody Home," by Roger Waters, in *The Wall*, Columbia Records, 1979, accessed February 27, 2017, https://genius.com/Pink-floyd-nobody-home-lyrics.

pg. 91: **most common form of family violence:** Murray A. Straus and Richard J. Gelles, *Physical Violence in American Families: Risk Factors and Adaptation to Violence in 8,145 Families* (New Brunswick, NJ: Transaction Publishers, 1990); Murray A. Straus, Richard J. Gelles, and Suzanne K. Steinmetz, *Behind Closed Doors: Violence in American Families* (Garden City, NY: Anchor/Doubleday, 1980).

pg. 91: **rarely reported to authorities:** Vernon R. Wiehe, "Sibling Abuse," in *Domestic Violence and Child Abuse Resource Sourcebook*, ed. Helene Henderson (Detroit: Omnigraphics, 2000), 409–492.

pg. 91: **legally ignored as a family problem:** Lisa Stock, "Sibling Abuse: It Is Much More Serious than Child's Play," *Child Legal Rights Journal* 14 (1993): 19–21.

pg. 91: **about one-third of children:** David Finkelhor et al., "Violence, Abuse, and Crime Exposure in a National Sample of Children and Youth," *Pediatrics* 124, no. 5 (2009): 1411–1423; Murray A. Straus and Richard J. Gelles, *Physical Violence in American Families: Risk Factors and Adaptation to Violence in 8,145 Families* (New Brunswick, NJ: Transaction Publishers, 1990); Murray A. Straus, Richard J. Gelles, and Suzanne K. Steinmetz, *Behind Closed Doors: Violence in American Families* (Garden City, NY: Anchor/Doubleday, 1980); Corinna J. Tucker, David Finkelhor, Anne M. Shattuck, and Heather Turner, "Prevalence and Correlates of Sibling Victimization Types," *Child Abuse and Neglect* 37, no. 4 (2013): 213–223.

pg. 91: **between one-half and three-quarters of young adults:** Shelley Eriksen and Vickie Jensen, "A Push or a Punch: Distinguishing the Severity of Sibling Violence," *Journal of Interpersonal Violence* 24, no. 1 (2009): 183–208; Megan P. Goodwin and Bruce Roscoe, "Sibling Violence and Agonistic Interactions Among Middle Adolescents," *Adolescence* 25, no. 98 (1990): 451–467; Marjorie S. Hardy, "Physical Aggression and Sexual Behavior Among Siblings: A Retrospective Study," *Journal of Family Violence* 16, no. 3 (2001): 255–268; Heather H. Kettrey and Beth C. Emery, "The Discourse of Sibling Violence," *Journal of Family Violence* 21, no. 6 (2006): 407–416; Catherine J. Simonelli et al., "Abuse by Siblings and Subsequent Experiences of Violence Within the Dating Relationship," *Journal of Interpersonal Violence* 17, no. 2 (2002): 103–121; Murray A. Straus and Richard J. Gelles, *Physical Violence in American Families: Risk Factors and Adaptation to Violence in 8,145 Families* (New Brunswick, NJ: Transaction Publishers, 1990); Murray A. Straus, Richard J. Gelles, and Suzanne K. Steinmetz, *Behind Closed Doors: Violence in American Families* (Garden City, NY: Anchor/Doubleday, 1980).

pg. 92: **even more frequent emotional abuse:** Murray A. Straus, Richard J. Gelles, and Suzanne K. Steinmetz, *Behind Closed Doors: Violence in American Families* (Garden City, NY: Anchor/Doubleday, 1980); Vernon R. Wiehe, *Understanding Family Violence* (Thousand Oaks, CA: Sage, 1998).

pg. 92: **threatened by a sibling with a gun or a knife:** Shelley Eriksen and Vickie Jensen, "A Push or a Punch: Distinguishing the Severity of Sibling Violence," *Journal of Interpersonal Violence* 24, no. 1 (2009): 183–208; Catherine J. Simonelli et al., "Abuse by Siblings and Subsequent Experiences of Violence Within the Dating Relationship," *Journal of Interpersonal Violence* 17, no. 2 (2002): 103–121.

pg. 92: **"children are the most violent persons":** Murray A. Straus and Richard J. Gelles, *Physical Violence in American Families: Risk Factors and Adaptation to Violence in 8,145 Families* (New Brunswick, NJ: Transaction Publishers, 1990), 110.

pg. 92: **Sibling violence may be pandemic:** David Finkelhor and Jennifer Dziuba-Leatherman, "Children as Victims of Violence: A National Survey," *Pediatrics* 94, no. 4 (1994): 413–420; Kristi L. Hoffman and John N. Edwards, "An Integrated Theoretical Model of Sibling Violence and Abuse," *Journal of Family Violence* 19, no. 3 (2004): 185–200.

pg. 92:   **ubiquity only contributes to it being seen as harmless:** Jonathan Caspi, *Sibling Aggression: Assessment and Treatment* (New York: Springer Publishing Company, 2012).

pg. 92:   **sisters can be chronically and seriously abusive:** Heather H. Kettrey and Beth C. Emery, "The Discourse of Sibling Violence," *Journal of Family Violence* 21, no. 6 (2006): 407–416; Jessie L. Krienert and Jeffrey A. Walsh, "My Brother's Keeper: A Contemporary Examination of Reported Sibling Violence Using National Level Data, 2000–2005," *Journal of Family Violence* 26, no. 5 (2011): 331–342.

pg. 92:   **minimize their own experiences, preferring labels:** Marjorie S. Hardy, "Physical Aggression and Sexual Behavior Among Siblings: A Retrospective Study," *Journal of Family Violence* 16, no. 3 (2001): 255–268; Heather H. Kettrey and Beth C. Emery, "The Discourse of Sibling Violence," *Journal of Family Violence* 21, no. 6 (2006): 407–416.

pg. 92:   **peaks before the teen years:** Jonathan Caspi, *Sibling Aggression: Assessment and Treatment* (New York: Springer Publishing Company, 2012); David Finkelhor, Richard K. Ormrod, and Heather A. Turner, "Lifetime Assessment of Poly-Victimization in a National Sample of Children and Youth," *Child Abuse and Neglect* 33, no. 7 (2009): 403–411; David Finkelhor, Heather Turner, and Richard Ormrod, "Kid's Stuff: The Nature and Impact of Peer and Sibling Violence on Younger and Older Children," *Child Abuse and Neglect* 30, no. 12 (2006): 1401–1421; Jacqueline L. Martin and Hildy S. Ross, "Sibling Aggression: Sex Differences and Parents' Reactions," *International Journal of Behavioral Development* 29, no. 2 (2005): 129–138; Corinna J. Tucker et al., "Sibling Proactive and Reactive Aggression in Adolescence," *Journal of Family Violence* 28, no. 3 (2013): 299–310.

pg. 93:   **"grow out of it":** Corinna J. Tucker, David Finkelhor, Heather Turner, and Anne M. Shattuck, "Sibling and Peer Victimization in Childhood and Adolescence," *Child Abuse and Neglect* 38, no. 10 (2014): 1599–1606.

pg. 93:   **parents often deny its significance:** Mark S. Kiselica and Mandy Morrill-Richards, "Sibling Maltreatment: The Forgotten Abuse," *Journal of Counseling and Development* 85, no. 2 (2007): 148–160.

pg. 93:   **can have long-lasting emotional effects:** John V. Caffaro and Allison Conn-Caffaro, *Sibling Abuse Trauma: Assessment and Intervention Strategies for Children, Families, and Adults* (London: Routledge, 1998); Shelley Eriksen and Vickie Jensen, "All in the Family? Family Environment Factors in Sibling Violence," *Journal of Family Violence* 21, no. 8 (2006): 497–507; Shelley Eriksen and Vickie Jensen, "A Push or a Punch: Distinguishing the Severity of Sibling Violence," *Journal of Interpersonal Violence* 24, no. 1 (2009): 183–208; David Finkelhor, Heather Turner, and Richard Ormrod, "Kid's Stuff: The Nature and Impact of Peer and Sibling Violence on Younger and Older Children," *Child Abuse and Neglect* 30, no. 12 (2006): 1401–1421.

pg. 93:   **Violence that does continue into high school:** Shelley Eriksen and Vickie Jensen, "A Push or a Punch: Distinguishing the Severity of Sibling Violence," *Journal of Interpersonal Violence* 24, no. 1 (2009): 183–208; David Finkelhor, Heather Turner, and Richard Ormrod, "Kid's Stuff: The Nature and Impact of Peer and Sibling Violence on Younger and Older Children," *Child Abuse and Neglect* 30, no. 12 (2006): 1401–1421; Corinna J. Tucker et al., "Sibling Proactive and Reactive Aggression in Adolescence," *Journal of Family Violence* 28, no. 3 (2013): 299–310.

pg. 93:   **by a brother or a sister than by a peer:** David Finkelhor, Heather Turner, and Richard Ormrod, "Kid's Stuff: The Nature and Impact of Peer and Sibling Violence on Younger and Older Children," *Child Abuse and Neglect* 30, no. 12 (2006): 1401–1421.

pg. 93:   **more closely than they watch their parents:** Linda M. Baskett, "Ordinal Position Differences in Children's Family Interactions," *Developmental Psychology* 20, no. 6 (1984): 1026–1031.

pg. 93:   **"traumatic expectations":** Robert S. Pynoos et al., "Issues in the Developmental Neurobiology of Traumatic Stress," *Annals of the New York Academy of Sciences* 821, no. 1

(1997): 176–193; Robert S. Pynoos, "The Transgenerational Repercussions of Traumatic Expectations" (paper presented at the 6th IPA Conference on Psychoanalytic Research, University of London, March 8–9, 1996).

pg. 93: **"anxiety of premonitions":** Jerome Kagan, "A Conceptual Analysis of the Affects," *Journal of American Psychoanalytic Association* 39 (1991): 109–130.

pg. 94: **"I lived in a world":** Jeannette Walls, *The Glass Castle: A Memoir* (New York: Scribner, 2009), 34.

pg. 94: **moments that precede the need for fight or flight:** Joseph E. LeDoux, "Emotion: Clues from the Brain," *Annual Review of Psychology* 46 (1995): 209–235.

pg. 94: **in uncertain and *potentially* dangerous situations:** John H. Krystal et al., "Neurobiological Aspects of PTSD: Review of Clinical and Preclinical Studies," *Behavior Therapy* 20, no. 2 (1989): 177–198; Lisa M. Shin, "The Amygdala in Post-Traumatic Stress Disorder," in *Post-Traumatic Stress Disorder: Basic Science and Clinical Practice*, eds. Joseph E. LeDoux, Terrence Keane, and Peter Shiromani (New York: Springer Science and Business Media, 2009), 319–336; Paul J. Whalen, "Fear, Vigilance, and Ambiguity: Initial Neuroimaging Studies of the Human Amygdala," *Current Directions in Psychological Science* (1998): 177–188.

pg. 94: **smoke detector principle:** Randolph M. Nesse, "Natural Selection and the Regulation of Defenses: A Signal Detection Analysis of the Smoke Detector Principle," *Evolution and Human Behavior* 26, no. 1 (2005): 88–105; Randolph M. Nesse, "The Smoke Detector Principle," *Annals of the New York Academy of Sciences* 935, no. 1 (2001): 75–85.

pg. 94: **creates long-lasting alterations:** Donald G. Rainnie and Kerry J. Ressler, "Physiology of the Amygdala: Implications for PTSD," in *Post-Traumatic Stress Disorder: Basic Science and Clinical Practice*, eds. Joseph E. LeDoux, Terrence Keane, and Peter Shiromani (New York: Springer Science and Business Media, 2009), 39–78.

pg. 94: **amygdalae of two groups of soldiers:** Guido A. van Wingen et al., "Perceived Threat Predicts the Neural Sequelae of Combat Stress," *Molecular Psychiatry* 16, no. 6 (2011): 664–671.

pg. 95: **exposed to family violence and twenty-three who had not:** Eamon J. McCrory et al., "Heightened Neural Reactivity to Threat in Child Victims of Family Violence," *Current Biology* 21, no. 23 (2011): R947–R948.

pg. 95: **larger amygdalae than their peers:** Sonia J. Lupien et al., "Larger Amygdala but No Change in Hippocampal Volume in 10-Year-Old Children Exposed to Maternal Depressive Symptomatology Since Birth," *Proceedings of the National Academy of Sciences* 108, no. 34 (2011): 14324–14329.

pg. 96: **"Once you've been there long enough":** Laurence Gonzales, *Surviving Survival: The Art and Science of Resilience* (New York: Norton, 2012), 70.

pg. 96: **already paying closer attention to certain details:** Karen A. Frankel, Elizabeth A. Boetsch, and Robert J. Harmon, "Elevated Picture Completion Scores: A Possible Indicator of Hypervigilance in Maltreated Preschoolers," *Child Abuse and Neglect* 24, no. 1 (2000): 63–70.

pg. 96: **Wechsler Preschool and Primary Scale of Intelligence:** David Wechsler, *Manual: Wechsler Preschool and Primary Scale of Intelligence, Revised* (San Antonio: Psychological Corporation, 1989).

pg. 96: **better than same-aged peers on one subtest: Picture Completion:** In this study, descriptive statistics were obtained only on WPPSI Performance scales. These include Object Assembly, Geometric Design, Block Design, Mazes, and Picture Completion.

pg. 97: **survival depends on reading and reacting to them:** First published in 1872. For a more recent edition, see Charles Darwin, Paul Ekman, and Phillip Prodger, *The Expression of the Emotions in Man and Animals, 3rd edition* (London: Harper Collins, 1998).

pg. 97: **specific movements of facial muscles:** Paul Ekman and Wallace V. Friesen, *Manual for the Facial Action Coding System* (Palo Alto, CA: Consulting Psychologists Press, 1978).

pg. 97: **Multiple studies:** Dante Cicchetti and Adrienne Banny, "A Developmental Psychopathology Perspective on Child Maltreatment," in *Handbook of Developmental Psychopathology,* eds. Michael Lewis and Karen D. Rudolph (New York: Springer, 2014), 723–741; Nikki Luke and Robin Banerjee, "Differentiated Associations Between Childhood Maltreatment Experiences and Social Understanding: A Meta-Analysis and Systematic Review," *Developmental Review* 33, no. 1 (2013): 1–28; Seth D. Pollak, "Mechanisms Linking Early Experience and the Emergence of Emotions: Illustrations from the Study of Maltreated Children," *Current Directions in Psychological Science* 17, no. 6 (2008): 370–375. See, for reviews, Willem E. Frankenhuis and Carolina de Weerth, "Does Early-Life Exposure to Stress Shape or Impair Cognition?" *Current Directions in Psychological Science* 22, no. 5 (2013): 407–412.

pg. 97: **In the first study:** Seth D. Pollak and Pawan Sinha, "Effects of Early Experience on Children's Recognition of Facial Displays of Emotion," *Developmental Psychology* 38, no. 5 (2002): 784–791.

pg. 98: **In a related study:** Seth D. Pollak et al., "Development of Perceptual Expertise in Emotion Recognition," *Cognition* 110, no. 2 (2009): 242–247.

pg. 98: **A third study:** Seth D. Pollak et al., "Physically Abused Children's Regulation of Attention in Response to Hostility," *Child Development* 76, no. 5 (2005): 968–977.

pg. 98: **"Pain or suffering of any kind":** Charles Darwin and Francis Darwin, ed., *The Life and Letters of Charles Darwin, Including an Autobiographical Chapter* (New York: D. Appleton and Company, 1887), 280.

pg. 99: **a shrewd observer:** See, for good discussion, Judith L. Herman, *Trauma and Recovery* (New York: Basic Books, 1997), 99.

pg. 99: **like a barometer, always gauging the moods of others:** Julien Worland et al., "St. Louis Risk Research Project: Comprehensive Progress Report of Experimental Studies," in *Children at Risk for Schizophrenia: A Longitudinal Perspective,* eds. Norman F. Watt et al. (New York: Cambridge University Press, 1984), 105–147.

pg. 101: **what unbroken prisoners do:** Judith L. Herman, *Trauma and Recovery* (New York: Basic Books, 1997), 90.

pg. 102: **like Sherlock Holmes:** See, for a description of a case study, Elwyn J. Anthony and Bertram J. Cohler, eds., *The Invulnerable Child* (New York: Guilford Press, 1987), 323.

pg. 102: **"Sherlock Holmes was just a superior human being":** Laurence Maslon and Michael Kantor, *Superheroes!: Capes, Cowls, and the Creation of Comic Book Culture* (New York: Crown Archetype, 2013), 136.

pg. 103: **by developing specialized survival skills:** Willem E. Frankenhuis and Carolina de Weerth, "Does Early-Life Exposure to Stress Shape or Impair Cognition?" *Current Directions in Psychological Science* 22, no. 5 (2013): 407–412.

pg. 103: **often associated with resilient children and teens:** Laura Campbell-Sills, Sharon L. Cohan, and Murray B. Stein, "Relationship of Resilience to Personality, Coping, and Psychiatric Symptoms in Young Adults," *Behaviour Research and Therapy* 44, no. 4 (2006): 585–599; Rebecca L. Shiner, Ann S. Masten, and Jennifer M. Roberts, "Childhood Personality Foreshadows Adult Personality and Life Outcomes Two Decades Later," *Journal of Personality* 71, no. 6 (2003): 1145–1170.

pg. 103: **low-power individuals watch others more:** See, for review, Dacher Keltner, Deborah H. Gruenfeld, and Cameron Anderson, "Power, Approach, and Inhibition," *Psychological Review* 110, no. 2 (2003): 265–284.

pg. 103: ***recognize* being in the right place:** Victor Goertzel and Mildred G. Goertzel, *Cradles of Eminence: Childhoods of More than Seven Hundred Famous Men and Women* (Scottsdale, AZ: Great Potential Press, 2004), 332.

pg. 103: **pay attention not only to danger but also to opportunity:** Michael Davis and Paul J. Whalen, "The Amygdala: Vigilance and Emotion," *Molecular Psychiatry* 6, no. 1 (2001): 13–34.

pg. 104: **when they are moderately aroused:** Rajnish P. Rao et al., "PTSD: From Neurons to Networks," in *Post-Traumatic Stress Disorder: Basic Science and Clinical Practice*, eds. Joseph E. LeDoux, Terrence Keane, and Peter Shiromani (New York: Springer Science and Business Media, 2009), 151–186.

pg. 104: **prefrontal cortex and the hippocampus:** Rajnish P. Rao et al., "PTSD: From Neurons to Networks," in *Post-Traumatic Stress Disorder: Basic Science and Clinical Practice*, eds. Joseph E. LeDoux, Terrence Keane, and Peter Shiromani (New York: Springer Science and Business Media, 2009), 151–186; Steven M. Southwick and Dennis S. Charney, *Resilience: The Science of Mastering Life's Greatest Challenges* (New York: Cambridge University Press, 2012), 56.

pg. 104: **locked in to their own hyperarousal:** Mark W. Miller et al., "Low Basal Cortisol and Startle Responding as Possible Biomarkers of PTSD: The Influence of Internalizing and Externalizing Comorbidity," in *Post-Traumatic Stress Disorder: Basic Science and Clinical Practice*, eds. Joseph E. LeDoux, Terrence Keane, and Peter Shiromani (New York: Springer Science and Business Media, 2009), 289.

pg. 104: **vigilance can persist for years, and even for a lifetime:** Rachel Yehuda, "Stress Hormones and PTSD," in *Post-Traumatic Stress Disorder: Basic Science and Clinical Practice*, eds. Joseph E. LeDoux, Terrence Keane, and Peter Shiromani (New York: Springer Science and Business Media, 2009), 257–276.

pg. 104: **"traumatic expectations":** Bessel A. van der Kolk, Alexander C. McFarlane, and Lars Weisaeth, *Traumatic Stress: The Effects of Overwhelming Experience on Mind, Body, and Society* (New York: Guilford, 2012).

pg. 104: **"anxiety of premonitions":** Jerome Kagan, "A Conceptual Analysis of the Affects," *Journal of American Psychoanalytic Association* 39 (1991): 109–130.

pg. 105: **take a toll on the brain and the body:** Dennis S. Charney, "Psychobiological Mechanisms of Resilience and Vulnerability," *Focus* 2, no. 3 (2004): 368–391; Bruce McEwen and Robert Sapolsky, "Stress and your Health," *Journal of Clinical Endocrinology and Metabolism* 91, no. 2 (2006); Hans Selye, "The General Adaptation Syndrome and the Diseases of Adaptation," *Journal of Clinical Endocrinology and Metabolism* 6, no. 2 (1946): 117–230; Steven M. Southwick and Dennis S. Charney, *Resilience: The Science of Mastering Life's Greatest Challenges* (New York: Cambridge University Press, 2012), 56.

pg. 105: **"I haven't really slept in 20 years":** Laurence Gonzales, *Surviving Survival: The Art and Science of Resilience* (New York: Norton, 2012), 167.

pg. 105: **spending less time in what is called delta sleep:** Klaus Bader et al., "Adverse Childhood Experiences Associated with Sleep in Primary Insomnia," *Journal of Sleep Research* 16, no. 3 (2007): 285–296; L. D. Sanford and X. Tang, "Effect of Stress on Sleep and Its Relationship to Post-Traumatic Stress Disorder," in *Post-Traumatic Stress Disorder: Basic Science and Clinical Practice*, eds. Joseph E. LeDoux, Terrence Keane, and Peter Shiromani (New York: Springer Science and Business Media, 2009), 231–256; Martin H. Teicher et al., "The Neurobiological Consequences of Early Stress and Childhood Maltreatment," *Neuroscience and Biobehavioral Reviews* 27, no. 1 (2003): 33–44.

CHAPTER 7: SUPERHUMAN

pg. 107: **"When I was at boarding school":** Oliver Sacks, *On the Move* (New York: Knopf, 2015), 1.

pg. 108: **I Am Adam Lanza's Mother:** Liza Long, "I Am Adam Lanza's Mother," *Blue Review*, Boise State University School of Public Service, December 15, 2012, http://the bluereview.org/i-am-adam-lanzas-mother.

pg. 110: **umbrella term intended to cover:** Merle McPherson et al., "A New Definition of Children with Special Health Care Needs," *Pediatrics* 102, no. 1 (1998): 137–139; Paul

W. Newacheck et al., "An Epidemiologic Profile of Children with Special Health Care Needs," *Pediatrics* 102, no. 1 (1998): 117–123.

pg. 110: **Such conditions most commonly include:** See also National Alliance on Mental Illness, North Carolina, "Understanding Serious Emotional Disorders in Children," accessed February 14, 2016, http://naminc.org/nn/publications/SED.pdf.

pg. 110: **National Survey of Children with Special Health Care Needs:** Christina D. Bethell et al., "What Is the Prevalence of Children with Special Health Care Needs? Toward an Understanding of Variations in Findings and Methods Across Three National Surveys," *Maternal and Child Health Journal* 12, no. 1 (2008): 1–14; Child and Adolescent Health Measurement Initiative, "Who Are Children with Special Health Care Needs?" accessed February 14, 2016, http://www.cahmi.org/wp-content/uploads/2014/06/CSHCNS-whoarecshcn_revised_07b-pdf.pdf; US Department of Health and Human Services, Health Resources and Services Administration, "Children with Special Health Care Needs in Context: A Portrait of States and the Nation 2007," accessed February 14, 2016, http://www.mchb.hrsa.gov/nsch/07cshcn/moreinfo/pdf/cshcn11.pdf; US Department of Health and Human Services, Health Resources and Services Administration, "The National Survey of Children with Special Health Care Needs Chartbook 2005–2006," accessed February 14, 2016, http://mchb.hrsa.gov/cshcn05.

pg. 111: **now are more likely to live at home:** Bruce E. Compas et al., "Coping with Chronic Illness in Childhood and Adolescence," *Annual Review of Clinical Psychology* 8 (2012): 455–480; Neal Halfon and Paul W. Newacheck, "Evolving Notions of Childhood Chronic Illness," *Journal of the American Medical Association* 303, no. 7 (2010): 665–666; Lidwine B. Mokkink et al., "Defining Chronic Diseases and Health Conditions in Childhood (0–18 Years of Age): National Consensus in the Netherlands," *European Journal of Pediatrics* 167, no. 12 (2008): 1441–1447.

pg. 111: **conditions that greatly affect their day-to-day lives:** US Department of Health and Human Services, Health Resources and Services Administration, "The National Survey of Children with Special Health Care Needs Chartbook 2005–2006," accessed February 14, 2016, http://mchb.hrsa.gov/cshcn05.

pg. 111: **stretch far into their adult years:** "Developmental Disabilities Assistance and Bill of Rights Act of 2000, Public Law 106–402," 106th US Congress, October 30, 2000, accessed February 14, 2016, http://www.acl.gov/Programs/AIDD/DDA_BOR_ACT_2000/docs/dd_act.pdf.

pg. 111: **"supersiblings":** See Karen Olsson, "Her Autistic Brothers," *New York Times Magazine*, February 18, 2007, accessed February 14, 2016, http://www.nytimes.com/2007/02/18/magazine/18autistic.t.html; "Supersiblings: Empowering and Supporting Siblings of People with Autism," accessed February 14, 2016, http://www.supersiblings.org.

pg. 112: **siblings of special-needs children are a special population:** Don Meyer and Patricia F. Vadasy, *Sibshops: Workshops for Siblings of Children with Special Needs* (Baltimore: Paul H. Brookes Publishing, 2007).

pg. 112: **Jordan Spieth:** Scott Michaux, "Star of Spieth Family Is Ellie," *Augusta Chronicle*, March 20, 2016, accessed January 23, 2017, http://www.augusta.com/masters/story/news/star-spieth-family-ellie.

pg. 113: **about half struggle with their own problems:** Gregory Jurkovic, *Lost Childhoods: The Plight of the Parentified Child* (New York: Brunner/Mazel, 1997); Suzanne Lamorey, "Parentification of Siblings of Children with Disability or Chronic Disease," in *Burdened Children: Theory, Research, and Treatment of Parentification*, ed. Nancy Chase (Thousand Oaks, CA: Sage, 1999), 75–91.

pg. 113: **"I set up my own [science] lab in the house":** Uncle Tungsten, quoted in Oliver Sacks, *On the Move* (New York: Knopf, 2015), 57–58.

pg. 113: **"partly to get away":** Oliver Sacks, *On the Move* (New York: Knopf, 2015), 65.

pg. 113: **"I could, I should, have been":** Oliver Sacks, *On the Move* (New York: Knopf, 2015), 63–64.

pg. 114:   **Winfrey described as "the speech of a lifetime":** Oprah Winfrey, *What I Know for Sure* (New York: Flatiron Books, 2014), 201.

pg. 116:   **"Lord yes, she had the stuff from the beginning":** Evelyn C. White, *Alice Walker: A Life* (New York: Norton, 2004), 15.

pg. 116:   **"Abe made books tell him more":** Carl Sandburg, *Abraham Lincoln: The Prairie Years and the War Years* (New York: Harcourt, 1954), 14.

pg. 116:   **"The teachers liked me":** Victor Bokris, *Warhol: The Biography* (Cambridge, MA: Da Capo Press, 2003), 37.

pg. 117:   **ability to control themselves:** Zhe Wang and Kirby Deater-Deckard, "Resilience in Gene-Environment Transactions," in *Handbook of Resilience in Children*, eds. Sam Goldstein and Robert B. Brooks (New York: Springer, 2012), 57–72.

pg. 117:   **ability to direct one's own thoughts, feelings, and behavior:** Roy F. Baumeister, Todd F. Heatherton, and Dianne M. Tice, *Losing Control: How and Why People Fail at Self-Regulation* (San Diego: Academic Press, 1994); Fred Rothbaum, John R. Weisz, and Samuel S. Snyder, "Changing the World and Changing the Self: A Two-Process Model of Perceived Control," *Journal of Personality and Social Psychology* 42, no. 1 (1982): 5–37.

pg. 117:   **A sort of catchall word:** Timothy A. Judge et al., "Are Measures of Self-Esteem, Neuroticism, Locus of Control, and Generalized Self-Efficacy Indicators of a Common Core Construct?" *Journal of Personality and Social Psychology* 83, no. 3 (2002): 693–710.

pg. 117:   **one of the hallmarks of civilization:** Sigmund Freud, *Beyond the Pleasure Principle* (London: Hogarth, 1922).

pg. 117:   **it comes from the prefrontal cortex:** See, for review, B. J. Casey et al., "A Developmental Functional MRI Study of Prefrontal Activation During Performance of a Go-No-Go Task," *Journal of Cognitive Neuroscience* 9, no. 6 (1997): 835–847; Todd A. Hare, Colin F. Camerer, and Antonio Rangel, "Self-Control in Decision-Making Involves Modulation of the vmPFC Valuation System," *Science* 324, no. 5927 (2009): 646–648.

pg. 117:   **"top-down" regulation:** Andre Fischer and Li-Huei Tsai, "Counteracting Molecular Pathways Regulating the Reduction of Fear: Implications for the Treatment of Anxiety Disorders," in *Post-Traumatic Stress Disorder: Basic Science and Clinical Practice*, eds. Joseph E. LeDoux, Terrence Keane, and Peter Shiromani (New York: Humana, 2009), 79–104.

pg. 117:   **where the executive functions reside, self-control being chief:** Russell A. Barkley, "The Executive Functions and Self-Regulation: An Evolutionary Neuropsychological Perspective," *Neuropsychology Review* 11, no. 1 (2001): 1–29; Adele Diamond, "Executive Functions," *Annual Review of Psychology* 64 (2013): 135–168.

pg. 117:   **"Marshmallow Test":** Harriet Nerlove Mischel and Walter Mischel, "The Development of Children's Knowledge of Self-Control Strategies," *Child Development* 54, no. 3 (1983): 603–619; Walter Mischel and Nancy Baker, "Cognitive Appraisals and Transformations in Delay Behavior," *Journal of Personality and Social Psychology* 31, no. 2 (1975): 254–261; Walter Mischel, Ebbe B. Ebbesen, and Antonette Raskoff Zeiss, "Cognitive and Attentional Mechanisms in Delay of Gratification," *Journal of Personality and Social Psychology* 21, no. 2 (1972): 204–218; Walter Mischel, Yuichi Shoda, and Monica I. Rodriguez, "Delay of Gratification in Children," *Science* 244, no. 4907 (1989): 933–938.

pg. 118:   **preschoolers who had enough self-control to wait:** See, for review, Walter Mischel et al., "'Willpower' Over the Life Span: Decomposing Self-Regulation," *Social Cognitive and Affective Neuroscience* 6, no. 2 (2011): 252–256.

pg. 118:   **pretty much all upside:** June P. Tangney, Roy F. Baumeister, and Angie Luzio Boone, "High Self-Control Predicts Good Adjustment, Less Pathology, Better Grades, and Interpersonal Success," *Journal of Personality* 72, no. 2 (2004): 271–324.

pg. 118:   **better outcomes in school, work, love, and health:** Denise de Ridder et al., "Taking Stock of Self-Control: A Meta-Analysis of How Trait Self-Control Relates to a Wide Range of Behaviors," *Personality and Social Psychology Review* 16, no. 1 (2012): 76–99.

pg. 118:   **better predictor of academic success than IQ:** Angela L. Duckworth and Martin Seligman, "Self-Discipline Outdoes IQ in Predicting Academic Performance of

Adolescents," *Psychological Science* 16, no. 12 (2005): 939–944; Raymond N. Wolfe and Scott D. Johnson, "Personality as a Predictor of College Performance," *Educational and Psychological Measurement* 55 (1995): 177–185.

pg. 118: **better relationships and tend to be popular:** Richard A. Fabes et al., "Regulation, Emotionality, and Preschoolers' Socially Competent Peer Interactions," *Child Development* 70, no. 2 (1999): 432–442; Patricia Maszk, Nancy Eisenberg, and Ivanna K. Guthrie, "Relations of Children's Social Status to Their Emotionality and Regulation: A Short-Term Longitudinal Study," *Merrill-Palmer Quarterly* 45, no. 3 (1999): 468–492; Harriet Nerlove Mischel and Walter Mischel, "The Development of Children's Knowledge of Self-Control Strategies," *Child Development* 54, no. 3 (1983): 603–619; Walter Mischel, Yuichi Shoda, and Philip K. Peake, "The Nature of Adolescent Competencies Predicted by Preschool Delay of Gratification," *Journal of Personality and Social Psychology* 54, no. 4 (1988): 687–696; Yuichi Shoda, Walter Mischel, and Phillip K. Peake, "Predicting Adolescent Cognitive and Self-Regulatory Competencies from Preschool Delay of Gratification: Identifying Diagnostic Conditions," *Developmental Psychology* 26, no. 6 (1990): 978–986.

pg. 118: **good at overriding their own desires:** Eli J. Finkel and W. Keith Campbell, "Ego Depletion and Accommodation in Romantic Relationships" (poster presented at the Society for Personality and Social Psychology, Nashville, TN, February 2000).

pg. 118: **better performance in sports:** Jed Jacobson and Leland Matthaeus, "Athletics and Executive Functioning: How Athletic Participation and Sport Type Correlate with Cognitive Performance," *Psychology of Sport and Exercise* 15, no. 5 (2014): 521–527; Chun-Hao Wang et al., "Open vs. Closed Skill Sports and the Modulation of Inhibitory Control," *PLOS One* 8, no. 2 (2013): e55773; Torbjörn Vestberg et al., "Executive Functions Predict the Success of Top-Soccer Players," *PLOS One* 7, no. 4 (2012): e34731.

pg. 119: **less likely to struggle with impulse-control problems:** R. Engels, C. Finkenauer, and Blokland Den Exter, "Parental Influences on Self-Control and Juvenile Delinquency," manuscript in preparation, Utrecht University, Netherlands (2000), in June P. Tangney, Roy F. Baumeister, and Angie Luzio Boone, "High Self-Control Predicts Good Adjustment, Less Pathology, Better Grades, and Interpersonal Success," *Journal of Personality* 72, no. 2 (2004): 271–324; James McGuire and Darice Broomfield, "Violent Offenses and Capacity for Self-Control," *Psychology Crime and Law* 2 (1994): 117–123; Terrie E. Moffitt et al., "A Gradient of Childhood Self-Control Predicts Health, Wealth, and Public Safety," *Proceedings of the National Academy of Sciences* 108, no. 7 (2011): 2693–2698; see also David M. Fergusson, Joseph M. Boden, and L. John Horwood, "Childhood Self-Control and Adult Outcomes: Results from a 30-Year Longitudinal Study," *Journal of the American Academy of Child and Adolescent Psychiatry* 52, no. 7 (2013): 709–717.

pg. 119: **less activity and connectivity in the prefrontal cortex:** Lisa M. Shin, "The Amygdala in Post-Traumatic Stress Disorder," in *Post-Traumatic Stress Disorder: Basic Science and Clinical Practice*, eds. Joseph E. LeDoux, Terrence Keane, and Peter Shiromani (New York: Humana, 2009), 319–336.

pg. 119: **inadequate "top-down" control:** Israel Liberzon and Sarah N. Garfinkel, "Functional Neuroimaging in Post-Traumatic Stress Disorder," in *Post-Traumatic Stress Disorder: Basic Science and Clinical Practice*, eds. Joseph E. LeDoux, Terrence Keane, and Peter Shiromani (New York: Humana, 2009), 297–318; Rajnish P. Rao et al., "PTSD: From Neurons to Networks," in *Post-Traumatic Stress Disorder: Basic Science and Clinical Practice*, eds. Joseph E. LeDoux, Terrence Keane, and Peter Shiromani (New York: Humana, 2009), 151–186; Scott L. Rauch, Lisa M. Shin, and Elizabeth A. Phelps, "Neurocircuitry Models of Posttraumatic Stress Disorder and Extinction: Human Neuroimaging Research—Past, Present, and Future," *Biological Psychiatry* 60, no. 4 (2006): 376–382; Lisa M. Shin, "The Amygdala in Post-Traumatic Stress Disorder," in *Post-Traumatic Stress Disorder: Basic Science and Clinical Practice*, eds. Joseph E. LeDoux, Terrence Keane, and Peter Shiromani (New York: Humana, 2009), 319–336.

pg. 119: **comparable to that of intelligence and socioeconomic status:** Angela L. Duckworth, "The Significance of Self-Control," *Proceedings of the National Academy of Sciences* 108, no. 7 (2011): 2639–2640.

pg. 119: **not the same as either of these:** Angela L. Duckworth and Martin Seligman, "Self-Discipline Outdoes IQ in Predicting Academic Performance of Adolescents," *Psychological Science* 16, no. 12 (2005): 939–944; T. Rohde, "Cross-Validation of Measures of Self-Control and Behavioral Inhibition in Young Adults" (2000), unpublished thesis in June P. Tangney, Roy F. Baumeister, and Angie Luzio Boone, "High Self-Control Predicts Good Adjustment, Less Pathology, Better Grades, and Interpersonal Success," *Journal of Personality* 72, no. 2 (2004): 271–324.

pg. 119: **will likely do better in life:** Kevin M. Beaver et al., "Genetic Influences on the Stability of Low Self-Control: Results from a Longitudinal Sample of Twins," *Journal of Criminal Justice* 36, no. 6 (2008): 478–485; see also Terrie E. Moffitt et al., "A Gradient of Childhood Self-Control Predicts Health, Wealth, and Public Safety," *Proceedings of the National Academy of Sciences* 108, no. 7 (2011): 2693–2698.

pg. 119: **built through practice and challenge:** Adele Diamond, "Activities and Programs That Improve Children's Executive Functions," *Current Directions in Psychological Science* 21, no. 5 (2012): 335–341; Adele Diamond and Kathleen Lee, "Interventions Shown to Aid Executive Function Development in Children 4 to 12 Years Old," *Science* 333, no. 6045 (2011): 959–964.

pg. 120: **through self-control and self-direction:** Thomas S. Bateman and Christine Porath, "Transcendent Behavior," in *Positive Organizational Scholarship: Foundations of a New Discipline*, eds. Kim Cameron, Jane Dutton, and Robert Quinn (San Francisco: Berrett-Koehler, 2003), 122–137.

pg. 120: **Kauai Longitudinal Study:** See Emmy E. Werner, "Risk, Resilience, and Recovery: Perspectives from the Kauai Longitudinal Study," *Development and Psychopathology* 5, no. 4 (1993): 503–515.

pg. 120: **believed in their own effectiveness:** Emmy Werner and Ruth S. Smith, *Overcoming the Odds: High Risk Children from Birth to Adulthood* (Ithaca, NY: Cornell University Press, 1992).

pg. 120: **felt in control of themselves and their lives:** Benjamin A. Shaw et al., "Emotional Support from Parents Early in Life, Aging, and Health," *Psychology and Aging* 19, no. 1 (2004): 4–12.

pg. 120: **put those raw materials to work:** Phillip L. Ackerman, "Nonsense, Common Sense, and Science of Expert Performance: Talent and Individual Differences," *Intelligence* 45, no. 1 (2014): 6–17.

pg. 122: **"dealing but not feeling":** Bessel A. van der Kolk, *The Body Keeps the Score: Brain, Mind, and Body in the Healing of Trauma* (New York: Penguin, 2014), 116.

pg. 123: **Guilt is a social, moral feeling:** Roy F. Baumeister, Arlene M. Stillwell, and Todd F. Heatherton, "Guilt: An Interpersonal Approach," *Psychological Bulletin* 115, no. 2 (1994): 243–267.

pg. 124: **closely related to self-control:** Ullrich Wagner et al., "Guilt-Specific Processing in the Prefrontal Cortex," *Cerebral Cortex* 21, no. 11 (2011): 2461–2470.

pg. 124: **feeling responsible for events one cannot control:** Sangmoon Kim, Ryan Thibodeau, and Randall S. Jorgensen, "Shame, Guilt, and Depressive Symptoms: A Meta-Analytic Review," *Psychological Bulletin* 137, no. 1 (2011): 68–96.

CHAPTER 8: ORPHAN

pg. 126: **"It must be pure bliss to arrange the furniture just as one likes":** Edith Wharton, *The House of Mirth* (New York: Vintage, 2012), 7.

pg. 127: **One in nine children:** Kate Stern, Jessica Malkin, and Arielle Densen, "Groundbreaking Survey of Childhood Loss Finds," *Comfort Zone Camps*, March 22, 2010, http://www.hellogrief.org/wp-content/uploads/2010/03/General-Population-Release-Revised1.pdf.

pg. 128: **accomplishments merited at least one column:** J. Marvin Eisenstadt, "Parental Loss and Genius," *American Psychologist* 33, no. 3 (1978): 211–223.

pg. 128: **say they are more resilient:** Kate Stern, Jessica Malkin, and Arielle Densen, "Groundbreaking Survey of Childhood Loss Finds," *Comfort Zone Camps*, March 22, 2010, http://www.hellogrief.org/wp-content/uploads/2010/03/General-Population-Release-Revised1.pdf.

pg. 128: **"Sonia, you have to be a big girl now":** Sonia Sotomayor, *My Beloved World* (New York: Vintage, 2014), 51.

pg. 128: **"My father left me with the feeling":** Bill Clinton, *My Life* (New York: Vintage, 2005), 8.

pg. 128: **take something bad and turn it into something good:** Lawrence J. Walker, Jeremy A. Frimer, and William L. Dunlop, "Varieties of Moral Personality: Beyond the Banality of Heroism," *Journal of Personality* 78, no. 3 (2010): 907–942.

pg. 129: **"much better" had they not:** Kate Stern, Jessica Malkin, and Arielle Densen, "Groundbreaking Survey of Childhood Loss Finds," *Comfort Zone Camps*, March 22, 2010, http://www.hellogrief.org/wp-content/uploads/2010/03/General-Population-Release-Revised1.pdf.

pg. 129: **would trade a year of their life for one more day:** Kate Stern, Jessica Malkin, and Arielle Densen, "Groundbreaking Survey of Childhood Loss Finds," *Comfort Zone Camps*, March 22, 2010, http://www.hellogrief.org/wp-content/uploads/2010/03/General-Population-Release-Revised1.pdf.

pg. 129: **"I love the thing":** Joel Lovell, "The Late, Great Stephen Colbert: Stephen Colbert on Making *The Late Show* His Own," *GQ*, August 17, 2015, accessed January 23, 2017, http://www.gq.com/story/stephen-colbert-gq-cover-story.

pg. 129: **"I am a more sensitive person":** Harold S. Kushner, *When Bad Things Happen to Good People* (New York: Schocken, 2001), xiii.

pg. 129: **"The Painted Guinea Pig":** Eugene Mahon and Dawn Simpson, "The Painted Guinea Pig," *The Psychoanalytic Study of the Child* 32 (1976): 283–303.

pg. 130: **"Children mourn on a skateboard":** Eugene Mahon and Dawn Simpson, "The Painted Guinea Pig," *The Psychoanalytic Study of the Child* 32 (1976): 283–303.

pg. 130: **Continuity is incredibly important:** James William Worden, *Children and Grief: When a Parent Dies* (New York: Guilford, 1996).

pg. 133: **US Citizenship and Immigration Services:** "Orphan," *US Citizenship and Immigration Services*, accessed June 21, 2016, https://www.uscis.gov/tools/glossary/orphan.

pg. 133: **United Nations goes further still:** "Orphans," UNICEF, last modified June 15, 2015, http://www.unicef.org/media/media_45279.html.

pg. 133: **live with surviving parents, grandparents, or other relatives:** "Orphans," UNICEF, last modified June 15, 2015, http://www.unicef.org/media/media_45279.html.

pg. 133: **"the effects should be more prominent":** J. Marvin Eisenstadt, "Parental Loss and Genius," *American Psychologist* 33, no. 3 (1978): 211–223.

pg. 134: **disenfranchised grief:** Kenneth J. Doka, *Disenfranchised Grief: New Directions, Challenges, and Strategies for Practice* (Champaign, IL: Research Press, 2002); Kenneth J. Doka, *Disenfranchised Grief: Recognizing Hidden Sorrow* (Lexington, MA: Lexington Books, 1989).

pg. 134: **"I found the mirror between the two stories":** Shawn Carter, *Jay-Z Decoded* (New York: Spiegel and Grau, 2010), 240.

pg. 135: **Lillian Rubin:** Lillian B. Rubin, *The Transcendent Child: Tales of Triumph Over the Past* (New York: Basic Books, 1996); Paul Vitello, "Lillian B. Rubin, 90, Is Dead; Wrote of Crippling Effects of Gender and Class Norms," *New York Times*, July 1, 2014.

pg. 135:   **good adjustment after adversity:** Ann S. Masten, "Ordinary Magic: Resilience Processes in Development," *American Psychologist* 56, no. 3 (2001): 227–238; Emmy Werner, "Resilience and Recovery: Findings from the Kauai Longitudinal Study," *Focal Point Research, Policy, and Practice in Children's Mental Health* 19, no. 1 (2005): 11–14.

pg. 135:   **"recruiting relationships":** Stuart T. Hauser and Joseph P. Allen, "Overcoming Adversity in Adolescence: Narratives of Resilience," *Psychoanalytic Inquiry* 26, no. 4 (2007): 549–576; Stuart T. Hauser, Joseph P. Allen, and Eve Golden, *Out of the Woods: Tales of Resilient Teens* (Cambridge, MA: Harvard University Press, 2006).

pg. 135:   **elicited positive attention:** Emmy E. Werner and Ruth S. Smith, *Overcoming the Odds: High Risk Children from Birth to Adulthood* (Ithaca, NY: Cornell University Press, 1992), 56.

pg. 136:   **number of adults with whom the child liked to associate:** Emmy E. Werner and Ruth S. Smith, *Overcoming the Odds: High Risk Children from Birth to Adulthood* (Ithaca, NY: Cornell University Press, 1992), 57, 178.

pg. 136:   **those who hide their distress:** Judith Herman, *Trauma and Recovery* (New York: Basic Books, 1997), 42–43, 100; Stephen P. Hinshaw, "Parental Mental Disorder and Children's Functioning: Silence and Communication, Stigma and Resilience," *Journal of Clinical Child and Adolescent Psychology* 33, no. 2 (2004): 400–411; Diane T. Marsh and Rex M. Dickens, *Troubled Journey: Coming to Terms with the Mental Illness of a Sibling or Parent* (New York: Tarcher/Penguin, 1997); Ronald Seifer, "Young Children with Mentally Ill Parents: Resilient Developmental Systems," in *Resilience and Vulnerability: Adaptation in the Context of Childhood Adversities*, ed. Suniya Luthar (New York: Cambridge University Press, 2003), 29–49; Rebecca L. Shiner, Ann S. Masten, and Jennifer M. Roberts, "Childhood Personality Foreshadows Adult Personality and Life Outcomes Two Decades Later," *Journal of Personality* 71, no. 6 (2003): 1145–1170; Zhe Wang and Kirby Deater-Deckard, "Resilience in Gene-Environment Transactions," in *Handbook of Resilience in Children*, eds. Sam Goldstein and Robert B. Brooks (New York: Springer, 2012), 57–72.

pg. 136:   **"Sylvia is an exceptionally fine girl":** Paul Alexander, *Rough Magic: A Biography of Sylvia Plath* (New York: Da Capo Press, 2003), 94.

pg. 136:   **"What is the normal child like?":** Donald W. Winnicott, "Some Psychological Aspects of Juvenile Delinquency," *Deprivation and Delinquency* (1946): 115.

pg. 137:   **they are her mom and dad:** Joyce Chen and Cara Sprunk, "Simone Biles Responds to NBC Sportscaster's Comment About Her Parents," *US Weekly*, August 10, 2016, accessed January 23, 2017, http://www.usmagazine.com/celebrity-news/news/simone -biles-responds-to-nbc-commentators-parents-comment-w433788; Juliet Macur, "Simone Biles Calms Her Mother, Then Sends Crowd into Frenzy," *New York Times*, August 11, 2016, accessed January 23, 2017, http://www.nytimes.com/2016/08/12/sports/ olympics/gymnastics-simone-biles-shines-brightest.html?_r=0.

pg. 138:   **"It's like a hotel":** Paula McLain, *Like Family: Growing Up in Other People's Houses, A Memoir* (New York: Back Bay, 2004), 4.

pg. 138:   **"Home is the place where":** Robert Frost, "The Death of a Hired Man," in *The Poetry of Robert Frost: The Collected Poems, Complete and Unabridged*, ed. Edward Connery Lathem (New York: Henry Holt, 1969), 34.

pg. 138:   **"Orphans always make the best recruits":** *Skyfall*, directed by Sam Mendes (2012; Los Angeles: Twentieth Century Fox, 2014), DVD.

pg. 138:   **"recruiting relationships":** Stuart T. Hauser and Joseph P. Allen, "Overcoming Adversity in Adolescence: Narratives of Resilience," *Psychoanalytic Inquiry* 26, no. 4 (2007): 549–576; Stuart T. Hauser, Joseph P. Allen, and Eve Golden, *Out of the Woods: Tales of Resilient Teens* (Cambridge, MA: Harvard University Press, 2006).

pg. 138:   **help or harm ourselves or others:** For a review, see Dacher Keltner, Deborah H. Gruenfeld, and Cameron Anderson, "Power, Approach, and Inhibition," *Psychological Review* 110, no. 2 (2003): 265–284.

pg. 139: **correlation between their smiles and how they really feel:** Dacher Keltner, Deborah H. Gruenfeld, and Cameron Anderson, "Power, Approach, and Inhibition," *Psychological Review* 110, no. 2 (2003): 265–284; Dacher Keltner et al., "Teasing in Hierarchical and Intimate Relations," *Journal of Personality and Social Psychology* 75, no. 5 (1998): 1231–1247; Paul Ekman and Wallace V. Friesen, "Felt, False, and Miserable Smiles," *Journal of Nonverbal Behavior* 6, no. 4 (1982): 238–252; Marvin A. Hecht and Marianne LaFrance, "License or Obligation to Smile: The Effect of Power and Sex on Amount and Type of Smiling," *Personality and Social Psychology Bulletin* 24, no. 12 (1998): 1332–1342.

pg. 139: **"The girls were now their mother's 'little women'":** Nancy Milford, *Savage Beauty: The Life of Edna St. Vincent Millay* (New York: Random House, 2002), 29.

pg. 140: **the less powerful are most mindful of punishments:** Dacher Keltner, Deborah H. Gruenfeld, and Cameron Anderson, "Power, Approach, and Inhibition," *Psychological Review* 110, no. 2 (2003): 265–284.

pg. 140: **"The families with whom I lived":** Marilyn Monroe and Ben Hecht, *My Story* (Lanham, MD: Taylor Trade, 2007), 36.

pg. 141: **"a sort of stray ornament":** Marilyn Monroe and Ben Hecht, *My Story* (Lanham, MD: Taylor Trade, 2007), 159.

CHAPTER 9: MASK

pg. 145: **"The persona is a kind of mask":** Carl Jung, *Two Essays on Analytical Psychology*, 2nd ed., trans. Richard F. C. Hull (London: Routledge, 1990), 192.

pg. 145: **"Nobody knows Johnny":** Marjorie Rosen, "Behind the Laughter: Numbed by Grief, Johnny Carson Reveals a Long-Hidden Side," *People Magazine* 36, no. 6, August 19, 1991, accessed January 24, 2017, http://www.people.com/people/archive/article/0,,20115734,00.html.

pg. 145: **"you get the impression":** Marjorie Rosen, "Behind the Laughter: Numbed by Grief, Johnny Carson Reveals a Long-Hidden Side," *People Magazine* 36, no. 6, August 19, 1991, accessed January 24, 2017, http://www.people.com/people/archive/article/0,,20115734,00.html.

pg. 146: **"was comfortable in front of":** Henry Bushkin, *Johnny Carson* (New York: Houghton Mifflin Harcourt, 2013), 13.

pg. 146: **through the medium and to the extent of his choosing:** W. R. D. Fairbairn, *Psychoanalytic Studies of the Personality* (New York: Routledge, 1994).

pg. 146: **"What surprised me":** National Public Radio, "Johnny Carson: 'King of Late Night,' A Man Unknown," *All Things Considered*, May 13, 2012, accessed January 24, 2017, http://www.npr.org/2012/05/13/152496256/johnny-carson-king-of-late-night-a-man-unknown.

pg. 147: **"the precursor of the mirror is the mother's face":** Donald W. Winnicott, "Mirror-Role of Mother and Family in Child Development," in *Playing and Reality* (New York: Routledge, 2005), 149.

pg. 149: **three to five million children are referred:** US Department of Health and Human Services, Administration for Children and Families, Administration on Children, Youth and Families, Children's Bureau, "Child Maltreatment 2013," January 15, 2015, accessed January 24, 2017, https://www.acf.hhs.gov/sites/default/files/cb/cm2013.pdf.

pg. 149: **estimated 85 percent of cases being unreported:** Valerie J. Edwards et al., "Relationship Between Multiple Forms of Childhood Maltreatment and Adult Mental Health in Community Respondents: Results from the Adverse Childhood Experiences Study," *American Journal of Psychiatry* 160, no. 8 (2003): 1453–1460.

pg. 149: **Fathers tend to be the offenders in the severest forms:** Neil B. Guterman and Yookyong Lee, "The Role of Fathers in Risk for Physical Child Abuse and Neglect:

Possible Pathways and Unanswered Questions," *Child Maltreatment* 10, no. 2 (2005): 136–149.

pg. 150: **most common perpetrators of child abuse:** US Department of Health and Human Services, Administration for Children and Families, Administration on Children, Youth and Families, Children's Bureau, "Child Maltreatment 2009," December 31, 2009, accessed January 24, 2017, https://www.acf.hhs.gov/sites/default/files/cb/cm2009.pdf.

pg. 150: **experience of being physically hurt by a parent is the same:** Luisa Sugaya et al., "Child Physical Abuse and Adult Mental Health: A National Study," *Journal of Traumatic Stress* 25, no. 4 (2012): 384–392.

pg. 150: **heightening their risk for stress-related illnesses:** Kristen W. Springer et al., "Long-Term Physical and Mental Health Consequences of Childhood Physical Abuse: Results from a Large Population-Based Sample of Men and Women," *Child Abuse and Neglect* 31, no. 5 (2007): 517–530.

pg. 150: **emotional abuse is an assault on a child's mind:** Douglas J. Besharov, *Recognizing Child Abuse: A Guide for the Concerned* (New York: Free Press, 1990); Danya Glaser, "Emotional Abuse and Neglect (Psychological Maltreatment): A Conceptual Framework," *Child Abuse and Neglect* 26, no. 6 (2002): 697–714.

pg. 150: **some of the most poignant studies in the field:** Robert Karen, *Becoming Attached: Unfolding the Mystery of the Infant–Mother Bond and Its Impact on Later Life* (New York: Warner Books, 1994); Leonard Shengold, *Soul Murder: The Effects of Childhood Abuse and Deprivation* (New Haven, CT: Yale University Press, 1989).

pg. 150: **"Give mother back to baby":** René Spitz, *Grief: A Peril in Infancy* [film] (New York: New York University Film Library, 1947).

pg. 151: **craving comfort above all else:** Harry F. Harlow, "Love in Infant Monkeys," *Scientific American* 200, no. 6 (1959): 68–74.

pg. 151: **single greatest protective factor:** Bekh Bradley et al., "Family Environment and Adult Resilience: Contributions of Positive Parenting and the Oxytocin Receptor Gene," *European Journal of Psychotraumatology* 18, no. 4 (2013): 21659, accessed January 24, 2017, doi: 10.3402/ejpt.v4i0.21659.

pg. 151: **emotional abuse is *more* likely than other adversities:** Daniel P. Chapman et al., "Adverse Childhood Experiences and the Risk of Depressive Disorders in Adulthood," *Journal of Affective Disorders* 82, no. 2 (2004): 217–225; Angelika H. Claussen and Patricia M. Crittenden, "Physical and Psychological Maltreatment: Relations Among Types of Maltreatment," *Child Abuse and Neglect* 15, no. 1–2 (1991): 5–18; Valerie J. Edwards et al., "Relationship Between Multiple Forms of Childhood Maltreatment and Adult Mental Health in Community Respondents: Results from the Adverse Childhood Experiences Study," *American Journal of Psychiatry* 160, no. 8 (2003): 1453–1460; Linda G. Russek and Gary E. Schwartz. "Feelings of Parental Caring Predict Health Status in Midlife: A 35-Year Follow-Up of the Harvard Mastery of Stress Study," *Journal of Behavioral Medicine* 20, no. 1 (1997): 1–13; Linda G. Russek and Gary E. Schwartz, "Narrative Descriptions of Parental Love and Caring Predict Health Status in Midlife: A 35-Year Follow-Up of the Harvard Mastery of Stress Study," *Alternative Therapies in Health and Medicine* 2, no. 6 (1996): 55–62; Martin H. Teicher et al., "Sticks, Stones, and Hurtful Words: Relative Effects of Various Forms of Childhood Maltreatment," *American Journal of Psychiatry* 163, no. 6 (2006): 993–1000; David D. Vachon et al., "Assessment of the Harmful Psychiatric and Behavioral Effects of Different Forms of Child Maltreatment," *JAMA Psychiatry* 72, no. 11 (2015): 1135–1142.

pg. 151: **"soul murder":** Leonard Shengold, "Assault on a Child's Individuality: A Kind of Soul Murder," *Psychoanalytic Quarterly* 47, no. 3 (1978): 419–424; Leonard Shengold, "Child Abuse and Deprivation: Soul Murder," *Journal of the American Psychoanalytic Association* 27, no. 3 (1979): 533–559; Leonard Shengold, *Soul Murder: The Effects of Childhood Abuse and Deprivation* (New Haven, CT: Yale University Press, 1989).

pg. 151: **"There is no such thing as a baby":** Donald W. Winnicott, *The Child, the Family, and the Outside World* (Cambridge, MA: Perseus, 1987), 88.

pg. 152: **"The good-enough mother":** Donald Winnicott, "Transitional Objects and Transitional Phenomena: A Study of the First Not-Me Possession," *International Journal of Psychoanalysis* 34 (1953): 89–97.

pg. 152: **becomes gifted at responding to them:** Alice Miller, *The Drama of the Gifted Child: The Search for the True Self* (New York: Basic, 1997).

pg. 152: **"I figured out by age ten":** James Rhodes, *Instrumental: A Memoir of Madness, Medication, and Music* (Edinburgh: Canongate, 2015), 50.

pg. 153: **cognitively and emotionally flexible:** Lea K. Hildebrandt et al., "Cognitive Flexibility, Heart Rate Variability, and Resilience Predict Fine-Grained Regulation of Arousal During Prolonged Threat," *Psychophysiology* 53, no. 6 (2016): 880–890; Christian E. Waugh, Renee J. Thompson, and Ian H Gotlib, "Flexible Emotional Responsiveness in Trait Resilience," *Emotion* 11, no. 5 (2011): 1059–1067.

pg. 153: **a way of life:** Donald W. Winnicott, "Ego Distortion in Terms of True and False Self (1960)," in *The Maturational Processes and the Facilitating Environment* (London, Hogarth Press, 1965), 140–152.

pg. 154: **"Never mind that I":** Andre Agassi, *Open* (New York: Vintage, 2010), 29.

pg. 154: **"I hate tennis":** Andre Agassi, *Open* (New York: Vintage, 2010), 27.

pg. 154: **"being alone while someone else is present":** Donald W. Winnicott, "The Capacity to Be Alone (1958)," in *The Maturational Processes and the Facilitating Environment* (London, Hogarth Press, 1965), 30.

pg. 154: **"going on being":** Steven Tuber, *Attachment, Play and Authenticity: A Winnicott Primer* (Lanham, MD: Jason Aronson, 2008), 141.

pg. 154: **spontaneity is not safe:** Donald W. Winnicott, "Ego Distortion in Terms of True and False Self (1960)," in *The Maturational Processes and the Facilitating Environment* (London, Hogarth Press, 1965), 140–152.

pg. 154: **false self:** Donald W. Winnicott, "Ego Distortion in Terms of True and False Self (1960)," in *The Maturational Processes and the Facilitating Environment* (London, Hogarth Press, 1965), 140–152.

pg. 155: **allowing the true self only a half-life:** Donald W. Winnicott, "Ego Distortion in Terms of True and False Self (1960)," in *The Maturational Processes and the Facilitating Environment* (London, Hogarth Press, 1965), 143.

pg. 155: **"To the casual observer":** Andre Agassi, *Open* (New York: Vintage, 2010), 57.

pg. 155: **feel like a sham:** Judith Herman, *Trauma and Recovery* (New York: Basic Books, 1997), 100.

pg. 155: **"as-if personalities":** Helene Deutsch, "Some Forms of Emotional Disturbance and Their Relation to Schizophrenia," *Psychoanalytic Quarterly* 11 (1942): 301–321; for more discussion of the as-if concept, see Helene Deutsch, "The Impostor: Contribution to Ego Psychology of a Type of Psychopath," *Psychoanalytic Quarterly* 24 (1955): 483–505; Ludwig Eidelberg, "Pseudo-Identification," *International Journal of Psychoanalytics* 19 (1938): 321–330; Phyllis Greenacre, "The Impostor," *Psychoanalytic Quarterly* 27, no. 3 (1958): 359–382; Phyllis Greenacre, "The Relation of the Impostor to the Artist," *Psychoanalytic Study of the Child* 13 (1958): 521–540; Ralph R. Greenson, "On Screen Defenses, Screen Hunger and Screen Identity," *Journal of the American Psychoanalytic Association* 6, no. 2 (1958): 242–262; Nathaniel Ross, "The 'As If' Concept," *Journal of the American Psychoanalytic Association* 15, no. 1 (1967): 59–82.

pg. 155: **"like the performance of an actor":** Helene Deutsch, "Some Forms of Emotional Disturbance and Their Relation to Schizophrenia," *Psychoanalytic Quarterly* 11 (1942): 303.

pg. 155: **appear entirely genuine:** Donald W. Winnicott, "Ego Distortion in Terms of True and False Self (1960)," in *The Maturational Processes and the Facilitating Environment* (London, Hogarth Press, 1965), 140–152.

pg. 155: **true self is not even on stage:** W. R. D. Fairbairn, *Psychoanalytic Studies of the Personality* (New York: Routledge, 1994).

pg. 155: **"He had not 'reached me' at all":** Tobias Wolff, *This Boy's Life: A Memoir* (New York: Grove, 1989), 252.

pg. 155: **"If you cannot get rid of the family skeleton":** Pearson Hesketh, *G.B.S.: A Full Length Portrait* (New York: Harper, 1942), 6.

pg. 157: **"It has not been pleasant":** Alan Cumming, *Not My Father's Son: A Family Memoir* (Edinburgh: Canongate, 2014), 4.

pg. 157: **"In regard to actors":** Donald W. Winnicott, "Ego Distortion in Terms of True and False Self (1960)," in *The Maturational Processes and the Facilitating Environment* (London, Hogarth Press, 1965), 145.

pg. 158: **"Jane says":** Eric Adam Avery, Perry Farrell, David Navarro, and Stephen Perkins, Sony/ATV Music Publishing LLC, Universal Music Publishing Group, 1988, accessed January 24, 2017, https://genius.com/Janes-addiction-jane-says-lyrics.

pg. 158: **"going on being":** Steven Tuber, *Attachment, Play and Authenticity: A Winnicott Primer* (Lanham, MD: Jason Aronson, 2008), 141.

pg. 159: **"Thou sayest":** Nick Madigan, "Abducted Girl's Relatives Say Her Captors Brainwashed Her," *New York Times*, March 17, 2003, accessed January 24, 2017, http://www.nytimes.com/2003/03/17/national/17UTAH.html.

pg. 159: **she did not know what they were anymore:** Henry Krystal and John H. Krystal, *Integration and Self-Healing: Affect, Trauma, Alexithymia* (Hillsdale, NJ: Analytic Press, 1988).

CHAPTER 10: ALIEN

pg. 161: **"Nobody realizes that some people":** Albert Camus, "Notebook IV," in *Notebooks: 1942–1951* (New York: Knopf, 1965), 80.

pg. 162: **low blood pressure:** Bjørn Hildrum et al., "Effect of Anxiety and Depression on Blood Pressure: 11-Year Longitudinal Population Study," *British Journal of Psychiatry* 193, no. 2 (2008): 108–113; Bjørn Hildrum et al., "Association of Low Blood Pressure with Anxiety and Depression: The Nord-Trøndelag Health Study," *Journal of Epidemiology and Community Health* 61, no. 1 (2007): 53–58.

pg. 166: **sexual assault against our most vulnerable:** See, for a review, Howard N. Snyder, "Sexual Assault of Young Children as Reported to Law Enforcement: Victim, Incident, and Offender Characteristics," Bureau of Justice Statistics, US Department of Justice (Washington, DC, 2000), 1–17, accessed August 27, 2016, http://www.bjs.gov/content/pub/pdf/saycrle.pdf.

pg. 166: **8 percent of boys and 25 percent of girls:** Rebecca M. Bolen and Maria Scannapieco, "Prevalence of Child Sexual Abuse: A Corrective Meta-Analysis," *Social Service Review* 73, no. 3 (1999): 281–313; David Finkelhor, "The International Epidemiology of Child Sexual Abuse," *Child Abuse and Neglect*, 18, no. 5 (1994): 409–417; Noemí Pereda et al., "The Prevalence of Child Sexual Abuse in Community and Student Samples: A Meta-Analysis," *Clinical Psychology Review* 29, no. 4 (2009): 328–338.

pg. 166: **people whom children know:** Howard N. Snyder, "Sexual Assault of Young Children as Reported to Law Enforcement: Victim, Incident, and Offender Characteristics," Bureau of Justice Statistics, US Department of Justice (Washington, DC, 2000), 1–17, accessed August 27, 2016, http://www.bjs.gov/content/pub/pdf/saycrle.pdf.

pg. 167: **betrayal is just as real:** Sandra Louise Kirby, Lorraine Greaves, and Olena Hankivsky, *The Dome of Silence: Sexual Harassment and Abuse in Sport* (Halifax: Fernwood, 2000); Roberto Maniglio, "The Impact of Child Sexual Abuse on Health: A Systematic Review of Reviews," *Clinical Psychology Review* 29, no. 7 (2009): 647–657; Elizabeth Oddone Paolucci, Mark L. Genuis, and Claudio Violato, "A Meta-Analysis of the Published Research on the Effects of Child Sexual Abuse," *Journal of Psychology* 135, no. 1 (2001): 17–36.

pg. 167: **"virtual incest":** Celia Brackenridge, "'He Owned Me Basically...': Women's Experience of Sexual Abuse in Sport," *International Review for the Sociology of Sport* 32, no. 2 (1997): 118.

pg. 167: **"I consider it incest":** Survivor quoted in Celia Brackenridge, "'He Owned Me Basically…': Women's Experience of Sexual Abuse in Sport," *International Review for the Sociology of Sport* 32, no. 2 (1997): 118.

pg. 168: **"compliant victims":** Kenneth V. Lanning, "A Law Enforcement Perspective on the Compliant Child Victim," *APSAC Advisor* 14, no. 2 (2002): 4–9.

pg. 168: **can never be consensual:** The age of consent is different around the world, and in the United States it varies from state to state, being either sixteen, seventeen, or eighteen years of age.

pg. 168: **swimming:** Rachel Sturtz, "The Sex Abuse Scandal Plaguing USA Swimming," Outside Online, accessed January 24, 2017, https://www.outsideonline.com/o/outdoor -adventure/water-activities/swimming/The-Sex-Abuse-Scandal-Plaguing-USA -Swimming.html.

pg. 168: **bicycling:** A. C. Shilton, "National Champion Missy Erickson Speaks Out About Her Sexual Abuse," *Bicycling*, January 4, 2017, accessed January 24, 2017, http://www.bicycling.com/ racing/people/national-champion-missy-erickson-speaks-out-about-her-sexual-abuse.

pg. 168: **soccer:** Katrin Bennhold, "Child Sexual Abuse Scandal Rocks UK Soccer," *New York Times*, December 13, 2016, accessed January 24, 2017, https://www.nytimes .com/2016/12/13/world/europe/soccer-uk-sexual-abuse-andy-woodward.html.

pg. 168: **gymnastics:** Tim Evans, Mark Alesia, and Marisa Kwiatkowski, "20-Year Toll: 368 Gymnasts Allege Sexual Exploitation," *Indianapolis Star*, December 15, 2016, accessed January 24, 2017, http://www.indystar.com/story/news/2016/12/15/20-year-toll-368-gymnasts-allege -sexual-exploitation/95198724/; Brit McCandless, "On *60 Minutes*, Former Gymnasts Allege Sexual Abuse," *CBS News*, February 19, 2017, accessed February 26, 2017, http:// www.cbsnews.com/news/on-60-minutes-former-gymnasts-allege-sexual-abuse.

pg. 168: **"near absolute power":** Katrin Bennhold, "Child Sexual Abuse Scandal Rocks UK Soccer," *New York Times*, December 13, 2016, accessed January 24, 2017, https://www .nytimes.com/2016/12/13/world/europe/soccer-uk-sexual-abuse-andy-woodward.html.

pg. 168: **"gatekeepers of dreams":** Katrin Bennhold, "Child Sexual Abuse Scandal Rocks UK Soccer," *New York Times*, December 13, 2016, accessed January 24, 2017, https://www.nytimes.com/2016/12/13/world/europe/soccer-uk-sexual-abuse-andy -woodward.html.

pg. 169: **"I was totally dependent on him":** Survivor quoted in Celia Brackenridge, "'He Owned Me Basically…': Women's Experience of Sexual Abuse in Sport," *International Review for the Sociology of Sport* 32, no. 2 (1997): 123.

pg. 169: **"cover stories":** Bessel A. van der Kolk, *The Body Keeps the Score: Brain, Mind, and Body in the Healing of Trauma* (New York: Penguin, 2014), 43.

pg. 170: **how they may feel:** Adapted from S. Rodgers, "Guilty Knowledge: The Sports Consultant's Perspective" (paper presented at Workshop on Guilty Knowledge, Cheltenham and Gloucester College of Higher Education, 1996), quoted in Celia Brackenridge, "'He Owned Me Basically…': Women's Experience of Sexual Abuse in Sport," *International Review for the Sociology of Sport* 32, no. 2 (1997): 115–130.

pg. 172: **"not only unhappy, but also ashamed of being unhappy":** Viktor Frankl, afterword to Edith Weisskopf-Joelson, *Father, Have I Kept My Promise? Madness as Seen from Within* (West Lafayette, IN: Purdue University Press, 1988), 137.

pg. 172: **half of Americans:** Ronald C. Kessler et al., "Lifetime Prevalence and Age-of-Onset Distributions of DSM-IV Disorders in the National Comorbidity Survey Replication," *Archives of General Psychiatry* 62, no. 6 (2005): 593–602.

pg. 172: **adapting well in the face of adversity, trauma, tragedy, or significant ongoing stressors:** American Psychological Association, "The Road to Resilience," accessed August 29, 2016, http://www.apa.org/helpcenter/road-resilience.aspx; see also Suniya S. Luthar and Dante Cicchetti, "The Construct of Resilience: Implications for Interventions and Social Policies," *Development and Psychopathology* 12, no. 4 (2000): 857–885; Ann S. Masten, "Resilience in Children Threatened by Extreme

Adversity: Frameworks for Research, Practice, and Translational Synergy," *Development and Psychopathology* 23, no. 2 (2011): 493–506; Ann S. Masten and Jenifer L. Powell, "A Resilience Framework for Research, Policy, and Practice," in *Resilience and Vulnerability: Adaptation in the Context of Childhood Adversities*, ed. Suniya S. Luthar (New York: Cambridge University Press, 2003), 1–25; Jennifer R. Riley and Ann S. Masten, "Resilience in Context," in *Resilience in Children, Families, and Communities: Linking Context to Practice and Policy*, eds. Ray D. Peters, Bonnie Leadbeater, and Robert J. McMahon (New York: Springer, 2005), 13–25.

pg. 173: **"the road to resilience":** American Psychological Association, "The Road to Resilience," accessed January 25, 2017, http://www.apa.org/helpcenter/road-resilience.aspx.

pg. 173: **any experience that is perceived as a potential danger:** Elaine Fox, Laura Griggs, and Elias Mouchlianitis, "The Detection of Fear-Relevant Stimuli: Are Guns Noticed as Quickly as Snakes?" *Emotion* 7, no. 4 (2007): 691–696.

pg. 173: **lifesaving adaptations can make us sick:** Bruce S. McEwen, "Stressed or Stressed Out: What Is the Difference?" *Journal of Psychiatry and Neuroscience* 30, no. 5 (2005): 315–318.

pg. 173: **"may be the leading cause of poor health":** "Breaking the Silence on Child Abuse: Protection, Prevention, Intervention, and Deterrence," Testimony of Robert W. Block on Behalf of the American Academy of Pediatrics Before the Senate Health, Education, Labor and Pensions Committee Hearing, December 13, 2011, accessed September 2, 2016, http://www.help.senate.gov/hearings/breaking-the-silence-on-child-abuse-protection-prevention-intervention-and-deterrence.

pg. 173: **Adverse Childhood Experiences (ACE) Study:** Vincent J. Felitti et al., "Relationship of Childhood Abuse and Household Dysfunction to Many of the Leading Causes of Death in Adults: The Adverse Childhood Experiences (ACE) Study," *American Journal of Preventive Medicine* 14, no. 4 (1998): 245–258.

pg. 173: **dose-dependent, generally linear relationship:** There may also be a "ceiling effect," such that after a certain point additional adversities increase risk but at a decreasing rate. See Corina Benjet, Guilherme Borges, and Maria Elizabeth Medina-Mora, "Chronic Childhood Adversity and Onset of Psychopathology During Three Life Stages: Childhood, Adolescence and Adulthood," *Journal of Psychiatric Research* 44, no. 11 (2010): 732–740.

pg. 173: **fatigue or ulcers or arthritis to the leading causes of death:** Vincent J. Felitti et al., "Relationship of Childhood Abuse and Household Dysfunction to Many of the Leading Causes of Death in Adults: The Adverse Childhood Experiences (ACE) Study," *American Journal of Preventive Medicine* 14, no. 4 (1998): 245–258.

pg. 174: **"sleeper effects":** Margaret O'Dougherty Wright, Ann S. Masten, and Angela J. Narayan, "Resilience Processes in Development: Four Waves of Research on Positive Adaptations in the Context of Adversity," in *Handbook of Resilience in Children*, eds. Sam Goldstein and Robert B. Brooks (New York: Springer, 2012), 26; Harvey Peskin, "Uses of the Past in Adult Psychological Health: Objective, Historical, and Narrative Realities," in *Handbook of Aging and Mental Health*, ed. Jacob Lomranz (New York: Springer, 1998), 297–318.

pg. 174: **health data from adults dating to 1900:** Shanta R. Dube et al., "The Impact of Adverse Childhood Experiences on Health Problems: Evidence from Four Birth Cohorts Dating Back to 1900," *Preventive Medicine* 37, no. 3 (2003): 268–277.

pg. 174: **stressed children show signs of chronic inflammation:** Andrea Danese et al., "Childhood Maltreatment Predicts Adult Inflammation in a Life-Course Study," *Proceedings of the National Academy of Sciences* 104, no. 4 (2007): 1319–1324; Gregory E. Miller and Steve W. Cole, "Clustering of Depression and Inflammation in Adolescents Previously Exposed to Childhood Adversity," *Biological Psychiatry* 72, no. 1 (2012): 34–40; Gregory Miller, Edith Chen, and Steve W. Cole, "Health Psychology: Developing Biologically Plausible Models Linking the Social World and Physical Health," *Annual Review of Psychology* 60 (2009): 501–524; Natalie Slopen et al., "Childhood Adversity and

Inflammatory Processes in Youth: A Prospective Study," *Psychoneuroendocrinology* 38, no. 2 (2013): 188–200.

pg. 174:   **shorter telomeres:** Stacy S. Drury et al., "Telomere Length and Early Severe Social Deprivation: Linking Early Adversity and Cellular Aging," *Molecular Psychiatry* 17, no. 7 (2012): 719–727; Laura Kananen et al., "Childhood Adversities Are Associated with Shorter Telomere Length at Adult Age Both in Individuals with an Anxiety Disorder and Controls," *PLOS One* 5, no. 5 (2010): e10826; Janice K. Kiecolt-Glaser et al., "Childhood Adversity Heightens the Impact of Later-Life Caregiving Stress on Telomere Length and Inflammation," *Psychosomatic Medicine* 73, no. 1 (2011): 16–22; Audrey R. Tyrka, "Childhood Maltreatment and Telomere Shortening: Preliminary Support for an Effect of Early Stress on Cellular Aging," *Biological Psychiatry* 67, no. 6 (2010): 531–534.

pg. 174:   **shorten the life span by up to twenty years:** David W. Brown et al., "Adverse Childhood Experiences and the Risk of Premature Mortality," *American Journal of Preventive Medicine* 37, no. 5 (2009): 389–396.

pg. 174:   **greatest when it comes to the most complex organ:** Paula S. Nurius, Edwina Uehara, and Douglas F. Zatzick, "Intersection of Stress, Social Disadvantage, and Life Course Processes: Reframing Trauma and Mental Health," *American Journal of Psychiatric Rehabilitation* 16, no. 2 (2013): 91–114; Sharon Schwartz and Cheryl Corcoran, "Theories of Psychiatric Disorders: A Sociological Analysis," in *A Handbook for the Study of Mental Health: Social Contexts, Theories and Systems*, 2nd ed., eds. Teresa L. Scheid and Tony N. Brown (New York: Cambridge University Press, 2010), 64–88; Jack P. Shonkoff et al., "The Lifelong Effects of Early Childhood Adversity and Toxic Stress," *Pediatrics* 129, no. 1 (2012): e232–e246.

pg. 174:   **wired into who we are:** Michael D. De Bellis et al., "Brain Structures in Pediatric Maltreatment-Related Posttraumatic Stress Disorder: A Sociodemographically Matched Study," *Biological Psychiatry* 52, no. 11 (2002): 1066–1078; Michael D. De Bellis et al., "Developmental Traumatology Part II: Brain Development," *Biological Psychiatry* 45 (1999): 1271–1284; Victor C. Carrion et al., "Attenuation of Frontal Asymmetry in Pediatric Post-Traumatic Stress Disorder," *Biological Psychiatry* 50, no. 12 (2001): 943–951; Danya Glaser, "Child Abuse and Neglect and the Brain: A Review," *Journal of Child Psychology and Psychiatry* 41, no. 1 (2000): 97–116; Christine Heim and Charles B. Nemeroff, "The Role of Childhood Trauma in the Neurobiology of Mood and Anxiety Disorders: Preclinical and Clinical Studies," *Biological Psychiatry* 49, no. 12 (2001): 1023–1039; Joan Kaufman and Dennis Charney, "Effects of Early Stress on Brain Structure and Function: Implications for Understanding the Relationship Between Child Maltreatment and Depression," *Development and Psychopathology* 13, no. 3 (2001): 451–471; Joan Kaufman et al., "Effects of Early Adverse Experiences on Brain Structure and Function: Clinical Implications," *Biological Psychiatry* 48, no. 8 (2000): 778–790; Sonia J. Lupien et al., "Effects of Stress Throughout the Lifespan on the Brain, Behaviour and Cognition," *Nature Reviews Neuroscience* 10, no. 6 (2009): 434–445; Jack P. Shonkoff et al., "The Lifelong Effects of Early Childhood Adversity and Toxic Stress," *Pediatrics* 129, no. 1 (2012): e232–e246; Martin H. Teicher, Carl M. Anderson, and Ann Polcari, "Childhood Maltreatment Is Associated with Reduced Volume in the Hippocampal Subfields CA3, Dentate Gyrus, and Subiculum," *Proceedings of the National Academy of Sciences* 109, no. 9 (2012): E563–E572; Martin H. Teicher, Akemi Tomoda, and Susan L. Andersen, "Neurobiological Consequences of Early Stress and Childhood Maltreatment: Are Results from Human and Animal Studies Comparable?" *Annals of the New York Academy of Sciences* 1071, no. 1 (2006): 313–323; Martin H. Teicher et al., "Childhood Neglect Is Associated with Reduced Corpus Callosum Area," *Biological Psychiatry* 56, no. 2 (2004): 80–85.

pg. 174:   **"brain health":** For a summary of Dr. Block's views, see the transcript of his talk at the 2015 meeting of the American Pediatric Surgical Association in the following paper: Robert W. Block, "All Adults Once Were Children," *Journal of Pediatric Surgery* 51, no. 1 (2016): 23–27; this term on p. 25.

pg. 174: **connection between early adversity and brain health:** Robert F. Anda et al., "The Enduring Effects of Abuse and Related Adverse Experiences in Childhood," *European Archives of Psychiatry and Clinical Neuroscience* 256, no. 3 (2006): 174–186; Oscar A. Cabrera et al., "Childhood Adversity and Combat as Predictors of Depression and Post-Traumatic Stress in Deployed Troops," *American Journal of Preventive Medicine* 33, no. 2 (2007): 77–82; Daniel P. Chapman, Shanta R. Dube, and Robert F. Anda, "Adverse Childhood Events as Risk Factors for Negative Mental Health Outcomes," *Psychiatric Annals* 37, no. 5 (2007): 359–364; Daniel P. Chapman et al., "Adverse Childhood Experiences and the Risk of Depressive Disorders in Adulthood," *Journal of Affective Disorders* 82, no. 2 (2004): 217–225; Mariette J. Chartier, John R. Walker, and Barbara Naimark, "Separate and Cumulative Effects of Adverse Childhood Experiences in Predicting Adult Health and Health Care Utilization," *Child Abuse and Neglect* 34, no. 6 (2010): 454–464; Ronald A. Cohen et al., "Early Life Stress and Adult Emotional Experience: An International Perspective," *International Journal of Psychiatry in Medicine* 36, no. 1 (2006): 35–52; Brian Draper et al., "Long Term Effects of Childhood Abuse on the Quality of Life and Health of Older People: Results from the Depression and Early Prevention of Suicide in General Practice Project," *Journal of the American Geriatrics Society* 56, no. 2 (2008): 262–271; Shanta R. Dube, Michelle L. Cook, and Valerie J. Edwards, "Health-Related Outcomes of Adverse Childhood Experiences in Texas, 2002," *Preventing Chronic Disease* 7, no. 3 (2010), A52; Valerie J. Edwards et al., "Relationship Between Multiple Forms of Childhood Maltreatment and Adult Mental Health in Community Respondents: Results from the Adverse Childhood Experiences Study," *American Journal of Psychiatry* 160, no. 8 (2003): 1453–1460; Jennifer Greif Green et al., "Childhood Adversities and Adult Psychiatric Disorders in the National Comorbidity Survey Replication I: Associations with First Onset of *DSM-IV* Disorders," *Archives of General Psychiatry* 67, no. 2 (2010): 113–123; Christine Heim et al., "The Link Between Childhood Trauma and Depression: Insights from HPA Axis Studies in Humans," *Psychoneuroendocrinology* 33, no. 6 (2008): 693–710; Carole Hooven et al., "Childhood Violence Exposure: Cumulative and Specific Effects on Adult Mental Health," *Journal of Family Violence* 27, no. 6 (2012): 511–522; Jeffrey G. Johnson et al., "Childhood Adversities Associated with Risk for Eating Disorders or Weight Problems During Adolescence or Early Adulthood," *American Journal of Psychiatry* 159, no. 3 (2002): 394–400; Ronald C. Kessler, Christopher G. Davis, and Kenneth S. Kendler, "Childhood Adversity and Adult Psychiatric Disorder in the US National Comorbidity Survey," *Psychological Medicine* 27, no. 5 (1997): 1101–1119; Weili Lu et al., "Correlates of Adverse Childhood Experiences Among Adults with Severe Mood Disorders," *Psychiatric Services* 59, no. 9 (2008): 1018–1026; Katie A. McLaughlin et al., "Childhood Adversities and Adult Psychiatric Disorders in the National Comorbidity Survey Replication II: Associations with Persistence of *DSM-IV* Disorders," *Archives of General Psychiatry* 67, no. 2 (2010): 124–132; Joshua P. Mersky, James Topitzes, and Arthur J. Reynolds, "Impacts of Adverse Childhood Experiences on Health, Mental Health, and Substance Use in Early Adulthood: A Cohort Study of an Urban, Minority Sample in the US," *Child Abuse and Neglect* 37, no. 11 (2013): 917–925; Elizabeth A. Schilling, Robert H. Aseltine, and Susan Gore, "Adverse Childhood Experiences and Mental Health in Young Adults: A Longitudinal Survey," *BMC Public Health* 7, no. 1 (2007): 30; Elizabeth A. Schilling, Robert H. Aseltine, and Susan Gore, "The Impact of Cumulative Childhood Adversity on Young Adult Mental Health: Measures, Models, and Interpretations," *Social Science and Medicine*, 66, no. 5 (2008), 1140–1151; R. Jay Turner and Donald A. Lloyd, "Lifetime Traumas and Mental Health: The Significance of Cumulative Adversity," *Journal of Health and Social Behavior* 36, no. 4 (1995): 360–376; Charles L. Whitfield et al., "Adverse Childhood Experiences and Hallucinations," *Child Abuse and Neglect* 29, no. 7 (2005): 797–810.

pg. 175: **Other disorders can be the result of stress, too:** Corina Benjet, Guilherme Borges, and María Elena Medina-Mora, "Chronic Childhood Adversity and Onset of

Psychopathology During Three Life Stages: Childhood, Adolescence and Adulthood," *Journal of Psychiatry Research* 44, no. 11 (2010): 732–740; Jennifer Greif Green et al., "Childhood Adversities and Adult Psychiatric Disorders in the National Comorbidity Survey Replication I: Associations with First Onset of *DSM-IV* Disorders," *Archives of General Psychiatry* 67, no. 2 (2010): 113–123.

pg. 175: ***trauma spectrum disorders:*** J. Douglas Bremner, *Does Stress Damage the Brain?: Understanding Trauma-Related Disorders from a Mind-Body Perspective* (New York: Norton, 2002); Christine J. Heim, Douglas Bremner, and Charles B. Nemeroff, "Trauma Spectrum Disorders," in *Principles of Molecular Medicine*, eds. Marschall S. Runge and Cam Patterson (Totowa, NJ: Humana, 2006), 1203–1210; Maryhelen Kreidler and Colleen Kurzawa, "Trauma Spectrum Disorders," *Journal of Psychosocial Nursing and Mental Health Services* 47, no. 11 (2009): 26–33.

pg. 175: **"child sexual abuse syndrome":** David Finkelhor, "Early and Long-Term Effects of Child Sexual Abuse: An Update," *Professional Psychology: Research and Practice* 21, no. 5 (1990): 325–330; David Finkelhor and Angela Browne, "Assessing the Long Term Impact of Child Sexual Abuse: A Review and Conceptualization," in *Family Abuse and Its Consequences: New Directions in Research*, eds. Gerald T. Hotaling et al. (Newburg Park, CA: Sage, 1988); Kathleen A. Kendall-Tackett, Linda M. Williams, and David Finkelhor, "Impact of Sexual Abuse on Children: A Review and Synthesis of Recent Empirical Studies," *Psychological Bulletin* 113, no. 1 (1993): 164–180; Alfred Lange et al., "Long-Term Effects of Childhood Sexual Abuse: Objective and Subjective Characteristics of the Abuse and Psychopathology in Later Life," *Journal of Nervous and Mental Disease* 187, no. 3 (1999): 150–158; Roberto Maniglio, "The Impact of Child Sexual Abuse on Health: A Systematic Review of Reviews," *Clinical Psychology Review* 29, no. 7 (2009): 647–657; Elliot C. Nelson et al., "Association Between Self-Reported Childhood Sexual Abuse and Adverse Psychosocial Outcomes: Results from a Twin Study," *Archives of General Psychiatry* 59, no. 2 (2002): 139–145; Elizabeth Oddone Paolucci, Mark L. Genuis, and Claudio Violato, "A Meta-Analysis of the Published Research on the Effects of Child Sexual Abuse," *Journal of Psychology* 135, no. 1 (2001): 17–36.

pg. 175: **nor is there any one way we would expect:** Jennifer Greif Green et al., "Childhood Adversities and Adult Psychiatric Disorders in the National Comorbidity Survey Replication I: Associations with First Onset of *DSM-IV* Disorders," *Archives of General Psychiatry* 67, no. 2 (2010): 113–123.

pg. 175: **the amount of unmitigated stress over time:** Corina Benjet, Guilherme Borges, and María Elena Medina-Mora, "Chronic Childhood Adversity and Onset of Psychopathology During Three Life Stages: Childhood, Adolescence and Adulthood," *Journal of Psychiatry Research* 44, no. 11 (2010): 732–740; Valerie J. Edwards et al., "Relationship Between Multiple Forms of Childhood Maltreatment and Adult Mental Health in Community Respondents: Results from the Adverse Childhood Experiences Study," *American Journal of Psychiatry* 160, no. 8 (2003): 1453–1460; Jennifer Greif Green et al., "Childhood Adversities and Adult Psychiatric Disorders in the National Comorbidity Survey Replication I: Associations with First Onset of *DSM-IV* Disorders," *Archives of General Psychiatry* 67, no. 2 (2010): 113–123; James Scott, Daniel Varghese, and John McGrath, "As the Twig Is Bent, the Tree Inclines: Adult Mental Health Consequences of Childhood Adversity," *Archives of General Psychiatry* 67, no. 2 (2010): 111–112.

pg. 175: **between nature and nurture that takes place over time:** Ronald C. Kessler et al., "Childhood Adversity and Adult Psychopathology," in *Stress and Adversity Over the Life Course: Trajectories and Turning Points*, eds. Ian H. Gotlib and Blair Wheaton (New York: Cambridge University Press, 1997), 29–49; Arnold Sameroff, "A Unified Theory of Development: A Dialectic Integration of Nature and Nurture," *Child Development* 81, no. 1 (2010): 6–22.

pg. 175: **Genetics, stress, and support:** Adriana Feder, Eric J. Nestler, and Dennis S. Charney, "Psychobiology and Molecular Genetics of Resilience," *Nature Reviews Neuroscience* 10, no. 6 (2009): 446–457; Charles F. Gillespie et al., "Risk and Resilience: Genetic and Environmental Influences on Development of the Stress Response," *Depression and Anxiety* 26, no. 11 (2009): 984–992; Joan Kaufman et al., "Social Supports and Serotonin Transporter Gene Moderate Depression in Maltreated Children," *Proceedings of the National Academy of Sciences* 101, no. 49 (2004): 17316–17321.

pg. 176: **"The research on the most effective treatments":** Bruce Perry, *The Boy Who Was Raised as a Dog* (New York: Basic Books, 2006), 80.

pg. 177: **as has some research:** Bonnie Carlson, "Sibling Incest: Adjustment in Adult Women Survivors," *Families in Society: The Journal of Contemporary Social Services* 92, no. 1 (2011): 77–83.

pg. 177: **"Being a stand-up, productive, normalised":** James Rhodes, *Instrumental: A Memoir of Madness, Medication, and Music* (Edinburgh: Canongate, 2015), 76.

pg. 178: **Freud himself said that normality was an "ideal fiction":** Sigmund Freud, "Analysis Terminable and Interminable," *International Journal of Psycho-Analysis* 18 (1937): 373–405; quote on pp. 388–389.

pg. 178: **"There's a notion I'd like to see buried":** Alan Moore, *Watchmen* (New York: DC Comics, 1987), 9.

pg. 179: **"Life itself":** Karen Horney, *Our Inner Conflicts: A Constructive Theory of Neurosis* (New York: Norton, 1992), 240.

CHAPTER 11: ANTIHERO

pg. 180: **"[Frankenstein was] made up of bad parts":** Johnny Cash, quoted in Robert Hilburn, *Johnny Cash: The Life* (New York: Little, Brown and Company, 2013), 17.

pg. 180: **when he drew the very first Spider-Man:** Laurence Maslon and Michael Kantor, *Superheroes!: Capes, Cowls, and the Creation of Comic Book Culture* (New York: Crown Archetype, 2013), 142–146.

pg. 181: **"Clark Kent was a disguise":** Laurence Maslon and Michael Kantor. *Superheroes!: Capes, Cowls, and the Creation of Comic Book Culture* (New York: Crown Archetype, 2013), 143.

pg. 181: **first antiheroic superhero:** Laurence Maslon and Michael Kantor, *Superheroes!: Capes, Cowls, and the Creation of Comic Book Culture* (New York: Crown Archetype, 2013), 129–146; also note that the Incredible Hulk briefly preceded Spider-Man in comic-book history and mirrored aspects of Frankenstein, as well as Dr. Jekyll and Mr. Hyde.

pg. 181: **brooding manner and revenge as his raison d'être:** Michael Spivey and Steven Knowlton, "Anti-Heroism in the Continuum of Good and Evil," in *The Psychology of Superheroes: An Unauthorized Exploration*, eds. Robin S. Rosenberg and Jennifer Canzoneri (Dallas: BenBella Books, 2008), 51–64; Chuck Tate, "An Appetite for Destruction: Aggression and the Batman," in *The Psychology of Superheroes: An Unauthorized Exploration*, eds. Robin S. Rosenberg and Jennifer Canzoneri (Dallas: BenBella Books, 2008), 135–146.

pg. 181: **"You can't have those characters":** Laurence Maslon and Michael Kantor, *Superheroes!: Capes, Cowls, and the Creation of Comic Book Culture* (New York: Crown Archetype, 2013), 137.

pg. 181: **eclipsed Superman as the country's most popular:** Laurence Maslon and Michael Kantor, *Superheroes!: Capes, Cowls, and the Creation of Comic Book Culture* (New York: Crown Archetype, 2013), 213.

pg. 181: **"I was always into the Spider-Man/Batman model":** Laurence Maslon and Michael Kantor, *Superheroes!: Capes, Cowls, and the Creation of Comic Book Culture* (New York: Crown Archetype, 2013), 291.

pg. 182: **more complicated than just good versus evil:** Laurence Maslon and Michael Kantor, *Superheroes!: Capes, Cowls, and the Creation of Comic Book Culture* (New York: Crown Archetype, 2013), 232.

pg. 182: **too good to be villains but too bad to get to feel like heroes:** Michael Spivey and Steven Knowlton, "Anti-Heroism in the Continuum of Good and Evil," in *The Psy-*

chology of Superheroes: An Unauthorized Exploration, eds. Robin S. Rosenberg and Jennifer Canzoneri (Dallas: BenBella Books, 2008), 52.

pg. 182: **two million children live with a parent who abuses drugs:** US Department of Health and Human Services, Children's Bureau, "Parental Drug Use as Child Abuse," Washington, DC, Child Welfare Information Gateway, 2016, accessed January 29, 2017, https://www.childwelfare.gov/topics/systemwide/laws-policies/statutes/drugexposed.

pg. 182: **significantly increased risk for mistreatment:** Neil McKeganey, Marina Barnard, and James McIntosh, "Paying the Price for Their Parents' Addiction: Meeting the Needs of the Children of Drug-Using Parents," *Drugs: Education, Prevention and Policy* 9, no. 3 (2002): 233–246; Christine Walsh, Harriet L. MacMillan, and Ellen Jamieson, "The Relationship Between Parental Substance Abuse and Child Maltreatment: Findings from the Ontario Health Supplement," *Child Abuse and Neglect* 27, no. 12 (2003): 1409–1425.

pg. 182: **mother who abuses substances:** Howard Dubowitz et al., "Identifying Children at High Risk for a Child Maltreatment Report," *Child Abuse and Neglect* 35, no. 2 (2011): 96–104.

pg. 182: **neglect is the most common problem:** Marina Barnard and Neil McKeganey, "The Impact of Parental Problem Drug Use on Children: What Is the Problem and What Can Be Done to Help?" *Addiction* 99, no. 5 (2004): 552–559; Paula Kienberger Jaudes, Edem Ekwo, and John Van Voorhis, "Association of Drug Abuse and Child Abuse," *Child Abuse and Neglect* 19, no. 9 (1995): 1065–1075.

pg. 183: **least amount of attention from professionals:** Ruth Gilbert et al., "Burden and Consequences of Child Maltreatment in High-Income Countries," *Lancet* 373, no. 9657 (2009): 68–81.

pg. 183: **"It's not bad people that become addicts":** Marina Barnard, "Between a Rock and a Hard Place: The Role of Relatives in Protecting Children from the Effects of Parental Drug Problems," *Child and Family Social Work* 8, no. 4 (2003): 291–299.

pg. 185: **in the face of family disadvantage:** David Autor et al., "Family Disadvantage and the Gender Gap in Behavioral and Educational Outcomes," National Bureau of Economic Research, 2016, accessed January 25, 2017, doi: 10.3386/w22267.

pg. 185: **perhaps girls are less negatively impacted:** Michael Baker and Kevin Milligan, "Boy-Girl Differences in Parental Time Investments: Evidence from Three Countries (Working Paper No. 18893)," *National Bureau of Economic Research*, April 2013, accessed January 29, 2017, http://www.nber.org/papers/w18893.pdf.

pg. 185: **less rowdy temperaments, and they are likely to act "in":** Angela Lee Duckworth and Martin Seligman, "Self-Discipline Gives Girls the Edge: Gender in Self-Discipline, Grades, and Achievement Test Scores," *Journal of Educational Psychology* 98, no. 1 (2006): 198–208; Irwin W. Silverman, "Gender Differences in Delay of Gratification: A Meta-Analysis," *Sex Roles* 49 (2003): 451–463.

pg. 186: **less affected by the quality of their neighborhoods:** Raj Chetty and Nathan Hendren, "The Impacts of Neighborhoods on Intergenerational Mobility: Childhood Exposure Effects and County-Level Estimates," May 2015, accessed January 29, 2017, http://cms.leoncountyfl.gov/coadmin/agenda/attach/150609/A0905.pdf.

pg. 186: **by the kind of parenting they receive:** David Autor, "Skills, Education, and the Rise of Earnings Inequality Among the 'Other 99 Percent,'" *Science* 344, no. 6186 (2014): 843–851; David Autor and Melanie Wasserman, "Wayward Sons: The Emerging Gender Gap in Education and Labor Markets," *Third Way*, Washington, DC, 2013, http://economics.mit.edu/files/8754; Marianne Bertrand and Jessica Pan, "The Trouble with Boys: Social Influences and the Gender Gap in Disruptive Behavior," *American Economic Journal: Applied Economics* 5, no. 1 (2013): 32–64.

pg. 187: **streak of rule-breaking or "delinquency" along the way:** Consider the data from the Kauai Longitudinal Study of at-risk youth: Although these were children who were born into families who struggled with significant disadvantages, the majority went on to be competent and law-abiding citizens; even among the teenagers who had criminal records as juveniles, 75 percent of the males and 90 percent of the females went on to have no such problems in adulthood; Emmy Werner, "Resilience and Recovery: Findings from the Kauai Longitudinal Study," *Focal Point Research, Policy, and Practice in Children's Mental Health* 19, no. 1 (2005): 11–14; Emmy E. Werner and Ruth S. Smith, *Overcoming the Odds: High Risk Children from Birth to Adulthood* (Ithaca, NY: Cornell University Press, 1992), 119.

pg. 187: **squandered potential and unfulfilled promise:** Donald W. Winnicott, "Ego Distortion in Terms of True and False Self (1960)," in *The Maturational Processes and the Facilitating Environment* (London: Hogarth Press, 1965), 140–152.

pg. 187: **"Delinquency as a Sign of Hope":** Donald W. Winnicott, "Delinquency as a Sign of Hope: A Talk Given to the Borstal Assistant Governors' Conference, King Alfred's College, Winchester (April 1967)," in *Home Is Where We Start From: Essays by a Psychoanalyst,* eds. Clare Winnicott, Ray Shepherd, and Madeleine Davis (New York: Norton, 1990), 90–100; see also Steven Tuber, *Attachment, Play and Authenticity: A Winnicott Primer* (Lanham, MD: Jason Aronson, 2008), 15; Donald W. Winnicott, "Some Aspects of Juvenile Delinquency," in *The Child, the Family, and the Outside World* (Cambridge, MA: Perseus, 1987), 229.

pg. 190: **at risk for similar troubles:** Joseph Biederman et al., "Patterns of Alcohol and Drug Use in Adolescents Can Be Predicted by Parental Substance Use Disorders," *Pediatrics* 106, no. 4 (2000): 792–797; Mary Jeanne Kreek et al., "Genetic Influences on Impulsivity, Risk Taking, Stress Responsivity and Vulnerability to Drug Abuse and Addiction," *Nature Neuroscience* 8, no. 11 (2005): 1450–1457; Suniya S. Luthar et al., "Multiple Jeopardy: Risk and Protective Factors Among Addicted Mothers' Offspring," *Development and Psychopathology* 10, no. 1 (1998): 117–136; Matt McGue, Irene Elkins, and William G. Iacono, "Genetic and Environmental Influences on Adolescent Substance Use and Abuse," *American Journal of Medical Genetics* 96, no. 5 (2000): 671–677; Ming T. Tsuang et al., "The Harvard Twin Study of Substance Abuse: What We Have Learned," *Harvard Review of Psychiatry* 9, no. 6 (2001): 267–279; Myrna M. Weissman et al., "Risk/Protective Factors Among Addicted Mothers' Offspring: A Replication Study," *American Journal of Drug and Alcohol Abuse* 25, no. 4 (1999): 661–679.

pg. 191: **regardless of whether or not one's parents were:** Robert F. Anda et al., "Adverse Childhood Experiences, Alcoholic Parents, and Later Risk of Alcoholism and Depression," *Psychiatric Services* 53, no. 8 (2002): 1001–1009; Robert F. Anda et al., "Adverse Childhood Experiences and Smoking During Adolescence and Adulthood," *Journal of the American Medical Association* 282, no. 17 (1999): 1652–1658; Robert F. Anda et al., "The Enduring Effects of Abuse and Related Adverse Experiences in Childhood," *European Archives of Psychiatry and Clinical Neuroscience* 256, no. 3 (2006): 174–186; Shanta R. Dube et al., "Adverse Childhood Experiences and the Association with Ever Using Alcohol and Initiating Alcohol Use During Adolescence," *Journal of Adolescent Health* 38, no. 4 (2006): 444.e1–444.e10; Shanta R. Dube et al., "Adverse Childhood Experiences and Personal Alcohol Abuse as an Adult," *Addictive Behaviors* 27, no. 5 (2002): 713–725; Brian M. Hicks et al., "Environmental Adversity and Increasing Genetic Risk for Externalizing Disorders," *Archives of General Psychiatry* 66, no. 6 (2009): 640–648; Susan D. Hillis et al., "Adverse Childhood Experiences and Sexual Risk Behaviors in Women: A Retrospective Cohort Study," *Family Planning Perspectives* 33, no. 5 (2001): 206–211; Ronald C. Kessler et al., "Posttraumatic Stress Disorder in the National Comorbidity Survey," *Archives of General Psychiatry* 52, no. 12 (1995): 1048–1060; Elizabeth A. Schilling, Robert H. Aseltine, and Susan Gore, "Adverse Childhood Experiences and Mental Health in Young Adults: A Longitudinal Survey," *BMC Public Health* 7, no. 1 (2007): 30.

pg. 191: **more likely to use and abuse substances as an adult:** Corina Benjet, Guilherme Borges, and María Elena Medina-Mora, "Chronic Childhood Adversity and Onset of Psychopathology During Three Life Stages: Childhood, Adolescence and Adulthood," *Journal of Psychiatric Research* 44, no. 11 (2010): 732–740; Rosana E. Norman et al., "The Long-Term Health Consequences of Child Physical Abuse, Emotional Abuse, and Neglect: A Systematic Review and Meta-Analysis," *PLOS Medicine* 9, no. 11 (2012): e1001349; Emily F. Rothman et al., "Adverse Childhood Experiences Predict Earlier Age of Drinking Onset: Results from a Representative US Sample of Current or Former Drinkers," *Pediatrics* 122, no. 2 (2008): e298–e304; Cathy Spatz Widom, "Childhood Victimization: Risk Factor for Delinquency," in *Adolescent Stress: Causes and Consequences*, eds. Mary Ellen Colten and Susan Gore (Hawthorne, NY: Aldine de Gruyter, 1991), 201–221.

pg. 191: **holds across four generations dating back to 1900:** Shanta R. Dube et al., "Childhood Abuse, Neglect, and Household Dysfunction and the Risk of Illicit Drug Use: The Adverse Childhood Experiences Study," *Pediatrics* 111, no. 3 (2003): 564–572.

pg. 191: **opt to drink more alcohol when given access:** J. Dee Higley et al., "Nonhuman Primate Model of Alcohol Abuse: Effects of Early Experience, Personality, and Stress on Alcohol Consumption," *Proceedings of the National Academy of Sciences* 88, no. 16 (1991): 7261–7265.

pg. 191: **one-half to two-thirds of serious problems with substance use:** Shanta R. Dube et al., "Childhood Abuse, Neglect, and Household Dysfunction and the Risk of Illicit Drug Use: The Adverse Childhood Experiences Study," *Pediatrics* 111, no. 3 (2003): 564–572.

pg. 191: **must include self-medication:** For reviews, see Susan L. Andersen and Martin H. Teicher, "Desperately Driven and No Brakes: Developmental Stress Exposure and Subsequent Risk for Substance Abuse," *Neuroscience and Biobehavioral Reviews* 33, no. 4 (2009): 516–524; Edward J. Khantzian, "The Self-Medication Hypothesis of Substance Use Disorders: A Reconsideration and Recent Applications," *Harvard Review of Psychiatry* 4, no. 5 (1997): 231–244; Edward J. Khantzian, *Treating Addiction as a Human Process* (Lanham, MD: Jason Aronson, 2007); Edward J. Khantzian, "Understanding Addictive Vulnerability: An Evolving Psychodynamic Perspective," *Neuropsychoanalysis* 5, no. 1 (2003): 5–21.

pg. 191: **chronic use of substances can be one way to cope:** Vincent J. Felitti et al., "Relationship of Childhood Abuse and Household Dysfunction to Many of the Leading Causes of Death in Adults: The Adverse Childhood Experiences (ACE) Study," *American Journal of Preventive Medicine* 14, no. 4 (1998): 245–258.

pg. 191: **"special adaptation":** Edward J. Khantzian, "Understanding Addictive Vulnerability: An Evolving Psychodynamic Perspective," *Neuropsychoanalysis* 5, no. 1 (2003): 5–21.

pg. 191: **shown to be neuroregulators:** Robert F. Anda et al., "Depression and the Dynamics of Smoking. A National Perspective," *Journal of the American Medical Association* 264, no. 12 (1990): 1541–1545; Timothy P. Carmody, "Affect Regulation, Nicotine Addiction, and Smoking Cessation," *Journal of Psychoactive Drugs* 21, no. 3 (1989): 331–342; Vincent J. Felitti et al., "Relationship of Childhood Abuse and Household Dysfunction to Many of the Leading Causes of Death in Adults: The Adverse Childhood Experiences (ACE) Study," *American Journal of Preventive Medicine* 14, no. 4 (1998): 245–258; Alexander H. Glassman et al., "Smoking, Smoking Cessation, and Major Depression," *Journal of the American Medical Association* 264, no. 12 (1990): 1546–1549; Ovide F. Pomerlau and Cynthia S. Pomerlau, "Neuroregulators and the Reinforcement of Smoking (Towards a Biobehavioral Explanation)," *Neuroscience and Biobehavioral Reviews* 8, no. 4 (1984): 503–513; Tara W. Strine et al., "Associations Between Adverse Childhood Experiences, Psychological Distress, and Adult Alcohol Problems," *American Journal of Health Behavior* 36, no. 3 (2012): 408–423.

pg. 192: **"These magical cylinders":** James Rhodes, *Instrumental: A Memoir of Madness, Medication, and Music* (Edinburgh: Canongate, 2015), 44.

pg. 192: **"If this bottle would just hold out 'til tomorrow":** Dwight Yoakam, "It Won't Hurt," Reprise Records, 1986, accessed January 25, 2017, https://genius.com/Dwight -yoakam-it-wont-hurt-lyrics; see also National Public Radio, "Dwight Yoakam Says

New Album Was Inspired by Coal Mining and Mountain Music," *Fresh Air*, December 6, 2016, accessed January 25, 2017, http://www.npr.org/2016/12/06/504543479/dwight-yoakam-says-new-album-was-inspired-by-coal-mining-and-mountain-music.

pg. 192:   ***The Short and Tragic Life of Robert Peace:*** Jeff Hobbs, *The Short and Tragic Life of Robert Peace: A Brilliant Young Man Who Left Newark for the Ivy League* (New York: Scribner, 2014).

pg. 192:   **try to be self-sufficient:** Henry Krystal and John H. Krystal, *Integration and Self-Healing: Affect, Trauma, Alexithymia* (Hillsdale, NJ: Analytic Press, 1988).

pg. 192:   **right their emotions through the use of substances:** Henry Krystal, "Adolescence and the Tendencies to Develop Substance Dependence," *Psychoanalytic Inquiry* 2, no. 4 (1982): 581–617.

pg. 192:   **cannot lean on others, so some may use substances:** Herbert Wieder and Eugene Kaplan, "Drug Use in Adolescents: Psychodynamic Meaning and Pharmacogenic Effect," *Psychoanalytic Study of the Child* 24 (1969): 399–431.

pg. 193:   **two-thirds of suicide attempts:** Shanta R. Dube et al., "Childhood Abuse, Household Dysfunction, and the Risk of Attempted Suicide Throughout the Life Span: Findings from the Adverse Childhood Experiences Study," *Journal of the American Medical Association* 286, no. 24 (2001): 3089–3096.

pg. 194:   **admired for bravery or great achievements or good qualities:** "Definition of 'Hero'—English Dictionary," *Cambridge Academic Content Dictionary*, Cambridge University Press, accessed January 25, 2017, http://dictionary.cambridge.org/us/dictionary/english/hero.

pg. 194:   ***Stories of Resilience in Childhood:*** Daniel D. Challener, *Stories of Resilience in Childhood: The Narratives of Maya Angelou, Maxine Hong Kingston, Richard Rodrigues, John Edgar Wideman, and Tobias Wolff* (New York: Garland, 1997).

pg. 194:   **the working title:** Daniel D. Challener, *Stories of Resilience in Childhood: The Narratives of Maya Angelou, Maxine Hong Kingston, Richard Rodrigues, John Edgar Wideman, and Tobias Wolff* (New York: Garland, 1997), 183.

pg. 194:   **obtained by any means necessary:** Michael Spivey and Steven Knowlton, "Anti-Heroism in the Continuum of Good and Evil," in *The Psychology of Superheroes: An Unauthorized Exploration*, eds. Robin S. Rosenberg and Jennifer Canzoneri (Dallas: BenBella Books, 2008), 51–64.

pg. 194:   **"the golden child":** Robert Hilburn, *Johnny Cash: The Life* (New York: Little, Brown and Company, 2013), 13.

pg. 195:   **"Too bad it wasn't you instead of Jack":** Robert Hilburn, *Johnny Cash: The Life* (New York: Little, Brown and Company, 2013), 20.

pg. 195:   **saw the rest of his years as a battle between lightness and dark:** Robert Hilburn, *Johnny Cash: The Life* (New York: Little, Brown and Company, 2013), 16.

pg. 195:   **change from feeling bad to feeling good:** Johnny Cash, *Cash: The Autobiography of Johnny Cash* (New York: HarperCollins, 1997), 141.

pg. 195:   **"it felt barely human":** Johnny Cash, *Cash: The Autobiography of Johnny Cash* (New York: HarperCollins, 1997), 169.

pg. 195:   **accuracy of this story has been disputed:** Robert Hilburn, *Johnny Cash: The Life* (New York: Little, Brown and Company, 2013), 321.

pg. 195:   **one he chose to tell in his autobiography:** This story is told in Johnny Cash, *Cash: The Autobiography of Johnny Cash* (New York: HarperCollins, 1997), 170–171.

pg. 195:   **"The truth is always more heroic than the hype":** "Misleading Information from the Battlefield," Hearing Before the Committee on Oversight and Government Reform, House of Representatives, 110th Congress, First Session, April 24, 2007, http://democrats.oversight.house.gov/sites/democrats.oversight.house.gov/files/documents/20071114152054.pdf, 23.

pg. 196:   **"On the average, only those prisoners":** Viktor E. Frankl, *Man's Search for Meaning: An Introduction to Logotherapy* (Boston: Beacon, 2006), 5–6.

Chapter 12: Reboot

pg. 197: **"I come from nowhere":** Andy Warhol, quoted in Victor Bockris, *Warhol: The Biography* (Cambridge, MA: Da Capo Press, 2003), 15.

pg. 197: **Wonder Woman is probably the earliest well-known example:** For a summary of rebooting, see Laurence Maslon and Michael Kantor, *Superheroes!: Capes, Cowls, and the Creation of Comic Book Culture* (New York: Crown Archetype, 2013), 270–271.

pg. 197: **Created in the 1940s by William Moulton Marston:** For the definitive history of Wonder Woman, see Jill Lepore, *The Secret History of Wonder Woman* (New York: Vintage, 2015).

pg. 198: **new writers gave Wonder Woman a new story:** For a detailed summary of Wonder Woman's 1960s and 1970s reboots, see Jill Lepore, *The Secret History of Wonder Woman* (New York: Vintage, 2015).

pg. 200: **"The world doesn't usually think about bank robbers":** Richard Ford, *Canada* (New York: Ecco, 2012), 285–289.

pg. 200: **over 50 percent are parents:** Lauren E. Glaze and Laura M. Maruschak, "Parents in Prison and Their Minor Children: Bureau of Justice Statistics Special Report," US Department of Justice, Office of Justice Programs, Washington, DC, August 2008, accessed January 26, 2017, https://www.bjs.gov/content/pub/pdf/pptmc.pdf.

pg. 200: **thirty years ago, it was 1 in every 125:** Pew Charitable Trusts, "Collateral Costs: Incarceration's Effect on Economic Mobility," Washington, DC, 2010, accessed January 26, 2017, http://www.pewtrusts.org/~/media/legacy/uploadedfiles/pcs_assets/2010/collateralcosts1pdf.pdf.

pg. 200: **serving sentences for nonviolent crimes:** Pew Charitable Trusts, "Collateral Costs: Incarceration's Effect on Economic Mobility," Washington, DC, 2010, accessed January 26, 2017, http://www.pewtrusts.org/~/media/legacy/uploadedfiles/pcs_assets/2010/collater alcosts1pdf.pdf.

pg. 200: **left with less money, food, structure, supervision, and security:** Yiyoon Chung, "The Effects of Paternal Imprisonment on Children's Economic Well-Being," *Social Service Review* 86, no. 3 (2012): 455–486; Kristin Turney, "Paternal Incarceration and Children's Food Insecurity: A Consideration of Variation and Mechanisms," *Social Service Review* 89, no. 2 (2015): 335–367; Christopher Uggen and Suzy McElrath, "Parental Incarceration: What We Know and Where We Need to Go," *Journal of Criminal Law and Criminology* 104, no. 3 (2014): 597–604.

pg. 200: **more likely to drop out of school and to break the law:** Joseph Murray, David P. Farrington, and Ivana Sekol, "Children's Antisocial Behavior, Mental Health, Drug Use, and Educational Performance After Parental Incarceration: A Systematic Review and Meta-Analysis," *Psychological Bulletin* 138, no. 2 (2012): 175–210; Emily Bever Nichols and Ann Booker Loper, "Incarceration in the Household: Academic Outcomes of Adolescents with an Incarcerated Household Member," *Journal of Youth and Adolescence* 41, no. 11 (2012): 1455–1471; Jeremy Travis, Elizabeth McBride, and Amy Solomon, "Families Left Behind: The Hidden Costs of Incarceration and Reentry," Urban Institute, Washington, DC, 2006, accessed January 26, 2017, http://www.urban.org/Uploaded PDF/310882_families_left_behind.pdf.

pg. 200: **In the body and the mind, there is more stress:** Kristin Turney, "Stress Proliferation Across Generations? Examining the Relationship Between Parental Incarceration and Childhood Health," *Journal of Health and Social Behavior* 55, no. 3 (2014): 302–319.

pg. 200: **Sesame Street took up the topic:** See Sesame Workshop, "Little Children, Big Challenges: Incarceration," *Sesame Street*, 2013, accessed January 26, 2017, http://www.sesame workshop.org/incarceration; "Little Children, Big Challenges: Incarceration," *Sesame Street*, 2013, accessed January 26, 2017, http://www.sesamestreet.org/toolkits/incarceration.

pg. 201: **orphans of justice:** Roger Shaw, "Imprisoned Fathers and the Orphans of Justice," in *Prisoners' Children: What Are the Issues?* (London: Routledge, 1992), 41–49.

pg. 201: **the children who are left behind:** Elizabeth I. Johnson and Beth A. Easterling, "Understanding Unique Effects of Parental Incarceration on Children: Challenges, Progress, and Recommendations," *Journal of Marriage and Family* 74, no. 2 (2012): 342–356; for an example of one of the few comprehensive programs for children of incarcerated parents, see: http://www.cpnyc.org.

pg. 201: **"one of the signature social changes":** Daniel P. Mears and Sonja E. Siennick, "Young Adult Outcomes and the Life-Course Penalties of Parental Incarceration," *Journal of Research in Crime and Delinquency* 53, no. 1 (2016): 24.

pg. 201: **adult children of incarcerated parents:** Rosalyn D. Lee, Xiangming Fang, and Feijun Luo, "The Impact of Parental Incarceration on the Physical and Mental Health of Young Adults," *Pediatrics* 131, no. 4 (2013): e1188–e1191; Daniel P. Mears and Sonja E. Siennick, "Young Adult Outcomes and the Life-Course Penalties of Parental Incarceration," *Journal of Research in Crime and Delinquency* 53, no. 1 (2016): 3–35; Joseph Murray, Rolf Loeber, and Dustin Pardini, "Parental Involvement in the Criminal Justice System and the Development of Youth Theft, Marijuana Use, Depression, and Poor Academic Performance," *Criminology* 50, no. 1 (2012): 255–302; Robert J. Sampson and John H. Laub, "A Life-Course View of the Development of Crime," *Annals* 602, no. 1 (2005): 12–45; Sara Wakefield and Christopher Wildeman, *Children of the Prison Boom: Mass Incarceration and the Future of American Inequality* (New York: Oxford University Press, 2014); Christopher Wildeman, "Parental Imprisonment, the Prison Boom, and the Concentration of Childhood Disadvantage," *Demography* 46, no. 2 (2009): 265–280.

pg. 201: **"I hadn't done anything personally":** Richard Ford, *Canada* (New York: Ecco, 2012), 167.

pg. 201: **"second-chance opportunities":** Emmy Werner, "Resilience and Recovery: Findings from the Kauai Longitudinal Study," *Focal Point Research, Policy, and Practice in Children's Mental Health* 19, no. 1 (2005): 11–14.

pg. 202: **left without even the few benefits they had before:** D. Wayne Osgood et al., "Introduction: Why Focus on the Transition to Adulthood for Vulnerable Populations," in *On Your Own Without a Net: The Transition to Adulthood for Vulnerable Populations*, eds. D. Wayne Osgood et al. (Chicago: University of Chicago Press, 2005), 1–26.

pg. 202: **Cumulative disadvantage:** Robert J. Sampson and John H. Laub, "A Life-Course Theory of Cumulative Disadvantage and the Stability of Delinquency," in *Developmental Theories of Crime and Delinquency: Advances in Criminological Theory*, vol. 7, ed. Terence P. Thornberry (New Brunswick, NJ: Transaction Publishers, 1997), 133–161; Robert J. Sampson and John H. Laub, "A Life-Course View of the Development of Crime," *Annals of the American Academy of Political and Social Science* 602 (2005): 12–45.

pg. 202: **Adulthood is when stress-related mental health problems:** John E. Schulenberg, Arnold J. Sameroff, and Dante Cicchetti, "The Transition to Adulthood as a Critical Juncture in the Course of Psychopathology and Mental Health," *Development and Psychopathology* 16, no. 4 (2004): 799–806.

pg. 202: **Young adulthood is, therefore, an inflection point:** Ann S. Masten et al., "Resources and Resilience in the Transition to Adulthood: Continuity and Change," *Development and Psychopathology* 16, no. 4 (2004): 1071–1094; Michael Rutter, "Transitions and Turning Points in Developmental Psychopathology: As Applied to the Age Span Between Childhood and Mid-Adulthood," *International Journal of Behavioral Development* 19, no. 3 (1996): 603–626; John E. Schulenberg, Arnold J. Sameroff, and Dante Cicchetti, "The Transition to Adulthood as a Critical Juncture in the Course of Psychopathology and Mental Health," *Development and Psychopathology* 16, no. 4 (2004): 799–806.

pg. 202: **able to see and to seize a second chance at life:** John A. Clausen, *American Lives: Looking Back at the Children of the Great Depression* (New York: Free Press, 1993); W. Andrew Collins, "More than Myth: The Developmental Significance of Romantic Relationships During Adolescence," *Journal of Research on Adolescence* 13, no. 1 (2003): 1–24; Glen

H. Elder, "Military Times and Turning Points in Men's Lives," *Developmental Psychology* 22, no. 2 (1986): 233–245; J. Kirk Felsman and George E. Vaillant, "Resilient Children as Adults: A 40-Year Study," in *The Invulnerable Child*, eds. Elwyn James Anthony and Bertram J. Cohler (New York: Guilford, 1987), 289–314; Frank F. Furstenberg Jr., Jeanne Brooks-Gunn, and S. Philip Morgan, *Adolescent Mothers in Later Life* (New York: Cambridge University Press, 1987); Susan Gore et al., "Life After High School: Development, Stress, and Well-Being," in *Stress and Adversity Over the Life Course: Trajectories and Turning Points*, eds. Ian H. Gotlib and Blair Wheaton (New York: Cambridge University Press, 1997), 197–214; Alice M. Hines, Joan Merdinger, and Paige Wyatt, "Former Foster Youth Attending College: Resilience and the Transition to Young Adulthood," *American Journal of Orthopsychiatry* 75, no. 3 (2005): 381–394; Ann S. Masten et al., "Resources and Resilience in the Transition to Adulthood: Continuity and Change," *Development and Psychopathology* 16, no. 4 (2004): 1071–1094; Terrie E. Moffitt et al., "Males on the Life-Course-Persistent and Adolescence-Limited Antisocial Pathways: Follow-Up at Age 26 Years," *Development and Psychopathology* 14, no. 1 (2002): 179–207; Glenn I. Roisman, Benjamin Aguilar, and Byron Egeland, "Antisocial Behavior in the Transition to Adulthood: The Independent and Interactive Roles of Developmental History and Emerging Developmental Tasks," *Development and Psychopathology* 16, no. 4 (2004): 857–871; Robert J. Sampson and John H. Laub, "A Life-Course Theory of Cumulative Disadvantage and the Stability of Delinquency," in *Developmental Theories of Crime and Delinquency: Advances in Criminological Theory*, vol. 7, ed. Terence P. Thornberry (New Brunswick, NJ: Transaction Publishers, 1997), 133–161; Elizabeth A. Schilling, Robert H. Aseltine, and Susan Gore, "Young Women's Social and Occupational Development and Mental Health in the Aftermath of Child Sexual Abuse," *American Journal of Community Psychology* 40, no. 1–2 (2007): 109–124; George E. Vaillant, "The Study of Adult Development," in *Looking at Lives: American Longitudinal Studies of the Twentieth Century*, eds. Erin Phelps, Frank F. Furstenberg, and Anne Colby (New York: Russell Sage Foundation, 2002), 116–132; Emmy Werner, "Resilience and Recovery: Findings from the Kauai Longitudinal Study," *Focal Point Research, Policy, and Practice in Children's Mental Health* 19, no. 1 (2005): 11–14; Emmy E. Werner, "Resilience in Development," *Current Directions in Psychological Science* 4, no. 3 (1995): 81–85; Emmy E. Werner and Ruth S. Smith, *Journeys from Childhood to Midlife: Risk, Resilience, and Recovery* (Ithaca, NY: Cornell University Press, 2001); Emmy E. Werner and Ruth S. Smith, *Overcoming the Odds: High Risk Children from Birth to Adulthood* (Ithaca, NY: Cornell University Press, 1992); Emmy E. Werner and Ruth S. Smith, *Vulnerable but Invincible: A Study of Resilient Children and Youth* (New York: McGraw-Hill, 1982).

pg. 202:   **"Marriage to Jim brought me escape":** George Barris, *Marilyn: Her Life in Her Own Words: Marilyn Monroe's Revealing Last Words and Photographs* (New York: Citadel, 1995), 42.

pg. 203:   **enlist in the armed forces:** John R. Blosnich et al., "Disparities in Adverse Childhood Experiences Among Individuals with a History of Military Service," *JAMA Psychiatry* 71, no. 9 (2014): 1041–1048; Jodie G. Katon et al., "Adverse Childhood Experiences, Military Service, and Adult Health," *American Journal of Preventive Medicine* 49, no. 4 (2015): 573–582.

pg. 205:   **hippocampus and the prefrontal cortex work together to evaluate:** Raffael Kalisch et al., "Context-Dependent Human Extinction Memory Is Mediated by a Ventromedial Prefrontal and Hippocampal Network," *Journal of Neuroscience* 26, no. 37 (2006): 9503–9511; Mohammed R. Milad et al., "Thickness of Ventromedial Prefrontal Cortex in Humans Is Correlated with Extinction Memory," *Proceedings of the National Academy of Sciences* 102, no. 30 (2005): 10706–10711; Scott L. Rauch, Lisa M. Shin, and Elizabeth A. Phelps, "Neurocircuitry Models of Posttraumatic Stress Disorder and Extinction: Human Neuroimaging Research—Past, Present, and Future," *Biological Psychiatry* 60, no. 4 (2006): 376–382.

pg. 205: **hippocampus and the prefrontal cortex may become overloaded:** Roee Admon et al., "Stress-Induced Reduction in Hippocampal Volume and Connectivity with the Ventromedial Prefrontal Cortex Are Related to Maladaptive Responses to Stressful Military Service," *Human Brain Mapping* 34, no. 11 (2013): 2808–2816; Karestan C. Koenen et al., "Measures of Prefrontal System Dysfunction in Posttraumatic Stress Disorder," *Brain and Cognition* 45, no. 1 (2001): 64–78; Bruce S. McEwen, "Stress and Hippocampal Plasticity," *Annual Review of Neuroscience* 22 (1999): 105–122; Fu Lye Woon, Shabnam Sood, and Dawson W. Hedges, "Hippocampal Volume Deficits Associated with Exposure to Psychological Trauma and Posttraumatic Stress Disorder in Adults: A Meta-Analysis," *Progress in Neuropsychopharmacology and Biological Psychiatry* 34, no. 7 (2010): 1181–1188.

pg. 206: **brain remembers best in context:** Mark E. Bouton, "Context, Ambiguity, and Unlearning: Sources of Relapse After Behavioral Extinction," *Biological Psychiatry* 52, no. 10 (2002): 976–986; Susan Engel, *Context Is Everything: The Nature of Memory* (New York: W. H. Freeman, 1999); Joseph E. LeDoux, *The Emotional Brain: The Mysterious Underpinnings of Emotional Life* (New York: Simon and Schuster, 1996), 250; Mohammed R. Milad et al., "Context Modulation of Memory for Fear Extinction in Humans," *Psychophysiology* 42, no. 4 (2005): 456–464; Steven M. Smith, "Remembering In and Out of Context," *Journal of Experimental Psychology: Human Learning and Memory* 5, no. 5 (1979): 460–471; Debora Vansteenwegen et al., "Return of Fear in Human Differential Conditioning Paradigm Caused by a Return to the Original Acquisition Context," *Behavior Research and Therapy* 43, no. 3 (2005): 323–336.

pg. 206: **classic experiment conducted in the United Kingdom in the 1970s:** Duncan R. Godden and Alan D. Baddeley, "Context-Dependent Memory in Two Natural Environments: On Land and Underwater," *British Journal of Psychology* 66, no. 3 (1975): 325–331.

pg. 207: **"Emotional memories may be forever":** Joseph E. LeDoux, *The Emotional Brain: The Mysterious Underpinnings of Emotional Life* (New York: Simon and Schuster, 1996), 145.

pg. 207: **never really forget or "unlearn" them:** Joseph E. LeDoux, *The Emotional Brain: The Mysterious Underpinnings of Emotional Life* (New York: Simon and Schuster, 1996), 251; Mohammed R. Milad et al., "Context Modulation of Memory for Fear Extinction in Humans," *Psychophysiology* 42, no. 4 (2005): 456–464.

pg. 207: **scarcely has time to think about its old ones:** Laurence Gonzales, *Surviving Survival: The Art and Science of Resilience* (New York: Norton, 2012), 149–152.

pg. 207: **"Memory lane was a sucker punch":** Paula McLain, *Like Family: Growing Up in Other People's Houses, A Memoir* (New York: Little, Brown and Company, 2009).

pg. 208: **"Erik, son of himself":** Erik H. Erikson, *Identity: Youth and Crisis* (New York: Norton, 1994).

pg. 208: **"I had to get born. And this time better than before":** Marilyn Monroe and Ben Hecht, *My Story* (Lanham, MD: Rowman and Littlefield, 2006), 65.

pg. 208: **Warhol changed his name, too:** This summary of Andy Warhol's life is taken from: Victor Bokris, *Warhol: The Biography* (Cambridge, MA: Da Capo Press, 2003).

pg. 208: **"The way he fought out of his background":** Victor Bokris, *Warhol: The Biography* (Cambridge, MA: Da Capo Press, 2003), 52.

pg. 208: **"compulsively, constantly, and amazingly":** Victor Bokris, *Warhol: The Biography* (Cambridge, MA: Da Capo Press, 2003), 52.

pg. 208: **"He never forgot what he saw":** Victor Bokris, *Warhol: The Biography* (Cambridge, MA: Da Capo Press, 2003), 50.

pg. 209: **"Never take Andy at face value":** Victor Bokris, *Warhol: The Biography* (Cambridge, MA: Da Capo Press, 2003), 543.

pg. 209: **thirty-two paintings of Campbell's Soup cans:** Andy Warhol. *Campbell's Soup Cans.* 1962, Museum of Modern Art, New York, accessed February 26, 2017, https://www.moma.org/learn/moma_learning/andy-warhol-campbells-soup-cans-1962.

pg. 209: **"Sometimes I wish I could reboot":** Alex Scarrow, *TimeRiders: The Pirate Kings* (New York: Penguin, 2013).

pg. 210: ***Freedom: My Book of Firsts:*** Jaycee Dugard, *Freedom: My Book of Firsts* (New York: Simon and Schuster, 2016).

pg. 210: **"It is a quick, easy read and perhaps a little boring":** Customer review, Amazon .com, accessed January 26, 2015, https://www.amazon.com/Freedom-Book-Firsts-Jaycee -Dugard/dp/1501147625.

CHAPTER 13: KRYPTONITE

pg. 213: **"I was determined to get away":** Nella Larsen, *Passing* (New York: Penguin, 1997), 26.

pg. 213: ***Some Freaks:*** David Mamet, *Some Freaks* (New York: Viking, 1989).

pg. 213: **Superman is a sham:** David Mamet, "Kryptonite," in *Some Freaks* (New York: Viking, 1989), 175–180.

pg. 213: **"Superman is the most vulnerable of beings":** David Mamet, *Some Freaks* (New York: Viking, 1989), 179.

pg. 213: **"Kryptonite is all that remains of his childhood home":** David Mamet, "Kryptonite: A Psychological Appreciation," in *Some Freaks* (New York: Penguin Books, 1989), 178.

pg. 213: **"no hope for him but constant hiding":** David Mamet, "Kryptonite: A Psychological Appreciation," in *Some Freaks* (New York: Penguin Books, 1989), 180.

pg. 214: **"adulation without intimacy":** David Mamet, "Kryptonite: A Psychological Appreciation," in *Some Freaks* (New York: Penguin Books, 1989), 178.

pg. 218: **"a chosen exile":** Allyson Hobbs, *A Chosen Exile: A History of Racial Passing in American Life* (Cambridge, MA: Harvard University Press, 2014).

pg. 218: **the management of a dangerous identity:** Erving Goffman, *Stigma: Notes on the Management of Spoiled Identity* (New York: Simon and Schuster, 2009).

pg. 218: **"Because of the great rewards":** Erving Goffman, *Stigma: Notes on the Management of Spoiled Identity* (New York: Simon and Schuster, 2009), 74.

pg. 219: **unsure of how to talk about what they had endured:** Arlene Stein, "As Far as They Knew I Came from France: Stigma, Passing, and Not Speaking About the Holocaust," *Symbolic Interaction* 32, no. 1 (2009): 44–60.

pg. 219: **"As far as they knew I came from France":** Arlene Stein, "As Far as They Knew I Came from France: Stigma, Passing, and Not Speaking About the Holocaust," *Symbolic Interaction* 32, no. 1 (2009): 44–60.

pg. 219: **it was her phone number:** Arlene Stein, "As Far as They Knew I Came from France: Stigma, Passing, and Not Speaking About the Holocaust," *Symbolic Interaction* 32, no. 1 (2009): 44–60.

pg. 219: **"Nobody talked about it":** Arlene Stein, "As Far as They Knew I Came from France: Stigma, Passing, and Not Speaking About the Holocaust," *Symbolic Interaction* 32, no. 1 (2009): 45.

pg. 219: **"like chalk from a blackboard":** Ruth Klüger, *Still Alive: A Holocaust Girlhood Remembered* (New York: Feminist Press at CUNY, 2003), 176.

pg. 219: **"The survivors kept silent. They passed for normal":** Eva Hoffman, *After Such Knowledge: Memory, History, and the Legacy of the Holocaust* (New York: Public Affairs, 2004), 46.

pg. 220: **"on the one side, a subject who doesn't tell":** Kimberlyn Leary, "Passing, Posing, and 'Keeping it Real,'" in *Relational Psychoanalysis*. Vol. 4, *Expansion of Theory*, eds. Lewis Aron and Adrienne Harris (New York: Routledge, 2010), 32.

pg. 220: **"no one ever asked if [they] were black":** Allyson Hobbs, *A Chosen Exile: A History of Racial Passing in American Life* (Cambridge, MA: Harvard University Press, 2014), 135.

pg. 220: **"I now inhabit a life I don't deserve":** David Carr, *The Night of the Gun: A Reporter Investigates the Darkest Story of His Life, His Own* (New York: Simon and Schuster, 2008), 382.

pg. 221: **"perils, not known, or imagined":** Nella Larsen, *Passing* (New York: Dover, 2004), 48.

pg. 221: **may be out of sight but it often is not be out of mind:** Judith A. Clair, Joy E. Beatty, and Tammy L. MacLean, "Out of Sight but Not Out of Mind: Managing Invisible Social Identities in the Workplace," *Academy of Management Review* 30, no. 1 (2005): 78–95; Laura Smart and Daniel M. Wegner, "The Hidden Costs of Hidden Stigma," in *The Social Psychology of Stigma*, eds. Todd Heatherton et al. (New York: Guilford, 2000), 220–242.

pg. 221: **keeping secrets requires a great deal of mental work:** Julie D. Lane and Daniel M. Wegner, "The Cognitive Consequences of Secrecy," *Journal of Personality and Social Psychology* 69, no. 2 (1995): 237–253.

pg. 221: **"must be alive to the social situation":** Erving Goffman, *Stigma: Notes on the Management of Spoiled Identity* (New York: Simon and Schuster, 2009), 88.

pg. 221: **"to display or not display":** Erving Goffman, *Stigma: Notes on the Management of Spoiled Identity* (New York: Simon and Schuster, 2009), 42.

pg. 221: **Keeping secrets is cognitively and even physically taxing:** John E. Pachankis, "The Psychological Implications of Concealing a Stigma: A Cognitive-Affective-Behavioral Model," *Psychological Bulletin* 133, no. 2 (2007): 328–345.

pg. 222: **double, even triple, lives, with disconnects:** Rich DeJordy, "Just Passing Through: Stigma, Passing, and Identity Decoupling in the Work Place," *Group and Organization Management* 33, no. 5 (2008): 504–531; Belle Rose Ragins, "Disclosure Disconnects: Antecedents and Consequences of Disclosing Invisible Stigmas Across Life Domains," *Academy of Management Review* 33, no. 1 (2008): 194–215.

pg. 223: **"every personal secret has the effect of sin or guilt":** Carl Jung, *Modern Man in Search of a Soul* (New York: Harvest Books, 1955), 33.

pg. 223: **required to conceal the information felt worse:** Michael J. Fishbein and James D. Laird, "Concealment and Disclosure: Some Effects of Information Control on the Person Who Controls," *Journal of Experimental Social Psychology* 15, no. 2 (1979): 114–121.

pg. 224: **"It is not that he must face prejudice against himself":** Erving Goffman, *Stigma: Notes on the Management of Spoiled Identity* (New York: Simon and Schuster, 2009), 42.

pg. 225: **"I am solitary":** Carl Jung, *Memories, Dreams, Reflections* (New York: Vintage, 1989), 42.

pg. 225: **perhaps passing's greatest burden of all: isolation:** Allyson Hobbs, *A Chosen Exile: A History of Racial Passing in American Life* (Cambridge, MA: Harvard University Press, 2014); John E. Pachankis, "The Psychological Implications of Concealing a Stigma: A Cognitive-Affective-Behavioral Model," *Psychological Bulletin* 133, no. 2 (2007): 328–345; Arlene Stein, "As Far as They Knew I Came from France: Stigma, Passing, and Not Speaking About the Holocaust," *Symbolic Interaction* 32, no. 1 (2009): 44–60.

pg. 225: **"Not close to a single soul":** Nella Larsen, *Passing* (New York: Dover, 2004), 52.

pg. 225: **Secrets separated him from everyone around:** Joseph Stokes, "The Relation of Loneliness and Self-Disclosure," in *Self-Disclosure: Theory, Research, and Therapy*, eds. Valerian Derlega and John Berg (New York: Springer Science and Business Media, 1987), 175–201.

pg. 225: **"adulation without intimacy":** David Mamet, "Kryptonite: A Psychological Appreciation," in *Some Freaks* (New York: Penguin Books, 1989), 178.

pg. 225: **"Fortress of Solitude, like Superman's retreat":** Charles Blow, *Fire Shut Up in My Bones: A Memoir* (New York: First Mariner, 2015), 94.

pg. 226: **"the safest place I knew":** Barack Obama, *Dreams from My Father: A Story of Race and Inheritance* (New York: Three Rivers, 2004), 4.

pg. 226: **loneliness and isolation have their own ways of putting us at risk:** Louise C. Hawkley and John T. Cacioppo, "Loneliness Matters: A Theoretical and Empirical Review of Consequences and Mechanisms," *Annals of Behavioral Medicine* 40, no. 2 (2010): 218–227.

pg. 226: **social isolation in early life was associated with poor health:** Avshalom Caspi et al., "Socially Isolated Children 20 Years Later: Risk of Cardiovascular Disease," *Archives of Pediatrics and Adolescent Medicine* 160, no. 8 (2006): 805–811.

pg. 226: **one that can raise blood pressure:** Louise C. Hawkley et al., "Loneliness Is a Unique Predictor of Age-Related Differences in Systolic Blood Pressure," *Psychology and Aging* 21, no. 1 (2006): 152–164.

pg. 226: **elevate levels of stress hormones:** Emma Adam et al., "Day-to-Day Dynamics of Experience-Cortisol Associations in a Population-Based Sample of Older Adults," *Proceedings of the National Academy of Sciences* 103, no. 45 (2006): 17058–17063.

pg. 226: **increase symptoms of depression and thoughts of suicide:** Liesl Heinrich and Eleonora Gullone, "The Clinical Significance of Loneliness: A Literature Review," *Clinical Psychology Review* 26, no. 6 (2006): 695–718.

pg. 226: **compromise the immune system:** John Cacioppo, Louise Hawkley, and Gary Berntson, "The Anatomy of Loneliness," *Current Directions in Psychological Science* 12, no. 3 (2003): 71–74.

pg. 226: **loneliness as a major risk factor for ill health and even death:** Beverly H. Brummett et al., "Characteristics of Socially Isolated Patients with Coronary Artery Disease Who Are at Elevated Risk for Mortality," *Psychosomatic Medicine* 63, no. 2 (2001): 267–272; James S. House, Karl R. Landis, and Debra Umberson, "Social Relationships and Health," *Science* 241, no. 4865 (1988): 540–545.

pg. 226: **more harmful to our well-being than many well-known risk factors:** Erika Friedmann et al., "Relationship of Depression, Anxiety, and Social Isolation to Chronic Heart Failure Outpatient Mortality," *American Heart Journal* 152, no. 5 (2006): 940.e1–940.e8; Julianne Holt-Lunstad, Timothy B. Smith, and J. Bradley Layton, "Social Relationships and Mortality Risk: A Meta-Analytic Review," *PLOS Medicine* 7, no. 7 (2010): e1000316; James S. House, Karl R. Landis, and Debra Umberson, "Social Relationships and Health," *Science* 241, no. 4865 (1988): 540–545.

pg. 226: **"One of the greatest diseases":** Quoted in Louis Cozolino, *The Neuroscience of Human Relationships: Attachment and the Developing Social Brain* (New York: Norton, 2014), 398.

pg. 226: **seeming unavailability of others, rather than objective:** Sheldon Cohen, "Social Relationships and Health," *American Psychologist* 59, no. 8 (2004): 676–684; Louise C. Hawkley and John T. Cacioppo, "Loneliness Matters: A Theoretical and Empirical Review of Consequences and Mechanisms," *Annals of Behavioral Medicine* 40, no. 2 (2010): 218–227; Robert S. Weiss, *Loneliness: The Experience of Emotional and Social Isolation* (Cambridge, MA: MIT Press, 1973).

pg. 226: **"What I felt at almost every stage of my development":** Oprah Winfrey, *What I Know for Sure* (New York: Flatiron Books, 2014), 32.

pg. 227: **"I went back to school and told no one":** Oprah Winfrey, *What I Know for Sure* (New York: Flatiron Books, 2014), 36.

CHAPTER 14: SECRET SOCIETY

pg. 228: **"Like burglars who secretly wish to be caught":** Ross Macdonald, quoted in Albin Krebs, "Ross Macdonald, Novelist, Dies at 67," *New York Times*, July 13, 1983, accessed February 27, 2017, http://www.nytimes.com/1983/07/13/obituaries/ross-macdonald-novelist-dies-at-67.html.

pg. 230: **"What the detective story is about":** P. D. James, quoted in interview, *Face Magazine* 80, December 1986.

pg. 231: **About half of adolescents who sexually assault another:** Natasha E. Latzman et al., "Sexual Offending in Adolescence: A Comparison of Sibling Offenders and Nonsibling Offenders Across Domains of Risk and Treatment Need," *Journal of Child Sexual Abuse* 20, no. 3 (2011): 245–263.

pg. 231: **goes beyond age-appropriate curiosity:** John V. Caffaro and Allison Conn-Caffaro, "Treating Sibling Abuse Families," *Aggression and Violent Behavior* 10, no. 5 (2005): 604–623; Jessie L. Krienert and Jeffrey A. Walsh, "Sibling Sexual Abuse: An Empirical Analysis of Offender, Victim, and Event Characteristics in National Incident-Based Reporting System (NIBRS) Data, 2000–2007," *Journal of Child Sexual Abuse* 20, no. 4 (2011): 353–372.

pg. 231: **tends to be more physically intrusive:** Mireille Cyr et al., "Intrafamilial Sexual Abuse: Brother–Sister Incest Does Not Differ from Father–Daughter and Stepfather–Stepdaughter Incest," *Child Abuse and Neglect* 26, no. 9 (2002): 957–973; Mary Jo McVeigh, "'But She Didn't Say No': An Exploration of Sibling Sexual Abuse," *Australian Social Work* 56, no. 2 (2003): 116–126; Inga Tidefors et al., "Sibling Incest: A Literature Review and A Clinical Study," *Journal of Sexual Aggression* 16, no. 3 (2010): 347–360.

pg. 231: **The more intrusive and frequent sibling sexual abuse is:** Margaret W. Ballantine, "Sibling Incest Dynamics: Therapeutic Themes and Clinical Challenges," *Clinical Social Work Journal* 40, no. 1 (2012): 56–65; Bronwyn Watson and W. Kim Halford, "Classes of Childhood Sexual Abuse and Women's Adult Couple Relationships," *Violence and Victims* 25, no. 4 (2010): 518–535.

pg. 232: **can be as damaging to a developing child as intercourse:** Mark S. Kiselica and Mandy Morrill Richards, "Sibling Maltreatment: The Forgotten Abuse," *Journal of Counseling and Development* 85, no. 2 (2007): 148–160; Kacie M. Thompson, "Sibling Incest: A Model for Group Practice with Adult Female Victims of Brother–Sister Incest," *Journal of Family Violence* 24, no. 7 (2009): 531–537.

pg. 232: **beliefs one held about the sexual experiences:** Bonnie Carlson, "Sibling Incest: Adjustment in Adult Women Survivors," *Families in Society: The Journal of Contemporary Social Services* 92, no. 1 (2011): 77–83.

pg. 232: **dangerous to let others get close, or that a normal life is not possible:** Bonnie Carlson, "Sibling Incest: Adjustment in Adult Women Survivors," *Families in Society: The Journal of Contemporary Social Services* 92, no. 1 (2011): 77–83.

pg. 232: **among the most unreported of all sex crimes:** John V. Caffaro and Allison Conn-Caffaro, "Treating Sibling Abuse Families," *Aggression and Violent Behavior* 10, no. 5 (2005): 604–623.

pg. 232: **for a multitude of reasons, victims rarely tell others:** Bonnie E. Carlson, Katherine Maciol, and Joanne Schneider, "Sibling Incest: Reports from Forty-One Survivors," *Journal of Child Sexual Abuse* 15, no. 4 (2006): 19–34.

pg. 232: **may worry about stressing their families even more:** Inga Tidefors et al., "Sibling Incest: A Literature Review and a Clinical Study," *Journal of Sexual Aggression* 16, no. 3 (2010): 347–360.

pg. 232: **responses they receive can be as hurtful and as harmful:** Margaret Rowntree, "Responses to Sibling Sexual Abuse: Are They as Harmful as the Abuse?" *Australian Social Work* 60, no. 3 (2007): 347–361.

pg. 232: **typical turns for abused and abusive siblings as they age:** Kathleen Monahan, "Themes of Adult Sibling Sexual Abuse Survivors in Later Life: An Initial Exploration," *Clinical Social Work Journal* 38, no. 4 (2010): 361–369.

pg. 233: **do not tell others about their experiences until many years after:** Ramona Alaggia, "Disclosing the Trauma of Child Sexual Abuse: A Gender Analysis," *Journal of Loss and Trauma* 10, no. 5 (2005): 453–470; Steven Kogan, "Disclosing Unwanted Sexual Experiences: Results from a National Sample of Adolescent Women," *Child Abuse and Neglect* 28, no. 2 (2004): 147–165; Daniel W. Smith et al., "Delay in Disclosure of Childhood Rape: Results from a National Survey," *Child Abuse and Neglect* 24, no. 2 (2000): 273–287.

pg. 233: **the relationship between opening up and health:** For a summary, see James W. Pennebaker, *Opening Up: The Healing Power of Expressing Emotions* (New York: Guilford, 1997).

pg. 233: **one early and revealing study:** James W. Pennebaker and Joan R. Susman, "Disclosure of Traumas and Psychosomatic Processes," *Social Science and Medicine* 26, no. 3 (1988): 327–332.

pg. 234: **"the act of not discussing or confiding":** James W. Pennebaker, "Traumatic Experience and Psychosomatic Disease: Exploring the Roles of Behavioural Inhibition, Obsession, and Confiding," *Canadian Psychology* 26, no. 2 (1985): 82.

pg. 234: **relief can come from talking about our darkest days:** James Pennebaker is actually best known for his work not with those who spoke about life's most difficult moments but for his work with those who wrote about them; for summaries, see James W. Pennebaker, *Opening Up: The Healing Power of Expressing Emotions* (New York: Guilford, 1997); James W. Pennebaker, "Putting Stress into Words: Health, Linguistic, and Therapeutic Implications," *Behaviour Research and Therapy* 31, no. 6 (1993): 539–548; James W. Pennebaker, "Writing About Emotional Experiences as a Therapeutic Process," *Psychological Science* 8, no. 3 (1997): 162–166; James W. Pennebaker and Janel D. Seagal, "Forming a Story: The Health Benefits of Narrative," *Journal of Clinical Psychology* 55, no. 10 (1999): 1243–1254.

pg. 234: **he interviewed Holocaust survivors:** James W. Pennebaker, Steven D. Barger, and John Tiebout, "Disclosure of Traumas and Health Among Holocaust Survivors," *Psychosomatic Medicine* 51, no. 5 (1989): 577–589.

pg. 235: **survivors who were willing and able to talk about the Holocaust:** Laura E. Finkelstein and Becca R. Levy, "Disclosure of Holocaust Experiences: Reasons, Attributions, and Health Implications," *Journal of Social and Clinical Psychology* 25, no. 1 (2006): 117–140.

pg. 235: **confession in Christianity, and it is the foundation of psychotherapy:** For a genealogy of confession, see Chloë Taylor, *The Culture of Confession from Augustine to Foucault: A Genealogy of the 'Confessing Animal'* (New York: Routledge, 2009).

pg. 235: **"talking cure":** Josef Breuer and Sigmund Freud, *Studies in Hysteria* (New York: Basic, 2000), 30.

pg. 235: **psychotherapies are more alike than they are different:** Stanley B. Messer and Bruce E. Wampold, "Let's Face Facts: Common Factors Are More Potent than Specific Therapy Ingredients," *Clinical Psychology: Science and Practice* 9, no. 1 (2002): 21–25; Bruce E. Wampold, "Absolute Efficacy: The Benefits of Psychotherapy Established by Meta-Analysis," in *The Great Psychotherapy Debate: Models, Methods, and Findings*, vol. 9 (New York: Routledge, 2013), 58–71; Bruce E. Wampold, "Relative Efficacy: The Dodo Bird Was Smarter than We Have Been Led to Believe," in *The Great Psychotherapy Debate: Models, Methods, and Findings*, vol. 9 (New York: Routledge, 2013), 72–118; Bruce E. Wampold et al., "A Meta-Analysis of Outcome Studies Comparing Bona Fide Psychotherapies: Empiricially, 'All Must Have Prizes,'" *Psychological Bulletin* 122, no. 3 (1997): 203–215.

pg. 235: **concluded that self-disclosure is beneficial:** Joanne Frattaroli, "Experimental Disclosure and Its Moderators: A Meta-Analysis," *Psychological Bulletin* 132, no. 6 (2006): 823–865.

pg. 235: **still no one knows exactly why:** Joanne Frattaroli, "Experimental Disclosure and Its Moderators: A Meta-Analysis," *Psychological Bulletin* 132, no. 6 (2006): 823–865; for theories as to why writing is good for us, see also Laura A. King, "Gain Without Pain? Expressive Writing and Self-Regulation," in *The Writing Cure: How Expressive Writing Promotes Health and Emotional Well-Being*, eds. Stephen J. Lepore and Joshua M. Smyth (Washington, DC: American Psychological Association, 2002), 119–134; Denise M. Sloan and Brian P. Marx, "Taking Pen to Hand: Evaluating Theories Underlying the Written Disclosure Paradigm," *Clinical Psychology: Science and Practice* 11, no. 2 (2004): 121–137; Joshua M. Smyth and James W. Pennebaker, "Exploring the Boundary Conditions of Expressive Writing: In Search of the Right Recipe," *British Journal of Health Psychology* 13, no. 1 (2008): 1–7.

pg. 235: **putting our experiences into words helps:** Anita E. Kelly et al., "What Is It About Revealing Secrets That Is Beneficial?" *Personality and Social Psychology Bulletin* 27, no. 6 (2001): 651–665; James W. Pennebaker, "Putting Stress into Words: Health, Linguistic, and Therapeutic Implications," *Behaviour Research and Therapy* 31, no. 6 (1993): 539–548.

pg. 236: **prefrontal cortex went up, while activity in the amygdala went down:** Ahmad R. Hariri, Susan Y. Bookheimer, and John C. Mazziotta, "Modulating Emotional Responses: Effects of a Neocortical Network on the Limbic System," *Neuroreport* 11, no. 1 (2000): 43–48.

pg. 237: **less activity in the amygdala and more in the prefrontal cortex:** Ahmad R. Hariri et al., "Neocortical Modulation of the Amygdala Response to Fearful Stimuli," *Biological Psychiatry* 53, no. 6 (2003): 494–501; see also Stephan F. Taylor et al., "Subjective Rating of Emotionally Salient Stimuli Modulates Neural Activity," *Neuroimage* 18, no. 3 (2003): 650–659.

pg. 237: **words force a shift from the amygdala to the prefrontal cortex:** Louis Cozolino, *The Neuroscience of Psychotherapy: Building and Rebuilding the Human Brain* (New York: Norton, 2010), 155.

pg. 237: **"A concept without a name":** Ruth Klüger and Lore Segal, *Still Alive: A Holocaust Girl Remembered* (New York: Feminist Press, 2003), 180.

pg. 238: **"Perhaps the narrative":** Annie Ernaux, *Shame* (Paris: Gallimard, 1997), 16–17, quoted in Chloe Taylor, *The Culture of Confession from Augustine to Foucault: A Genealogy of the 'Confessing Animal'* (New York: Routledge, 2009), 111.

pg. 238: **words and sentences have the potential to create order:** Crystal L. Park, "Making Sense of the Meaning Literature: An Integrative Review of Meaning Making and Its Effects on Adjustment to Stressful Life Events," *Psychological Bulletin* 136, no. 2 (2010): 257–301; Laura Jacobsen Wrenn, "Trauma: Conscious and Unconscious Meaning," *Clinical Social Work Journal* 31, no. 2 (2003): 123–137.

pg. 238: **telling study about the relationship between secrets and community:** Deborrah Frable, Linda Platt, and Steve Hoey, "Concealable Stigmas and Positive Self-Perceptions: Feeling Better Around Similar Others," *Journal of Personality and Social Psychology* 74, no. 4 (1998): 909–922.

pg. 238: **social support is crucial:** Sheldon Cohen, "Social Relationships and Health," *American Psychologist* 59, no. 8 (2004): 676–684; Bert N. Uchino, "Social Support and Health: A Review of Physiological Processes Potentially Underlying Links to Disease Outcomes," *Journal of Behavioral Medicine* 29, no. 4 (2006): 377–387; Debra Umberson and Jennifer Karas Montez, "Social Relationships and Health: A Flashpoint for Health Policy," *Journal of Health and Social Behavior* 51, no. 1 (2010): S54–S66.

pg. 238: **key difference between those who are and are not happy:** Ed Diener and Martin E. P. Seligman, "Very Happy People," *Psychological Science* 13, no. 1 (2002): 81–84.

pg. 238: **less likely to struggle with anxiety and depression:** Paula S. Nurius, Patricia Logan-Greene, and Sara Green, "ACEs Within a Social Disadvantage Framework: Distinguishing Unique, Cumulative, and Moderated Contributions to Adult Mental Health," *Journal of Prevention and Intervention in the Community* 40, no. 4 (2012): 278–290.

pg. 239: **not the severity of the event but how alone one feels afterward:** Chris R. Brewin, Bernice Andrews, and John D. Valentine, "Meta-Analysis of Risk Factors for Posttraumatic Stress Disorder in Trauma-Exposed Adults," *Journal of Consulting and Clinical Psychology* 68, no. 5 (2000): 748–766; Lori Davis and Lawrence J. Siegel, "Posttraumatic Stress Disorder in Children and Adolescents: A Review and Analysis," *Clinical Child and Family Psychology Review* 3, no. 3 (2000): 135–154; Emily J. Ozer et al., "Predictors of Posttraumatic Stress Disorder and Symptoms in Adults: A Meta-Analysis," *Psychological Bulletin* 129 (2003): 52–73; Daniel S. Pine and Judith A. Cohen, "Trauma in Children and Adolescents: Risk and Treatment of Psychiatric Sequelae," *Biological Psychiatry* 51 (2002): 519–531; David Trickey et al., "A Meta-Analysis of Risk

Factors for Post-Traumatic Stress Disorder in Children and Adolescents," *Clinical Psychology Review* 32, no. 2 (2012): 122–138; Ana-Maria Vranceanu, Stevan E. Hobfoll, and Robert J. Johnson, "Child Multi-Type Maltreatment and Associated Depression and PTSD Symptoms: The Role of Social Support and Stress," *Child Abuse and Neglect* 31, no. 1 (2007): 71–84.

pg. 239: **sharing our secrets and having people in our lives who support us:** Kim M. Anderson and Catherine Hiersteiner, "Recovering from Childhood Sexual Abuse: Is a 'Storybook Ending' Possible?" *American Journal of Family Therapy* 36, no. 5 (2008): 413–424.

pg. 239: **a person who can be discreet, and who can be trusted not to judge:** Anita E. Kelly and Kevin J. McKillop, "Consequences of Revealing Personal Secrets," *Psychological Bulletin* 120, no. 3 (1996): 450–465.

pg. 239: **allow each group member to see that he or she is not the only one:** Kim M. Anderson and Catherine Hiersteiner, "Recovering from Childhood Sexual Abuse: Is a 'Storybook Ending' Possible?" *American Journal of Family Therapy* 36, no. 5 (2008): 413–424; Carolyn Knight, "Groups for Individuals with Traumatic Histories: Practice Considerations for Social Workers," *Social Work* 51, no. 1 (2006): 20–30; see also Janel D. Seagal and James W. Pennebaker, "Expressive Writing and Social Stigma: Benefits from Writing About Being a Group Member" (unpublished manuscript, University of Texas–Austin, 1997), described in James W. Pennebaker and Janel D. Seagal, "Forming a Story: The Health Benefits of Narrative," *Journal of Clinical Psychology* 55, no. 10 (1999): 1243–1254.

pg. 239: **tend to be caring friends or supportive partners:** Emmy E. Werner and Ruth S. Smith, *Overcoming the Odds: High Risk Children from Birth to Adulthood* (Ithaca, NY: Cornell University Press, 1992), 195.

pg. 239: **roughly 20 percent of children who had been sexually assaulted:** Noemi Pereda et al., "The Prevalence of Child Sexual Abuse in Community and Student Samples: A Meta-Analysis," *Clinical Psychology Review* 29, no. 4 (2009): 328–338.

pg. 240: **there are risks in telling them:** Stephenie R. Chaudoir and Jeffrey D. Fisher, "The Disclosure Processes Model: Understanding Disclosure Decision Making and Postdisclosure Outcomes Among People Living with a Concealable Stigmatized Identity," *Psychological Bulletin* 136, no. 2 (2010): 236–256; Anita E. Kelly and Kevin J. McKillop, "Consequences of Revealing Personal Secrets," *Psychological Bulletin* 120, no. 3 (1996): 450–465; Julia Omarzu, "A Disclosure Decision Model: Determining How and When Individuals Will Self-Disclose," *Personality and Social Psychology Review* 4, no. 2 (2000): 174–185.

pg. 240: **"cruel paradox":** Kent D. Harber and James W. Pennebaker, "Overcoming Traumatic Memories," in *The Handbook of Emotion and Memory*, ed. Sven-Ake Christiansen (Hillsdale, NJ: Erlbaum, 1992), 359–387; see also Dan Coates and Tina Winston, "The Dilemma of Distress Disclosure," in *Self-Disclosure: Theory, Research, and Therapy*, eds. Valerian J. Derlega and John H. Berg (New York: Springer Science Business Media, 1987), 229–255.

pg. 240: **more likely to suffer from depression and PTSD:** Matthew D. Jeffreys et al., "Trauma Disclosure to Health Care Professionals by Veterans: Clinical Implications," *Military Medicine* 175, no. 10 (2010): 719–724; Ruth Q. Leibowitz et al., "Veterans' Disclosure of Trauma to Healthcare Providers," *General Hospital Psychiatry* 30, no. 2 (2008): 100–103; Norman Solkoff, Philip Gray, and Stuart Keill, "Which Vietnam Veterans Develop Posttraumatic Stress Disorders?" *Journal of Clinical Psychology* 42, no. 5 (1986): 687–698.

pg. 240: **only insofar as their social groups were supportive:** Valerian J. Derlega et al., "Reasons for HIV Disclosure/Nondisclosure in Close Relationships: Testing a Model of HIV–Disclosure Decision Making," *Journal of Social and Clinical Psychology* 23, no. 6 (2004): 747–767; Philip M. Ulrich, Susan K. Lutgendorf, and Jack T. Stapleton, "Concealment of Homosexual Identity, Social Support, and CD4 Cell Count Among HIV-Seropositive Gay Men," *Journal of Psychosomatic Research* 54, no. 3 (2003): 205–212.

pg. 240: **full support of those they told, were less likely to become depressed:** Brenda Major et al., "Mixed Messages: Implications of Social Conflict and Social Support Within Close Relationships for Adjustment to a Stressful Life Event," *Journal of Personality and Social Psychology* 72, no. 6 (1997): 1349–1363.

pg. 240: **women struggling with infertility:** Mariana V. Martins et al., "Interactive Effects of Social Support and Disclosure on Fertility-Related Stress," *Journal of Social and Personal Relationships* 30, no. 4 (2013): 371–388.

pg. 240: **only if they felt understood by others:** Kristin P. Beals, Letitia Anne Peplau, and Shelly L. Gable, "Stigma Management and Well-Being: The Role of Perceived Social Support, Emotional Processing, and Suppression," *Personality and Social Psychology Bulletin* 35, no. 7 (2009): 867–879.

pg. 240: **how others handled their disclosures:** Elisa E. Bolton et al., "The Relationship Between Self-Disclosure and Symptoms of Posttraumatic Stress Disorder in Peacekeepers Deployed to Somalia," *Journal of Traumatic Stress* 16, no. 3 (2003): 203–210.

pg. 240: **negative reactions of others were more predictive of PTSD:** Bernice Andrews, Chris R. Brewin, and Suzanna Rose, "Gender, Social Support, and PTSD in Victims of Violent Crime," *Journal of Traumatic Stress* 16, no. 4 (2003): 421–427; Rebecca Campbell et al., "Social Reactions to Rape Victims: Healing and Hurtful Effects on Psychological and Physical Health Outcomes," *Violence and Victims* 16, no. 3 (2001): 287–302; Myriam S. Denov, "To a Safer Place? Victims of Sexual Abuse by Females and Their Disclosures to Professionals," *Child Abuse and Neglect* 27, no. 1 (2003): 47–61; Sarah E. Ullman et al., "Psychosocial Correlates of PTSD Symptom Severity in Sexual Assault Survivors," *Journal of Traumatic Stress* 20, no. 5 (2007): 821–831.

pg. 241: **hurt and even devastated by negative comments and attacks:** Katelyn Y. A. McKenna and John A. Bargh, "Coming Out in the Age of the Internet: Identity 'Demarginalization' Through Virtual Group Participation," *Journal of Personality and Social Psychology* 75, no. 3 (1998): 681–694.

pg. 241: **often determine whether or when one might open up again:** Courtney E. Ahrens, "Being Silenced: The Impact of Negative Social Reactions on the Disclosure of Rape," *American Journal of Community Psychology* 38, no. 3–4 (2006): 263–274; Courtney E. Ahrens et al., "Deciding Whom to Tell: Expectations and Outcomes of Rape Survivors' First Disclosures," *Psychology of Women Quarterly* 31, no. 1 (2007): 38–49; Stephenie R. Chaudoir and Diane M. Quinn, "Revealing Concealable Stigmatized Identities: The Impact of Disclosure Motivations and Positive First-Disclosure Experiences on Fear of Disclosure and Well-Being," *Journal of Social Issues* 66, no. 3 (2010): 570–584.

pg. 241: **"A man who tells secrets or stories":** John Steinbeck, *The Winter of Our Discontent* (New York: Penguin, 2001), 70.

pg. 241: **"culture of confession":** Chloe Taylor, *The Culture of Confession from Augustine to Foucault: A Genealogy of the 'Confessing Animal'* (New York: Routledge, 2009).

pg. 242: **it does not follow:** Leigh Gilmore, *The Limits of Autobiography: Trauma and Testimony* (Ithaca, NY: Cornell University Press, 2001).

pg. 242: **"champion of sincerity":** Quoted in Chloe Taylor, *The Culture of Confession from Augustine to Foucault: A Genealogy of the 'Confessing Animal'* (New York: Routledge, 2009), 174–187; see also Jean-Paul Sartre, *Being and Nothingness* (New York: Gallimard, 1984), 107–109.

pg. 242: **Judith Butler:** Judith Butler, *On Giving an Account of Oneself* (New York: Fordham University Press, 2005).

pg. 243: **"You don't know me, anonymity insists":** Leigh Gilmore, *The Limits of Autobiography: Trauma and Testimony* (Ithaca, NY: Cornell University Press, 2001), 144.

pg. 243: **"define ourselves by the best that is in us":** Quoted in Lorraine A. DarConte, ed., *Pride Matters: Quotes to Inspire Your Personal Best* (Kansas City, MO: Andrews McMeel Publishing, 2001), 176.

pg. 243: **"There are two types of people on planet Earth":** David Wong, *This Book Is Full of Spiders: Seriously, Dude, Don't Touch It* (New York: St. Martin's Press, 2012), 52.

pg. 244: **family heroes may leave clues:** Ramona Alaggia, "Many Ways of Telling: Expanding Conceptualizations of Child Sexual Abuse Disclosure," *Child Abuse and Neglect* 28, no. 11 (2004): 1213–1227.

pg. 244: **what friends and acquaintances do and do not say:** Dorothy Miell and Steve Duck, "Strategies in Developing Friendships," in *Friendship and Social Interaction*, eds. Valerian J. Derlega and Barbara A. Winstead (New York: Springer-Verlag, 1986), 129–143.

pg. 245: **"it takes one to know one":** Amy Robinson, "It Takes One to Know One: Passing and Communities of Common Interest," *Critical Inquiry* 20, no. 4 (1994): 715–736.

pg. 245: **to disrupt our most meaningful bonds but also to create them:** Kai Erikson, "Notes on Trauma and Community," in *Trauma: Explorations in Memory*, ed. C. Caruth (Baltimore, MD: Johns Hopkins University Press, 1995), 183–199.

CHAPTER 15: CAPE

pg. 247: **"The world is a dangerous place to live":** Albert Einstein, quoted in Robert I. Fitzhenry, ed., *The Harper Book of Quotations*, 3rd ed. (New York: Collins Reference, 1993), 356.

pg. 247: **"With great power":** Stan Lee and Steve Ditko, *Spider-Man!: Amazing Fantasy* #15 (New York: Marvel Comics, August 1962); Laurence Maslon and Michael Kantor, *Superheroes!: Capes, Cowls, and the Creation of Comic Book Culture* (New York: Crown Archetype, 2013), 144.

pg. 247: **"Where there is great power":** Winston Churchill, *The Parliamentary Debates* (Authorized Edition), Fourth Series, First Session of the Twenty-Eighth Parliament of the United Kingdom of Great Britain and Ireland, Vol. 152, February 28, 1906 (London: Wyman and Sons), 1239.

pg. 247: **"Great power involves":** Franklin D. Roosevelt, "Undelivered Address Prepared for Jefferson Day," April 13, 1945, online by Gerhard Peters and John T. Woolley, *The American Presidency Project*, accessed July 31, 2016, http://www.presidency.ucsb.edu/ws/?pid=16602.

pg. 249: **nearly 20 percent of adults suffer from depression:** Referring here to unipolar depression; DSM-5 diagnostic criteria: A. Five (or more) of the following symptoms have been present most of the day, nearly every day during the same 2-week period and represent a change from previous functioning; (1) Depressed mood; (2) Markedly diminished interest or pleasure in activities; (3) Significant change in weight and/or appetite; (4) Insomnia or hypersomnia; (5) Psychomotor agitation or retardation; (6) Fatigue or loss of energy; (7) Feelings of worthlessness or excessive or inappropriate guilt; (8) Diminished ability to think or concentrate, or indecisiveness; (9) Recurrent thoughts of death; B. The symptoms cause clinically significant distress or impairment in social, occupational, or other important areas of functioning; C. The episode is not attributable to the physiological effects of a substance or to another medical condition.

pg. 249: **most prevalent mental health disorder in the United States:** Center for Behavioral Health Statistics and Quality, "Behavioral Health Trends in the United States: Results from the 2014 National Survey on Drug Use and Health," HHS Publication No. SMA 15-4927, NSDUH Series H-50, 2015, accessed July 21, 2016, http://www.samhsa.gov/data/sites/default/files/NSDUH-FRR1-2014/NSDUH-FRR1-2014.pdf; Ronald C. Kessler et al., "Prevalence, Severity, and Comorbidity of 12-Month DSM-IV Disorders in the National Comorbidity Survey Replication," *Archives of General Psychiatry* 62, no. 6 (2005): 617–627.

pg. 249: **many do not recognize its invisible burden:** Christopher J. L. Murray and Alan D. Lopez, eds., *The Global Burden of Disease: A Comprehensive Assessment of Mortality and Disability* *from Diseases, Injuries and Risk Factors in 1990 and Projected to 2020* (Geneva, Switzerland: Harvard University Press, 1996).

pg. 249: **shorten not our life span but our "health span":** Christopher J. L Murray and Alan D. Lopez, eds., *The Global Burden of Disease: A Comprehensive Assessment of Mortality and Disability from Diseases, Injuries and Risk Factors in 1990 and Projected to 2020* (Geneva, Switzerland: Harvard University Press, 1996), 22.

pg. 249: **second leading cause of years lived with a disability:** Alize J. Ferrari et al., "Burden of Depressive Disorders by Country, Sex, Age, and Year: Findings from the Global Burden of Disease Study 2010," *PLOS Medicine* 10, no. 11 (2013): e1001547; Institute for Health Metrics and Evaluation (IHME), GBD Compare, Seattle, WA: IHME, University of Washington, 2015, accessed July 21, 2016, http://vizhub.healthdata.org/gbd-compare; Harvey A. Whiteford et al., "Global Burden of Disease Attributable to Mental and Substance Use Disorders: Findings from the Global Burden of Disease Study 2010," *Lancet* 382, no. 9904 (2013): 1575–1586.

pg. 249: **not only of parents but also of their children:** For a summary, see Sherryl H. Goodman, "Depression in Mothers," *Annual Review of Clinical Psychology* 3 (2007): 107–135.

pg. 250: **equally impacted by their parents' poor mental health:** William R. Beardslee et al., "Children of Parents with a Major Affective Disorder: A Review," *American Journal of Psychiatry* 140, no. 7 (1983): 825–832; Geraldine Downey and James C. Coyne, "Children of Depressed Parents: An Integrative Review," *Psychological Bulletin* 108, no. 1 (1990): 50–76.

pg. 250: **Parenting is one of the greatest challenges:** Geraldine Downey and James C. Coyne, "Children of Depressed Parents: An Integrative Review," *Psychological Bulletin* 108, no. 1 (1990): 50–76; Brenda M. Gladstone et al., "Children's Experiences of Parental Mental Illness: A Literature Review," *Early Intervention in Psychiatry* 5, no. 4 (2011): 271–289; Constance Hammen, "Risk and Protective Factors for Children of Depressed Parents," in *Resilience and Vulnerability: Adaptation in the Context of Childhood Adversities*, ed. Suniya S. Luthar (New York: Cambridge University Press, 2003), 51–75; Sydney L. Hans, "Mothering and Depression," in *Women's Mental Health*, eds. Sarah E. Romans and Mary V. Seeman (Philadelphia: Lippincott, Williams and Wikins, 2006), 311–320; M. Christine Lovejoy et al., "Maternal Depression and Parenting Behavior: A Meta-Analytic Review," *Clinical Psychology Review* 20, no. 5 (2000): 561–592.

pg. 250: **the inability to experience positive emotions:** David Watson and Auke Tellegen, "Toward a Consensual Structure of Mood," *Psychological Bulletin* 98, no. 2 (1985): 219–235.

pg. 250: **As adults, many children of depressed parents do fare well:** Hsing-Jung Chen and Pamela Kovacs, "Working with Families in Which a Parent Has Depression: A Resilience Perspective," *Families in Society: The Journal of Contemporary Social Services* 94, no. 2 (2013): 114–120; Constance Hammen, "Risk and Protective Factors for Children of Depressed Parents," in *Resilience and Vulnerability: Adaptation in the Context of Childhood Adversities*, ed. Suniya S. Luthar (New York: Cambridge University Press, 2003), 51–75; Rebecca Pargas et al., "Resilience to Maternal Depression in Young Adulthood," *Developmental Psychology* 46, no. 4 (2010): 805–814.

pg. 250: **longest-running such study to date:** Myrna M. Weissman et al., "Offspring of Depressed Parents: 20 Years Later," *American Journal of Psychiatry* 163, no. 6 (2006): 1001–1008; for a four-year longitudinal study with similar findings, see also Roselind Lieb et al., "Parental Major Depression and the Risk of Depression and Other Mental Disorders in Offspring: A Prospective-Longitudinal Community Study," *Archives of General Psychiatry* 59, no. 4 (2002): 365–374.

pg. 251: **family heroes may look more like parents than children:** Hanita Zimrin, "A Profile of Survival," *Child Abuse and Neglect* 10, no. 3 (1986): 339–349.

pg. 252: **two-thirds functioned as the family heroes:** Bruce Lackie, "Family Correlates of Career Achievement in Social Work" (doctoral dissertation, Rutgers University,

1982); Bruce Lackie, "The Families of Origin of Social Workers," *Clinical Social Work Journal* 11, no. 4 (1983): 309–322.

pg. 253: **choose professions that are an extension of that role:** Sharon Wegscheider-Cruse, *Another Chance: Hope and Health for the Alcoholic Family* (Palo Alto, CA: Science and Behavior Books, 1989).

pg. 253: **"When the Family Hero Turns Pro":** Barbara L. Wood, *Children of Alcoholism: The Struggle for Self and Intimacy in Adult Life* (New York: New York University Press, 1987), 144–157.

pg. 253: **80 percent of social work students:** Sara Rae Marsh, "Antecedents to Choice of a Helping Career: Social Work vs. Business Majors," *Smith College Studies in Social Work* 58, no. 2 (1988): 85–100.

pg. 253: **nearly half of students of social work:** Robin Russel et al., "Dysfunction in the Family of Origin of MSW and Other Graduate Students," *Journal of Social Work Education* 29, no. 1 (1993): 121–129.

pg. 253: **common in the histories of social work, guidance, and counseling:** Phyllis Black, Dorothy Jeffreys, and Elizabeth Kennedy Hartley, "Personal History of Psychosocial Trauma in the Early Life of Social Work and Business Students," *Journal of Social Work Education* 29, no. 2 (1993): 171–180; Catherine A. Hawkins and Raymond C. Hawkins, "Alcoholism in the Families of Origin of MSW Students: Estimating the Prevalence of Mental Health Problems Using Standardized Measures," *Journal of Social Work Education* 32, no. 1 (1996): 127–134; Elizabeth Lewis Rompf and David Royse, "Choice of Social Work as a Career: Possible Influences," *Journal of Social Work Education* 30, no. 2 (1994): 163–171; Robin Russel et al., "Dysfunction in the Family of Origin of MSW and Other Graduate Students," *Journal of Social Work Education* 29, no. 1 (1993): 121–129.

pg. 253: **early adversities did indeed influence their vocational choice:** Marilyn Barnett, "What Brings You Here? An Exploration of the Unconscious Motivations of Those Who Choose to Train and Work as Psychotherapists and Counselors," *Psychodynamic Practice* 13, no. 3 (2007): 257–274; Kara Coombes and Ruth Anderson, "The Impact of Family of Origin on Social Workers from Alcoholic Families," *Clinical Social Work Journal* 28, no. 3 (2000): 281–302; Barry A. Farber et al., "Choosing Psychotherapy as a Career: Why Did We Cross That Road?" *Journal of Clinical Psychology* 61, no. 8 (2005): 1009–1031; Hallie Frank and Joel Paris, "Psychological Factors in the Choice of Psychiatry as a Career," *Canadian Journal of Psychiatry* 32, no. 2 (1987): 118–122; Stephen P. Hinshaw, *Breaking the Silence: Mental Health Professionals Disclose Their Personal and Family Experiences of Mental Illness* (New York: Oxford University Press, 2008); Thomas Maeder, "Wounded Healers," *Atlantic Monthly* 263, no. 1 (1989): 37–47; Robert A. Murphy and Richard P. Halgin, "Influences on the Career Choice of Psychotherapists," *Professional Psychology: Research and Practice* 26, no. 4 (1995): 422–426; Sherrill L. Sellers and Andrea G. Hunter, "Private Pains, Public Choices: Influence of Problems in the Family Origin on Career Choices Among a Cohort of MSW Students," *Social Work Education* 24, no. 8 (2005): 869–881.

pg. 253: **moving, and rare, qualitative study:** L. Knutsson-Medin, Birgitta Edlund, and Mia Ramklint, "Experiences in a Group of Grown-Up Children of Mentally Ill Parents," *Journal of Psychiatric and Mental Health Nursing* 14, no. 8 (2007): 744–752.

pg. 255: **"heroic helpers":** Ervin Staub, "The Psychology of Bystanders, Perpetrators, and Heroic Helpers," in *Understanding Genocide: The Social Psychology of the Holocaust*, eds. Leonard S. Newman and Ralph Erber (New York: Oxford University Press, 2002): 11–42.

pg. 255: **"The opposite of a hero isn't a villain; it's a bystander":** Quoted in Aditya Chakrabortty, "The Psychology of Heroism: How Can Normal People Be Made to Act Heroically?" *Guardian*, March 8, 2010, accessed February 26, 2017, https://www.theguardian.com/science/2010/mar/09/brain-food-psychology-heroism.

pg. 255: **to do what you are good at, and to do what moves you:** Frank Parsons, *Choosing a Vocation* (Boston, MA: Houghton Mifflin, 1909).

pg. 255: **story of Howard Schultz:** Howard Schultz and Dori Jones Yang, *Pour Your Heart into It: How Starbucks Built a Company One Cup at a Time* (New York: Hachette, 1999).

pg. 256: **"I knew in my heart":** Howard Schultz and Dori Jones Yang, *Pour Your Heart into It: How Starbucks Built a Company One Cup at a Time* (New York: Hachette, 1999), 4.

pg. 256: **"Although I didn't consciously plan it that way":** Howard Schultz and Dori Jones Yang, *Pour Your Heart into It: How Starbucks Built a Company One Cup at a Time* (New York: Hachette, 1999), 7.

pg. 256: **there are a lot of ways to help people, to be a hero:** Alice H. Eagly, "The His and Hers of Prosocial Behavior: An Examination of the Social Psychology of Gender," *American Psychologist* 64, no. 8 (2009): 644–658; Zeno E. Franco, Kathy Blau, and Philip G. Zimbardo, "Heroism: A Conceptual Analysis and Differentiation Between Heroic Action and Altruism," *Review of General Psychology* 15, no. 2 (2011): 99–113; Sara Staats et al., "The Hero Concept: Self, Family, and Friends Who Are Brave, Honest, and Hopeful," *Psychological Reports* 104, no. 3 (2009): 820–832.

pg. 256: **"altruism born of suffering":** Ervin Staub, "The Roots of Goodness: The Fulfillment of Basic Human Needs and the Development of Caring, Helping and Nonaggression, Inclusive Caring, Moral Courage, Active Bystandership, and Altruism Born of Suffering," in *Moral Motivation Through the Life Span: Theory, Research, Applications,* eds. Gustavo Carlo and Carolyn Edwards (Lincoln: Nebraska University Press, 2005), 33–72; Ervin Staub and Johanna Vollhardt, "Altruism Born of Suffering: The Roots of Caring and Helping After Victimization and Other Trauma," *American Journal of Orthopsychiatry* 78, no. 3 (2008): 267–280.

pg. 256: **Raoul Wallenberg:** "Raoul Wallenberg and the Rescue of the Jews in Budapest," US Holocaust Museum, Washington, DC, last modified July 2, 2016, accessed February 26, 2017, https://www.ushmm.org/wlc/en/article.php?ModuleId=10005211.

pg. 257: **reportedly died later in a Soviet prison:** Sewell Chan, "71 Years After He Vanished, Raoul Wallenberg Is Declared Dead," *New York Times,* October 31, 2016, accessed January 29, 2017, https://www.nytimes.com/2016/11/01/world/europe/71-years-after -he-vanished-raoul-wallenberg-is-declared-dead.html?_r=0.

pg. 257: **grow up too fast or carry far too heavy a load:** Nancy Chase, *Burdened Children: Theory, Research, and Treatment of Parentification* (Thousand Oaks, CA: Sage, 1999); David Elkind, *The Hurried Child: Growing Up Too Fast Too Soon* (Boston, MA: Da Capo Press, 1981); Gregory J. Jurkovic, *Lost Childhoods: The Plight of the Parentified Child* (New York: Routledge, 1997); Bruce Lackie, "The Families of Origin of Social Workers," *Clinical Social Work Journal* 11, no. 4 (1983): 309–322.

pg. 257: **pathways to compassion and competence:** Jo Aldridge and Saul Becker, *Children Caring for Parents with Mental Illness: Perspectives of Young Carers, Parents and Professionals* (Cambridge, MA: MIT Press, 2003); Kara Coombes and Ruth Anderson. "The Impact of Family of Origin on Social Workers from Alcoholic Families," *Clinical Social Work Journal* 28, no. 3 (2000): 281–302; Brenda M. Gladstone, Katherine M. Boydell, and Patricia McKeever, "Recasting Research into Children's Experiences of Parental Mental Illness: Beyond Risk and Resilience," *Social Science and Medicine* 62, no. 10 (2006): 2540–2550; Brenda M. Gladstone et al., "Children's Experiences of Parental Mental Illness: A Literature Review," *Early Intervention in Psychiatry* 5, no. 4 (2011): 271–289.

pg. 257: **more likely to help others:** Ervin Staub and Johanna Vollhardt, "Altruism Born of Suffering: The Roots of Caring and Helping After Victimization and Other Trauma," *American Journal of Orthopsychiatry* 78, no. 3 (2008): 267–280.

pg. 257: **"survivor mission":** Judith Herman, *Trauma and Recovery* (New York: Basic Books, 1997), 201.

pg. 257: **"The great illusion of leadership":** Henri J. M. Nouwen, *The Wounded Healer: Ministry in Contemporary Society* (New York: Image, 1979), 72.

pg. 257: **"The doctor is effective":** Carl Jung, *Memories, Dreams, Reflections* (New York: Vintage, 1989), 134.

pg. 258:   **linked to improved health and well-being:** See, for review, Stephen G. Post, ed., *Altruism and Health: Perspectives from Empirical Research* (New York: Oxford University Press, 2007); see also Carolyn Schwartz et al., "Altruistic Social Interest Behaviors Are Associated with Better Mental Health," *Psychosomatic Medicine* 65, no. 5 (2003): 778–785.

pg. 258:   **higher levels of happiness and satisfaction, and lower mortality rates:** Gian V. Caprara and Patrizia Steca, "Self-Efficacy Beliefs as Determinants of Prosocial Behavior Conducive to Life Satisfaction Across Ages," *Journal of Social and Clinical Psychology* 24, no. 2 (2005): 191–217; P. L. Dulin and R. D. Hill, "Relationships Between Altruistic Activity and Positive and Negative Affect Among Low-Income Older Adult Service Providers," *Aging and Mental Health* 7, no. 4 (2003): 294–299; Robert Grimm, Kimberly Spring, and Nathan Dietz, "The Health Benefits of Volunteering: A Review of Recent Research," Corporation for National and Community Service, Office of Research and Policy Development, Washington, DC, 2007, http://www.nationalservice .gov/pdf/07_0506_hbr.pdf; Nancy Morrow-Howell, Song-Iee Hong, and Fengyan Tang, "Who Benefits from Volunteering? Variations in Perceived Benefits," *Gerontologist* 49, no. 1 (2009): 91–102; Nancy Morrow-Howell et al., "Effects of Volunteering on the Well-Being of Older Adults," *Journals of Gerontology Series B* 58, no. 3 (2003): S137–S145; Marc A. Musick and John Wilson, "Volunteering and Depression: The Role of Psychological and Social Resources in Different Age Groups," *Social Science and Medicine* 56, no. 2 (2003): 259–269; Doug Oman, Carl E. Thoresen, and Kay McMahon, "Volunteerism and Mortality Among the Community-Dwelling Elderly," *Journal of Health Psychology* 4, no. 3 (1999): 301–316; Marieke Van Willigen, "Differential Benefits of Volunteering Across the Life Course," *Journals of Gerontology* 55, no. 5 (2000): S308–S318.

pg. 258:   **shown to reduce one's heart rate and blood pressure:** Stephanie L. Brown, R. Michael Brown, and Ashley Schiavone, "Close Relationships and Health Through the Lens of Selective Investment Theory," in *Altruism and Health: Perspectives from Empirical Research*, ed. Stephen G. Post (New York: Oxford University Press, 2007).

pg. 258:   **key predictor of physical health and emotional health:** Aaron M. Eakman, "A Prospective Longitudinal Study Testing Relationships Between Meaningful Activities, Basic Psychological Needs Fulfillment, and Meaning in Life," *OTJR: Occupation, Participation and Health* 34, no. 2 (2014): 93–105; Aaron M. Eakman, "Relationships Between Meaningful Activity, Basic Psychological Needs, and Meaning in Life: Test of the Meaningful Activity and Life Meaning model," *OTJR: Occupation, Participation and Health* 33, no. 2 (2013): 100–109; Aaron M. Eakman and Mona Eklund, "The Relative Impact of Personality Traits, Meaningful Occupation and Occupational Value on Meaning in Life and Life Satisfaction," *Journal of Occupational Science* 19, no. 2 (2012): 165–177; Ann Marie Roepke, Eranda Jayawickreme, and Olivia M. Riffle, "Meaning and Health: A Systematic Review," *Applied Research in Quality of Life* 9, no. 4 (2014): 1055–1079.

pg. 258:   **lead to more positive feelings for the caregiver:** Michael J. Poulin et al., "Does a Helping Hand Mean a Heavy Heart? Helping Behavior and Well-Being Among Spouse Caregivers," *Psychology and Aging* 25, no. 1 (2010): 108–117.

pg. 259:   **reduce one's own risk of death:** Stephanie L. Brown et al., "Caregiving Behavior Is Associated with Decreased Mortality Risk," *Psychological Science* 20, no. 4 (2009): 488–494.

pg. 259:   **recover from grief and depression faster:** Stephanie L. Brown et al., "Coping with Spousal Loss: Potential Buffering Effects of Self-Reported Helping Behavior," *Personality and Social Psychology Bulletin* 34, no. 6 (2008): 849–861.

pg. 259:   **Cardiac patients who help new patients learn about and cope:** Gwynn B. Sullivan and Martin J. Sullivan, "Promoting Wellness in Cardiac Rehabilitation: Exploring the Role of Altruism," *Journal of Cardiovascular Nursing* 11, no. 3 (1997): 43–52.

pg. 259:   **associated with longer survival with HIV:** Gail Ironson et al., "Spirituality and Religiousness Are Associated with Long Survival, Health Behaviors, Less Distress, and Lower Cortisol in People Living with HIV/AIDS: The IWORSHIP Scale, Its Validity and Reliability," *Annals of Behavioral Medicine* 24, no. 1 (2002): 34–48.

pg. 259: **participating in a research study can help us feel better:** Beth J. Seelig and William H. Dobelle, "Altruism and the Volunteer: Psychological Benefits from Participating as a Research Subject," *ASAIO Journal* 47, no. 1 (2001): 3–5; see also Natalie McClain and Angela Frederick Amar, "Female Survivors of Child Sexual Abuse: Finding Voice Through Research Participation," *Issues in Mental Health Nursing* 34, no. 7 (2013): 482–487.

pg. 259: **"it's good to be good":** Stephen G. Post, "Altruism, Happiness, and Health: It's Good to Be Good," *International Journal of Behavioral Medicine* 12, no. 2 (2005): 66–77.

pg. 259: **may even outweigh that of receiving help:** Stephanie L. Brown et al., "Providing Social Support May Be More Beneficial than Receiving It: Results from a Prospective Study of Mortality," *Psychological Science* 14, no. 4 (2003): 320–327; Jersey Liang, Neal M. Krause, and Joan M. Bennett, "Social Exchange and Well-Being: Is Giving Better than Receiving?" *Psychology and Aging* 16, no. 3 (2001): 511–523.

pg. 259: **patients with multiple sclerosis provided social support to others:** Carolyn E. Schwartz and Rabbi Meir Sendor, "Helping Others Helps Oneself: Response Shift Effects in Peer Support," *Social Science and Medicine* 48, no. 11 (1999): 1563–1575.

pg. 259: **a similar study of more than one thousand churchgoers:** Carolyn Schwartz et al., "Altruistic Social Interest Behaviors Are Associated with Better Mental Health," *Psychosomatic Medicine* 65, no. 5 (2003): 778–785.

pg. 259: **found to reduce the risk of death:** Stephanie L. Brown et al., "Providing Social Support May Be More Beneficial than Receiving It: Results from a Prospective Study of Mortality," *Psychological Science* 14, no. 4 (2003): 320–327.

pg. 260: **we forget for a time about our own problems:** George Vaillant, "Adaptive Mental Mechanisms: Their Role in a Positive Psychology," *American Psychologist* 55, no. 1 (2000): 89–98.

pg. 260: **we even feel happier, too:** Barbara L. Fredrickson, "The Role of Positive Emotions in Positive Psychology: The Broaden-and-Build Theory of Positive Emotions," *American Psychologist* 56, no. 3 (2001): 218–226; Barbara L. Fredrickson et al., "The Undoing Effect of Positive Emotions," *Motivation and Emotion* 24, no. 4 (2000): 237–258; Andrea H. Marques and Esther M. Sternberg, "The Biology of Positive Emotions and Health," in *Altruism and Health: Perspectives from Empirical Research*, ed. Stephen G. Post (New York: Oxford University Press, 2007), 149–188; Michele M. Tugade and Barbara L. Fredrickson, "Resilient Individuals Use Positive Emotions to Bounce Back from Negative Emotional Experiences," *Journal of Personality and Social Psychology* 86, no. 2 (2004): 320–333.

pg. 261: **hang up the cape on a regular basis and save themselves:** Elaine Mordoch and Wendy A. Hall, "Children's Perceptions of Living with a Parent with a Mental Illness: Finding the Rhythm and Maintaining the Frame," *Qualitative Health Research* 18, no. 8 (2008): 1127–1144; David Sloan Wilson and Mihaly Csikszentmihalyi, "Health and the Ecology of Altruism," in *Altruism and Health: Perspectives from Empirical Research*, ed. Stephen G. Post (New York: Oxford University Press, 2007), 314–331.

pg. 261: **feels freely chosen is more likely to be effective:** Kyle D. Killian, "Helping Till It Hurts? A Multimethod Study of Compassion Fatigue, Burnout, and Self-Care in Clinicians Working with Trauma Survivors," *Traumatology* 14, no. 2 (2008): 32–44; Wilmar B. Schaufeli and Bram P. Buunk, "Burnout: An Overview of 25 Years of Research and Theorizing" in *The Handbook of Work and Health Psychology*, 2nd ed., eds. Marc J. Schabracq, Jacques A. M. Winnubst, and Cary L. Cooper (West Sussex, UK: John Wiley and Sons, 2003), 383–428; Netta Weinstein and Richard M. Ryan, "When Helping Helps: Autonomous Motivation for Prosocial Behavior and Its Influence on Well-Being for the Helper and Recipient," *Journal of Personality and Social Psychology* 98, no. 2 (2010): 222–244.

pg. 262: **addicted to stress:** Louis Cozolino, *The Neuroscience of Psychotherapy: Building and Rebuilding the Human Brain* (New York: Norton, 2010), 279.

pg. 263: **"Part of the art of being a hero":** Alan Moore, *Watchmen* (New York: DC Comics, 1987), 101.

CHAPTER 16: AVENGER

pg. 264: **"The best revenge is to be unlike him who":** Although the exact source of this quote is unclear, it is widely attributed to Marcus Aurelius.

pg. 266: **children are like little scientists:** Deborah Byrd, "Neil deGrasse Tyson: Learning How to Think Is Empowerment," *Human World*, December 15, 2011, http://earthsky .org/human-world/neil-degrasse-tyson; "Neil deGrasse Tyson: Kids Are Born Scientists," Youtube video, 2:14, November 22, 2012, accessed January 29, 2017, https:// www.youtube.com/watch?v=bvFOeysaNAY; Alison Gopnik, Andrew N. Meltzoff, and Patricia K. Kuhl, *The Scientist in the Crib: Minds, Brains, and How Children Learn* (New York: Perennial, 2001).

pg. 266: **"I'd not only never been in love":** Marilyn Monroe and Ben Hecht, *My Story* (Lanham, MD: Taylor Trade, 2007), 88.

pg. 267: **"I couldn't help but stare at them":** Elizabeth Smart with Chris Stewart, *My Story* (New York: St. Martin's Press, 2013), 210-211.

pg. 267: **from an evolutionary perspective, positive emotions such as love:** Michael A. Cohn and Barbara L. Fredrickson, "Beyond the Moment, Beyond the Self: Shared Ground Between Selective Investment Theory and the Broaden-and-Build Theory of Positive Emotions," *Psychological Inquiry* 17, no. 1 (2006): 39–44.

pg. 267: **most often they come home alone:** Stephanie R. deLuse, "Coping with Stress… The Superhero Way," in *The Psychology of Superheroes: An Unauthorized Exploration*, ed. Robin S. Rosenberg (Dallas: Benbella Books, 2008), 196.

pg. 268: **"superheroes are anything but super in these terms":** Christopher Peterson and Nansook Park, "The Positive Psychology of Superheroes," in *The Psychology of Superheroes: An Unauthorized Exploration*, ed. Robin S. Rosenberg (Dallas: Benbella Books, 2008), 11.

pg. 269: **the leading cause of injury to women:** Patricia A. Barrier, "Domestic Violence," *Mayo Clinic Proceedings* 73, no. 3 (1998): 271-274; Jennifer L. Truman and Rachel E. Morgan, "Nonfatal Domestic Violence, 2003-2012," *Journal of Current Issues in Crime, Law, and Law Enforcement* 8, no. 4 (2015).

pg. 270: **killed by their husbands than troops were killed by war:** Mansur Gidfar, "Don't Believe in a War on Women? Would a Body Count Change Your Mind?" *Upworthy*, June 19, 2012, accessed January 29, 2017, http://www.upworthy .com/dont-believe-in-the-war-on-women-would-a-body-count-change-your.mind.

pg. 270: **women with disabilities:** Douglas A. Brownridge, "Partner Violence Against Women with Disabilities," *Violence Against Women* 12, no. 9 (2006): 805–822; Sandra L. Martin et al., "Physical and Sexual Assault of Women with Disabilities," *Violence Against Women* 12, no. 9 (2006): 823–837; Diane L. Smith, "Disability, Gender and Intimate Partner Violence: Relationships from the Behavioral Risk Factor Surveillance System," *Sexuality and Disability* 26, no. 1 (2008): 15–28.

pg. 270: **because of money:** Kim Pentico, "What Is Financial Abuse and How Can We Help Victims?" National Network to End Domestic Violence, November 11, 2015, accessed February 26, 2017, http://nnedv.org/news/4583-what-is-financial-abuse-how-can-we -help victims.html.

pg. 270: **about 20 percent of youth:** Sherry Hamby et al., "Children's Exposure to Intimate Partner Violence and Other Family Violence: Nationally Representative Rates Among US Youth," *Office of Justice and Juvenile Delinquency Prevention Juvenile Justice Bulletin* NCJ 232272 (2011): 1–11, accessed January 29, 2017, https://www.ncjrs.gov/pdffiles1/ ojjdp/232272.pdf; Alice Kramer, Darcy Lorenzon, and George Mueller, "Prevalence of Intimate Partner Violence and Health Implications for Women Using Emergency Departments and Primary Care Clinics," *Women's Health Issues* 14, no. 1 (2004): 19–29; Renee McDonald et al., "Estimating the Number of American Children Living in Partner-Violent Families," *Journal of Family Psychology* 20, no. 1 (2006): 137–142.

pg. 270: **mean number of incidents is eleven:** Sherry Hamby et al., "Children's Exposure to Intimate Partner Violence and Other Family Violence: Nationally Representative Rates Among US Youth," *Office of Justice and Juvenile Delinquency Prevention Juvenile Justice Bulletin* NCJ 232272 (2011): 1–11, accessed January 29, 2017, https://www.ncjrs.gov/pdffiles1/ojjdp/232272.pdf.

pg. 270: **Children may be exposed to partner violence:** Stephanie Holt, Helen Buckley, and Sadhbh Whelan, "The Impact of Exposure to Domestic Violence on Children and Young People: A Review of the Literature," *Child Abuse and Neglect* 32, no. 8 (2008): 797–810.

pg. 270: **directly witnessed one adult physically hurting another:** Sherry Hamby et al., "Children's Exposure to Intimate Partner Violence and Other Family Violence: Nationally Representative Rates Among US Youth," *Office of Justice and Juvenile Delinquency Prevention Juvenile Justice Bulletin* NCJ 232272 (2011): 1–11, accessed January 29, 2017, https://www.ncjrs.gov/pdffiles1/ojjdp/232272.pdf.

pg. 270: **silent witnesses:** Jennifer E. McIntosh, "Children Living with Domestic Violence: Research Foundations for Early Intervention," *Journal of Family Studies* 9, no. 2 (2003): 219–234.

pg. 270: **yelling at one of the adults involved in the hope of making it stop:** Sherry Hamby et al., "Children's Exposure to Intimate Partner Violence and Other Family Violence: Nationally Representative Rates Among US Youth," *Office of Justice and Juvenile Delinquency Prevention Juvenile Justice Bulletin* NCJ 232272 (2011): 1–11, accessed January 29, 2017, https://www.ncjrs.gov/pdffiles1/ojjdp/232272.pdf.

pg. 271: **similar developmental consequences as being the victim:** Katherine M. Kitzmann et al., "Child Witnesses to Domestic Violence: A Meta-Analytic Review," *Journal of Consulting and Clinical Psychology* 71, no. 2 (2003): 339–352; David A. Wolfe et al., "The Effects of Children's Exposure to Domestic Violence: A Meta-Analysis and Critique," *Clinical Child and Family Psychology Review* 6, no. 3 (2003): 171–187.

pg. 271: **more likely than their peers to suffer from stress-related illnesses:** Valerie J. Edwards et al., "Relationship Between Multiple Forms of Childhood Maltreatment and Adult Mental Health in Community Respondents: Results from the Adverse Childhood Experiences Study," *American Journal of Psychiatry* 160, no. 8 (2003): 1453–1460; Sarah E. Evans, Corrie Davies, and David DiLillo, "Exposure to Domestic Violence: A Meta-Analysis of Child and Adolescent Outcomes," *Aggression and Violent Behavior* 13, no. 2 (2008): 131–140; Stephanie Holt, Helen Buckley, and Sadhbh Whelan, "The Impact of Exposure to Domestic Violence on Children and Young People: A Review of the Literature," *Child Abuse and Neglect* 32, no. 8 (2008): 797–810; Dean G. Kilpatrick et al., "Violence and Risk of PTSD, Major Depression, Substance Abuse/Dependence, and Cormorbidity: Results from the National Survey of Adolescents," *Journal of Consulting and Clinical Psychology* 71, no. 4 (2003): 692–700; Beatriz Olaya et al., "Mental Health Needs of Children Exposed to Intimate Partner Violence Seeking Help from Mental Health Services," *Children and Youth Services Review* 32, no. 7 (2010): 1004–1011; Joy D. Osofsky, "The Impact of Violence on Children," *The Future of Children* 9, no. 3 (1999): 33–49.

pg. 272: **children learn by observing others:** Albert Bandura, *Social Learning Theory* (Upper Saddle River, NJ: Prentice Hall, 1977).

pg. 272: **groundbreaking experiments by Albert Bandura:** Albert Bandura, Dorothea Ross, and Sheila A. Ross, "Transmission of Aggression Through Imitation of Aggressive Models," *Journal of Abnormal and Social Psychology* 63, no. 3 (1961): 575–582.

pg. 273: **"cycle of violence":** Cathy S. Widom, "The Cycle of Violence," *Science* 244, no. 4901 (1989): 160–166.

pg. 273: **evidence for the cycle of violence is rather sparse:** Ilgi Ozturk Ertem, John M. Leventhal, and Sara Dobbs, "Intergenerational Continuity of Child Physical Abuse: How Good Is the Evidence?" *Lancet* 356, no. 9232 (2000): 814–819; Cathy S. Widom, "Does Violence Beget Violence? A Critical Examination of the Literature," *Psychological Bulletin* 106, no. 1 (1989): 3–28.

pg. 273: **evidence for the cycle of violence was inconsistent at best:** Ilgi Ozturk Ertem, John M. Leventhal, and Sara Dobbs, "Intergenerational Continuity of Child Physical Abuse: How Good Is the Evidence?" *Lancet* 356, no. 9232 (2000): 814–819.

pg. 273: **family history of violence had only a small to moderate effect:** Sandra M. Stith et al., "The Intergenerational Transmission of Spouse Abuse: A Meta-Analysis," *Journal of Marriage and Family* 62, no. 3 (2000): 640–654; see also Miriam K. Ehrensaft et al., "Intergenerational Transmission of Partner Violence: A 20-Year Prospective Study," *Journal of Consulting and Clinical Psychology* 71, no. 4 (2003): 741–753.

pg. 273: **Further studies conducted since the year 2000:** David M. Fergusson, Joseph M. Boden, and L. John Horwood, "Examining the Intergenerational Transmission of Violence in a New Zealand Birth Cohort," *Child Abuse and Neglect* 30, no. 2 (2006): 89–108.

pg. 273: **except in the severest of cases:** Timothy O. Ireland and Carolyn A. Smith, "Living in Partner-Violent Families: Developmental Links to Antisocial Behavior and Relationship Violence," *Journal of Youth and Adolescence* 38, no. 3 (2009): 323–339.

pg. 273: **will not themselves become involved in violent relationships:** Cathy S. Widom, "Does Violence Beget Violence? A Critical Examination of the Literature," *Psychological Bulletin* 106, no. 1 (1989): 3–28.

pg. 274: **most will not:** Ashley F. Jespersen, Martin L. Lalumière, and Michael C. Seto, "Sexual Abuse History Among Adult Sex Offenders and Non-Sex Offenders: A Meta-Analysis," *Child Abuse and Neglect* 33, no. 3 (2009): 179–192; Ian Lambie et al., "Resiliency in the Victim–Offender Cycle in Male Sexual Abuse," *Sexual Abuse: A Journal of Research and Treatment* 14, no. 1 (2002): 31–48; Daniel Salter et al., "Development of Sexually Abusive Behaviour in Sexually Victimised Males: A Longitudinal Study," *Lancet* 361, no. 9356 (2003): 471–476.

pg. 274: **Parenting style has not been shown to be passed cleanly:** Marinus H. van IJzendoorn, "Adult Attachment Representations, Parental Responsiveness, and Infant Attachment: A Meta-Analysis on the Predictive Validity of the Adult Attachment Interview," *Psychological Bulletin* 117, no. 3 (1995): 387–403; Marinus H. van IJzendoorn, "Intergenerational Transmission of Parenting: A Review of Studies in Nonclinical Populations," *Developmental Review* 12, no. 1 (1992): 76–99.

pg. 274: **neither has divorce:** Jaap Dronkers and Juho Härkönen, "The Intergenerational Transmission of Divorce in Cross-National Perspective: Results from the Fertility and Family Surveys," *Population Studies* 62, no. 3 (2008): 273–288.

pg. 274: **such as depression:** Falk W. Lohoff, "Overview of the Genetics of Major Depressive Disorder," *Current Psychiatry Reports* 12, no. 6 (2010): 539–546.

pg. 274: **and alcoholism:** Justine M. Campbell and Tian P. Oei, "A Cognitive Model for the Intergenerational Transference of Alcohol Use Behavior," *Addictive Behaviors* 35, no. 2 (2010): 73–83; National Institute on Alcohol Abuse and Alcoholism, "Genetics of Alcohol Use Disorder," National Institutes of Health, accessed January 29, 2017, http://www.niaaa.nih.gov/alcohol-health/overview-alcohol-consumption/alcohol-use -disorders/genetics-alcohol-use-disorders.

pg. 274: **a risk for such problems:** Cathy S. Widom, "Does Violence Beget Violence? A Critical Examination of the Literature," *Psychological Bulletin* 106, no. 1 (1989): 3–28.

pg. 274: **a parable that a minister shared with me:** My thanks to the Reverend Chip Edens of Christ Church in Charlotte, North Carolina, for sharing this story with me.

pg. 275: **follow-up study to his famous Bobo doll experiment:** Albert Bandura, Dorothea Ross, and Sheila A. Ross, "Vicarious Reinforcement and Imitative Learning," *Journal of Abnormal and Social Psychology* 67, no. 6 (1963): 601–607.

pg. 275: **"A wise man learns from the mistakes":** Although the exact source of this quote is unclear, it is widely attributed to Otto von Bismarck.

pg. 275: **We watch them go down paths that we decidedly do not follow:** Javier C. Hernandez, "From His Father's Decline, de Blasio 'Learned What Not to Do,'" *New York Times*, October 13, 2013, accessed January 29, 2017, http://www.nytimes

.com/2013/10/14/nyregion/from-his-fathers-decline-de-blasio-learned-what
-not-to-do.html; Steven M. Southwick and Dennis S. Charney, *Resilience: The Science of Mastering Life's Greatest Challenges* (New York: Cambridge University Press, 2012), 121.

pg. 275: **In one qualitative study of youth who had been exposed:** Hadass Goldblatt, "Strategies of Coping Among Adolescents Experiencing Interparental Violence," *Journal of Interpersonal Violence* 18, no. 5 (2003): 532–552.

pg. 275: **"To see the parent is not to be the parent":** Leonard Shengold, *Soul Murder: The Effects of Childhood Abuse and Deprivation* (New Haven, CT: Yale University Press, 1989), 315.

pg. 276: **"very, very powerful personal lessons in terms of how to live life":** Ana Sale, "Exclusive: Bill de Blasio Speaks with WNYC About His Father's Suicide," WNYC, September 30, 2013, accessed January 29, 2017, http://www.wnyc.org/ story/exclusive-bill-de-blasio-speaks-wnyc-about-his-fathers-suicide.

pg. 276: **"I learned what not to do":** Javier C. Hernandez, "From His Father's Decline, de Blasio 'Learned What Not to Do,'" *New York Times*, October 13, 2013, accessed January 29, 2017, http://www.nytimes.com/2013/10/14/nyregion/from-his-fathers -decline-de-blasio-learned-what-not-to-do.html.

pg. 276: **"Whenever people ask me about having children":** Mitch Albom, *Tuesdays with Morrie: An Old Man, a Young Man, and Life's Greatest Lesson* (New York: Broadway Books, 1997), 93.

pg. 277: **"a stand-up, productive, normalised member of society":** James Rhodes, *Instrumental: A Memior of Madness, Medication, and Music* (Edinburgh: Canongate, 2015), 88–92.

pg. 277: **"my son being born was the beginning":** James Rhodes, *Instrumental: A Memior of Madness, Medication, and Music* (Edinburgh: Canongate, 2015), 92.

pg. 278: **interview on National Public Radio:** National Public Radio, "Jonathan Safran Foer on Marriage, Religion and Universal Balances," *Fresh Air*, October 11, 2016, accessed January 29, 2017, http://www.npr.org/2016/10/11/497515290/jonathan-safran-foer-on-marriage -religion-and-universal-balances.

pg. 279: **ordinary experiences make us happier as we age:** Amit Bhattacharjee and Cassie Mogilner, "Happiness from Ordinary and Extraordinary Experiences," *Journal of Consumer Research* 41, no. 1 (2014): 1–17.

pg. 279: **hardly unusual:** Roy F. Baumeister et al., "Some Key Differences Between a Happy Life and a Meaningful Life," *Journal of Positive Psychology* 8, no. 6 (2013): 505–516; S. Katherine Nelson et al., "In Defense of Parenthood: Children Are Associated with More Joy than Misery," *Psychological Science* 24, no. 1 (2013): 3–10; see also Angus Deaton and Arthur A. Stone, "Evaluative and Hedonic Wellbeing Among Those With and Without Children at Home," *Proceedings of the National Academy of Sciences* 111, no. 4 (2014): 1328–1333; S. Katherine Nelson, Kostadin Kushlev, and Sonja Lyubomirsky, "The Pains and Pleasures of Parenting: When, Why, and How Is Parenthood Associated with More or Less Well-Being?" *Psychological Bulletin* 140, no. 3 (2014): 846–895; Debra Umberson and Walter R. Gove, "Parenthood and Psychological Well-Being Theory, Measurement, and Stage in the Family Life Course," *Journal of Family Issues* 10, no. 4 (1989): 440–462.

Chapter 17: Redemption

pg. 282: **"Love is the prerogative of the brave":** Although the exact source of this quote is unclear, it is widely attributed to Gandhi.

pg. 282: **longest-running study of well-being in history:** See, for summary, George Vaillant, *Triumphs of Experience: The Men of the Harvard Grant Study* (Cambridge, MA: Belknap, 2012), 54–107.

pg. 282: **intellectually, physically, and emotionally sound:** George Vaillant, *Triumphs of Experience: The Men of the Harvard Grant Study* (Cambridge, MA: Belknap, 2012), 38.

pg. 283: **opened his memoir with his experience of being a subject:** Ben Bradlee, *A Good Life: Newspapering and Other Adventures* (New York: Touchstone, 1996), 15–16.

pg. 283: **President John F. Kennedy was revealed:** Joshua Wolf Shenk, "What Makes Us Happy," *The Atlantic*, June 2009, accessed January 7, 2017, http://www.theatlantic .com/magazine/archive/2009/06/what-makes-us-happy/307439.

pg. 283: **"one of Harvard's most important contributions":** Dan H. Fann, "Grant Study Analyzes 'Normal' Individuals," *Harvard Crimson*, May 13, 1942, accessed January 7, 2017, http://www.thecrimson.com/article/1942/5/13/grant-study-analyzes-normal-individuals -pin; quoted in George Vaillant, *Triumphs of Experience: The Men of the Harvard Grant Study* (Cambridge, MA: Belknap, 2012), 56.

pg. 283: **"superachievers":** George Vaillant, *Triumphs of Experience: The Men of the Harvard Grant Study* (Cambridge, MA: Belknap, 2012), 61.

pg. 284: **"hanging length of [the] scrotum":** George Vaillant, *Triumphs of Experience: The Men of the Harvard Grant Study* (Cambridge, MA: Belknap, 2012), 72; see also Scott Stos-sel, "What Makes Us Happy, Revisited: A New Look at the Famous Harvard Study of What Makes People Thrive," *The Atlantic*, May 2013, accessed January 7, 2017, http:// www.theatlantic.com/magazine/archive/2013/05/thanks-mom/309287.

pg. 284: *Triumphs of Experience:* George Vaillant, *Triumphs of Experience: The Men of the Har-vard Grant Study* (Cambridge, MA: Belknap, 2012).

pg. 285: **"They were normal when I picked them":** Quoted in Joshua Wolf Shenk, "What Makes Us Happy," *The Atlantic*, June 2009, accessed January 7, 2017, http://www .theatlantic.com/magazine/archive/2009/06/what-makes-us-happy/307439.

pg. 285: **one the study's founders had really never considered at all:** George Vail-lant, *Triumphs of Experience: The Men of the Harvard Grant Study* (Cambridge, MA: Belknap, 2012), 52.

pg. 285: **"psychologists not only show no interest in the origin":** Harry F. Harlow, "The Nature of Love," *American Psychologist* 13, no. 12 (1958): 673–685; also quoted in George Vaillant, *Triumphs of Experience: The Men of the Harvard Grant Study* (Cambridge, MA: Belknap, 2012), 64.

pg. 285: **took the form of a good childhood:** George Vaillant, *Triumphs of Experience: The Men of the Harvard Grant Study* (Cambridge, MA: Belknap, 2012), 112–113.

pg. 285: **life-altering warmth and care:** See also L. Alan Sroufe, "Attachment and Develop-ment: A Prospective, Longitudinal Study from Birth to Adulthood," *Attachment and Human Development* 7, no. 4 (2005): 349–367; L. Alan Sroufe et al., *The Development of the Person: The Minnesota Study of Risk and Adaptation from Birth to Adulthood* (New York: Guilford, 2005).

pg. 285: **close to a brother or a sister:** Joshua Wolf Shenk, "What Makes Us Happy," *The Atlantic*, June 2009, accessed January 7, 2017, http://www.theatlantic.com/magazine/ archive/2009/06/what-makes-us-happy/307439.

pg. 286: **children:** George Vaillant, *Triumphs of Experience: The Men of the Harvard Grant Study* (Cambridge, MA: Belknap, 2012), 48.

pg. 286: **"You know what I learned from my children?":** George Vaillant, *Triumphs of Experience: The Men of the Harvard Grant Study* (Cambridge, MA: Belknap, 2012), 48.

pg. 286: **"love is love":** George Vaillant, *Triumphs of Experience: The Men of the Harvard Grant Study* (Cambridge, MA: Belknap, 2012), 48.

pg. 286: **"The follow-up is the great exposer of truth":** Quoted in Donald W. Goodwin, Samuel B. Guze, and Eli Robins, "Follow-Up Studies in Obsessional Neurosis," *Archives of General Psychiatry* 20, no 2 (1969): 182.

pg. 286: **"Happiness is love. Full stop.":** George Vaillant, *Triumphs of Experience: The Men of the Harvard Grant Study* (Cambridge, MA: Belknap, 2012), 52.

pg. 286: **most important source of meaning in our lives:** See, for review, Harry T. Reis and Shelly L. Gable, "Toward a Positive Psychology of Relationships," in *Flourishing: The*

Positive Person and the Good Life, eds. Corey L. M. Keyes and Jonathan Haidt (Washington, DC: APA, 2003), 129–159.

pg. 286: **love emerges as a powerful force for good:** See, for summary, Margaret O'Dougherty Wright, Ann S. Masten, and Angela J. Narayan, "Resilience Processes in Development: Four Waves of Research on Positive Adaptations in the Context of Adversity," in *Handbook of Resilience in Children*, eds. Sam Goldstein and Robert B. Brooks (New York: Springer, 2012), 25.

pg. 286: **feeling connected to a parent or a teacher or a mentor:** Michael D. Resnick et al., "Protecting Adolescents from Harm: Findings from the National Longitudinal Study on Adolescent Health," *Journal of the American Medical Association* 278, no. 10 (1997): 823–832.

pg. 286: **"lifelines":** Robert B. Cairns and Beverley D. Cairns, *Lifelines and Risks: Passages of Youth in Our Time* (New York: Cambridge University Press, 1994).

pg. 286: **tracing the lives of three hundred teenage mothers:** Frank F. Furstenberg Jr., Jeanne Brooks-Gunn, and S. Philip Morgan, *Adolescent Mothers in Later Life* (New York: Cambridge University Press, 1987); Frank F. Furstenberg Jr. et al., *Managing to Make It: Urban Families and Adolescent Success* (Chicago: University of Chicago Press, 1999).

pg. 287: **those who felt connected to work and love in adulthood:** John H. Laub and Robert J. Sampson, "Turning Points in the Life Course: Why Change Matters to the Study of Crime," *Criminology* 31, no. 3 (1993): 301–325.

pg. 287: **only one in six of the struggling teens became struggling adults:** Emmy E. Werner and Ruth S. Smith, *Overcoming the Odds: High Risk Children from Birth to Adulthood* (Ithaca, NY: Cornell University Press, 1992).

pg. 287: **one of the most pivotal "second-chance opportunities":** See, for summary, Emmy Werner, "Resilience and Recovery: Findings from the Kauai Longitudinal Study," *Research, Policy, and Practice in Children's Mental Health* 19, no. 1 (2005): 11–14, accessed January 29, 2017, https://www.pathwaysrtc.pdx.edu/pdf/fpS0504.pdf; Emmy Werner, "What Can We Learn About Resilience from Large-Scale Longitudinal Studies?" in *Handbook of Resilience in Children*, eds. Sam Goldstein and Robert B. Brooks (New York: Springer, 2012), 91–106.

pg. 287: **one of the most consistent findings in social science research:** Louis Cozolino, *The Neuroscience of Human Relationships: Attachment and the Developing Social Brain*, 2nd ed. (New York: Norton, 2014), 244.

pg. 288: **"The Nature of the Child's Tie to His Mother":** John Bowlby, "The Nature of the Child's Tie to His Mother," *International Journal of Psycho-Analysis* 39 (1958): 350–373.

pg. 288: **According to Bowlby:** For a full treatment of Bowlby's work on attachment, see John Bowlby, *Attachment and Loss*. Vol. 1, *Attachment* (New York: Basic, 1969); John Bowlby, *Attachment and Loss*. Vol. 2, *Separation* (New York: Basic, 1973); John Bowlby, *Attachment and Loss*. Vol. 3, *Loss, Sadness, and Depression* (New York: Basic, 1980).

pg. 288: **"All of us, from cradle to grave":** John Bowlby, *The Making and Breaking of Affectional Bonds* (London: Tavistock, 1979), 129; see also Cindy Hazan and Phillip Shaver, "Romantic Love Conceptualized as an Attachment Process," *Journal of Personality and Social Psychology* 52, no. 3 (1987): 511–524; for a summary, see R. Chris Fraley and Phillip R. Shaver, "Adult Romantic Attachment: Theoretical Developments, Emerging Controversies, and Unanswered Questions," *Review of General Psychology* 4, no. 2 (2000): 132–154.

pg. 288: **"I consider myself a hero":** John Lahr, "Viola Davis's Call to Adventure: How the Star of 'Fences' and 'How to Get Away with Murder' Got Away from Her Difficult Past," *New Yorker*, December 19 and 26, 2016, accessed January 8, 2017, http://www.newyorker.com/magazine/2016/12/19/viola-davis-call-to-adventure.

pg. 289: **"the sum of all of the moments of our lives":** Thomas Wolfe, *Look Homeward, Angel* (New York: Scribner Paperback Fiction, 1995), xv.

pg. 289: **amygdalae are quieted and our stress hormone levels are lowered:** Louis Cozolino, *The Neuroscience of Psychotherapy: Building and Rebuilding the Human Brain* (New York: Norton, 2010), 225–226; Louis Cozolino, *The Neuroscience of Human Relationships: Attachment and the Developing Social Brain*, 2nd ed. (New York: Norton, 2014), 243.

pg. 290: **Physical intimacy:** Beate Ditzen, Christiane Hoppmann, and Petra Klumb, "Positive Couple Interactions and Daily Cortisol: On the Stress-Protecting Role of Intimacy," *Psychosomatic Medicine* 70, no. 8 (2008): 883–889; Beate Ditzen et al., "Effects of Different Kinds of Couple Interaction on Cortisol and Heart Rate Responses to Stress in Women," *Psychoneuroendocrinology* 32, no. 5 (2007): 565–574.

pg. 290: **boosts our levels of oxytocin and vasopressin:** James A. Coan, Hillary S. Schaefer, and Richard J. Davidson, "Lending a Hand: Social Regulation of the Neural Response to Threat," *Psychological Science* 17, no. 12 (2006): 1032–1039; Sheldon Cohen et al., "Does Hugging Provide Stress-Buffering Social Support? A Study of Susceptibility to Upper Respiratory Infection and Illness," *Psychological Science* 26, no. 2 (2015): 135–147; Beate Ditzen and Markus Heinrichs, "Psychobiology of Social Support: The Social Dimension of Stress Buffering," *Restorative Neurology and Neuroscience* 32, no. 1 (2014): 149–162; Megan Galbally et al., "The Role of Oxytocin in Mother-Infant Relations: A Systematic Review of Human Studies," *Harvard Review of Psychiatry* 19, no. 1 (2011): 1–14; Karen M. Grewen et al., "Effects of Partner Support on Resting Oxytocin, Cortisol, Norepinephrine, and Blood Pressure Before and After Warm Partner Contact," *Psychosomatic Medicine* 67, no. 4 (2005): 531–538; Julianne Holt-Lunstad, Wendy A. Birmingham, and Kathleen C. Light, "Influence of a 'Warm Touch' Support Enhancement Intervention Among Married Couples on Ambulatory Blood Pressure, Oxytocin, Alpha Amylase, and Cortisol," *Psychosomatic Medicine* 70 no. 9 (2008): 976–985; Kathleen C. Light, Karen M. Grewen, and Janet A. Amico, "More Frequent Partner Hugs and Higher Oxytocin Levels Are Linked to Lower Blood Pressure and Heart Rate in Premenopausal Women," *Biological Psychology* 69, no. 1 (2005): 5–21.

pg. 290: **seeing photos of our loved ones:** Andreas Bartels and Semir Zeki, "The Neural Basis of Romantic Love," *Neuroreport* 11, no. 17 (2000): 3829–3834; Sarah L. Master et al., "A Picture's Worth: Partner Photographs Reduce Experimentally Induced Pain," *Psychological Science* 20, no. 11 (2009): 1316–1318.

pg. 290: **love quiets the amygdala and reduces stress hormones:** Andreas Bartels and Semir Zeki, "The Neural Correlates of Maternal and Romantic Love," *Neuroimage* 21, no. 3 (2004): 1155–1166; A. De Boer, E. M. Van Buel, and G. J. Ter Horst, "Love Is More than Just a Kiss: A Neurobiological Perspective on Love and Affection," *Neuroscience* 201, no. 10 (2012): 114–124.

pg. 290: **more open to newer, more expansive learning:** Louis Cozolino and Susan Sprokay, "Neuroscience and Adult Learning," *New Directions for Adult and Continuing Education* 2006, no. 110 (2006): 11–19.

pg. 290: **"the greatest contributor to [neuroplasticity] *is* love":** Louis Cozolino and Susan Sprokay, "Neuroscience and Adult Learning," *New Directions for Adult and Continuing Education* 2006, no. 110 (2006): 11–19; italics in this quote are mine.

pg. 290: **birds learn their songs more quickly from other birds:** Louis Cozolino and Susan Sprokay, "Neuroscience and Adult Learning," *New Directions for Adult and Continuing Education* 2006, no. 110 (2006): 11–19.

pg. 290: **children learn better from interactions with others than from videos:** Sarah Roseberry, Kathy Hirsh Pasek, and Roberta M. Golinkoff, "Skype Me!: Socially Contingent Interactions Help Toddlers Learn Language," *Child Development* 85, no. 3 (2014): 956–970; Sarah Roseberry et al., "Live Action: Can Young Children Learn Verbs from Video?" *Child Development* 80, no. 5 (2009): 1360–1375.

pg. 290: **host of benefits for the body and the brain:** Louis Cozolino, *The Neuroscience of Human Relationships: Attachment and the Developing Social Brain*, 2nd ed. (New York: Norton,

2014), 245; A. De Boer, E. M. Van Buel, and G. J. Ter Horst, "Love Is More than Just a Kiss: A Neurobiological Perspective on Love and Affection," *Neuroscience* 201, no. 10 (2012): 114–124; Barbara L. Fredrickson, "The Broaden-and-Build Theory of Positive Emotions," *Philosophical Transactions of the Royal Society of London Series B: Biological Sciences* 359, no. 1449 (2004): 1367–1378; Barbara L. Fredrickson, "Positive Emotions Broaden and Build," *Advances in Experimental Social Psychology* 47 (2013): 1–53; Barbara L. Fredrickson, "The Role of Positive Emotions in Positive Psychology: The Broaden-and-Build Theory of Positive Emotions," *American Psychologist* 56, no. 3 (2001): 218–226; Alice M. Isen, "Positive Affect, Cognitive Processes, and Social Behavior," *Advances in Experimental Social Psychology* 20 (1987): 203–253.

pg. 290: **"may be the leading cause of poor health":** "Breaking the Silence on Child Abuse: Protection, Prevention, Intervention, and Deterrence," Testimony of Robert W. Block on Behalf of the American Academy of Pediatrics Before the Senate Health, Education, Labor and Pensions Committee Hearing, December 13, 2011, accessed September 2, 2016, http://www.help.senate.gov/hearings/breaking-the-silence-on-child-abuse-protection-prevention-intervention-and-deterrence.

pg. 291: **"undoing effect":** Barbara L. Fredrickson, "The Role of Positive Emotions in Positive Psychology: The Broaden-and-Build Theory of Positive Emotions," *American Psychologist* 56, no. 3 (2001): 218–226; Barbara L. Fredrickson et al., "The Undoing Effect of Positive Emotions," *Motivation and Emotion* 24, no. 4 (2000): 237–258; Andrea H. Marques and Esther M. Sternberg, "The Biology of Positive Emotions and Health," in *Altruism and Health: Perspectives from Empirical Research*, ed. Stephen G. Post (New York: Oxford University Press, 2007), 149–188; Michele M. Tugade and Barbara L. Fredrickson, "Resilient Individuals Use Positive Emotions to Bounce Back from Negative Emotional Experiences," *Journal of Personality and Social Psychology* 86, no. 2 (2004): 320–333.

pg. 291: **an umbrella term for the good feelings we experience:** Barbara L. Fredrickson, "Positive Emotions Broaden and Build," *Advances in Experimental Social Psychology* 47 (2013): 1–53; see also Carroll E. Izard, *Human Emotions* (New York: Springer, 1977).

pg. 291: **"bad emotions, bad parents, and bad feedback":** Roy F. Baumeister et al., "Bad Is Stronger than Good," *Review of General Psychology* 5, no. 4 (2001): 323–370.

pg. 294: **"as much about remembering":** Bessel A. van der Kolk, *The Body Keeps the Score: Brain, Mind, and Body in the Healing of Trauma* (New York: Penguin, 2014), 213.

pg. 295: **reparative relationship is first found in therapy:** Louis Cozolino, *The Neuroscience of Human Relationships: Attachment and the Developing Social Brain*, 2nd ed. (New York: Norton, 2014); Linda A. Travis, Nancy G. Bliwise, Jeffrey L. Binder, and H. Lynn Horne-Moyer, "Changes in Clients' Attachment Styles Over the Course of Time-Limited Dynamic Psychotherapy," *Psychotherapy: Theory, Research, Practice, Training* 38, no. 2 (2001): 149–159.

pg. 295: **"Psychoanalysis is in essence a cure through love":** Sigmund Freud in a letter to Carl Jung (1906), as quoted in Bruno Bettelheim, *Freud and Man's Soul* (New York: Vintage Books, 1984).

pg. 295: **"Love is love":** George Vaillant, *Triumphs of Experience: The Men of the Harvard Grant Study* (Cambridge, MA: Belknap, 2012), 48.

pg. 295: **"I had a weak father, domineering mother":** Quoted in Glenn I. Roisman et al., "Earned–Secure Attachment Status in Retrospect and Prospect," *Child Development* 73, no. 4 (2002): 1204–1219.

pg. 296: **what goes right matters more than what goes wrong:** George Vaillant, *Triumphs of Experience: The Men of the Harvard Grant Study* (Cambridge, MA: Belknap, 2012), 141–142.

pg. 296: **poor predictors of the future:** George Vaillant, *Triumphs of Experience: The Men of the Harvard Grant Study* (Cambridge, MA: Belknap, 2012), 52.

pg. 296: **death of a parent foretold little:** George Vaillant, *Triumphs of Experience: The Men of the Harvard Grant Study* (Cambridge, MA: Belknap, 2012), 140.

pg. 296: **successes, and not their failures, that most influenced their lives:** George Vaillant, *Triumphs of Experience: The Men of the Harvard Grant Study* (Cambridge, MA: Belknap, 2012), 141–142.

pg. 296: **Learning (or relearning) to love and be loved in adulthood is possible:** Mark W. Baldwin and Beverley Fehr, "On the Instability of Attachment Style Ratings," *Personal Relationships* 2, no. 3 (1995): 247–261; Joanne Davila, Dorli Burge, and Constance Hammen, "Why Does Attachment Style Change?" *Journal of Personality and Social Psychology* 73, no. 4 (1997): 826–838; Joanne Davila and Rebecca J. Cobb, "Predictors of Change in Attachment Security During Adulthood," in *Adult Attachment: Theory, Research, and Clinical Implications*, eds. W. Steven Rholes and Jeffry A. Simpson (New York: Guilford, 2004), 133–156; Louis Cozolino, *The Neuroscience of Human Relationships: Attachment and the Developing Social Brain*, 2nd ed. (New York: Norton, 2014), 155.

pg. 296: **find their way into stable, satisfying relationships in adulthood:** Jay Belsky and Jude Cassidy, "Attachment: Theory and Evidence," in *Development Through Life: A Handbook for Clinicians*, eds. Michael J. Rutter and Dale F. Hay (Oxford, UK: Blackwell, 1994), 373–402; Jami Grich, "Earned Secure Attachment in Young Adulthood: Adjustment and Relationship Satisfaction," *Dissertation Abstracts International: The Sciences and Engineering*, 62, no. 7-B (2002): 3419; Blair Paley et al., "Attachment and Marital Functioning: Comparison of Spouses with Continuous-Secure, Earned-Secure, Dismissing, and Preoccupied Attachment Stances," *Journal of Family Psychology* 13, no. 4 (1999): 580–597; Glenn I. Roisman et al., "Earned–Secure Attachment Status in Retrospect and Prospect," *Child Development* 73, no. 4 (2002): 1204–1219.

pg. 296: **positive sleeper effects as well:** Louis Cozolino and Susan Sprokay, "Neuroscience and Adult Learning," *New Directions for Adult and Continuing Education* 2006, no. 110 (2006): 11–19; George Vaillant, *Triumphs of Experience: The Men of the Harvard Grant Study* (Cambridge, MA: Belknap, 2012), 108–109.

pg. 297: **"positivity effect":** Laura L. Carstensen, Helene H. Fung, and Susan T. Charles, "Socioemotional Selectivity Theory and the Regulation of Emotion in the Second Half of Life," *Motivation and Emotion* 27, no. 2 (2003): 103–123; Susan Charles and Laura L. Carstensen, "Social and Emotional Aging," *Annual Review of Psychology* 61 (2010): 383–409; Mara Mather and Laura L. Carstensen, "Aging and Motivated Cognition: The Positivity Effect in Attention and Memory," *Trends in Cognitive Sciences* 9, no. 10 (2005): 496–502; Andrew E. Reed, Larry Chan, and Joseph A. Mikels, "Meta-Analysis of the Age-Related Positivity Effect: Age Differences in Preferences for Positive Over Negative Information," *Psychology and Aging* 29, no. 1 (2014): 1–15.

pg. 297: **faith in others tends to become stronger:** Judith A. Crowell, Dominique Treboux, and Everett Waters, "Stability of Attachment Representations: The Transition to Marriage," *Developmental Psychology* 38, no. 4 (2002): 467–479; Tamara L. Fuller and Frank D. Fincham, "Attachment Style in Married Couples: Relation to Current Marital Functioning, Stability Over Time, and Method of Assessment," *Personal Relationships* 2, no. 1 (1995): 17–34; Fang Zhang and Gisela Labouvie-Vief, "Stability and Fluctuation in Adult Attachment Style Over a 6-Year Period," *Attachment and Human Development* 6, no. 4 (2004): 419–437.

pg. 297: **arc of history bends toward justice:** See the quote, "The arc of the moral universe is long but it bends toward justice," by Martin Luther King Jr., "Sermon at Temple Israel of Hollywood," delivered February 26, 1965, *American Rhetoric Online Speech Bank*, accessed January 29, 2017, http://www.americanrhetoric.com/speeches/mltemple israelhollywood.htm.

CHAPTER 18: NEVER-ENDING

pg. 298: **"Real life is messy, inconsistent":** Alan Moore, quoted in Alan Moore and Dave Gibbons, *Watchmen* (New York: DC Comics, 1987), 99.

pg. 298: **_Superheroes: A Never-Ending Battle:_** _Superheroes: A Never-Ending Battle,_ documentary, Public Broadcasting Service, accessed February 26, 2017, http://www.pbs.org/show/super heroes-neverending-story.

pg. 300: **fighting a hard battle:** The sentiment probably originated with Ian Maclaren; "Ian Maclaren," _Wikipedia, The Free Encyclopedia,_ accessed February 26, 2017, https:// en.wikipedia.org/wiki/Ian_Maclaren.

ACKNOWLEDGMENTS

Above all else, this is the place to acknowledge those I cannot name: the truly amazing women and men who have shared their stories with me. You are the ones who taught me that resilience is more about strength and bravery than it is about elasticity—and that living outside of the average and expectable is a complicated place to be. Here, I have gathered together glimpses of just a few of the clients and students it has been my privilege to fight for and care for, in the hope that you—and supernormals everywhere— may feel less alone. Although I could not tell your stories in full, I have tried to do your experiences justice. Normality, if there is such a thing, has nothing on you.

This is also the place to take my own advice and express my deep gratitude to the good people who have fought for and cared for me—and who have done the same for this book:

At Twelve, my publisher. Brian McLendon, marketing phenom, I am starting with you because editors may come and go but you always have my back. We have been through a lot together, and your unwavering kindness and friendship have made it all quite wonderful. Deb Futter, *Supernormal*'s first editor, you championed me and this book from the start, and I thank you for your continuing enthusiasm and support. Sean Desmond, *Supernormal*'s last editor, thank you for saving the day by taking on this book, and for making sure it would be published in a way that supernormals out there deserve. I am so appreciative also for the many others at Hachette who have supported me over the years, especially Jamie Raab, Paul Samuelson, Rachel Kambury, Bailey Donoghue, Elizabeth Kulhanek, Sonya Safro, Libby Burton, and Michael Pietsch.

Jon Gray, cover designer. Thank you for creating such a strong, beautiful, mysterious jacket, one that truly represents the experience of being supernormal.

My trusted colleagues, Cathleen Clerkin, Robert Emery, Krista Jana, and especially Steve Lagerfeld. It takes a lot of trust indeed to share drafts of chapters with those you admire. I appreciate your making it possible for me to do so, and for giving me your time and your honest opinions—two of the world's most valuable resources as far as I am concerned. You made the book better, and I thank you.

Colleagues, supervisors, and friends, Linda Cozzarelli, Nancy Chodorow, Deborah Raphael, Laurie Case, Carol Manning, Eric Turkheimer, and Emily Lape. You have shown me what it looks like to be a clinician who makes a difference; who cures with love. You made me a better therapist and a better person, and I thank you.

Molly Davis Foukal, clinical psychologist, research assistant, and quote investigator extraordinaire. I mean it sincerely when I say this book would not have been possible without you. Your spirited, tireless hard work. Your ability to tie anything back to *Hamilton*, which is, of course, a supernormal story, too. I look forward to a lifetime of singing your praises, recommending you for the next great thing, and being in your corner. (Fantastic job on your twenties, too, by the way. You nailed 'em.)

Tina Bennett, my agent. You are my kind of woman: indefatigable and compassionate and committed to doing good in the world. I am indebted to you for being the wisest adviser, ally, and confidante imaginable, far beyond what your job requires. Most of all, I thank you for the sparkly earrings, and for being the kind of person who would send them. I'm holding on to those earrings, and to you, for life.

The Jays, you know who you are. Thank you for the laughter and the love. As long as I can remember, I have wanted to be a writer, probably because, also as long as I can remember, I've been listening to our family stories. #4. #9. #11. #27. Among other things, they taught me that heartbreak and humor can—and maybe should—go side by side. That's a whole other book, as you know, and maybe it will be.

My husband, my partner. You are generous and kind and, as long as I have known you, you have supported my ambitions in ways big and small. It seems too plain to thank you for sharing your life with me, but that is what you have done. You have taken your days and years and lent them to my happiness and my dreams. I'm not sure you knew quite what you were getting into when you married me, but I love you for being brave enough to join your life with mine.

My children, my emerald and my ruby. You are precious to me beyond words. It is insufficient, but still I must say thank you for always caring about how the book was going, and for letting me get away sometimes to write it. It has been my absolute joy and privilege to be there for your childhoods, and no matter how old you get, I will never be able to stop telling you how much I love you. The most important job and greatest achievement of my life has been being your mom.

ABOUT THE AUTHOR

Meg Jay is a clinical psychologist and an associate professor of education at the University of Virginia. She earned a doctorate in clinical psychology, and in gender studies, from the University of California, Berkeley. Her work has appeared in the *New York Times, Los Angeles Times, USA Today, Wall Street Journal,* and on NPR, the BBC, and TED. Her books have been translated into more than a dozen languages.